The Meaning and Practice of Confirmation

American University Studies

Series VII
Theology and Religion

Vol. 31

PETER LANG
New York · Bern · Frankfurt am Main · Paris

Paul Turner

The Meaning and Practice of Confirmation

Perspectives from a Sixteenth-Century Controversy

PETER LANG
New York · Bern · Frankfurt am Main · Paris

Library of Congress Cataloging-in-Publication Data

Turner, Paul
  The meaning and practice of confirmation.

  (American university studies. Series VII, Theology and religion ; vol. 31)
  Bibliography: p.
  1. Confirmation—History—16th century. 2. Confirmation. I. Title. II. Series: American university
studies. Series VII, Theology and religion ; v. 31.
BV815.T87 1988   265'.2   87-3056
ISBN 0-8204-0456-X
ISSN 0740-0446

CIP-Kurztitelaufnahme der Deutschen Bibliothek

Turner, Paul:
The meaning and practice of confirmation :
perspectives from a sixteenth-century
controversy / Paul Turner. – New York; Bern;
Frankfurt am Main; Paris: Lang, 1987.
  (American University Studies: Ser. 7,
  Theology and Religion; Vol. 31)
  ISBN 0-8204-0456-X

NE: American University Studies / 07

BV
815
.T87
1987

Nihil obstat
Rev. Michael Coleman

Imprimatur
Most Rev. John J. Sullivan
Bishop of Kansas City-St. Joseph

March 5, 1987

Printed by Weihert-Druck GmbH, Darmstadt, West Germany

IOHANNI EPISCOPO SULLIVANO
SUIS DISSENSURO CONCLUSIONIBUS
DEDICAT AUCTOR
UT
GRATUM EI FIAT A GRATO

I wish to thank

Ghislain Lafont, *who inspired*
Doug Ferraro *and* Andrew Clark, *who read*
Bob Cameron *and* Michael Coleman, *who pored*
Susan Walker, *who poured*
Reginaldo Foster, *qui docuit*
Bishop John J. Sullivan, *who prayed*
The Diocese of Kansas City-St. Joseph, *who paid*
Bill & Alice Turner, *who loved*
Tom Powers, *who hosted*
Mary O'Driscoll, *who guided*
Martin Luther, *who challenged*
Robert Bellarmine, *who disputed*
God, *Who confirms our faith.*

P.T.

Table of Contents

Abbreviations

Wherever possible these abbreviations are taken from TRE: Abkürzungsverzeichnis (Berlin: Walter de Gruyter, 1976).

AAS   *Acta apostolicae sedis. Commentarium officiale.* Rome: Typographia Polyglotta, vol. 1, 1909.

AHP   *Archivum historiae pontificiae.* Rome: Pontificia Universitas Gregoriana Facultas Historiae Ecclesiasticae, vol. 1, 1963.

APTh   *Arbeiten zur Pastoraltheologie.* Göttingen: Vandenhoeck & Ruprecht, vol. 1, 1962.

ARCEG   *Acta Reformationis Catholicae ecclesiam Germaniae concernentia saeculi xvi: Die Reformverhandlungen des Deutschen Episkopats von 1520 bis 1570.* Ed. Georg Pfeilschifter. Regensburg: Verlag Friedrich Pustet, vol. 1, 1959.

ASS   *Acta sanctae sedis.* Rome: Typis Polyglottis Vaticanis, vol. 1, 1865.

BAC   *Biblioteca de autores cristianos.* Madrid: La Editorial Católica, S.A., 1947ff.

BRHE   *Bibliothèque de la revue d'histoire ecclésiastique.* Louvain: Publications Universitaires de Louvain, vol. 1, 1927.

CCath   *Corpus catholicorum: Werke Katholischer Schriftsteller im Zeitalter der Glaubensspaltung.* Münster in Westfalen: Verlag der Aschendorffschen Verlagsbuchhandlung, vol. 1, 1919.

CChr.CM   *Corpus Christianorum – Continuatio medievalis.*
Turnhout: Brepols, vol. 1, 1971.

CChr.SL   *Corpus Christianorum – Serie Latina.* Turnhout:
Brepols, vol. 1, 1954.

CFI   *Concilium Florentinum documenta et scriptores.* Rome:
Pontificium Institutum Orientalium Studiorum, vol. 1,
1940.

CIC   *Corpus Iuris Canonici.* Ed. Emil Friedberg. Editio
Lipsiensis secunda. Graz: Akademische Druck-U.
Verlagsanstalt, 1955.

COGP   *Concilia omnia, tam generalia, quam particularia, ab
apostolorum temporibus in hunc usque diem a
sanctissimis patribus celebrata, & quorum acta literis
mandata, ex vetustissimis diversarum regionum
bibliothecis haberi potuere.* Ed. Petrus Crabbe. Cologne:
Petrus Quentel, 1538.

CorpAp   *Corpus apologetarum Christianorum saeculi secundi.*
Jena: Libraria Hermanni Dvfft, vol. 1, 1847.

CR   *Corpus reformatorum. Philippi Melanthonis, opera
quae supersunt omnia.* Ed. Carolus Gottlieb
Bretschneider and Henricus Ernestus Bindseil. 28 vols.
Halis Saxonum: C. A. Schwetschke et filium, 1834-
1860; reprint ed. New York and London: Johnson Reprint
Corporation, 1963.

Ioannis Calvini opera quae supersunt omnia. Ed.
Guilielmus Baum et al. Brunsvigae: C. A. Schwetschke
et filium, vol. 1 (CR 29), 1863.

*Huldreich Zwinglis Sämtliche Werke Unter
Mitwirkung des Zwingli-Vereins in Zürich.* Ed. Emil
Egli, Georg Finsler, Walter Köhler. Leipzig: M.
Heinsius Nachfolger, vol. 1 (CR 88), 1905.

CSEL   *Corpus scriptorum ecclesiasticorum Latinorum.* Vienna:
F. Tempsky, vol. 1, 1866.

CT   *Concilium Tridentinum Diariorum, Actorum,*
Epistularum, Tractatuum. Nova collectio. Ed. Societas
Goerresiana. 13 vols. Freiburg: Herder and Co., 1901-
1938.

CTh   *Cahiers théologiques.* Neuchâtel: Editions Delachaux
& Niestlé, S.A., vol. 1, 1949.

DThC   *Dictionnaire de théologie catholique.* Paris: Letouzey
et Ané, Éditeurs, vol. 1, 1910.

ETR   *Etudes Théologiques et Religieuses: Revue publiée par*
la Faculté libre de Théologie Protestante de
Montpellier. Montpellier: Imprimeries Reunies Valence-
surRhone, vol. 1, 1926.

GCS   *Die griechischen christlichen Schriftsteller der ersten*
drei Jahrhunderte. Berlin, Leipzig: J. C. Hinrichs'sche
Buchhandlung, vol. 1, 1897.

JThS   *Journal of Theological Studies.* Oxford et al.: Clarendon
Press, vol. 1, 1899.

LBW   *Lutheran Book of Worship.* Ed. Inter-Lutheran
Commission on Worship: Lutheran Church in America,
The American Lutheran Church, The Evangelical
Lutheran Church of Canada, and The Lutheran
Church– Missouri Synod. Minnneapolis: Augsburg
Publishing House, 1982.

LThK   *Lexikon für Theologie und Kirche.* Ed. Michael
Buchberger et al. Freiburg: Verlag Herder, vol. 1, 1957.

LuthW   *Luther's Works, American Edition.* General editors
Jaroslav Pelikan and Helmut T. Lehmann. St. Louis:
Concordia Publishing House and Philadelphia:
Fortress Press, vol. 1, 1958.

Mansi   *Sacrorum conciliorum nova et amplissima collectio.* Ed.
             Johannes Dominicus Mansi et al. Florence: Antonius
             Zatta Venetus, vol. 1, 1759.

NCE   *New Catholic Encyclopedia.* New York: McGraw-Hill,
             vol. 1, 1967.

PG   *Patrologiae cursus completus.* Ed. Jacques-Paul Migne.
             Series Graeca. Paris: J.-P. Migne, vol. 1, 1857.

PL   *Patrologiae cursus completus.* Ed. Jacques-Paul Migne.
             Series Latina. Paris: J.-P. Migne, vol. 1, 1841.

PMAAR   *Papers and Monographs of the American Academy in
             Rome.* Rome, New Haven: Yale University Press, vol. 1,
             1919.

PosLuth   *Positions luthériennes.* Paris: Corbière & Jugain, vol. 1,
             1953.

QD   *Quaestiones disputatae.* Ed. Karl Rahner and Heinrich
             Schlier. Freiburg: Herder, vol. 1, 1958.

QFRG   *Quellen und Forschungen zur Reformationsgeschichte.*
             Gütersloh et al.: Verlagshaus Gerd Mohn, vol. 1, 1911.

RBen   *Revue Bénédictine.* Belgium: Abbaye de Maredsous,
             vol. 7, 1890.

RRef   *La Revue Réformée. Bulletin Trimestriel de l'Alliance
             Evangélique.* Paris: Alliance Evangélique, vol. 1, 1950.

SC   *Sources chrétiennes.* Paris: Editions du Cerf, vol. 1, 1941.

SpicBon   *Spicilegium Bonaventurianum.* Quaracchi,
             Grottaferrata: Editiones Collegii S. Bonaventurae ad
             Claras Aquas, vol. 1, 1963.

StT   *Studi e Testi.* Vatican City: Biblioteca apostolica
             Vaticana, vol. 1, 1900.

TRE   *Theologische Realenzyklopädie*. Berlin: Walter de
             Gruyter, vol. 1, 1977.

TU   *Texte und Untersuchungen zur Geschichte der
             altchristlichen Literatur*. Berlin, Leipzig: J. C.
             Hinrichs'sche Buchhandlung, vol. 1, 1882.

WA   *D. Martin Luthers Werke. Kritische Gesammtausgabe*.
             Weimar: Hermann Böhlau, vol. 1, 1883.

WABr   *D. Martin Luthers Werke. Kritische Gesamtausgabe.
             Briefwechsel*. Weimar: Hermann Böhlaus Nachfolger,
             vol. 1, 1930.

The Meaning and Practice
of Confirmation

No rite in the history of Christianity has proven as puzzling as confirmation. What began as imposition of hands became anointing. What once was part of initiation has become a mature act of commitment to the Church. What is a sacrament to one Christian tradition remains an ecclesial rite to another. Confirmation has the embarrassing distinction of being the one rite about which people keep asking, "Just what does it mean?"

Take the Catholic tradition for example. Confirmation is celebrated in two different ways, depending on the age of the recipient. If the person is an adult, it is part of the rites of initiation into the Church, celebrated at the time of baptism or profession of the Catholic faith. However, if one was baptized as a child, confirmation is celebrated at a later age, at the conclusion of a post-baptismal period of catechesis. The difference is not simply one of age – There is a difference in meaning and efficacity as well. For adults, confirmation has the meaning of initiation, and it brings about a gift of God: the seal of the Holy Spirit on the covenant of baptism. But for children, confirmation marks the conclusion of a period of Christian catechesis, and as a result it strengthens the individual by ritualizing the renewed commitment he or she makes to the Christian life. Thus, for the adult confirmation is a beginning, for the child it is a conclusion. In the one case it emphasizes God's free gift of the Spirit, in the other it ritualizes the individual's commitment. For the adult it is the seal of the Spirit, for the child it is the Spirit's strength.

The Catholic tradition has also varied in regard to the minister and the matter of confirmation, which in turn betrays an instability in its practice. There is a long tradition attributing the administration of confirmation to a bishop alone. But there is an equally long history of dispensations for priests to confer it under certain circumstances. Today, dioceses which would have petitioned Rome for the appointment of an auxiliary bishop just to help with the administration of many confirmations no longer have such a pressing need: A bishop may delegate the ministry to a diocesan vicar. Regarding the matter of confirmation, it has been consistently identified with anointing with chrism; still, the Church has preserved imposition of hands as an integral part of the rite because that was the original gesture of the Apostles. Thus, while the liturgy of Vatican Council II balances both anointing and imposition of hands at the pivotal moment of administering confirmation, the Church hesitates to call imposition the essential gesture of the rite.

Another difficulty in the Catholic tradition is that for the first time in history the order of administering four of the sacraments has been changed, raising questions about their relationship to and dependency on one another. Up until this century the three sacraments of initiation into the Church were preserved in order (in theory, if not universally in practice): Those baptized as infants were confirmed seven or ten years later and received the Eucharist after that. Pope Pius X's eagerness to open reception of the Eucharist to children can be heralded as a great advance in the Church's understanding of communion, but at the same time his zeal did not resolve what to do about confirmation. Consequently, for the first time in Church history, it became quite normal for children to receive communion *before* confirmation. Moreover, when Eucharist came down to children it brought first penance along with it, pushing confirmation from second in order of reception to fourth. And in the years since Vatican II, many episcopal conferences have allowed a further step, removing confirmation farther yet from both baptism and Eucharist to an age when children are passing into adulthood. Throughout this period there has been no satisfactory treatment of the relation of confirmation to Eucharist or the place of penance in or out of initiation.

This calls to mind another curious aspect of the Catholic rites. In infant baptism, after the water is poured, the minister anoints the crown of the child's head with chrism, calling to mind Christ's anointing as priest, prophet, and king. However, in adult initiation, the minister anoints with chrism the *forehead* of the newly baptized, while invoking the sevenfold gift of the Holy Spirit. That is, the priest confirms the adult, and the postbaptismal anointing with chrism found in infant baptism is dropped from the rites of adult initiation. Or, perhaps more accurately, the anointing with chrism on the crown of the head is *inserted* into the rite of infant baptism. Perhaps it is a fore-shadowing of the neophyte's confirmation, or perhaps it is a vestige of a practice long forsaken – the complete celebration of the rites of initiation for infants.

Leaving the Catholic practice behind for a moment, let us examine the Churches of the Reformation. Here confirmation was never considered part of initiation. Since the time of Luther it was a non-sacramental invocation of the Holy Spirit for children baptized as infants who now professed their faith before the community, at the end of a period of catechesis. This celebration patently borrowed from the way Catholics celebrated the rite for children, except the Churches of the Reform never regarded confirmation as a sacrament. In addition, the mechanics of the celebration differed from those of the Catholics in two aspects which, as mentioned above, betrayed some instability in the tradition: minister and matter. The Reformers allowed any pastor to function as the minister, and the matter was the action introduced by the Apostles: imposition of hands, not anointing with chrism.

As in the Catholic tradition, innovation has come to the liturgical celebration of the Reformers. For the first time in their history, baptismal initiation includes the possibility of a ritual of sealing: imposition of hands, invocation of the Holy Spirit, and even anointing with oil. Although the rite is not considered a separate sacrament, it clearly shares the same history as the Catholic sacrament of confirmation.

It is not surprising that confirmation is such a puzzling rite. Within each Church and among the Churches there are and have been so many variations that to survey the history of confirmation is to venture into a desert of mirages: When no clear way can be found, one adopts and explains what only appears to be there.

Given this situation, one wonders is it possible to arrive at a theology and practice of confirmation which can weave together its many threads? Can the meaning of confirmation be so established that its celebration may express a unified purpose? How does one reconcile the individual's need for catechesis and commitment with God's free gift of the Holy Spirit? What is the proper relation of confirmation to Eucharist and penance? And can the pieces of confirmation's puzzle be assembled in an ecumenical framework so that a theoretical and pastoral agreement could be envisioned at some future date for Catholics and the Churches of the Reformation?

The way here selected to respond to these questions is through the study of a post-Reformation controversy about confirmation. This approach will present the beginning and growth of the Reformers' theory and practice of confirmation and the affirmation of the post-Tridentine Catholic doctrine of the same. It is from this starting point that the Churches developed up to modern times the positions they reached and defended in this controversy. Consequently, a study of post-Reformation controversy will help one understand the ordinary celebrations of confirmation in Catholic and Reform Churches during the three subsequent centuries. This study will also provide clues for a new perspective on confirmation by observing the shortcomings of the controversies surrounding the theology of confirmation in the sixteenth century, under which the Churches have remained divided for far too long.

Specifically, the one around whom this investigation is organized is Robert Bellarmine, sixteenth century controversialist. Historian, defender of the faith, Bellarmine unleashed his energies against the threat of the Reformation. He is not the only possible starting point, but he is a good one. Bellarmine was a member of the Society of Jesus and taught at the Roman College. The mission of both community and school was to counter the Reform. Writing in 1588, he stands at an age a generation after Trent when the positions of both Catholics and Reformers had been firmly established. His presentation provides a summary of both his own tradition and that of his adversaries. To open Bellarmine is to open a compendium of both sides of the controversy. For this reason he is an apt choice for focusing this study. In writing on confirmation, Bellarmine confronts in particular two adversaries filled with the spirit of Reform – in love with the Scriptures, indignant against abuses: Martin Chemnitz and John Calvin. Together with Bellarmine they stand at the gate of an untravelled path toward revised theology and practice.

There are five parts. The first chapter examines the history of the theology of confirmation from Martin Luther till the Council of Trent. It lays bare the roots of the controversy. The second chapter presents the positions of the protagonists, the mature development of early Reformation and controversialist thought. Third is a list of the complete collection of sources which Calvin, Chemnitz, and Bellarmine cite, followed by a discussion on the method of these controversialists. This provides an analytical tool for evaluating the benefit of controversies in theology. Fourth, individual sources will be examined to familiarize the reader with some of the history of confirmation and the conflicting interpretation of these sources. Finally, in the light of post-Reformation controversy, the fifth chapter examines the contemporary Roman Catholic and Lutheran liturgical practice of confirmation. Thus, chapters one and two present the theology of confirmation at the time of and immediately after the Reformation, three and four present the method of the sixteenth century controversy concerning that theology, and in the final chapter, having learned from the process of controversy, contemporary methods will reveal a revised theology of confirmation, leading to a proposal for its practice.

This study hopes to resolve some of the puzzlement over confirmation so that one day all Christian Churches may celebrate it with understanding and enjoy its benefits in unity.

CHAPTER I

History

This journey toward a juncture in the theology of confirmation begins at the Reformation, where the road first divided. Robert Bellarmine, the focus for this study, appears some years later, but it is the Reformation which influenced his work.

On the question of confirmation, Bellarmine's work disputed the writings of many Reformers, but especially of John Calvin, who promoted the Reform in France and Switzerland in the mid-sixteenth century, and Martin Chemnitz, who continued the Lutheran Reform in Germany after the Council of Trent. The theological background for post-Reformation controversy lies in the writings prior to the pronouncements of Trent. This first chapter will trace the development of that theology.

The chapter begins with the writings of Martin Luther, who first questioned the sacramentality of confirmation in depth. His work was challenged early by controversialists in the Catholic tradition. After presenting their position, the chapter returns to the thought of the Reformers in the work of Philipp Melanchthon and the Augsburg Confession. Finally, it gives the Catholic pronouncements from the Council of Trent, which closed this first period.

A. Martin Luther
1. *De captivitate Babylonica ecclesiae praeludium*

Martin Luther's *De captivitate Babylonica ecclesiae praeludium* was the starting point for the sixteenth century controversies on the sacraments. Although John Wyclif[1] and John Hus[2] had broached the

---

[1] See, for example, *Trialogus cum supplemento Trialogi*, ed. Gotthard Lechler (Oxford: Clarendon Press, 1869).

[2] Hus was condemned for his errors concerning the sacraments, "Consilium doctorum facultatis theologicae studii Pragensis. Pragae, 1413, 6 Febr.," *Documenta Mag.*

topic, it was Luther's "little song about Rome"[3] which provoked a flurry of theological activity. Focusing on this work one can observe the evolution of sacramental theology up to the Council of Trent.

De captivitate Babylonica ecclesiae praeludium is the second of three great Reformation treatises Luther composed in the latter half of 1520.[4] He expresses how the Church is held in a Babylonian captivity by the sacramental abuses of the Popes and their theologians. The work has a simple structure: After an introduction during which Luther hardens his position against indulgences and the papacy and strengthens his position for communion under both kinds, he presents for analysis each of the seven sacraments of the Roman Church.

Luther's sacramental theology unfolds in the very structure of his work: He first discusses Eucharist, baptism, and penance, which he accepts as sacraments. Then, having established principles for the definition of a sacrament from these three, he dismisses the other four as merely sacramental ceremonies.

Luther begins his presentation of sacramental principles in his first major section, regarding the Eucharist. He says there are three captivities of this sacrament: first, its substance since the laity receive it under one species only; second, the concept of transubstantiation for which he finds no Scriptural support; and third, that the Mass has been reduced to a good work or a sacrifice. In denying that Mass is a good work, Luther begins to reveal what, for him, constitutes a sacrament. He starts with the concept of testament:

> Let it stand, therefore, first and infallibly – the Mass or Sacrament of the Altar is Christ's testament, which He, dying, left behind Him to be distributed among His believers. For thus His words go, "This cup is the new testament in my blood." . . . Thus, let us inquire what a testament is, and we

---

Joannis Hus vitam, doctrinam, causam in Constantiensi Concilio actam et controversias de religione in Bohemia annis 1403-1418 motas, pp. 475-480; even though in an earlier work he treated all seven as sacraments, "Liber IV, distinccio vii," *Super IV. Sententiarum,* ed. Wenzel Flajshans & Marie Hominková, Mag. Joannis Hus opera omnia II (Osnabrück: Biblio-Verlag, 1966), pp. 550-553 on confirmation.

[3] ". . . ein lidlen von Rom." Luther himself refers to his forthcoming work in this way in *An dem christlichen Adel deutscher Nation von des christlichen Standes Besserung.* 1520, WA 6:469.

[4] The treatises are *An dem christlichen Adel deutscher Nation von des christlichen Standes Besserung.* 1520, WA 6:404-469; *De captivitate Babylonica ecclesiae praeludium.* 1520, WA 6:497-573; and *Ein Sendbrief an den Papst Leo X. Von der Freiheit eines Christenmenschen.* 1520, WA 7:3-38.

shall learn at the same time what the Mass is, what its right
use, its fruit, its abuse.[5]

Luther then explains that a testament is a promise made by one about
to die.[6] Having a record of Christ's promise is his first criterion for
what constitutes the Eucharist as a sacrament.

> You see, therefore, that the Mass, which we call such, is a
> promise of the forgiveness of sins made to us by God, and
> such a promise as has been confirmed by the death of the
> Son of God.[7]

Here Luther returns to why Mass should not be called a good work and
introduces another essential element to what constitutes the Eucharist:
faith.

> If <the Mass> is a promise, as has been said, then access to it
> is gained by no works, no powers, no merits, but by faith
> alone.[8]

Then he expands on his principles with a third essential element of the
sacrament: the sign.

> This is surely true, that in the case of every promise of his,
> God was almost accustomed to add some sign as a
> remembrance or memorial of His promise, so that thereby it
> may be kept the more diligently and admonish the more
> effectually.[9]

Luther has been explaining how the promise of God is operative simply
in the Mass, but he will expand this to mean that every sacrament must
have a promise of God and an accompanying sign.

---

[5] "Stet ergo primum et infallibiliter, Missam seu sacramentum altaris esse
testamentum Christi, quod moriens post se reliquit distribuendum suis fidelibus. Sic
enim habent eius verba 'Hic calix novum testamentum in meo sanguine'. . . . "Quaeramus
ergo quid sit testamentum, et simul habebimus quid sit missa, quis usus, quis fructus, quis
abusus eius." De captivitate Babylonica ecclesiae praeludium, WA 6:513.

[6] Luther seems to make a linguistic error here, equivocating on the word
"testamentum".

[7] "Vides ergo, quod Missa quam vocamus sit promissio remissionis peccatorum, a
deo nobis facta, et talis promissio, quae per mortem filii dei firmata sit." WA 6:513.

[8] "Si enim <Missa> promissio est, ut dictum est, nullis operibus, nullis viribus,
nullis meritis ad eam acceditur, sed sola fide." WA 6:514.

[9] "Hoc sane verum est, in omni promissione sua deus fere solitus est adiicere
signum aliquod, ceu monumentum, ceu memoriale promissionis suae, quo fidelius
servaretur et efficatius moneret." WA 6:517-518.

We learn from which things that in any promise whatsoever
of God two things are presented, the word and the sign, so
that we understand the word to be the testament, but the
sign to be the sacrament.[10]

Luther will test each sacrament against these criteria. He searches
Scripture for a record of God's promise and its accompanying sign, to be
encountered with faith in the sacrament.

Thus, in the next section on baptism, Luther looks for these
elements. "First of all the divine promise must be considered in
baptism, which says 'Whoever will have believed and been baptized
will be saved.'"[11]   Here is both the recorded promise and the
requirement of faith. He adds later, "The other thing which pertains
to baptism is the sign or sacrament, which is the very immersion into
water from which it also derives its name."[12]

Luther's capricious position on penance further illuminates his
theology. He begins with a strong affirmation: "First I have to reject
the seven sacraments, and for the present I have to posit only three:
baptism, penance, and the bread."[13]   When he takes up penance itself
he says, "For this sacrament, like the other two, consists in the word of
divine promise and our faith."[14] His omission of the requirement of a
sign is noteworthy here, for at the end of his work he concludes penance
is not a sacrament on that basis.

For only in <baptism and the bread> do we see both the
divinely instituted sign and the promise of forgiveness of sins.
For the sacrament of penance, which I added to these two,
lacks the visible and divinely instituted sign, and I said it is
nothing but a way and a return to baptism.[15]

[10] "Ex quibus intelligimus, in qualibet promissione dei duo proponi, verbum et
signum, ut verbum intelligamus esse testamentum, signum vero esse sacramentum." WA
6:518.

[11] "Primum itaque in Baptismo observanda est divina promissio, quae dicit: Qui
crediderit et baptisatus fuerit, salvus erit." WA 6:527.

[12] "Alterum, quod ad baptismum pertinet, est signum seu sacramentum, quod est
ipsa mersio in aquam, unde et nomen habet." WA 6:531.

[13] "Principio neganda mihi sunt septem sacramenta, et tantum tria pro tempore
ponenda, Baptismus, Poenitentia, Panis. . . ." WA 6:501.

[14] "Nam cum et ipsum, sicut et alia duo, constet verbo promissionis divinae et fide
nostra. . . ." WA 6:543.

[15] ". . . cum in his solis <Baptismo et pane> et institutum divinitus signum et
promissionem remissionis peccatorum videamus. Nam poenitentiae sacramentum quod
ego his duobus accensui, signo visibili et divinitus instituto caret, et aliud non esse dixi,
quam viam ac reditum ad baptismum." WA 6:572.

Having seen Luther's theology of sacrament at work among the rites he does accept, one may see more clearly how it works in a rite he does not regard as sacramental, namely confirmation.

Luther rejects confirmation on the basis of his definition of a sacrament:

> But for this time we seek sacraments that have been divinely instituted, among which we find no reason that we should number confirmation. Indeed, for the constitution of a sacrament there is required above all things a word of divine promise, by which faith may be exercised. But we read that Christ promised nothing anywhere concerning confirmation.[16]

Luther does not condemn the seven sacraments, but he esteems confirmation "as a certain ecclesiastical rite or sacramental ceremony."[17] He then stresses the importance of the promise. There are ceremonies which have a word and a prayer, but no promise. Such ceremonies

> cannot be called sacraments of faith, because they have no divine promise connected with them. Neither do they work salvation; but the sacraments do preserve those who believe the divine promise.[18]

Because confirmation lacks this promise, Luther wonders why the Roman Church made a sacrament out of the imposition of hands, which is such an ambiguous gesture – Jesus touched children with it; and the Apostles imparted the Holy Spirit, ordained presbyters, and cured the sick all with that same gesture. Then he proposes an alternate mode of

---

[16] "Nos autem pro hac vice sacramenta divinitus instituta quaerimus, inter quae ut Confirmationem numeremus, nullam invenimus causam. Ad sacramenti enim constitutionem ante omnia requiritur verbum divinae promissionis, quo fides exerceatur. At nihil legimus Christum uspiam de confirmatione promisisse." WA 6:550.

[17] "Quare satis est pro ritu quodam Ecclesiastico seu cerimonia sacramentali confirmationem habere." WA 6:550. Although the terminology may vary, the Reformers consistently establish two distinct groups: sacraments and "sacramental ceremonies." The sacraments number two, baptism and Eucharist. Other ceremonies are "sacramental", meaning "imitative of sacraments," not "pertaining to sacraments." In modern English, what appears to be contrary to Luther is actually clearer: There are sacraments and non-sacramental ceremonies. For the Reformers, confirmation continually falls to this second group; it is a religious rite, but not a sacrament.

[18] ". . . quia promissionem divinam non habent, sacramenta fidei dici non possunt? Neque enim salutem operantur. At sacramenta servant credentes promissioni divinae." WA 6:550.

confirmation: In Acts 9 and Psalm 104 it is bread which gives strength, or "confirms". So he says there could be three sacraments that confirm: the bread, ordination, and · confirmation itself. Luther reduces the Roman position to absurdity by asking, "if whatever the Apostles did is a sacrament, why have they not rather made preaching a sacrament?"[19] Luther argues that the sign and means by which the Christian receives strength are ambiguous in Scripture, and that the Roman Church has erred in making a sacrament out of the actions of the Apostles, not the promise of Jesus.

Next Luther challenges the practice of confirmation. From Scriptural evidence, he shows that the present practice does not correspond to the miracles of apostolic times. Confirmation, he says, is a not too burdensome rite to adorn the office of bishops, "that they may not be entirely without work in the Church."[20] He charges that bishops have relinquished their work, despising what is divine, and holding human wisdom in honor. Far from celebrating a sacrament found in Scripture, bishops have turned away from their pastoral responsibilities of preaching the Gospel and caring for souls, and replaced them with a rite of mere human fabrication. Luther argues that the current practice, invented by the Church, does not correspond to Scripture.

De captivitate Babylonica concludes with similar reflections on marriage, ordination, and extreme unction. One of Luther's comments about ordination is pertinent to this discussion. He denies ordination is a sacrament, since there is no Scriptural evidence. And without a text from Scripture, the Church cannot institute a sacrament on its own:

> Nor does the Church have power to establish new divine promises of grace, as some babble, because what is decreed by the Church is of no less authority than what is decreed by God, since it is ruled by the Holy Spirit. . . .
>
> Let this then be certain, that the Church is not able to promise grace, which is the property of God alone, for which reason neither to institute a sacrament.[21]

---

[19]   "Si autem sacramentum est, quicquid Apostoli fecerunt, cur non magis praedicationem fecerunt sacramentum?" WA 6:549.

[20]   ". . . ne penitus sint sine opere in Ecclesia." WA 6:549.

[21]   "Nec habet Ecclesia potestatem novas promissiones gratiae divinas statuere, sicut quidam garriunt, quod non minoris sit autoritatis, quicquid ab Ecclesia, quam quod a deo statuitur, cum regatur spiritu sancto....

"Sit itaque certum, Ecclesiam non posse promittere gratiam, quod solius dei est, quare nec instituere sacramentum." WA 6:560-561.

Concluding this treatise, Luther admits that other things might appear to be sacraments – e.g., prayer, the Word, the cross of Christ – because they have a divine promise. But the promise needs a sign.

> However it seemed good that those things be properly called sacraments which have been promised, after signs have been attached. The remainder, because they have not been bound to signs, are bare promises. Hence, it happens that, if we want to speak strictly, there are only two sacraments in the Church of God – baptism and the bread.[22]

In the third Reformation treatise, *Von der Freiheit eines Christenmenschen*, Luther lists confirmation among the duties of a bishop, but gives it no special rank.

> A bishop, when he consecrates a church, confirms or performs some other duty belonging to his office, is not made a bishop by these works.[23]

For Luther, then, sacraments are signs celebrated in accordance with a promise of Jesus recorded in the Gospels. They call for a response of faith. Confirmation – lacking a promise and a sign – is therefore not a sacrament.

2. Other Works

De captivitate Babylonica remains the single work most expressive of Luther's sacramental theology. Nonetheless, during the previous year and in many other writings spanning the decade between its publication and the pronouncement of the Augsburg Confession, he both accented and expanded his earlier position.[24]

In the year before the great Reformation treatises, Luther was already exploring the sacraments. A trilogy of treatises on penance,

---

[22] "Proprie tamen ea sacramenta vocari visum est, quae annexis signis promissa sunt. Caetera, quia signis alligata non sunt, nuda promissa sunt. Quo fit, ut, si rigide loqui volumus, tantum duo sunt in Ecclesia dei sacramenta, Baptismus et panis." WA 6:572.

[23] "Item gleych wie eyn geweyheter Bischoff wen der kirchen weyhet, fermelt oder sonst seynis ampts werck ubet, ßo machen yhn die selben werck nit zu eynem bischoff." WA 7:31.

[24] There was one occasion early on when Luther spoke of baptism and confirmation as being unrepeatable and on the same level: "Unde et ab omnibus dicitur theologis sacramentum baptismatis et confirmationis non esse iterabile." *Commentariolus in epistolam divi Pauli Apostoli ad Hebreos*–1517 6, WA 57,III:180.

baptism, and Eucharist announced his theme. In "The Holy and Blessed Sacrament of Baptism," Luther makes faith in the promise of God a necessary component of baptism.

> This faith is of all things the most necessary, for it is the ground of all comfort. ...
> This faith a person must hold so firmly that he would cling to it even though everything and all sins attacked him. For he who lets himself be forced away from this faith makes God a liar in his promise in the sacrament of baptism.[25]

In the same year Luther wrote a letter anticipating *De captivitate Babylonica* to his friend Georg Spalatin. Since he had just treated only three sacraments, Luther explains:

> Concerning the other sacraments, there is no reason why you or anyone of humanity should hope or expect from me any statement until I be informed at which place I may be able to prove those things. For to me, a sacrament remains a sacrament only [26] where a clear divine promise is given, which may exercise faith, since without the Word of the One promising and the faith of the one receiving there can be nothing of contact for us with God. You will hear another time the things which those people have pronounced concerning those seven sacraments.[27]

Heralding a more discursive essay, this passage already enunciates that a sacrament requires a divine promise from the Word of God, which will be met in faith.

In the ensuing years Luther alluded to the practice of confirmation, first reiterating the principles of *De captivitate Babylonica*, then

---

[25] Dißer glaub ist der aller notigst, denn er der grund ist alles trostis. . . . <An> dem glauben muß man alßo fest halten, das, ob auch alle creature und alle sund eynen ubirfielen, er dennoch dran hange, angesehen, das, wer sich davon lest dringen, der macht gott zu eynem lugner in seynem vorpinden an dem sacrament der tauff." "Ein Sermon von der heiligen hochwürdigen Sakrament der Taufe, 1519," WA 2:732-733; translation from LuthW 35:36-37.

[26] I have simplified the triple negative in this translation.

[27] "De aliis sacramentis non est, quod tu vel ullus hominum ex me speret aut expectet ullum sermonem, donec docear, quo loco queam illa probare. Non enim ullum mihi reliquum est sacramentum, quod sacramentum non sit, nisi ubi expressa detur promissio divina, que fidem exerceat, cum sine verbo promittentis & fide suscipientis nihil possit nobis esse cum Deo negotii. Quę autem de sacramentis illis septem fabulati illi sunt, alio tempore audies." "Luther an Spalatin. Wittenberg, 18. Dezember 1519," WABr 1:594-595.

expanding on them. In a sermon on impediments to marriage in 1522 he says,

> But it is important to avoid the deceitful jugglery of the idol-bishops, confirmation, which has no foundation in the Scriptures. And the bishops only deceive the people with their lies that they will give grace, character, a mark inside. It is much more the character of the beasts, (Rev. 13).[28]

Here he underlines the importance of finding sacraments in Scripture. In another sermon the same year, he says,

> I allow that confirmation be administered provided that it is known that God has said nothing about it, and knows nothing of it, and that what the bishops allege about it is false. They mock our God in saying that it is a sacrament of God, when it is merely human invention.[29]

So, while permitting the ceremony, he denies it is a sacrament and claims it is a human invention, not of divine origin.

At Christmas the same year, Luther preached on Paul's letter to Titus 3, 5 against the practice of confirmation, again because it is not Scriptural. But here he adds that because the Holy Spirit comes in baptism, the apostolic imposition of hands in Acts, although analogous to confirmation, must have been a temporary measure whose miraculous signs no longer continue in the Church.

> Here you hear, "the water," that is the bath: you hear: "to be born again," that is the regeneration and the renewal, and the Spirit, Whom here St. Paul interprets as the Holy Spirit. And here it is to be noticed that the Apostle knows nothing of the sacrament of confirmation. For he teaches that the Holy Spirit is given in baptism, as Christ also teaches, indeed, in

---

[28] "Sonderlich aber ist tzu meyden der Bisschoffgotzen lugenhafftig gauckelwerck, die fermelung, wilche keyn grund ynn der schrifft hatt Und die Bisschoff nur die leutt mit yhren lugen betriegen, das gnade, Character, maltzeychen drynnen geben werden. Es ist viel mehr der Bestien Character, Apoc. 13." *Welche Personen verboten sind zu ehelichen*, 1522, WA 10,2:266.

[29] "Ich laß zu, das man fermele ßo fern, das man wisse, das gott nicht davon gesagt hatt, auch nichts darumb wisse, und das es erlogen sey, was die Bisschoffe darynnen fur geben. Sie spotten unßers gottis, sagen, es sey eyn Sacrament gottis, und ist doch eygen menschen fundle." *Vom ehelichen Leben*, 1522, WA X,II:282. Translation from J.D.C. Fisher, *Christian Initiation: The Reformation Period. Some Early Reformed Rites of Baptism and Confirmation and Other Contemporary Documents*, Alcuin Club Collections, No. 51 (London: S.P.C.K., 1970), pp. 172-173.

baptism we are reborn by the Holy Spirit. We read in the
Acts of the Apostles that the Apostles laid their hands on the
heads of the baptized, so that they might receive the Holy
Spirit, which is analogous to confirmation; but there it
happens that they themselves receive the Holy Spirit with
outward signs and would speak in many tongues in order to
preach the gospel. But this was a temporary measure and
does not continue any more.[30]

This argument will reappear – Luther's followers use it to require that
sacraments be universally applicable to all times. In addition, the
passages from Acts 8 and 19 are hinges for the whole controversy on
confirmation. Continually the Roman Church will open them as the
Scriptural evidence the Reformers seek, while the Reformers dismiss
them as insufficient.

In the following year Luther revealed a form of confirmation he
would tolerate. He defines the proper minister (the pastor) and content
(an examination of children's faith) of the rite.

Confirmation should not be bothered with as the bishops
desire, but nevertheless we do not find fault that every pastor
might investigate the faith from children and if it be good and
sincere, he may impose hands and confirm.[31]

In suggesting that confirmation is an examination of children's faith,
Luther accepts an interpretation common among the Reformers
throughout the controversy.

Near the end of the decade Luther addressed the problem of the
Anabaptists by reiterating the necessity of faith (now more nuanced
than in the 1519 Sermon on baptism because of the need to defend the

---

[30] "Hie horistu: das wasser, das ist das badt, du horist: anderweyt geporn werden,
das ist, die widdergepurt und vornewrung, unnd den geyst, den hie S. Paulus außdruckt,
den heyligen geyst. Und ist hie tzu mercken, das der Apostell von dem sacrament der
firmelung nichts weyß; denn er leret, der heylig geyst werd ynn der tawff geben, wie
auch Christus leret, ia, ynn der tawff werden wyr auß dem heyligen geyst gepornn. Wyr
leßen wol ynn Act. Apostolorum, das die Apostelln yhr hend legten auff die hewbt der
getawfften, das sie den heyligen geyst empfingen, wilchs sie tzu der firmelung tzihen,
ßo dasselb darumb geschah, das dieselben den heyligen geyst yn offentlichem zeychen
empfingen und mit viel tzungen reden mochten, das Euangelium tzu predigen. Aber
dasselb ist tzeytlich abgangen und nit mehr blieben. . . ." Zu der frue Christmeß Epistell
Pauli, WA 10,1,1:117. Translation from Fisher, p. 172, alt.

[31] "Confirmatio, ut volunt Episcopi, non curanda, sed tamen quisque pastor posset
scrutari a pueris fidem, quae si bona et germana esset, ut imponeret manus et confirmaret,
non improbamus." Predigt am Sonntag Lätare Nachmittags (15. März 1523), WA 11:66.
See fn. 53 and 55 below.

validity of infant baptism) and the certainty of the Word and command of God. Now Luther stresses the importance of the *command* of God, which his followers will require as part of the Scriptural evidence for a sacrament.

> True, one should add faith to baptism. But we are not to base baptism on faith. There is quite a difference between having faith, on the one hand, and depending on one's faith and making baptism depend on faith, on the other. . . . But a baptism on the Word and command of God even when faith is not present is still a correct and certain baptism if it takes place as God commanded.
> . . . <Nothing> is lacking in baptism. Always something is lacking in faith. However long our life, always there is plenty to learn in regard to faith.[32]

He chides the Anabaptists for devaluing the sacrament of baptism. As he had complained that the Roman Church made confirmation a sacrament out of a human act, now he complains that the Anabaptists made human a divinely-instituted sacrament.

> In sum, the Anabaptists are too frivolous and insolent. For they consider baptism not as a God-given ordinance or command, but as a human trifle, like many other customs under the papacy relating to the consecration of salt, water, or herbs.[33]

In 1529 Luther contributed his Large Catechism and Small Catechism for the religious education of his followers. They refined the genre of catechism and are still, together with the Augsburg Confession and other texts, normative handbooks in the Lutheran Church. No longer the polemicist, Luther simply applies his sacramental theology to baptism and Eucharist.

---

[32] "War ists, das man glewben sol zur tauffe, Aber auff den glawben sol man sich nicht teuffen lassen. Es ist gar viel ein ander ding, den glawben haben und sich auff den glawben verlassen und also sich drauff teuffen lassen. . . . Welcher aber getaufft wird auff Gottes wort und gebot, wenn da gleich kein glawbe were, dennoch were die tauffe recht und gewis, denn sie geschicht, wie sie Gott geboten hat. . . .

"An der tauffe seilet nichts, am glauben seilets ymer dar, Denn wir haben an dem glawben gnug zu lernen unser leben lang." *Von Der Widdertauffe an zween Pfarherrn. Ein brieff Mart. Luther.* WA 26:164-166; translation from LuthW 40:252-253.

[33] "Summa, die widderteuffer sind ze frevel und frech, Denn sie sehen die tauffe nicht an fur eine Göttliche ordnung odder gebot, sondern als were es menschen tand, wie viel andere kirchen breuche sind unter dem Bapst als von saltz, wasser, kreuter weihen." WA 26:169-170; LuthW 40:258.

It remains for us to speak of our two sacraments, instituted by Christ, in which every Christian should have at least some short elementary instruction.[34]

He then quotes Jesus' injunction for his disciples to teach and baptize all nations (Mt 28, 19) and his promise that whoever believes and is baptized shall be saved (Mk 16, 16). From these he deduces the divine institution of baptism.

Observe first, that these words contain God's command and ordinance; we should not doubt, then, that baptism is of divine origin, and was not devised and invented by humanity.[35]

Late in his life Luther wrote a pastor who had scruples about confirming at all. He assured him he would not betray his faith since even political authority denied it was a sacrament.

If you wish, you will even be able to anoint the sick and to confirm adults for the time being, because <the prince> denies that they are sacraments and established only a ceremony with a clear conscience.[36]

Arthur C. Repp suggests that Luther approved confirmation as a "concession he was ready to make for the time being as long as no compromise was involved."[37] Repp concludes,

---

[34] "Uber die selbige ist noch zu sagen von unsern zweien Sacramenten von Christo eingesetzt, davon auch ein yglicher Christ zum wenigsten ein gemeinen kurtzen unterricht haben sol. . . ." *Deudsch Catechismus (Der Große Katechismus)*. 1529. WA 30,I:212, *Luther's Large Catechism*, trans. J. N. Lenker, (Minneapolis: Augsburg Publishing House, 1967), p. 124.

[35] "Yn diesen worten soltu zum ersten wercken, das hie stehet Gottes gebot und einsetzung, des man nicht zweivele, die Tauffe sey ein Götlich ding, nicht von menschen erdacht noch erfunden." WA 30,I:212; Lenker, p. 124.

[36] "Si vis, poteris etiam ad tempus aegrotos ungere et confirmare Adultos, quia <princeps> negat esse sacramenta, solam ceremoniam libera conscientia statuit." "Luther an Gregor Solinus in Tangermünde, Wittenberg, 13 September 1540, No. 3534," WABr 9:232.

[37] Arthur C. Repp, Confirmation in the Lutheran Church (St. Louis: Concordia Publishing House, 1964), p. 18. I accept this observation more readily than Max Thurian's opinion: "Luther n'a pas eu sur la confirmation une pensée bien définie. Il semble avoir hésité à l'accepter ou à la rejeter comme sacrement." *La Confirmation: Consécration des laïcs* (Neuchatel: Delachaux & Niestle, 1957), p. 7. Perhaps he means Luther's opinion about confession. Otherwise, it is hard to reconcile Thurian with *De captivitate Babylonica*, WA 6:550 (see fn. 16 above).

> Actually, confirmation did not play an important role in his
> thoughts. His interest took a different tack. He was
> concerned primarily with catechetical instruction.[38]

In context, sacraments are only a part of Luther's theological
framework. He was more concerned with justification by faith, the
nature of sin, and the primacy of Scripture. His depreciation of the role
of confirmation is a result of other issues which preoccupied him.

Luther maintained his principal arguments to the end: a sacrament
must have a promise and a sign in Scripture, and must be met with
faith. In addition he stressed the efficacy of God's command. He called
the imposition of hands in Acts a temporary measure no longer in effect.
He concluded that confirmation may be celebrated only as an
examination of children's faith.

Here then are the thoughts which inspired a theological
revolution about the sacraments. Luther so well formulated his
position that neither converts nor opponents could remain silent. These
thoughts were promoted, criticized, expanded, and attacked by
succeeding generations of theologians.

B. Early Controversialists

Theologians of the Roman Church quickly responded to the
challenge of Luther's theology of sacraments. The issue was heated
from the beginning and positions hardened on each side.

One of the first to respond to *De captivitate Babylonica* was a man
who sought to secure for himself a reputation as a great theologian for
the Church: Henry VIII of England. *Assertio septem sacramentorum*
defended the Church's teaching on all the sacraments, and Henry
shows a good grasp of the issues at stake. His principal argument
concerning confirmation opposes Luther's requirement for a text from
Scripture to support the dominical institution of the sacrament.

> <Why> does he so maliciously judge concerning the whole
> Church, as if she took up a sacrament gratuitously, because
> he reads no word of promise in these places? As if Christ has
> promised, said or done nothing at all which the evangelists do
> not include.[39]

---

[38] Repp, p. 18.

[39] "<Cur> tam maligne de tota iudicat ecclesia, quasi temere sacramentum suscipiat,
propterea quia in illis locis nullum legit verbum promissionis? quasi nihil omnino
promiserit, dixerit, fecerit Christus, quod non complectantur euangelistae." Henry VIII,

He suggests that the sacraments were very likely celebrated by the apostolic community even before the Gospels were written.

> If none of them had ever been written, yet the Gospel would remain written in the hearts of the faithful, which was older than the manuscripts of all the evangelists; and the sacraments would remain, which themselves I doubt not are older than all the books of the evangelists, so that Luther should not think it an effective proof of a sacrament having been received in vain if he does not find it instituted in the Gospels.[40]

Henry insightfully focuses the argument on what constitutes a Christological institution of confirmation. The Scriptures do record the promise of the Spirit (Jn 15; 16), and the imposition of hands by the Apostles (Acts 8; 19). Perhaps the Word of Christ regarding the sacrament was given but simply not recorded, he argues, for that confirmation is a sacrament is attested not only by the

> testimony of holy doctors and by the faith of the whole Church, but also in the clearest passages of holy Scripture it is shown that by the visible sign of the episcopal hand it confers not only grace but also the Spirit of grace Himself.[41]

Henry's refutation so moved Leo X, to whom he dedicated the Assertio, that the Pope praised the work and bestowed on Henry the title *Fidei Defensor*.[42]

Meanwhile, John Eck was becoming a theological champion of the Roman Church for his debates against Martin Luther and his followers.

Assertio septem sacramentorum adversus Marti. Lutherum, (London: Pyrson, 1521; reprint ed., Ridgewood, NJ: The Gregg Press Incorporated, 1966), "De confirmatione," pages not numbered.

[40] "Quorum si nullum unquam scriptum esset, maneret tamen euangelium scriptum in cordibus fidelium, quod antiquius fuit omnium euangelistarum codicibus, manerent sacramenta, quae & ipsa non dubito euangelistarum libris esse omnibus antiquiora, ne putet Lutherus efficax argumentum esse, frustra suscepti sacramenti, si non reperiat institutum in euangeliis." Henry VIII, "De confirmatione."

[41] ". . . quae non solum sanctorum testimonio doctorum, & totius ecclesiae fide, sed etiam sacrae scripturae clarissimis locis ostenditur: visibili signo manus pontificiae, non gratiam tantum, sed & ipsum gratiae spiritum conferre." Henry VIII, "De confirmatione."

[42] Leo X, "LI.: Ex supernae dispositionis," *Bullarum Diplomatum et privilegiorum sanctorum romanorum Pontificum*, ed. Collegium Adlectum Romae Virorum S. Theologiae et SS. Canonum Peritorum, Taurinensis editio, 22 vols. (Turin: Seb. Franco et Henrico Dalmazzo, 1860), vol. 5, pp. 773-775.

From 1525 on, Eck composed his *Enchiridion locorum communium*, a handbook which underwent several revisions, providing ready responses to the Reformers. Eck treated specific issues, and his work reads like a random confrontation on theological points: One chapter deals with the diverse topics of not eating meats and degrees of consanguinity, and the chapters on the sacraments are scattered throughout the book. Chapter 6, "De Confirmatione" concerns two axioms: that confirmation is a sacrament, and that bishops alone confirm now as a continuation of the charism of the Apostles.

For the first axiom, Eck argues from reason and from authorities.

> But because in confirmation there is a sensible sign, having the infallible assistance of the grace of the Holy Spirit, it is accordingly a sacrament.[43]

He summons Acts 8 and 19 to endorse his view.

> Note that after baptism, there was a sensible sign, namely the imposition of hands, whereby the grace of the Holy Spirit was conferred, and thus it was a sacrament.[44]

For the second axiom, Eck collects testimony from Dionysius the Areopagite, Miltiades, the Council of Orleans, and Jerome, to show that this gift has always been present in the Church. In the 1529 edition, Eck raises the question of scriptural proof of dominical institution.

> When the heretics object that Christ did not institute this sacrament, it must be said that Christ did indeed institute this sacrament not indeed by showing it forth, but by promising. He says in the last chapter of Luke: 'But stay in the city until you are invested with power from above.' And in the sixteenth chapter of John: 'If I do not go away, the Paraclete will not come to you. . . .'[45]

[43] "At quia in confirmatione est signum sensibile, habens infallibilem assistentiam gratiae Spiritus sancti, ideo est sacramentum." John Eck, "De confirmatione VI," *Enchiridion locorum communium adversus Lutherum et alios hostes ecclesiae (1525-1543)*, CCath 34:104.

[44] "Ecce, post baptismum erat signum sensibile, scilicet impositio manuum, quo conferebatur gratia Spiritus sancti, et ita erat sacramentum." CCath 34:104.

[45] "Obiicientibus hereticis Christum hoc sacramentum non institutisse, dicendum est, quod Christus utique hoc sacramentum instituit: non quidem exhibendo, sed promittendo. Lucae ultimo dicit: 'Vos autem sedete in civitate quousque induamini virtute ex alto.' Et Iohannis XVI: 'Si non abiero, Paracletus non venerit ad vos. . . .'" CCath 34:106.

He also suggests, "When Christ laid his hands on the children he either instituted or hinted at this sacrament."[46]

Eck initially argues for the sacramentality of confirmation from the scholastic notion of sacrament as sign, rather than from Luther's concept of it as promise rooted in the Word of God. Although he quotes from Acts in the earliest edition, he reports the practice of imposition of hands, not the promise and command of Christ demanded by Luther's school.

In 1535 Eck included a chapter on the character.

> The Church believes, and also the faithful, that a certain sign which is called a character is impressed on the soul in three sacraments: namely, in baptism, confirmation, and orders.[47]

Against Luther's objection that the character is unknown to Scripture, Eck contends,

> The character is not a thing invented by the Fathers, but since the Holy Spirit is the teacher, people of God understood it, as has been shown from Paul.[48]

As a simple handbook, Eck's work provides the reader with answers to objections but does not refine the argument.

In summary, the early controversialists challenged the Reformation's principle of sacramental theology: They questioned the necessity of scriptural evidence to prove the dominical institution of sacraments. They recorded the practice of imposition of hands in Acts and its continuation in history as confirmation, and they incorporated the doctrine of character in connection with it. These arguments would prove unconvincing since they begin from a contrary position regarding what kind of scriptural testimony is required for sacraments. Thus this becomes one instance of the much larger controversy between Catholics and Reformers weighing the value of tradition against that of Scripture.

---

[46] "Christus quando imposuit manus parvulis, hoc sacramentum vel instituit, vel insinuavit." CCath 34:106 (see Mark 10, 16).

[47] "Credit ecclesia et fideles in tribus sacramentis imprimi animae quoddam signaculum quod "character" nominatur: scilicet in baptismo, confirmatione, et ordine." CCath 34:365.

[48] "Character non est res a patribus ficta, sed, Spiritu sancto doctore, homines Dei eum intellexerunt, ut ex Paulo ostensum est." CCath 34:368 (see Ephesians 4, 30; 1, 13-14).

C. Philipp Melanchthon
and the Augsburg Confession

Among Luther's companions Philipp Melanchthon arose as a dedicated theologian striving for the truth. Already in 1521 his *Loci Theologici* was developing the doctrine of the Reformation.

> Now indeed as we speak in the Church, a sacrament is called a ceremony instituted in the Gospel, so that it may be a witness of the promise which is proper to the Gospel, namely of promised reconciliation or grace. [49]

Melanchthon stresses Luther's concept of reconciliation in his definition of the promised grace of a sacrament. [50] He is thus more easily able to include penance among the sacraments. [51] He also adds orders to the list because of the manifold references to ministry in the Pauline corpus and the Gospels themselves. [52]

Nevertheless, confirmation is another matter.

> There was once an examination of doctrine in which individuals used to recite a summary of doctrine and show that they dissented from Gentiles and heretics, and it was a very useful way for educating people, likewise for separating the profane and the religious. Afterwards it became a public prayer, and the Apostles imposed hands on them. Thus they were being presented with manifest gifts of the Holy Spirit. But now the rite of confirmation, which bishops retain, is an utterly empty ceremony. It would be useful however that an investigation and profession of doctrine be made and a public prayer for the sake of good people, nor would that prayer be futile. [53]

[49] "Sacramentum nunc quidem, ut in Ecclesia loquimur, vocatur ceremonia in Evangelio instituta, ut sit testimonium promissionis, quae est Evangelii propria, videlicet promissae reconciliationis seu gratiae." Philipp Melanchthon, *Loci Theologici*, CR 21:847.

[50] See fn. 15 above.

[51] CR 21:849.

[52] CR 21:850.

[53] "Olim fuit exploratio doctrinae, in qua singuli recitabant summam doctrinae et ostendebant se dissentire ab Ethnicis et Haereticis, et erat mos ad erudiendos homines, item ad discernendos profanos et pios admodum utilis. Postea fiebat publica precatio, et Apostoli imponebant eius <sic> manus. Ita donabantur manifestis donis Spiritus sancti. Sed nunc ritus Confirmationis, quem retinent Episcopi, est prorsus otiosa ceremonia. Utile autem esset, explorationem et professionem doctrinae fieri et publicam precationem pro piis, nec ea precatio esset inanis." CR 21:853.

So while rejecting confirmation as a sacrament, Melanchthon values an examination of faith, which he believes was its original purpose. This belief is popular among the Reformers, and Melanchthon is the first to mention it. His text predates Luther's 1523 sermon [54] where he also favors this interpretation of confirmation. [55] But early patristic literature does not support examination as the origin of the rite.

The Augsburg Confession, drafted by Melanchthon in 1530, attempted to restore unity by emphasizing common elements between the opponents, using the Council of Nicaea as a starting point. The Confession itself avoids defining what a sacrament is and how many of them there are. However, it explains that "sacraments and the word because of the ordination and command of Christ are efficacious, even if they are produced through evil people,"[56] thus calling the word and command of Jesus efficacious sacramental elements. The following sections present baptism, Eucharist, and penance. Article 13 considers the use of the sacraments, that

> sacraments were instituted not in the way that they might be signs of profession among people, but rather that they might be signs and witnesses of the will of God toward us, for stirring up and confirming faith in those who use them as proposed. And so sacraments must be used so that faith, which believes the promises which are brought forth and shown through sacraments, may give assent.
>
> <The Churches of the Reform> condemn therefore those who teach that sacraments justify *ex opere operato*, but do not teach that faith, which believes sins are remitted, is

---

[54] See fn. 31 above.

[55] These writers do not relate the origin of the historically unsupportable idea that confirmation was originally an examination of faith. Chemnitz says in #25 of his section on Confirmation that this interpretation of history is consonant with canon 7 of the Council of Laodicaea, canon 8 of the Council of Arles, a canon of the Council of Orleans, and with Dionysius at the end of the *Ecclesiastica hierarchia*. In each case the reference is vague enough to impose this interpretation, but the earliest explicit reference I have found is this text of Melanchthon.

Theóbald Suss writes that the origin is traditionally assigned to Erasmus (see Chapter III, fn. 61 for text), "Remarques sur le problème de la confirmation," *Positions Lutheriennes* (July 1957):190, but Melanchthon's suggestion is older by one year.

[56] "Et sacramenta et verbum propter ordinationem et mandatum Christi sunt efficacia, etiamsi per malos exhibeantur." Confessio Augustana Ipsa, 8, CR 26:277. This point echoes a text which will be presented in more detail in Chapter IV, Augustine's *De baptismo* 3:16,21.

required in the use of the sacraments.[57]

Orders and ecclesiastical rites follow.   By not presenting the other sacraments, the Confession may imply their position among these ecclesiastical rites, but the assignment is not explicit.

John Eck, Johannes Faber, and other theologians contributed to the *Confutatio Romana Confessionis Augustanae*, which sought a clarification on the number of sacraments through its comment on Article 13.

> Article 13 causes no offense, but is accepted, as long as they say that sacraments were instituted not only that they might be signs of profession among people, but more so that they might be signs and witnesses of the will of God toward us; nevertheless it will need to be asked of them that what they show forth here in general concerning the sacraments, they profess also specifically concerning the seven sacraments of the Church, and that they take care that it be observed by their followers.[58]

Since they asked, Melanchthon explained in his *Apologia Confessionis Augustanae* of 1531:

> If we call the sacraments rites which have the command of God, and to which has been added the promise of grace, it is easy to judge which are properly sacraments.   For rites instituted by humans will not be in this way properly called sacraments.   For it is not of human authority to promise grace, wherefore signs instituted without the command of God are not certain signs of grace, even if perhaps they teach ignorant people and advise something.   Truly therefore baptism, the Supper of the Lord, and absolution, which is the

[57] "De usu sacramentorum docent, quod sacramenta instituta sint, non modo ut sint notae professionis inter homines, sed magis ut sint signa et testimonia voluntatis Dei erga nos, ad excitandam et confirmandam fidem in his qui utuntur proposita <sic>. Itaque utendum est sacramentis ita, ut fides accedat, quae credat promissionibus, quae per sacramenta exhibentur et ostenduntur.
"Damnant igitur <Ecclesiae Reformationis> illos qui docent, quod sacramenta ex opere operato iustificent, nec docent fidem requiri in usu sacramentorum, quae credat remitti peccata." Confessio Augustana, 13, CR 26:279-280. (This last sentence seems to be a later addition to the *Confessio*. See note in CR 26.)

[58]   "Tredecimus articulus nihil offendit, sed acceptatur, dum sacramenta aiunt instituta, non modo ut sint notae professionis inter homines, sed magis ut sint signa et testimonia voluntatis Dei erga nos; petendum tamen ab eis erit, ut, quod hic in genere de sacramentis perhibent, speciatim quoque de septem sacramentis ecclesiae fateantur, et a subditis suis observari procurent." Confutatio Confessionis Augustanae, "Ad artic. XIII.," CR 27:114.

sacrament of penance, are sacraments. For these rites have the command of God and the promise of grace which is characteristic of the New Testament. . . . Confirmation and extreme unction [59] are rites received from the Fathers, which not even the Church requires as necessary for salvation, because they do not have the command of God. Therefore it is not useless to distinguish these rites from those above which have the express command of God and a clear promise of grace. [60]

On one occasion Melanchthon had the opportunity to express his position on confirmation together with Luther. Frederick of Saxony, at the request of the Holy Roman Emperor, asked the Reformers at Wittenberg for a theological statement on several positions. Martin Luther, Johann Bugenhagen, Caspar Creutziger, Georg Maior, and Philipp Melanchthon signed the "Wittenberg Reformation" of 1545, which included a piece on confirmation. It called for an imposition of hands on children who made a confession of their faith. [61]

In summary, Melanchthon's attempts at reconciliation failed

---

[59] Georges Tavard says Melanchthon could have accepted the sacramentality of the other 5 rites, but these two were always excluded from the list because of their clear ecclesial institution. *Protestantism*, trans. Rachel Attwater, ed. Henri Daniel-Rops, Twentieth Century Encyclopedia of Catholicism, vol. 137 (New York: Hawthorn Books, 1959), pp. 34-35.

[60] "Si Sacramenta vocamus ritus, qui habent mandatum Dei, et quibus addita est promissio gratiae, facile est iudicare quae sint proprie Sacramenta. Nam ritus ab hominibus instituti non erunt hoc modo proprie dicta Sacramenta. Non est enim autoritatis humanae, promittere gratiam, Quare signa sine mandato Dei instituta, non sunt certa signa gratiae, etiam si fortasse rudes docent, aut admonent aliquid. Vere igitur sunt sacramenta, Baptismus, Coena Domini, Absolutio, quae est sacramentum poenitenciae. Nam hi ritus habent mandatum Dei, et promissionem gratiae, quae est propria noui Testamenti. . . .

"Confirmatio et Extrema unctio sunt ritus accepti a patribus, quos ne Ecclesia quidem tanquam necessarios ad salutem requirit, quia non habent mandatum Dei. Propterea non est inutile hos ritus discernere a superioribus, qui habent expressum mandatum Dei, et claram promissionem gratiae." Melanchthon, "Apologia Confessionis Augustanae," CR 27:570.

[61] The text is as follows: "Dieses wäre hochnöthig in allen Kirchen, den *Catechismum* auf bestimpte Tage zu halten, die Jugend in allen nöthigen Artikeln christlicher Lehre zu unterweisen. Dazu möcht die Confirmation angericht werden, nämlich, so ein Kind zu seinen mündigen Jahren kommen, öffentlich sein Bekenntniß zu hören, und zu fragen, ob es bei dieser einigen göttlicher Lehre und kirchen bleiben wollt, und nach der Bekenntniß und Zufage mit Auflegung der Hände ein Gebeth thuen. Dieses wäre ein nüßliche Ceremonien, nicht allein zum Schein, sondern viel mehr zu Erhaltung rechter Lahr und reines Verstands und zu guter Zucht dienlich." "Wittenbergische Reformation," CR 5:584.

because the Roman Church insisted the Reformers adhere to traditional teaching. The Catholics' demands ignored the new definition of sacraments proposed by the Reformers, who believed that confirmation, not having a scriptural institution, was a human fabrication distinct from the sacraments of Scripture. Once again, the two sides are clearly influenced by the debate of Scripture and tradition: The revelatory value the Catholics place on tradition is of little consequence to Melanchthon.

D. Martin Bucer

Although he does not figure in directly with Bellarmine's controversy over confirmation, an examination of the work of Martin Bucer will not only add a dimension to the total position of the Reformation, but will also provide valuable information about the importance of this controversy for the Reformers themselves.

Bucer (1491-1551) led the Reform in Strasbourg, travelled widely, and was a consultant in other regions, as far away as England. In *De regno Christi* he agreed with other Reformers that confirmation is not a sacrament, but has a dignity in the Church:

> Instead we read that the early Churches used the sign of imposing hands, both in the reconciliation of penitents and in the confirmation of the baptized in the faith of Christ, which bishops used to do according to the example of the Apostles who were conferring the Holy Spirit on the baptized with this sign (Acts 8). Therefore, those who desire that the kingdom of Christ be restored before themselves ought to take care first of all that the rightful administration of baptism and Eucharist be recalled.[62]

In the actual celebration of confirmation, Bucer stressed the importance of readiness for reception. G. J. Van de Poll writes,

> In order to be admitted to the Lord's Supper, a certain maturity in Christian growth must be attained. Holy Baptism

---

[62] "Vsas praeterea legimus priscas Ecclesias signo imponendi manus, etiam in reconciliatione poenitentium, et in confirmatione in fide Christi baptizatorum, quam episcopi facere solebant ad exemplum apostolorum, qui baptizatis conferebant hoc signo Spiritum sanctum. Act. 8. Qui itaque Christi regnum apud se rite cupiunt restaurari, in primis elaborare debent, ut legitima reuocetur administratio baptismatis et eucharistiae." Ed. François, Wendel, Opera Latina 15 (Paris: Presses Universitaires de France, 1955), Liber I, caput VII, "De sacramentorum dispensatione," p. 66.

gradually acquired a more objective meaning for Bucer,
whereas confirmation threw light upon the subjective sense
of faith.[63]

Thus, unlike the other Reformers, Bucer acknowledged the relationship
between confirmation and Eucharist. He saw it as the celebration of a
mature acceptance of faith which prepared the recipient for full
participation in the Eucharist.

Commenting on the rite in England's Book of Common Prayer, Bucer
writes,

> Finally, it is ordered in this place that no one be admitted to
> holy communion unless he will have been confirmed. This
> precept will be exceedingly salutary if also people be not
> solemnly confirmed except those who will have confirmed
> the confession of their mouth with a proper life, and if it will
> be able to be known also from their morals that they are
> making a confession of their own and not another's faith.[64]

Of extreme interest to the theology of the Reformers regarding
confirmation is Bucer's situation with the Anabaptists. It appears that
he developed his theology of confirmation, underlining the importance
of a personal confession of faith, as a response to the objection from the
Anabaptists that infant baptism was unacceptable because of the need
to confess faith in order to be baptized. Bucer sought to defuse their
objections by developing a rite of acceptance of faith – confirmation – at
an age when the baptized child could make such a profession. George
Huntston Williams writes,

> The formularies in the rite of confirmation in the Church of
> England indirectly reflect Bucer's extended efforts to cope
> with the demands of the Strassburg and the Hessian
> Anabaptists.[65]

---

[63] G. J. Van de Poll, *Martin Bucer's Liturgical Ideas: The Strasburg Reformer and His Connection with the Liturgies of the Sixteenth Century* (Assen: Van Gorcum & Comp. N.V., 1954), pp. 101-102.

[64] "Postremo praecipitur hoc loco, ne quis ad sacram communionem admittatur, nisi confirmatus. Hoc praeceptum valde salutare erit, si etiam non solenniter confirmentur, nisi qui oris sui confessionem, vita consentanea confirmaverint: agnoscique potuerit & ex moribus, suae, non alienae fidei facere confessionem." E. C. Whitaker, *Martin Bucer and the Book of Common Prayer: Censura Martini Buceri Super Libro Sacrorum Seu Ordinationis Ecclesiae atque Ministerii Ecclesiastici in Regno Angliae ad petitionem R. Archiepiscopi Cantuarensis Thomae Cranmeri Conscripta,* Alcuin Club Collections, No. 55 (Great Wakering: Mayhew-McCrimmon, 1974), p 115.

[65] *The Radical Reformation* (Philadelphia: The Westminster Press, 1962), p. 780.

Although Bucer left no rite of confirmation, there exists a rite from the church of St. Nicholas in Strassbourg about the year 1550, which may well have continued his own tradition. It explains the importance of confirmation as a response to the Anabaptists:

> Among other reasons why the Anabaptists reject infant baptism is this, that (as they claim) through the introduction of infant baptism the order and discipline of the church are bound to fall into decay, and that these will never be rightly restored without the abolition of this infant baptism. [66]

Then the value of instructing children is explained. The introduction continues,

> Such a Christian and altogether necessary ceremony is once more provided in the church, whereby baptized children after they have now learned the catechism are openly brought before the church and after an open and voluntary confession submit to the discipline and obedience of the church with hand-laying and faithful prayer to commend them to the Lord our God and his dear congregation. [67]

This may explain why the Reformers kept the celebration of confirmation at all. They were not only battling the Catholics on one side, they battled the Anabaptists on the other side as well. By keeping confirmation, the Reformers had a convenient method of responding to demands that those to be baptized have faith.

E. The Council of Trent

The Council of Trent, convened to oppose the threat of the Reformers, reviewed the sacraments in session 7 and issued its decree on 3 March 1547. It contains thirteen canons on the sacraments in general, and then explores each of the seven.

The first canon rings like a verdict in a trial of De captivitate Babylonica:

> If anyone shall have said that the sacraments of the New Law were not all instituted by our Lord Jesus Christ, or that there

---

[66] Quoted from Fisher, p. 174, who refers to Friedrich Hubert's *Die Strassburger Liturgischen Ordnungen im Zeitalter der Reformation* (Göttingen: Vandenhoed & Ruprecht, 1900), p. 132.

[67] Fisher, p. 175.

are more or fewer than seven, namely, baptism, confirmation, Eucharist, penance, extreme unction, orders and matrimony, or even that some one of these seven is not truly and properly a sacrament–anathema sit. [68]

Canon 9 continues the rebuke of Luther's work by sustaining the sacramental character:

If anyone shall have said that in three sacraments, namely baptism, confirmation, and orders, there is not imprinted on the soul a character, that is, a certain spiritual and indelible sign, by reason of which they cannot be repeated– anathema sit. [69]

Trent's preoccupation with *De captivitate Babylonica* in these and other canons of Session 7 is evidence of the impact of Luther's work 27 years before. [70]

Canon 8 considers the necessity of faith, a question initially raised by Luther and formalized by Article 13 of the Augsburg Confession:

If anyone shall have said that by the sacraments of the New Law grace is not conferred *ex opere operato*, but that faith alone in the divine promise is sufficient for obtaining grace–anathema sit. [71]

The Roman Church perceived Luther as saying sacraments required faith alone without the power of God. Luther perceived the Roman Church as advocating *ex opere operato* without the power of God behind the efficacy of the sacraments.

---

[68] "Si quis dixerit, sacramenta novae legis non fuisse omnia a Iesu Christo Domino nostro instituta, aut esse plura vel pauciora, quam septem, videlicet baptismum, confirmationem, Eucharistiam, poenitentiam, extremam unctionem, ordinem et matrimonium, aut etiam aliquod horum septem non esse vere et proprie sacramentum: anathema sit." Sessio septima sacrosancti oecumenici et generalis concilii Tridentini sub Paulo III Pont. Max. 3. martii 1547: Canones de sacramentis in genere, CT 5 (1911):995.

[69] "Si quis dixerit, in tribus sacramentis, baptismo scilicet, confirmatione et ordine, non imprimi characterem in anima, hoc est signum quoddam spirituale et indelebile, unde ea iterari non possunt: anathema sit." CT 5:995.

[70] The Council fathers' dependence on this and other material is evident from the drafts of the canons considered on 17 January 1547. The argument of this section draws upon CT 5:835-839 and Hubert Jedin, *A History of the Council of Trent*, trans. Ernest Graf, 2 vols. (London: Thomas Nelson and Sons Ltd., 1957-1961), vol. 2, pp. 370-395.

[71] "Si quis dixerit, per ipsa novae legis sacramenta ex opere operato non conferri gratiam, sed solam fidem divinae promissionis ad gratiam consequendam sufficere: anathema sit." CT 5:995.

The canons on confirmation leave aside these arguments and instead assert the true sacramental nature of confirmation. The first canon condemns Luther's position that confirmation is not a sacrament and Melanchthon's (in the *Apologia*, not the Augsburg Confession itself) that it was handed down by the Fathers:

> If anyone shall have said that the confirmation of those baptized is an empty ceremony and not rather a true and proper sacrament; or that of old it was nothing more than a sort of instruction in which those approaching adolescence gave an account of their faith before the Church – anathema sit.[72]

Canon 2 warns:

> If anyone shall have said that those who ascribe any power to the holy chrism of confirmation are insulting to the Holy Spirit–anathema sit.[73]

The third canon reacted to the "Cologne Reformation,"[74] drawn up by the Reformers under the approval of the lenient local archbishop, Hermann von Wied. It favored a broad opinion of who can be the minister of confirmation.

> If anyone shall have said that the ordinary minister of holy confirmation is not the bishop alone but any simple priest – anathema sit.[75]

The anathemas of Trent solidified the Roman position that confirmation is a sacrament administered by a bishop with the use of chrism, in opposition to the teaching of the Reformers that it is an ecclesial ceremony of instruction for adolescents. Trent gave traditional

---

[72] "Si quis dixerit, confirmationem baptizatorum otiosam caeremoniam esse et non potius verum et proprium sacramentum, aut olim nihil aliud fuisse, quam catechesim quandam, qua adolescentiae proximi fidei suae rationem coram ecclesia exponebant: anathema sit." Canones de sacramento confirmationis, CT 5:996.

[73] "Si quis dixerit, iniurios esse Spiritui Sancto eos, qui sacro confirmationis chrismati virtutem aliquam tribuunt: anathema sit." CT 5:996.

[74] Hermann, Ertzbisschof von Köln, *Einfaltigs bedencken warauff ein Christliche inn dem wort Gottes gegrünte Reformation an Lehr brauch der Heiligen Sacramenten vnd Ceremonien Seelsorge vnd anderem Kirchen dienst biß avff eines freyen Christlichenn Gemeinen oder Nationals Concilij oder des Reichs Teutscher Nation Stende im Heiligen Geist versamlet verbesserung bei denen so unserer Seelsorge befohlenn anzurichten seye,* (Marpurg: Antonium Tirolt, 1544).

[75] "Si quis dixerit, sanctae confirmationis ordinarium ministrum non esse solum episcopum, sed quemvis simplicem sacerdotem: anathema sit." CT 5:996.

theology the added weight of conciliar teaching. Afterwards the battle lines were drawn more clearly. Just as in the preceding years all rendered their arguments in the light of Luther's teaching, now they did so with the knowledge of Trent. Martin Luther died in 1546. Session 7 of Trent in 1547 tried to bury his teachings as well, but the battle raged on.

F. After Trent

In the decades after the Council of Trent, writers seized upon aspects of the Council to continue the discussion of its theology. In fact, there is some question about how faithful the post-Tridentine era was to the intention of the actual Council.[76]

To judge this situation it is good first to situate the Council within its own historical milieu. The era from the fifteenth to the sixteenth century was marked by many movements of Reform. Savanarola called for a new political order, Erasmus preached the doctrine of humanism, Luther personalized the need for reform into a quest for his justification before God, and the whole Protestant Reformation called for dramatic changes in the Church. Against the whole background of the sixteenth century, Trent may be seen as one more voice in Western Europe shouting the Spirit of Reform. Besides combatting the threat of division, Trent also strove for moral renewal of the Church.

However, as time went on after the Council, and the threat of the Reformation loomed ever more large to the Church at Rome, Trent became a club Rome wielded against those she perceived as heretics. In short, the call for internal renewal became secondary to the call to theological arms against the Reform.

This development is not altogether surprising, given the historical development of Roman Catholic theology. Since the time of the Middle Ages, the progress of dogmatic theology had become bound to a study of canonical legislation. Gratian's Decretals were decisive for casting theological discourse into a canonical frame. The impact of canonical study on liturgical and sacramental theology cannot be overestimated. The whole development of scholastic theology became possible only after Gratian provided a point of reference for documenting theological

---

[76] Two articles by Giuseppe Alberigo were helpful for this section. "Dinamiche religiose del Cinquecento italiano tra Riforma, Riforma cattolica, Controriforma," *Cristianesimo nella storia* 6 (October 1985):543-560; and "Du Concile de Trente au tridentinisme," *Irenikon* 54 (1981):192-210.

positions.

Trent provided the Church with a new point of reference for theology. The period after Trent gave Bellarmine and others the same opportunity Aquinas and his school had after Gratian; namely, now that new canonical material was handy, theological statements could be made. So the development of sacramental theology fell back to an expansion of the canons of Trent. Bellarmine, then, stands at the end of an age of theological interpretation begun not with the Reformation, but several centuries earlier. (Even the Reformation only fed the development of theology by legislation.) In addition, the influence of Bellarmine and the post-Tridentine school would be felt in the Catholic Church for the next three hundred years.

To take confirmation as an example, Trent left three canons based on specific issues raised by Luther, Melanchthon, and Hermann von Wied. It did not provide a comprehensive statement on the theology of confirmation, it was putting out fires from the Reformation. But the interpreters of the Council, including Bellarmine, turned to Trent as a rallying point for unity in the Church. Thus, whereas the overall desire of the Council may have been for a restoration of unity in the Church through a spirit of renewal, the outcome was an acceptance of division in the Church and a renewed sense of authority among the hierarchy for carrying out the decrees of the Council.

Now, to return to the question about how faithful post-Tridentine writers were to the spirit of the Council, one might be inclined to permit Trent a broader scope than became evident. However, in the context of confirmation, a case may be made that the post-Tridentine school was faithful to the Council. In the decrees on confirmation, Trent was already engaging in the controversial theology which Bellarmine would bring to fruition. It is more evident in this case that the Council was concerned not simply with the general spirit of reform which pervaded the age, but with a particular Reform, as evidenced by specific threats to the theology of confirmation. As will be seen below, the kind of theology which Bellarmine endorses as a representative of the post-Tridentine age is well in keeping with the authoritative spirit of Trent's three little canons raining absolute condemnation on her adversaries.

G. Summary

This chapter has presented the beginnings of the controversy over confirmation during the Reformation. Both sides formulated opinions which would be elaborated in the next generation.

The Reformers have stated confirmation is not a sacrament. Luther explains that there is no promise concerning confirmation, no sign is given, and the Scriptures do not know the sacrament. Melanchthon agrees and stresses Luther's later point, that there is no command from Christ regarding it.

Many of their arguments will recur. Since the Holy Spirit comes in baptism, Luther argues that the imposition of hands for the sending of the Holy Spirit in Acts 8 and 19 was only a temporary measure, not a sacramental one. He sees no reason why only a bishop may confirm. In fact, Luther and Melanchthon both value confirmation as a rite for examining the faith of children, and the pastor may preside. Melanchthon believes that the early history of confirmation supports his point.

The Roman Church has reiterated that confirmation is a sacrament. The *Confutatio* to the Augsburg Confession asks the Reformers to agree that there are seven sacraments; the number rooted in tradition strengthens their argument. Henry VIII suggests that the celebration of sacraments predates the written Gospel. These positions look to tradition, not just Scripture, to define sacraments.

Yet, in response to the Reformers' demand for scriptural evidence, the Roman Church proposes several texts and thus accepts the criterion of Scripture. Acts 8 and 19 are cited by both Henry and Eck as evidence that the sign accompanies the action of the Holy Spirit. The promise of the Spirit is found from Jesus in John 15 and 16. Eck adds the testimony of several ancient sources–Dionysius, Miltiades, the Council of Orleans, and Jerome–and thus opens a whole new area of investigation which will be expanded by his successors. The Council of Trent reaffirms as conciliar teaching that confirmation is a sacrament, not an examination of children's faith, and that the ordinary minister is a bishop.

In fairness to both sides, the good motives of the disputants must be acknowledged. Martin Luther's intense love for the Scriptures led him to wrestle with a Church community he felt had lost its roots. The Roman Church's sense of history, destiny, and unity led it to react strongly in favor of the traditions it had retained for centuries. The classic struggle between Scripture and tradition is especially evident in the confirmation controversy where these are the fundamental principles which guide the conflict: The Catholics accepted it as a sacrament because of its tradition, the Reformers rejected it because of Scripture.

In some ways this resembles a family squabble. The followers of Luther were like a young child growing into maturity who notices weakness in the parent. Testing its own strength against the parent's will, the child provokes a harsh response, which in turn is motivated by the fear of discord and the need for finding protection in tradition. The child makes a challenge to authority and an assertion of independence. The parent scolds and punishes to re-establish the traditional roles. This analogy works in some measure for the entire Reformation, and is applicable in a special way to confirmation. For confirmation is a celebration of faith – how people confess it, how God seals it. For the Roman Church the acceptance of seven sacraments became a symbol for the restoration of unity. Confirmation, which they saw as a strengthening of baptismal faith and an arming for the battle of life, was doubly symbolic for the whole Reformation controversy: It was the sacrament which strengthened their one faith and prepared them to fight the troublesome adversary. The Reformers, on the other hand, saw confirmation as an independent confession of faith by one baptized as an infant who expressed the maturity of his personal faith before the Church. It was then a symbolic expression of the whole Reformation – the young child was asserting the independence of his faith. For the Catholics, belief in the sacramentality of confirmation meant restoration of unity; for the Reformers, the public examination of faith meant an independent expression of belief. The very theologies of confirmation, then, are expressive of the dynamics of the entire Reformation controversy.

CHAPTER II:
The Protagonists

The historical and theological roots of the confirmation controversy having been exposed, this second chapter will examine the works of the three protagonists behind this study. Each will be presented with his background, together with a description of the principal work pertaining to this controversy. Some secondary works are included for additional detail. Their writings demonstrate the results of historical research and theological reflection in the development of both sides of the controversy.

A. John Calvin (1509-1564)

1. Background

Many educational influences shaped John Calvin's theology. Several biographers have traced the geneology of the Genevan Reformer's thought.[1] The list includes Augustine's definition of a sacrament, Ratramnus's Platonic presuppositions of the sacramental structure, Berengarius's fear of sacramental materialism,[2] and John Wyclif's refusal to put God at the disposal of humanity.[3] Other pre-

---

[1] See especially François Wendel, *Calvin: Sources et évolution de sa pensée religieuse*, Etudes d'histoire et de philosophie religieuses publiées par la faculté de théologie protestante de l'Université de Strasbourg 41 (Paris: Presses Universitaires de France, 1950). This work is available in English under the title *Calvin: The Origins and Development of His Religious Thought,* trans. Philip Mairet (New York: Harper & Row, 1963).

[2] Berengarius was the first to introduce the terms "matter" and "form", "substance" and accidents" to Eucharistic theology, although only later were they joined to the aristotelian sense. See Hans Jorissen, *Die Entfaltung der Transubstantiationslehre bis zum Beginn der Hochscholastik,* ed. Bernhard Kötting and Joseph Ratzinger, Münsterische Beiträge zur Theologie, vol. 28,1 (Münster Westfalen: Aschendorffsche Verlagsbuchhandlung, 1965), pp. 6-7.

[3] Kilian McDonnell, *John Calvin, the Church, and the Eucharist* (Princeton: Princeton University Press, 1967), pp. 58-59.

Reformation influences include William of Occam's nominalism, the *devotio moderna* personalist devotional tradition, and the humanism of Erasmus.[4] Even the Scholastics contributed,[5] as will be evident in Calvin's presentation of confirmation. Like Luther, Calvin respected Augustine, on whom he depended for his sacramental theology. McDonnell writes,

> Calvin believes himself supported by the authority of Augustine on three aspects of general sacramental doctrine: the constitutive importance of Word and faith for the sacrament, the peculiar relationship of the reality and sign in their unity and distinction, and, finally, the sacramental way of speaking, namely, metonymy or the use of the name of one thing for that of another associated with or suggested by it.[6]

Among the Reformers Luther was a font. Calvin introduces sacramental concepts from *De captivitate Babylonica*, e.g., sacrament as a testament and promise, and the requirement of faith.[7] August Lang[8] believes Calvin borrowed from Melanchthon's *Loci communes*, and as is shown below with regard to the history of confirmation, he even borrowed inaccuracies.

The influences on Calvin were many, yet he remained his own man – theologically and even geographically a bit separated from the German Reformers. Not a direct disciple of Luther, he was caught up in the outcry against the abuses in the Church of his day, and, as a layman, forged a new vision of the Church, a political and theological unity rooted in Scripture, reformed by theology.

2. Institutio Christianae religionis

The masterpiece of Calvin's corpus, and the work Bellarmine chiefly challenges, was *Institutio Christianae religionis*. First published in Basel in 1536 under the title *Christianae religionis*

[4] Ibid., pp. 18-32.

[5] See Karl Reuter, *Das Grundverständnis der Theologie Calvins: Unter Einbeziehung ihrer geschichtlichen Abhängigkeiten*, ed. Paul Jacobs et al., Beiträge zur Geschichte und Lehre der Reformerten Kirche, vol. 15, part 1 (Neukirchen: Verlag des Erziehungsvereins GmbH, 1963), p. 47.

[6] McDonnell, p. 42.

[7] McDonnell invites a comparison of CR 29:118-119 with WA 6:513-515; and of CR 29:119-120 with WA 6:517.

[8] McDonnell (p. 95) cites "Sources," *Evangelical Quarterly*, vol. 8, 133, 134; and "Melanchthon und Calvin," *Reformation und Gegenwart, Gesammelte Aufsätze* (Detmold, 1918), p. 91; which were unavailable to me.

institutio, it was revised every few years throughout Calvin's life. Calvin composed the *Institutio* to prepare and instruct candidates in sacred theology for reading the divine Word.[9] Its character is manifold: It is at once a reflection on the plan of God, a discussion of the mystery of redemption, an encouragement for the spiritual life, and a refutation of Catholics and Anabaptists. To Calvin's surprise, the *Institutio* was so popular even among the faithful that he translated it into the vernacular French in a late edition.

The *Institutio* comprises four books: "Concerning the Knowledge of God the Creator," "Concerning the Knowledge of God the Redeemer in Christ, Which Was Disclosed First to the Fathers Under the Law, Then Also to Us in the Gospel," "Concerning the Way of Receiving the Grace of Christ and What Fruits Come Forth to Us from There and What Effects Follow," and "Concerning the External Means or Supports by Which God Invites Us Into the Community of Christ and Keeps Us in It."[10] Through this outline, Calvin traces the plan of God from the Father's revelation of Himself through the mystery of Christ, the personal effect of redemption on the believer, and the nature of the Church community in which the believer lives.

This full outline of Calvin's book is helpful in situating his position on confirmation. His is a comprehensive theological treatise and not primarily a work of controversy. However, in dealing with confirmation, Calvin will need to take the role of controversialist in order to accomplish his broader goal of helping the reader's spiritual growth. But he does not devote as much of his corpus to controversy as, for example, Luther did.

3. Sacraments

It is in the final book that Calvin classifies the sacraments of the Church as one of the external means (together with the Church herself and civil government) which increase faith. Calvin knows Augustine's brief definition of a sacrament, "a visible sign of a sacred thing," "or a

[9] "Ioannes Calvinus lectori," *Institutio christianae religionis,* 1559, CR 30:1-2. I have chosen to cite here and in future references from Calvin's 1559 edition of the *Institutio,* the last Latin edition in his lifetime.

[10] "De cognitione Dei Creatoris," "De cognitione Dei Redemptoris in Christo, quae patribus sub lege primum, deinde et nobis in evangelio patefacta est," "De modo percipiendae Christi gratiae, et qui inde fructus nobis proveniant, et qui effectus consequantur," "De externis mediis vel adminiculis quibus Deus in Christi societatem nos invitat et in ea retinet." CR 30:passim.

visible form of an invisible grace,"[11] but he elaborates on these to clarify them. He proposes two definitions: a sign by which God sustains our weak faith, and a testimony of God's grace confirmed by a sign.

> At the start it is appropriate to consider what a sacrament is. However, it seems this definition will be simple and proper if we will have said it is an external symbol by which the Lord seals on our consciences the promises of his kindness toward us for sustaining the weakness of our faith, and <by which> we on the other hand witness our piety toward Him, as much before Him and the angels as with humans.[12] One can even define with more brevity in another way, so that it is called a witness of divine grace toward us, confirmed by an external sign, with the mutual evidence of our piety toward Him.[13]

Calvin reiterates this basic definition in his 1537 *Instruction et confession de foy*, where he organizes his teaching for catechesis and apologetics. Concerning the sacraments in general, he writes that they exercise faith and are given as a promise in God's word and in a sign.

> The sacraments were instituted for this purpose, that they be exercises of our faith as much before God as before others. And certainly before God they exercise our faith when they confirm it in the truth of God. . . . <By> the word of the Lord they are marked in this signification. For always the promise which is included in the word precedes: the sign is added, which confirms and seals that promise and makes it better certified for us, as the Lord sees that it pertains to the capacity of our coarseness. . . . Now by the sacraments <our faith> is also exercised toward others, when it emerges in public confession and is spurred to render praises to the Lord.
>
> A sacrament then is an exterior sign by which the Lord

---

[11] Calvin writes that a sacrament is "rei sacrae visibile signum" in Augustine, "aut invisibilis gratiae visibilem formam." Augustine himself wrote "signacula quidem rerum diuinarum esse uisibilia." *De catechizandis rudibus* 26:50,2, CChr.SL 46:173.

[12] According to Bellarmine, Calvin derived this definition of a sacrament from the other principal Reformers – the first part from Luther, the second from Zwingli. See *Disputationum de controversiis Christianae fidei adversus hujus temporis haereticos* III, "Prefatio in scholis habita, de haereticorum levitate in re sacramentaria," (Milan: Natale Battezzati, 1857-1862):8.

[13] "Principio animadvertere convenit quid sit sacramentum. Videtur autem mihi haec simplex et propria fore definitio, si dixerimus, externum esse symbolum, quo benevolentiae erga nos suae promissiones conscientiis nostris Dominus obsignat, ad sustinendam fidei nostrae imbecillitatem, et nos vicissim pietatem erga eum nostram tam coram eo et angelis quam apud homines testamur. Licet etiam maiore compendio aliter definire: ut vocetur divinae in nos gratiae testimonium externo signo confirmatum, cum mutua nostrae erga ipsum pietatis testificatione." Book 4: chapter 14, section 1, CR 30:941-942.

presents to us and confirms his good will toward us, to prop
up the weakness of our faith, or (to speak more briefly and
more clearly) it is a witness of the grace of God declared by an
exterior sign. The Christian Church makes as much use of
only two sacraments, viz., baptism and the Supper. [14]

For Calvin a sacrament ratifies a preceding promise of God to stir
up the believer's faith. To this end, it must be celebrated with an
accompanying, intelligible, preached word. Sacraments may be
likened to government seals and human covenants.[15] Their efficacy
comes from the Holy Spirit, not by magic.[16]

Calvin's sacramental theology is Christocentric in that Christ is
the substance of all the sacraments.[17] It is for this reason that the
efficacy of the sacraments depends on Christ, the One Who made the
promises and instituted the sacraments.[18]

Thus sacraments do not justify, but they are instruments of Christ's
justification. "From which another thing is deduced, that assurance of
salvation does not depend on the participation in a sacrament as if
justification were situated there."[19] Similarly, Calvin rejects Trent's
concept of *ex opere operato* on the grounds that it introduces human
work rather than human need into the accomplishment of sacramental
efficacy.[20] However, although assurance of salvation does not depend

---

[14] "Les sacremens sont instituez a ceste fin quilz feussent exercices de nostre foy
tant devant Dieu que devant les hommes. Et certes devant Dieu ilz exercent nostre foy
quand ilz la confirment en la verite de Dieu. . . . <Par> la parolle du Seigneur elles sont
marquees en ceste signification. Car tousiours la promesse precede laquelle est comprinse
en la parolle: le signe est adiouste, lequel confirme et seelle icelle promesse et la nous
rend comme plus testifiee, ainsi que le Seigneur voit quil convient a la capacite de nostre
rudesse. . . . Or elle est aussi par les sacremens exercee envers les hommes, quand elle sort
en confession publique et est incitee a rendre louanges au Seigneur.
"Sacrement doncques est un signe exterieur par lequel le Seigneur nous represente et
testifie sa bonne volunte envers nous, pour soustenir limbecillite de nostre foy, ou (pour
dire plus briefvement et plus clairement) cest un tesmoignage de la grace de Dieu declare
par signe exterieur. LEglise chrestienne use tant seulement de deux sacremens, cest a
scavoir du baptesme et de la cene." *Instruction et confession de foy dont on use en leglise
de Geneve*, CR 50:68. This passage shows the influence of Luther. See Chapter I, fn. 16.

[15] 4:14,3-6, CR 30:942-945.

[16] 4:14,9 and 14, CR 30:947-948, 950-951.

[17] 4:14,14 and 16, CR 30:592-953.

[18] See also Alexandre Ganoczy, *Calvin: théologien de l'église et du ministére*,
Unam Sanctam 48 (Paris: Les éditions du Cerf, 1964), p. 112.

[19] "Ex quo alterum etiam conficitur, non pendere ex sacramenti participatione
salutis fiduciam, ac si iustificatio sita illic foret," 4:14,14, CR 30:951.

[20] 4:14,26, CR 30:962.

on the sacraments, Calvin believes they give that assurance.[21]
Calvin stresses God's promise when he describes baptism.

> Furthermore, <baptism> was given to us by God for this
> purpose (which I have taught is a common thing with regard
> to all the mysteries): first, that it may serve our faith before
> Him, and then our confession before peoples. . . . <But the
> chief point of baptism> is that it must be received by us with
> this promise, that whoever will have believed and been
> baptized will be saved (Mark 16, 16).[22]

Similarly, the Eucharist comes from a divine promise for the interior
benefit of the believer.

> We now know to what purpose this mystical blessing
> pertains. Namely, so that it may confirm for us that the Body
> of the Lord was thus sacrificed for our sake once, so that now
> we may eat It, and by eating feel the efficacy of that single
> sacrifice in us; that His Blood was thus poured out for our
> sake once, so that It might be a perpetual drink for us. And in
> this way sound the words of the promise added in that place:
> "Take, this is my Body which is handed over for your sake (Mt
> 26, 26; Mark 14, 22; Luke 22, 19; 1 Cor 11, 24)."[23]

Calvin criticizes those who accept the other five ceremonies as
sacraments because of Augustine's definition.

> For those who posit seven sacraments attribute to all
> together that definition that they are visible forms of invisible
> grace; they make all together vessels of the Holy Spirit,
> instruments for conferring justice, causes for obtaining
> grace.[24]

He cites the example of extreme unction which his opponents call a
sacrament because of its outward sign and word, whereas Calvin finds

---

[21] See McDonnell, p. 201.

[22] "Porro in hunc finem <baptismus> nobis a Deo datus est (quod mysteriis omnibus commune esse docui), primum ut fidei nostrae apud se, deinde ut confessioni apud homines serviret. . . . Id vero est, quod a nobis accipiendus sit cum hac promissione, quicunque crediderint et baptizati fuerint salvos fore (Marc. 16, 16)." 4:15,1, CR 30:962.

[23] "Iam ergo habemus in quem finem spectet mystica haec benedictio. Nempe quo nobis confirmet, corpus Domini sic pro nobis semel esse immolatum, ut nunc eo vescamur, ac vescendo unici illius sacrificii efficaciam in nobis sentiamus; sanguinem eius sic pro nobis semel fusum, ut sit nobis perpetuus potus. Atque ita sonant verba promissionis illic additae: accipite, hoc est corpus meum quod pro vobis traditur (Matth. 26, 26; Marc. 14, 22; Luc. 22, 19; 1 Cor. 11, 24)." 4:17,1, CR 30:1003.

[24] "Nam qui septem ponunt, simul illam definitionem omnibus tribuunt, ut sint gratiae invisibilis visibiles formae; omnia simul faciunt vasa spiritus sancti, instrumenta conferendae iustitiae, causas obtinendae gratiae." 4:19,1, CR 30:1066.

neither command nor promise.[25] Furthermore, God alone can establish a sacrament by His promise recorded in His Word.

> Since indeed, by a sure promise of God, a sacrament ought to build up and encourage the consciences of the faithful, which could never receive that certainty from a human, . . . <therefore> it is He alone Who witnesses to us concerning Himself through His Word with legitimate authority. A sacrament is a seal by which God's testament or promise is sealed. But it could not be sealed by physical things and elements of this world, unless they be shaped and designated by the power of God. Therefore, a human cannot institute a sacrament, because to cause such great mysteries of God to hide under such lowly things—that is just not of human power. It is necessary for the Word of God to precede, that it may make a sacrament a sacrament, as Augustine teaches best.[26]

He concludes his general comments with patristic texts which corroborate for him that the sacraments number two, not seven.

Calvin accepts, then, a philosophical notion of sacramental sign (something which seals God's grace), but insists that as signs of God they must be confirmed by Him in His Word. Only God institutes sacramental signs.

4. Confirmation

At this point of the *Institutio* Calvin presents for analysis each of the five rites individually, beginning with confirmation. He structures his discussion along scholastic lines. Thomas Aquinas, for example, ordered the material for confirmation in this way: sacrament, matter, form, effect, minister, and ceremonies.[27] Calvin frames this section of

---

[25] 4:19,1, CR 30:1067.

[26] "Siquidem sacramentum certa Dei promissione erigere fidelium conscientias ac consolari debet, quae eam certitudinem nunquam ab homine acciperent. . . . Solus ergo ipse est qui de se nobis per verbum suum testificatur legitima autoritate. Sacramentum, sigillum est, quo Dei testamentum seu promissio obsignatur. Obsignari vero non posset rebus corporeis et elementis huius mundi, nisi virtute Dei ab hoc formentur et designentur. Instituere ergo sacramentum homo non potest: quia facere, ut sub rebus tam abiectis tanta Dei mysteria lateant, id vero humanae virtutis non est. Verbum Dei praeeat oportet quod sacramentum esse sacramentum faciat, ut Augustinus optime docet." 4:19,2, CR 30:1067.

[27] "Summa Theologiae," III:72,1-12. *S. Thomae Aquinatis opera omnia*, ed. Roberto Busa, 6 vols. (Stuttgart-Bad Cannstatt: Friedrich Frommann Verlag Günther Holzboog KG, 1980), 2:885-888. Apparently this division is original with Aquinas. Peter Lombard divided the material on confirmation into five chapters: form and matter, minister, effect, dignity, and irrepeatability. Bonaventure, Aquinas's contemporary, comments on Peter and establishes a threefold division of integrity (including form,

his work (Book 4, Chapter 19, 4-13)[28] describing the origins of confirmation in the Church (4) and his desire to return to that practice (13). In between, he follows the scholastic structure, responding each time to texts drawn from Gratian: Confirmation is not a *sacrament* because it lacks a promise and command (5), even though the Apostles imposed hands for another purpose (6); the use of oil as *matter* has no apostolic foundation, and the *form* used is not in Scripture (7); the *effects* ascribed to confirmation belong more properly to baptism (8-9); appointing a bishop as the more worthy *minister* of confirmation is not only not scriptural, but even Donatist (10); the *ceremonies* of anointing the forehead with oil give no dignity to the sacrament (10-11). Calvin then adds a comment on the methodology of his opponents in their appeal to tradition (12).

Although the *Institutio* contains Calvin's most complete treatise on confirmation, other works make contributions. Principal among them is the *Acta Synodi Tridentinae cum Antidoto* of 1547. Its release in the same year as the seventh session of Trent signified Calvin's enthusiasm for rebuttal. Bellarmine selected it as a secondary work of Calvin to challenge in his disputation on confirmation. Its structure is simple: It refutes each of the three canons on confirmation in turn. This work and others in which Calvin teaches about confirmation will now be cited following the outline of the *Institutio*.

a. Confirmation Not a Sacrament

i. Origin of the Rite

Calvin believes that the true origin of confirmation is as a rite for children who were baptized as infants to come before the bishop and the people to confess the faith in which they were being instructed.

> In times past this was the custom, that the children of Christians after they had grown up were stood up before the bishop that they might fulfill that duty which was required of those who as adults were offering themselves for baptism. . . . Therefore, those who had been initiated at baptism as

---

matter, and minister), efficacy, and use. Aquinas's division is naturally followed by those who comment on the "Summa" (e.g., Suarez), but also by both Calvin and Bellarmine.

[28] Section numbers are based on the later editions. The first edition (1536) is not only not numbered, but the material of section 4 had not even been written. If Calvin's theology was developing in a way similar to Bucer, this additional material (which erroneously describes the origins of confirmation) could have been added in good faith as a response to pressure from the Anabaptists regarding Calvin's practice of infant baptism.

infants, because they had not then performed a confession of faith before the Church, towards the end of childhood--or as adolescence was beginning--were again presented by the parents, were examined by the bishop according to a formula of catechism which then people had definite and universal. But so that this action, which otherwise deservedly ought to have been weighty and holy, might have all the more of reverence and dignity, the ceremony of the imposition of hands was also being used.[29]

Melanchthon had held the same opinion.[30] Calvin cites Leo and Jerome for support [31] and wishes the rite were restored to its pure use.[32]

Other works reject the sacrament too. Introducing the reader to his catechism of 1545, Calvin reasserts his interpretation of the rite and ridicules the Roman practice.

It is what is called confirmation which is nothing but monkey business, without any foundation. Thus that which we are putting forward is nothing if not the usage which has from all antiquity been observed among Christians: and has never been abandoned, except when the Church has been thoroughly corrupted.[33]

Two years after Trent's proclamation on the sacraments, Calvin published a commentary on the Letter to the Hebrews. He draws on chapter six to support his belief about the ancient practice of confirmation.

[29] "Hic mos olim fuit ut Christianorum liberi, postquam adoleverant, coram episcopo sisterentur, ut officium illud implerent quod ab iis exigebatur qui se ad baptismum adulti offerebant. . . . Qui ergo baptismo initiati erant infantes, quia fidei confessione apud ecclesiam tunc defuncti non erant, sub finem pueritiae, aut ineunte adolescentia, repraesentabantur iterum a parentibus, ab episcopo examinabantur secundum formulam catechismi, quam tunc habebant certam ac communem. Quo autem haec actio, quae alioqui gravis sanctaque merito esse debebat, plus reverentiae haberet ac dignitatis, caeremonia quoque adhibebatur manuum impositionis." 4:19,4, CR 30:1068. Similar to Luther, Calvin reserves the word "sacrament" for baptism and Eucharist. He does not use the phrase "sacramental ceremonies" for the others, but he does refer to confirmation here as a ceremony.

[30] Fischer comments upon this erroneous belief widely held among the Reformers. "In actual fact the practice of the ancient Church does not support Calvin's claim at all. The *Apostolic Tradition of Hippolytus* (c. A.D. 217) and the sixth-century *Gelasian Sacramentary*, for example, show that, when infants were baptized, they were confirmed and communicated immediately afterwards," p. 259.

[31] Ironically, these texts do not support Calvin's position at all. They will be analyzed in Chapter III.

[32] 4:19,4, CR 30:1068-69.

[33] "C'est la confirmation qu'on appelle, où il n'y a que singerie, sans aucun fondement. Ainsi ce que nous mettons en avant, n'est sinon l'usage qui a de toute ancienneté esté observé entre les Chrestiens: et n'a iamais esté delaissé, que quand l'Eglise a esté du tout corrumpue." *Le Catechisme de l'Eglise de Geneve*, 1545, CR 34:3.

> But the children of the faithful, because they had been
> adopted from the womb, and were belonging to the body of
> the Church by right of the promise, were baptized as infants:
> but when the time of infancy had been completed, after they
> had been instructed in the faith, they were offering
> themselves also for catechesis, which in those cases was later
> than baptism: but another symbol was then used, namely the
> imposition of hands. This one passage abundantly witnesses
> that the origin of this ceremony flowed away from the Apos-
> tles, which yet afterwards was turned into a superstition, as
> the world almost always degenerates from the best insti-
> tutions into corruptions. . . . For which reason today the pure
> institution ought to be retained, while the superstition ought
> to be removed.[34]

Calvin thus follows the lead of Melanchthon before him, calling
confirmation an examination of faith in accordance with the dubious
witness of earliest Christianity.

ii. Not in Scripture

In the *Institutio*, having presented this basic position, Calvin
condemns the Roman Church for fashioning a sacrament out of a rite
which has no promise or command in Scripture.

> But where is the Word of God, which promises the presence
> of the Holy Spirit here? Not even an iota can they produce.
> From which place therefore will they inform us that their
> chrism is a vessel of the Holy Spirit? . . . This is the first law of
> a minister, that he not undertake anything without a
> command. Come, let them produce some command of this
> ministry, and I will not add a word. If they are wanting a
> command, they cannot excuse a sacrilegious audacity.[35]

He makes the same point in the *Antidotum* to Trent's first canon on
confirmation.

---

[34] "At liberi fidelium, quoniam ab utero adoptati erant, et iure promissionis
pertinebant ad corpus ecclesiae, infantes baptizabantur: transacta vero infantia,
postquam instituti erant in fide, se quoque ad catechesin offerebant, quae in illis
baptismo erat posterior. Sed aliud symbolum tunc adhibebatur, nempe manuum
impositio. Hic unus locus abunde testatur huius caeremoniae originem fluxisse ab
apostolis: quae tamen postea in superstitionem versa fuit: ut mundus semper fere ab
optimis institutis ad corruptelas degenerat....Quamobrem hodie retinenda pura istitutio
est: superstitio autem corrigenda." *Commentarius in epistolam ad Hebraeos,* CR 83:69.

[35] "Sed ubi Dei verbum quod spiritus sancti praesentiam hic promittat? Ne iota
quidem obtendere possunt. Unde ergo nos certiores facient, chrisma suum esse vas spiritus
sancti? . . . Haec prima ministri lex est ne quid sine mandato obeat. Age, mandatum huius
ministerii aliquod producant, et verbum non addam. Si mandato deficiuntur, sacrilegam
audaciam excusare non possunt." 4:19,5, CR 30:1069.

> Let us remember that what they have made a sacrament is never entrusted to us in Scripture, neither with this name nor with this rite nor this signification.[36]

Calvin responded to the *Acts of Regensburg*, which reaffirmed the traditional Roman teaching on the sacraments, including confirmation. He denies that confirmation is a sacrament, again since it carries no command or divine promise.

> It is because the Book defines a sacrament to be an invisible sign of grace, that this description does not pertain at all to these ceremonies which are now called confirmation and extreme unction, which have neither a command nor a divine promise.[37]

iii. Temporary Gift

Continuing in the *Institutio*, Calvin posits the possibility that the Roman Church imitates the practice of the Apostles. He responds that whereas the Apostles were being faithful to their ministry, its form and results have since ceased.

> I hear what the Apostles did: namely that they carried out their ministry faithfully. Those visible and wonderful graces of the Holy Spirit, which He was then pouring out upon His people, the Lord wanted to be administered and distributed by His Apostles through the imposition of hands. . . . But where that grace has ceased to be conferred, to what purpose does the imposition of hands pertain? . . . For it was necessary that the new preaching of the Gospel, the new kingdom of Christ, be illustrated and magnified by unheard-of and unusual miracles.[38]

---

[36] "Meminerimus, nusquam in scriptura nobis commendari quod fingunt sacramentum, neque hoc nomine, neque hoc ritu, neque hac significatione." "In primum Canonem," *Acta Synodi Tridentinae cum Antidoto. 1547*, CR 35:501.

[37] "C'est puis que le Livre deffinit Sacrement estre un signe invisible de la grace, que ceste description ne convient point à ces Ceremonies, qu'on appelle maintenant confirmation et extreme unction, lesquelles n'ont ne commandement ne promesse divine." *Les Actes de la iournée imperiale tenue en la cité de Regespourg, aultrement dicte Ratispone.* 1541, CR 33:595.

[38] "Audio quid apostoli fecerint: nempe suum ministerium fideliter exsequuti sunt. Visibiles illas et admirabiles spiritus sancti gratias, quas tunc in populum suum effundebat, voluit Dominus a suis apostolis per manuum impositionem administrari et distribui. . . . <Sed> ubi gratia illa conferri desiit, quorsum pertinet manuum impositio? . . . Oportuit enim novam evangelii praedicationem, novum Christi regnum, inauditis et inusitatis miraculis illustrari et magnificari." 4:19,6, CR 30:1070.

The argument that the imposition of hands was a temporary gift borrows from the writings of Luther.[39] But Calvin has accented his interpretation to show that sacraments stir up the faith of believers.

The position is restated in Calvin's 1544 response to the faculty of theology in Paris, who proposed articles relating to matters of controversy. He tells what practice of confirmation he favors, based on his belief that the Scriptures evidence a temporary gift of the Spirit which has now ceased.

> We read that the Apostles conferred visible graces of the Spirit by the imposition of hands (Acts 19,6). But experience demonstrates that this was a temporary gift. Indeed the most ancient writers testify that it ceased immediately after the death of the Apostles. We admit that the ceremony of imposing hands was retained by the successors when children brought forth a confession of their faith: but not with this purpose, that it be considered a sacrament instituted by Christ. For Augustine affirms that it is nothing else than a prayer.[40]

In 1549-1550 Calvin gave a thorough treatment of confirmation in his *Vera christianae pacificationis et ecclesiae reformandae ratio*, a response to the *Interim adultero-germanum*, which had reaffirmed the position of the Roman Church. Surprisingly he admits that the Apostles surely would not have imposed hands without the command of Christ and allows the practice of imposition, but he does not call it a sacrament.

> But nevertheless the imposition of hands ought to be preserved. For if it is believable that the Apostles used it only on the command of Christ, their observance is like a law for us. To this another thing is also added, that it was not a futile symbol. It is deduced therefore that it must be had as a sacrament. And I admit both of those things. But our

---

[39] See Chapter I, fn. 30.

[40] "Legimus apostolos, impositione manuum, visibiles spiritus gratias contulisse (Act. 19, 6). Sed hoc fuisse temporale donum, experientia demonstrat. Imo statim post mortem apostolorum desiisse, vetustissimi scriptores testantur. Caeremoniam imponendi manus retentam a successoribus fuisse fatemur, quum fidei suae confessionem ederent adulescentes: sed non hoc fine, ut sacramentum haberetur a Christo institutum. Nam Augustinus nihil aliud esse affirmat, quam orationem." *Articuli a facultate sacrae theologiae parisiensi determinati super materiis fidei nostrae hodie controversis. Cum Antidoto.* 1544, CR 35:21. The pertinent passage of Augustine will be presented in Chapter IV.

mediators, not considering that which should have been
disregarded in no way, namely of what essence a sacrament
was, ignorantly make a perpetual thing out of a temporal
one.[41]

Again, it is noteworthy that although he did not regard
confirmation as a sacrament, Calvin wanted to keep the imposition of
hands as a fruitful celebration for the community because of its
apostolic antiquity.

In his commentary on the Acts of the Apostles published in 1552
and 1554, at the two passages commonly used by his opponents Calvin
again criticizes the Roman practice of confirmation. He offers in his
comment on Acts 8 another reason for the apostolic gesture: Peter and
John imposed hands on those whom Philip had baptized only for a
sense of unity since Philip himself could have done it.

> Indeed <God> was able to complete through Philip what He
> had begun; but so that the Samaritans might learn better how
> to cultivate the fraternal union in a holy way with the first
> Church, He wanted to bind them as it were with this chain;
> then, He wanted to honor the Apostles, to whom He had
> given the command of promulgating the Gospel everywhere
> in the whole world, with this privilege, that all might grow
> together better into the one faith of the Gospel.[42]

Thus for Calvin, confirmation was originally a rite for children to
profess their faith before the people. He condemns the Roman Church
for making this into a sacrament since confirmation has no command or
divine promise in Scripture, where it is only an apostolic practice
whose benefits have long ceased.

---

[41] "At manuum tamen impositio servanda est. Nam si credibile non est, ea nisi
Christi mandato usos fuisse apostolos, nobis instar legis est eorum observatio. Huic
alterum quoque annexum est, inane symbolum non fuisse. Pro sacramento igitur habendum
esse conficitur. Ego vero utrumque istorum fateor. Sed quod minime praetereundum erat
non considerantes mediatores nostri, cuius rei scilicet fuerit sacramentum, ex temporali
imperite perpetuum faciunt." *Interim adultero-germanum: cui adiecta est vera
christianae pacificationis et ecclesiae reformandae ratio. 1549-1550,* CR 35:628.

[42] "Poterat <Deus> quidem per Philippum, quod coeperat, absolvere: sed ut
melius discerent Samaritani fraternam coniunctionem sancte cum prima ecclesia colere,
hoc quasi vinculo obstringere eos voluit: deinde, apostolos, quibus promulgandi ubique in
toto orbe evangelii mandatum dederat, hoc privilegio ornare voluit, ut in unam
evangelii fidem melius   omnes coalescerent." Caput viii:14, *Commentarius in Acta
Apostolorum,* CR 76:181.

b. Matter and Form

Calvin proceeds by turning to the intrinsic principles of a sacrament: matter and form. He has already observed there is no promise or command for confirmation in the Word, now he adds that neither is there an apostolic precedent for oil. Sacraments require a substance formed by the Word of God.

> I reply, in the divinely delivered sacraments two things must be observed: the substance of the physical thing which is placed before us, and the form which has been impressed upon it by the Word of God, in which lies all the power. To what extent therefore bread, wine, water, that are offered to our sight in the sacraments retain their substance, that statement of Paul is always sound: "Food for the belly, and the belly for food; God will destroy both (1 Cor 6, 13)." For they pass away and vanish with the form of this world. But to what extent they are sanctified by the Word of God in order that they might be sacraments, they do not keep us in the flesh, but truly and spiritually teach us.[43]

In the *Antidotum* Calvin tries a different angle – the absence of testimony from the ancients.

> The question is whether by the decision of humans oil receives a new and secret power of the Spirit as soon as it will have pleased them that it be called chrism. For there is no one who makes mention of oil, from the ancients, nor even from that middle age which abounded with many faults. Therefore although they may clatter, they will accomplish nothing by denying that they are insolent toward the Spirit of God as long as they transfer His power to fetid oil.[44]

This a surprising argument for two reasons: He does not mention the silence of Scripture, and what he does mention – the absence of patristic testimony – is wildly inaccurate.[45]

---

[43] "Respondeo, in sacramentis divinitus traditis duo spectanda esse: substantiam rei corporeae quae nobis proponitur, et formam quae illi a verbo Dei impressa est, in qua tota vis iacet. Quatenus ergo substantiam suam retinent panis, vinum, aqua, quae aspectui nostro in sacramentis offeruntur, valet semper illud Pauli: esca ventri, et venter escis; Deus utrumque destruet (1 Cor. 6, 13). Praetereunt enim et evanescunt cum figura huius mundi. Quatenus autem verbo Dei sanctificantur, ut sacramenta sint, non in carne nos retinent, sed vere et spiritualiter docent." 4:19,7, CR 30:1071.

[44] "Quaestio est an ab hominum arbitrio novam et arcanam spiritus virtutem oleum accipiat, simul atque illis placuerit vocari chrisma. Olei enim qui faciat mentionem, nemo est ex veteribus, imo nec ex media illa aetate, quae iam multis vitiis abundabat. Crepent igitur licet, nihil proficient negando, se in spiritum Dei esse contumeliosos, eius virtutem dum ad putidum oleum transferunt." "In II," *Antidotum*, CR 35:502.

[45] Fischer writes, "Every Western rite of initiation from the time of Tertullian at the end of the second century included an anointing with oil after the act of baptism; and

c. Effect

One of Calvin's strongest arguments is how confirmation in the Roman Church impoverishes baptism. Paul's Letter to the Romans says that baptism makes us partakers in Christ's death, sharers in His resurrection; it crucifies the old self that one may walk in newness of life. The Roman Church says confirmation equips a person for battle, even though baptism more nearly fits that description in Paul. Calvin draws additional support from Luke and from the Council of Milevis. For him, to attribute the effects of baptism to confirmation is satanic.

> You who are of God, look at the wicked and dangerous fraud of Satan. What was truly given in baptism, he lies that it is given in his confirmation; so that he may by stealth lead away the incautious from baptism. . . . The word of God is that all who have been baptized in Christ have put on Christ with his gifts (Gal 3, 27). The word of the anointers is that no promise has been received in baptism by which people are prepared for struggles. If the former is the voice of truth, it must be that the latter is of falsehood. Therefore, I can define this confirmation more truly than they have defined it up to now: namely, it is a singular insult to baptism, which obscures, indeed, abolishes, its use; it is a false promise of the devil, which pulls us away from God's truth. Or, if you prefer, it is oil polluted by the devil's lie, which deceives the minds of simple people as when darkness has been poured out. [46]

In the *Antidotum* Calvin says confirmation cuts off half of baptism's efficacy:

> <Popes pronounce that> baptism is sufficient for those immediately about to die, but those who are going to be victorious are armed with confirmation, so that they may be able to sustain the struggles.[47] Thus a half part of efficacy is

the Fathers frequently referred to it," p. 255, n.1.   Bellarmine will challenge Calvin here with an army of witnesses.

[46] "Videte malitiosam et sonticam satanae fraudem, qui ex Deo estis. Quod vere in baptismo dabatur, in sua confirmatione dari mentitur; ut furtim incautos a baptismo abducat. . . . Dei verbum est: omnes, qui in Christo baptizati sunt, Christum induisse cum suis donis (Gal. 3, 27). Verbum unctorum: nullam promissionem in baptismo percepisse, qua in agonibus instruantur <Gratian, De consecr. dist. 5. c. 2: Spiritus sanctus>. Illa vox est veritatis, hanc mendacii esse oportet. Verius ergo definire hanc confirmationem possum quam ipsi hactenus definierint: nempe insignem esse baptismi contumeliam, quae usum ipsius obscurat, imo abolet; falsam esse diaboli pollicitationem, quae nos a veritate Dei abstrahit. Aut, si mavis, oleum diaboli mendacio pollutum, quod velut offusis tenebris simplicium mentes fallit." 4:19,8, CR 30:1072.

[47] Calvin alludes to the letter of Miltiades from the False Decretals of Pseudo-Isidore, which drew from Pseudo-Eusebius of Gaul and Faustus of Riez ("Prolegomena," *Collectio Homiliarum*, ed. Fr. Glorie, CChr.SL 101 <1970>:vii-xxiii). It had an

cut off from baptism, as if it were said for nothing, that the old person is crucified in baptism, so that we may walk in newness of life (Rom 6, 6).[48]

In his commentary on Acts, Calvin rails against the Roman Church for opposing confirmation to the power of baptism:

> But the papists are deserving of no indulgence, who not being content with an ancient rite, have dared to force in fetid anointing, which is supposed to be not only a confirmation of baptism, but even a more worthy sacrament, by which they talk the nonsense that faithful are perfected who earlier had been only half full; by which they are armed for battle, for whom earlier only sins had been remitted. For they have not hesitated to vomit forth these execrable blasphemies.. [49]

Calvin rages on about another effect the Roman Church claims for confirmation – that it completes Christians. He says this is not in Scripture, and if accepted it would condemn the Apostles and martyrs who were never confirmed; besides, the small numbers actually anointed indicate it is not very important at all.[50]

The same point is made in the *Antidotum:*

> For there exists a decree of the Council of Orleans that no one should be esteemed a Christian who has not been chrismated by an episcopal anointing. For their words are worthy to be toasted also to children for sport. A sacrilege so stuffed with execrable blasphemies differs much from an idle ceremony.[51]

extraordinary influence on the entire development of the theology of confirmation. From one Pentecost sermon of the fifth century distinguishing the effects of baptism and confirmation the Roman Church derived its theology of the sacrament for centuries to come and the Reformers rejected confirmation from the list of the sacraments centuries later. See Thurian, p. 66.

[48] "<Papae pronunciant> Baptismum sufficere statim morituris, sed confirmatione armari victuros, ut agones sustinere valeant <De consecrat. dist. 5>. Ita dimidia pars efficaciae a baptismo truncatur: quasi de nihilo dictum sit, crucifigi veterem hominem in baptismo, ut in vitae novitate ambulemus (Rom. 6,6)." "In primum Canonem," *Antidotum,* CR 35:501.

[49] "Papistae autem nulla venia digni sunt, qui vetusto ritu non contenti putidam unctionem obtrudere ausi sunt: quae non tantum esset baptismi confirmatio, sed dignius etiam sacramentum, quo fideles perfici nugantur, qui prius tantum semipleni erant: quo armantur ad pugnam, quibus tantum remissa prius erant peccata. Has enim exsecrabiles blasphemias evomere non dubitarunt." *Commentarius in Acta Apostolorum,* 19:8, CR 76:443.

[50] 4:19,9, CR 30:1072-1073.

[51] "Exstat etiam decretum Aurelianensis concilii: neminem debere existimari christianum, qui non episcopali unctione fuerit chrismatus. Digna enim sunt eorum verba, quae pueris quoque propinentur in ludibrium. Multum ab otiosa caeremonia differt

d. Minister

Calvin says that the Roman Church places more value on confirmation than on baptism since the former is administered by a bishop, the latter by priests. He argues that it is Donatist to judge a sacrament on the worthiness of the minister. And if bishops alone may administer what the Apostles did, surely only bishops may give the Eucharist too.[52]

The *Antidotum* asserts that Scripture does not distinguish bishop from priest.

> But how, I ask, will they prove that these offices pertain to bishops more than the other priests, unless that it has so pleased questionable authors? For if a reason be demanded from Scripture, there is by everyone's admission no distinction of bishop and presbyter there. . . . Then what they want has been sanctioned either by a law of God or by human principle. If the law is of God, why are they not afraid to violate it? For they concede extraordinarily the right of confirming to presbyters. But thundering so according to a human principle, in whom will they strike fear?[53]

e. Ceremonies

Calvin has little regard for using oil in confirmation, so it is offensive to him that because the oil is placed on the forehead and not on the crown of the head, the Roman Church calls confirmation a worthier sacrament than baptism. Nor does he accept that a greater increase of virtues is conferred in confirmation than in baptism, since the visible gifts of the Spirit resulting from the imposition of hands in Acts have ceased.[54]

f. Method

Finally, Calvin weighs the historical witnesses gathered by the Roman Church and finds them powerless against the Word of God.

sacrilegium, tam exsecrandis blasphemiis refertum." "In primum Canonem," *Antidotum*, CR 35:501.

[52] 4:19,10, CR 30:1073.

[53] "Sed unde, quaeso, probabunt, episcopis magis quam reliquis sacerdotibus convenire has partes, nisi quia incertis autoribus ita placuit? Nam si ex scriptura petatur ratio, nullum illic est, omnium confessione, presbyteri et episcopi discrimen. . . . Denique vel Dei lege sancitum est quod volunt, vel humano placito. Si Dei lex est: cur eam violare non verentur? Nam presbyteris extra ordinem concedunt ius confirmandi. Pro humano autem placito ita fulminantes, cui formidinem incutient?" "In III," *Antidotum*, CR 35:502.

[54] 4:19,10-11, CR 30:1073-1074.

> A sacrament is not from the earth, but from heaven; not from
> humans, but from the one God. They must prove that God is
> the author of their confirmation if they want it to be
> considered a sacrament.[55]

Calvin says the ancients accept only two sacraments, and the
imposition of hands is not among them.[56]

g. Conclusion

Calvin concludes by proposing a return to the former custom of
children giving an account of their faith before the Church. This would
do no injustice to baptism. Such a practice, he suggests, would even
arouse slothful parents to know their faith. "In short, it would be as a
certain method of Christian doctrine for all."[57]

In his response to the *Acts of Regensburg,* Calvin writes of his
hopes for using the imposition of hands in language reminiscent of
Melanchthon's *Loci theologici,*[58] accepting it as a useful examination of
faith, though not as a sacrament.

> We would prefer that the catechism be made in all the
> Churches, as the Book encourages, and that after the
> examination of children and the profession which they would
> make, the people pray for them. We think that this <prayer>
> would not be futile, and we would not find fault if it were done
> with the imposition of hands, as it is done even in some of our
> churches.[59]

Thus, when Calvin inserts a revised rite of confirmation into the
Reform tradition, he – together with the other Reformers – turns not to
the patristic origins of confirmation but to the later practice of
confirming children years after infant baptism, forming a non-
sacramental rite he erroneously believes is truer to historical sources.

---

[55] "<Non> e terra est sacramentum, sed e coelo; non ex hominibus, sed ab uno Deo.
Deum suae confirmationis autorem probent oportet, si sacramentum haberi volunt." 4:19,
12, CR 30:1074.

[56] 4:19,12, CR 30:1074. Calvin cites book 3, chapter 16 of Augustine's *De baptismo,*
which will become a central text in the controversy.

[57] "<Omnibus> denique esset quaedam velut methodus doctrinae christianae."
4:19,13, CR 30:1075.

[58] See Chapter I, fn. 53.

[59] "Nous vouldrions bien que le Catechisme se fit par toutes les Eglises, comme le
Livre admoneste, et que apres l'examen des enfans, et la profession qu'ilz feroient, le
peuple fit priere pour eulx. Nous pensons que icelle ne seroit pas vaine, et ne
improuverions pas qu'on usast avec d'imposition de mains, comme mesme il se faict en
aucunes de noz eglises." *Les Actes de Ratispone,* CR 33:595.

5. Summary

Calvin promotes and embellishes many of the themes begun by Luther and Melanchthon. He says confirmation is not a sacrament because there is no promise regarding it in Scripture. He rejects the non-apostolic anointing with chrism. He continues the theological objection that confirmation detracts from the efficacy of baptism. He proposes that a proper use of the rite would be for examining the faith of children before the bishop and the assembly; the imposition of hands at that time would be acceptable, but not sacramental.

Although Calvin reaches the same conclusion as Luther about confirmation, there are differences in their approach. They agree on what constitutes a sacrament – a promise and divinely instituted sign from the Word of God.[60] But Calvin says sacraments are symbols of realities and do not themselves cause the effects they signify – God is the cause. Luther and the Roman tradition on the other hand do accept some sort of sacramental causality.[61] Bellarmine observed that the two saw the purpose of sacraments differently: Luther for present justification, Calvin for eternal election.[62]

The two have different starting points. Luther begins with the Word of God. He reads about baptism and Eucharist in the Gospels and develops his sacramental principles from the texts: Both contain a promise and a divinely instituted sign. Calvin though begins from the philosophy of symbol. A sacrament, he says, is a sign which confirms the promise of God. Baptism and Eucharist, because they have a divinely instituted sign and promise in the Word, confirm the divine action within believers and allow them to confess faith before God and others. Even Calvin's orderly, scholastic outline betrays his search for a philosophical idea of symbol, whereas Luther starts from the raw texts themselves.

Their conclusion regarding confirmation, though, is the same: It is not a sacrament. This conclusion deceptively places Luther and Calvin in the same sacramental tradition since it ends the discussion early. An examination of their Eucharistic theology would show a more clear divergence in their sacramental theology: Both accept the Eucharist as

---

60 See Chapter I, fn. 15 and Chapter II, fn. 26 above.

61 Compare for example Calvin 4:14,1 (Chapter II, fn. 13 above) and 4:19,2 (Chapter II, fn. 26) with Luther WA 6:517-518 (Chapter I, fn. 9) and Bellarmine 1:2,9 (Chapter II, fn. 102 below).

62 *Disputationum* III, "Praefatio," Battezzati:8.

a sacrament, and both accept the real presence of Christ in the Eucharist, but where Luther connects that presence consubstantially to the elements of bread and wine, Calvin connects it spiritually; for him the real presence has ascended into heaven.[63] With confirmation, Calvin and Luther never approach the subtler questions because they have rejected it as a sacrament from the start. So although from the conclusion it looks like they might always agree, from the starting points and other conclusions about sacraments, they do not.

B. Martin Chemnitz (1522-1586)
1. Life

It is unjust that Martin Chemnitz is not popularly remembered among those who shaped the progress of the Reformation. His clarity of style won him recognition as a great controversialist in his day, and his concern for the unity of the congregations which followed Luther actually saved the Lutheran Church in Germany from splintering into so many independent entities.

Although he studied for a time with Melanchthon, Chemnitz was a self-taught man. A prolific writer, he became known more for his erudition than his originality. In the last years of his life, he strove for the unity of the German churches left behind after Luther's death. Concerned that these congregations subscribe to a unified expression of belief, Chemnitz contributed significantly to the Formula of Concord of 1577. Not all the pastors and dukes signed the formula, but its acceptance helped the early unification of the Lutheran Church.[64]

Chemnitz was a reconciler within his own tradition. His object therefore differed from that of Melanchthon, who attempted

---

[63] See Carl F. Wisløff, *The Gift of Communion: Luther's Controversy with Rome on Eucharistic Sacrifice*, trans. Joseph M. Shaw (Minneapolis: Augsburg Publishing House, 1964), p. 150; and Calvin's "Petit Traicté de la Saincte Cene de Nostre Seigneur ' Iesus Christ (Geneva, 1541)," CR 33:429-460.

[64] The *Konkordienformel*, the definitive statement of Lutheran orthodoxy, was incorporated into the Book of Concord of 1580 together with the three creeds (the Apostles', the Nicene, and the Athanasian), the Augsburg Confession and Apology (1530), the Schmalkaldic Articles (1537), Luther's two catechisms, and the three earlier drafts on which it was based (the Swabian and Saxon Formula 1574-1575, the Maulbronn Formula of 1575, and the Torgau Articles of 1576). Published in German at Dresden, it was signed by 86 representatives of the Lutheran state-churches and 8000 pastors and teachers. Regarding Chemnitz's contribution to the Formula of Concord, L. Loevenbruck boasts "ainsi, grâce à Chemnitz, la doctrine luthérienne parut solidement établie aussi bien dans la foi du peuple que dans l'enseignement officiel des Etats de l'Allemagne du Nord." "Chemnitz (Chemnitzius, Kemnitz) Martin," DThC II, 2:2355.

reconciliations with the Roman Church through the Augsburg Confession and also through a series of Interims arranged by Charles V to establish temporary theological concord for the growing confessional diffusion of his Empire. The Reformers criticized Melanchthon for granting too many concessions to the Romans,[65] and Bellarmine criticized those who accepted Melanchthon's Leipzig Interim for abandoning its confession of faith.[66] Chemnitz, however, saw the need for unity within his own camp, and labored successfully there.[67]

2. *Examen concilii Tridentini*

The work of Chemnitz cited by Bellarmine for his disputation on confirmation was the *Examen concilii Tridentini*, four large volumes composed between 1565 and 1573.[68] The sheer length of the work indicates the controversy had extended far beyond the need for a small handbook like Eck's, and Bellarmine's tomes would be yet more voluminous. The *Examen* is indeed an examination of the decrees of the Council of Trent, but its history – and its provocation of Bellarmine – is more complex.

Johannes Monheim composed *Doctrina caelestis*, an evangelical catechism printed in Düsseldorf in 1560.[69] A group of the newly-founded Jesuits from Cologne refuted its theology the same year with *Censura de praecipuis doctrinae caelestis capitibus*. Chemnitz responded in turn with *Theologiae jesuitarum praecipua capita ex quadam ipsorum*

---

[65] See J. Paquier, "Mélanchthon, Philippe" DThC X, 1:504.

[66] *Disputationum* III, "De Baptismo et Confirmatione," liber 2, caput 1, Battezzati:211.

[67] Eduard Preuss records a saying in his "Vita Martini Chemnicii," "Si Martinus non fuisset, Martinus vix stetisset." Martin Chemnitz, *Examen Concilii Tridentini*, ed. Eduard Preuss (Berlin: Gust. Schlawitz, 1861):956.

[68] Theodor Mahlmann records that volumes I and II were printed in 1565 and 1566, III and IV in 1573, "Chemnitz, Martin (1522-1586)", TRE 7:716 and 719. Bellarmine, who comments only on volume II here, says in the preface to his work (Battezzati:24) he actually has the 1566 edition of the *Examen*.

[69] This information comes from Loevenbruck's DThC article. Joseph Kuckhoff refers to the title as *Catechismus, in quo christianae religionis elementa. . . explicantur* ("Monheim, Johannes," LThK 7 (1935):275. (This gives a fuller title than August Franzen's article in the 1962 edition of LThK.) This catechism must have set off an immediate furor. Johann Kühn (under the pseudonym of Henricus Artopoeus) begins his *Ad theologogastrorum Coloniensium censuram responsio* saying, "Multa statim ab initio verba profundunt Censores Catechismi Monhemiani," (Grenoble: Petrus Cephalius Duromontanus, 1561).

censura, quae Coloniae, anno 1560 edita est, adnotata, printed in Leipzig in 1562. The theological rivalry between Chemnitz and the Jesuits had a history even before Bellarmine entered the struggle. Chemnitz knew that the Jesuits had established a college in Rome to train German scholars for the Roman Church who could curb the progress of the Reformation in its native land.[70] Once Chemnitz began the argument in 1562, several adversaries rebutted, especially a Portuguese theologian, Diego Andrada de Payva, whose book bore a ponderous title which itself summed up the controversy thus far: *Ten Books of Orthodox Explanations, in Which Almost All the Points about Religion Which Are Being Called into Controversy by the Heretics at These Times Are Explained Openly and Plainly; Especially Against the Impudent Audacity of Martin Chemnitz, Who Thoughtlessly Undertook Misrepresenting the Cologne Censure, Which He Says Had Been Composed by Men of the Society of Jesus, Together with the System of Life of the Same Most Holy Society.*[71] Andrada argued from the Council of Trent, and it was for that reason that Chemnitz produced, over a period of 9 years, his *Examen*, first published in Frankfurt.[72] Grégoire de Valence, Ravenstein of Louvain, and Andrada himself rejoined, as did the Jesuit at the center of this study, Robert Bellarmine.

Chemnitz directs his *Examen* specifically against Andrada in order to make the issues and the adversary as concrete as possible. He writes,

> But I have had many and weighty reasons why I have
> wanted to oppose some response to Andrada since he is
> provoking me to this contest so proudly and even insolently
> enough. . . . I thought that a response should rather have
> been begun concerning the issues themselves, so that
> therefore something of usefulness might return to the
> Church from this controversy, if God assists well. Also, I

---

[70] See *Examen*, "Prefatio" 5, Preuss:2.

[71]   *Orthodoxarvm explicationvm libri decem, In quibus omnia ferè de religione capita, quae his temporibus ab haereticis in controuersiam vocantur, apertè & dilucidè explicantur; Praesertim contra Martini Kemnicij petulantem audaciam, qui Coloniensem Censuram, quam à uiris societatis Iesu compositam esse ait, unà cum eiusdem sanctissimae societatis uitae ratione, temerè calumniandam suscepit* (Venice: Iordanus Ziletus, 1564). The material on confirmation is on pages 275-279.

[72]   Loevenbruck says of the *Examen* "qu'il mit son auteur au premier rang parmi les théologiens protestants du XVIe siècle," DThC II, 2: 2356.

[73]   "Multas autem et graves habui causas, quod volui responsionem aliquam Andradio opponere, cum ad hoc certamen tam superbe, et quidem satis contumeliose me

consider that the material of the response has been offered
and shown to me divinely.[73]

Chemnitz does not presume that one should blindly follow conciliar
decrees. Since the norm of Scripture judges even a council, he argues
against the very logic of the decrees.

> But the bare label of "council" having been heard should
> not–as it were the head of Gorgon–turn us immediately into
> rocks, tree trunks, and logs, so that we heedlessly embrace
> whatever decrees you please without examination, without
> inquiry and judicious distinction. . . . Therefore it is rightly
> done, and necessarily from the command of God this must
> be done, that the decrees of the councils be formulated
> according to the norm of sacred Scripture, as the saying of
> Jerome has it: The doctrine of the Holy Spirit is that which has
> been brought forth by the canonical writings, against which if
> the councils decide something, I consider it sinful.[74]

With this method of criticism, Chemnitz logically arrives at
conclusions different from those of a council whose single-minded
purpose was to confront the Reform, not to explore the Scriptures.

The *Examen* is ordered by the canons of the Council of Trent. Its
schema then is not an original outline, but a comment on another
structure.[75] For this reason, the material on confirmation is found
between baptism and Eucharist, two rites Chemnitz accepts as
sacraments.[76] In Luther and Calvin, confirmation appears after these
two sacraments as the first of five rites rejected from the list of the
Roman Church. Chemnitz also rejects its sacramentality, but he
formulates his criticisms not by their integral relationship in his own
mind but according to the outline of Trent.

---

provocet. . . . <Cogitavi> responsionem potius de rebus ipsis instituendam esse, ut ita
aliquid utilitatis ex illa concertatione ad Ecclesiam, Deo bene juvante, redire posset. Et
existimo, materiam responsionis divinitus mihi oblatam et monstratam esse."
"Prefatio" 7, Preuss:3.

[74] "Sed nudus Concilii titulus exauditus non debet nos statim tanquam caput
Gorgonis in saxa, truncos et stipites convertere, ut quaevis decreta sine examine, sine
inquisitione et dijudicatione, temere amplectamur. . . . Recte igitur fit, et ex mandato Dei
necessario hoc faciendum est, ut decreta Conciliorum exigantur ad normam sacrae
Scripturae, sicut Hieronymi sententia habet: Spiritus sancti doctrina quae Canonicis
literis prodita est, contra quam si quid statuant Concilia, nefas duco." "Prefatio" 10-11,
Preuss:3.

[75] The schema in fact had been used by Calvin in the *Antidotum*.

[76] See "Examen secundae partis decretorum concilii tridentini, de sacramentis, etc.,
Locus III, "De Confirmatione," Preuss:284-298.

3. Sacraments

Chemnitz begins with a discussion of sacraments in general, and then proceeds through each in particular.

In the Preface to Part II, Chemnitz contrasts the method of the Council of Trent with that of the Council of Jerusalem in Acts 15. From the start Scripture is the primary criterion for him. He says the fathers at Jerusalem explained the basis, reasons, and proof for their decrees as they placed them before the churches.[77] Trent, however, gives only canons which presume their own authority regardless of their association with Scripture. Chemnitz proposes to supply the doctrine which the canons omit.

> For reasons and explanations will have to be sought out of the lacunas of the disputations which exist among the scholastic and papist writers.[78]

The first issue in Section I is the use of the term "sacrament". Chemnitz knows the pitfalls: the number and meaning have varied in history, and the term itself is not Scriptural. He shows from the Augsburg Confession that the Church must preserve what has a command and a promise of grace in Scripture. As Chemnitz distinguishes between what is and what is not a sacrament, he gives one of the most precise treatments of sacraments in the Reformation. For Chemnitz, the matter will be clear

> . . . if it can be kept in this way, that those things which have a command of God and promises in Scripture, whether with special rites or without rites, be retained, and indeed be treated and used in that way as they have been handed on in the Word of God, whether they are called sacraments or not.
> Second, that those rites which have the express command of God in Scripture, and a clear promise of grace added on which is characteristic of the New Testament, may be precisely distinguished from the other things which indeed have a command of God but do not have divinely instituted special and specific rites. They also have a promise, but not that which is about the application and sealing of gratuitous

---

[77] Chemnitz is not entirely accurate here. The fathers at the Council of Jerusalem explained the reasons for their decrees among themselves. When the time came to deliver the results to the faithful, Paul and Barnabas, Judas and Silas presented a letter containing no proofs, only bare decrees (Acts 15, 23-29). It was a technique the fathers at Trent unwittingly followed only too closely.

[78] "Petendae enim erunt rationes et explicationes ex lacunis disputationum, quae exstant apud scriptores Scholasticos et Pontificios." "Prefatio, secundae partis" 4, Preuss:226.

reconciliation.

Third, that the rites which do not have an express command and clear promise of grace in the Scripture of the New Testament, but were either received from the Fathers or instituted by other humans, may be distinguished from those above about which mention has already been made.

Fourth, that a distinction be preserved between the promise of grace, which offers and applies to the ones believing the benefits of redemption promised in the Gospel, by a single and bare word, and that same <promise> when it has been clothed in rites or ceremonies divinely instituted in the Word of God.[79]

Thus a sacrament for Chemnitz must have a command, a promise of reconciliation, and a divinely instituted rite in Scripture. It differs from commands and promises which have no rite in Scripture, or whose rites were invented later. This places him in the Lutheran tradition more so than in Calvin's. Although he therefore accepts only baptism and the Eucharist as true sacraments, he praises the other five of the Roman Church with characteristic deference:

> This declaration is also necessary at the beginning: In no way do we want to diminish or detract from that truth, reverence, dignity, and usefulness, which they have and should have from the statement of Scripture, when we contend that they are not truly and properly sacraments instituted by Christ in that way as baptism and the Lord's Supper are truly and properly sacraments: indeed, we do this only, that we may so judge and speak about these things in the Church as Scripture prescribes and hands on: for in this way they possess and retain their true worth.[80]

[79] ". . . si modo hoc servetur, ut res illae, quae in scriptura, sive cum peculiaribus ritibus, sive absque ritibus habent mandatum Dei, et promissiones, retineantur: et quidem eo modo tractentur et usurpentur, sicut in verbo Dei traditae sunt: sive Sacramenta appellentur, sive non.

"Secundo, ut ritus illi, qui habent expressum mandatum Dei in Scriptura, et additam claram promissionem gratiae, quae Novi Testamenti propria est, accurate discernantur a reliquis rebus, quae habent quidem mandatum Dei, sed non habent peculiares et certos ritus divinitus institutos. Habent etiam promissionem, sed non illam, quae est de applicatione et obsignatione gratuitae reconciliationis.

"Tertio, et <sic, more probably 'ut'> ritus qui non habent expressum mandatum et claram promissionem gratiae in Scriptura Novi Testamenti, sed vel a Patribus accepti, vel ab aliis hominibus instituti sunt, discernantur a superioribus de quibus jam dictum est.

"Quarto, ut discrimen conservetur inter promissionem gratiae, quae beneficia redemptionis in Evangelio promissa, solo et nudo verbo offert, et applicat credentibus et inter eandem, quando vestita est ritibus seu ceremoniis divinitus in verbo Dei institutis." "Locus I, Sectio I, Canon I. Examen" 1, Preuss:226.

[80] "Necessaria etiam in principio est haec contestatio. Nos. . . nullo modo, eam, quam ex Scripturae sententia habent et habere debent, veritatem, reverentiam, dignitatem, et utilitatem, vel imminuere, vel detrahere velle, quando pugnamus non esse vere et proprie Sacramenta a Christo instituta, eo modo, sicut Baptismus et Coena

He discerns three parts to Trent's first canon on sacraments in general: that the authority of sacramental institution is God's (a point he concedes), that there are seven sacraments, and that each is truly and properly a sacrament.

Regarding the number of sacraments, Chemnitz says the Roman Church holds seven from the testimonies of the ancients, but it cannot be clearly justified in Scripture or early tradition. Regarding the term "sacrament", he adopts it by custom since Scripture does not use it.[81]

> And the use of the word "sacrament" with this meaning–namely, that it may be applied to the efficacious signs of grace, as are baptism and the Lord's Supper in the New Testament without controversy–indeed has some affinity with those examples of Scripture of which it was spoken above: nevertheless it was not taken up from Scripture but from the ecclesiastical manner of speaking. For Scripture never calls either baptism or the Eucharist mysteries or sacraments. Therefore the name is up to this point *agraphos* <unwritten>.[82]

Chemnitz explains why the other five rites cannot be called sacraments. He introduces confirmation, which he will develop in its place, with observations by now familiar to the Reformation: that it was used by the Apostles as a temporary gift from God, that the gifts of the Spirit may be conferred by other means which are divinely ordered, that the Church is audacious to devise a new rite purporting to confer these gifts. He remarks that the Apostles imposed hands, whereas the Roman Church uses anointing with the sign of the cross.

In conclusion, Chemnitz expresses his desire for the restoration of purity and simplicity, based on the Word of God.

Domini vere et proprie sunt sacramenta: imo hoc tantum agimus, ut de illis rebus in Ecclesia ita sentiamus et loquamur, sicut scriptura praescribit et tradit: hoc enim modo habent et retinent veram suam dignitatem." "Canon I. Examen" 2, Preuss:227.

[81] At first it may seem surprising that Chemnitz abandons Scripture for tradition's term "sacramentum", but it is a sensible way to continue the discussion: Scripture does not offer a different word.

[82] "Et usurpatio vocabuli sacramenti in hac significatione, ut scilicet accommodetur ad signa gratiae efficacia, qualia, in Novo Testamento extra controversiam sunt Baptismus et Coena Domini, habet quidem aliquam affinitatem cum illis Scripturae exemplis, de quibus supra dictum est: non tamen ex Scriptura, sed ex Ecclesiastica loquendi consuetudine sumpta est. Scriptura enim nusquam vel Baptismum vel Eucharistiam vocat mysteria vel sacramenta. Hactenus ergo est appellatio *agraphos*." "Canon I, Examen, Articulus I" 7, Preuss:229.

In order that therefore the genuine purity and simplicity may be restored to these things from the Word of God, and having been restored be preserved, and lest an occasion be given to posterity of departing from that simplicity again and of fashioning in its place strange and counterfeit things, this disputation is useful and necessary, whether the remaining five which the papists number are truly and properly sacraments in that way as baptism and the Lord's Supper are.[83]

Although Chemnitz holds his own ideas, he shows both sides of the questions. True to his promise to present the argumentation Trent omitted, he refers to ancient sources which held varying opinions. His distinctions between what is and what is not a sacrament refine the best of the Lutheran tradition.[84]

Concluding his reflections on sacraments in general, Chemnitz says they are efficacious for those who use them in faith, and the efficacy comes from the Holy Spirit.[85] Drawing an image from the Trojan War, he calls *ex opere operato* the beautiful Helen of the battle, and charges the Roman Church with a tumbled-down version of sacramental theology.[86]

In another book, *De duabus naturis in Christo*, Chemnitz speaks of the presence of God in the sacraments in relation to His presence in Christ.

Fifth, by the external ministry of the Word and sacraments in the Church, God is truly present, acting with us through those means and effectually working in us; and even in the external signs in the use of the sacraments God is present, dispensing and communicating through those visible signs His invisible grace, according to the Word.[87]

[83] "Ut igitur rebus illis genuina puritas et simplicitas ex verbo Dei restitui, et restituta conservari possit: neve posteritati occasio detur, a simplicitate illa rursus discedendi, et ejus loco, peregrina et adulterina affingendi: utilis et necessaria est illa disputatio, an reliqua quinque, quae Pontificii numerant, vere et proprie sint sacramenta, eo modo, sicut Baptismus et Coena Domini." "Canon I, Examen, Articulus I" 28, Preuss:236.

Like Calvin, without using Luther's categories of sacraments and sacramental ceremonies, Chemnitz clearly sets apart five rites into a group of useful ceremonies, though not sacraments. See fn. 29 above.

[84] Chemnitz's sacramental theology naturally reflects more the Christocentrism of his age than the ecclesiology of more recent writers.

[85] "Sectio V," Preuss:245-249. The point is reminiscent of Calvin's stress on the efficacious role of the Holy Spirit; see fn. 16 above.

[86] "Sectio VI," Preuss:250-253.

[87] "Quintò, Externo ministerio Verbi & Sacramentorum in Ecclesia Deus verè adest, agens per illa media nobiscum, ac efficaciter in nobis operans: & externis etiam symbolis Sacramentorum in vsu Deus adest, dispensans & communicans, per visibilia illa signa,

There is a freer expression here of the role of the signs as means of dispensing God's grace than Calvin allows them as seals on our consciences of God's promise.

Chemnitz begins the analysis of individual sacraments with baptism. Fundamentally, he agrees with the baptismal doctrine of Trent. There are minor disputes over the meaning of New Testament passages, the possibility of loss of baptismal grace, obligations, remission of venial sins, and the work of the Holy Spirit, but the basic doctrine of baptism is accepted. Chemnitz elaborates on Trent, correcting it and defending the Reformers where necessary, but the real struggle over baptism is revealed in the following section, where he accuses the Roman Church of robbing baptism of its merit through confirmation.[88]

4. Confirmation

The examination of the decrees on confirmation is in four sections: the teachings of the Roman Church, their agreement and conflict with Scripture, the writings of the ancients concerning confirmation, and an examination of the canons to show how the rite may be used fruitfully. Chemnitz faithfully weighs both sides before pronouncing a judgment; he believes his example consonant with that of the Council of Jerusalem, abandoned by the Council of Trent.

Chemnitz reveals the elaborate extra-scriptural nature of confirmation in the Roman Church. His principal objection is that the effects attributed to confirmation are denied to baptism.

> The principal point of this controversy is this, how they speak concerning the efficacy of this confirmation of theirs. And this whole disputation cannot be set forth in a shorter abridgment nor be more rightly understood than if this is considered, that in this doctrine of theirs the antithesis of baptism and confirmation is perpetual, so that whatever effects are attributed to confirmation are by that very fact denied to and drawn away from baptism.[89]

---

inuisibilem suam gratiam, iuxta verbum." *De dvabvs natvris in Christo: De hypostatica earvm vnione: De commvnicatione idiomatvm, et aliis qvaestionibus inde dependentibus libellus*, Leipzig (1600).

88 "Locus II, De baptismo," Preuss:264-284.

89 "Praecipuum vero caput hujus controversiae illud est, quomodo de efficacia hujus suae Confirmationis loquantur. Et non potest breviori compendio, tota illa disputatio proponi, nec rectius intelligi, quam si hoc consideretur, quod in hac illorum doctrina, perpetua est antithesis Baptismi et Confirmationis: ita ut quicumque effectus tribuuntur

He exposes many spurious documents proposed by his adversaries, and quotes from the rite of confirmation itself to show how beggarly it leaves the sacrament of baptism.

His second section presents the Scriptures used by the Roman Church. Agreeing that the Church needs the Holy Spirit, Chemnitz responds that He operates only through divinely instituted means, of which confirmation–a humanly devised rite – is not one. He argues that the Roman Church's support – scholastic derivations, counterfeit documents, and selective Scripture texts – is weak. He maintains that Scripture speaks of imposing hands for a temporary benefit, not for the universal Church for all times.

> Therefore this proof presses upon the papists, that they show a command of God that that deed of the Apostles in Acts 8 and 19 ought to be imitated, used, and repeated in the Church up to the consummation of the age, until Christ comes for judgment.[90]

In addition, he says the manifold versions of the formula betray the non-scriptural origin of the texts, which offer neither matter (chrism) nor form (words); thus, calling the rite a sacrament actually militates against God's Word.[91] He concludes this section with his theme that confirmation detracts from baptism:

> For whatever things are attributed to chrism, those things are taken away from baptism by antithesis. . . . so that the papist doctrine concerning chrism cannot be accepted and approved without injury and insult to sacrosanct baptism.[92]

Third, Chemnitz criticizes the Roman Church's use of the ancients writers. He raises several objections: They favor forgeries; many early writers were Montanist; the Fathers imposed hands in non-sacramental ceremonies; in using chrism they preserved the effects of baptism. He includes a lengthy analysis of Cyril of Jerusalem. He

---

Confirmationi, eo ipso denegentur et detrahantur Baptismo." "Locus III, De Confirmatione, Examen" 3, Preuss:285.

[90] "Incumbit igitur Pontificiis haec probatio, ut ostendant mandatum Dei, quod illud Apostolorum factum, Act. 8 et 19 usque ad consummationem seculi, donec Christus ad judicium veniat, in Ecclesia imitandum, usurpandum et frequentandum sit." 11, Preuss:289.

[91] 12-18, Preuss:289-291.

[92] "Quae enim chrismati tribuuntur, ea ex antithesi baptismo detrahuntur. . . . ut sine injuria et contumelia sacrosancti baptismi, Pontificia doctrina de chrismate, recipi et approbari non possit." 19, Preuss: 291.

concludes that the Roman Church's anointing differs from that of the ancients by its omission of the imposition of hands and by its separation from baptism in ritual and effect.[93]

Finally, Chemnitz examines the canons of Trent. Contrary to the first canon, Chemnitz says a profession of faith for children preceded by instruction would be a more fit celebration of the rite, in keeping with Scripture and tradition.[94] He regrets that instead of having a rite that reminds one of baptism and offers strengthening grace, the Roman Church confirms at an age making instruction impossible and relies on the spontaneous conferral of grace.[95] The second canon claims that chrism has the power of the Holy Spirit, but Chemnitz cannot agree.

> That which pertains to the second canon: What kind of and how great a power they attribute to their chrism without any command and divine promise, and how great is the wrong and abuse of baptism to draw away that power from baptism and transfer it to the chrism, which has no word of God at all, has been shown up to now with many words.[96]

Treating the third canon, he denies that only bishops have the authority to confirm. Paraphrasing Luther, Chemnitz says,

> What kind of bishops they are, such also the ministry they want to have. For because they have cast off the preaching of the Word and the administration of true sacraments from themselves and to inferior others, they invented the smearing of the chrism, as laborious and troublesome to the least degree, lest they themselves nevertheless have nothing such that they might do.[97]

---

[93] 22-24, Preuss:291-297.

[94] For all his scholarship, this is still a blindspot for Chemnitz. 25, Preuss:297.

[95]　Ibid. Chemnitz's proposals for a proper celebration of confirmation were so influential among his followers that he is called the Father of Lutheran Confirmation. See Bjarne Hareide, *Die Konfirmation in der Reformationszeit: Eine Untersuchung der lutherischen Konfirmation in Deutschland 1520-1585*, Arbeiten zur Pastoraltheologie 8 (Göttingen: Vandenhoeck & Ruprecht, 1971), pp. 278-285.

[96]　"Quod secundum Canonem attinet: Qualem et quantam virtutem suo chrismati, sine ullo mandato et promissione divina tribuant, et quanta sit injuria et contumelia Baptismi, illam virtutem Baptismo detrahere, et ad Chrisma, quod nullum omnino habet verbum Dei, transferre, hactenus multis ostensum est." 26, Preuss:297-298.

[97]　"Quales sunt Episcopi, tale etiam volunt habere ministerium. Quia enim praedicationem verbi, et administrationem verorum Sacramentorum a se et ad alios inferiores rejecerunt: ne tamen ipsi nihil quod agerent, haberent, delibutionem Chrismatis, ut minime laboriosam et molestam invenerunt." 26, Preuss:298. See WA 6:549 (Chapter I, fn. 20).

Chemnitz knows from history that priests confirmed in certain instances, and that ordinaries resided far from their dioceses and let others administer their flock.

5. Summary

Chemnitz's sacramental theology is a child of Luther's. Both composed polemical works, one against abuses in the Church, another against a Council. Calvin's is a more synthetic summary of his theology. A hallmark of Reformation theology was the singular importance of Scripture, over and above the traditions which were handed down through the history of the Church. Even the confirmation debate bears the stamp of this hallmark, since the Reformers rejected it as a sacrament because of the silence of Scripture. Chemnitz, Calvin, and Luther all agree that a promise and a sign from the Scriptures produce a sacrament, but the sign is causative only for Chemnitz and Luther. For Luther the importance of one's faith makes sacraments an integral part of the economy of salvation. This is less true for Calvin, whose sacraments are signs of what God does for impoverished humanity. The requirement for a universal command is emphasized by Chemnitz. Luther does not mention the command in *De captivitate Babylonica*[98], and Calvin speaks of it only as what determines the work of a minister.[99] Chemnitz sees the universal command as a logical result of seeking the definition of a sacrament from the institution narratives of baptism and Eucharist. Chemnitz demonstrates well the differences between the rites of the ancients and those of the Roman Church in his day. He summarizes the history of the separation of the rites. But his fundamental accusation, repeated over and over again, is that the Roman Church's theology of confirmation detracts from the sacrament of baptism. It is a point Calvin and Luther have already introduced. He objects that what is ascribed to one is denied to the other. Surprisingly, Bellarmine never fully responds to this criticism. The Roman Church generally explains the efficacy of confirmation as a sealing or strengthening of the grace of baptism–more a question of support or degree than of displacement. Chemnitz's argument is based on a necessary antithesis between the rites that was never fully challenged, and hence remained strong.

Before the Reformers are left behind one nagging question remains.

[98] He does mention it twice in 1529, see Chapter I, fn. 33 and 35.

[99] See Chapter II, fn. 35 and 37 above.

Why did they really keep the rite of confirmation at all? In the spirit of reform, would it not have been more true to the bare written Word to eliminate its celebration altogether? Its retention seems all the more odd considering the Reformers' flimsy historical argument that the original purpose of confirmation both in Scripture and in the early Church was as an examination of the faith of those who were baptized as infants. There are several possible answers. First is the influence of Erasmus. As a humanist and scholar, the idea of educating children and examining them ritually would understandably appeal to him. His suggestion in 1523 that the faith of children be examined may well have convinced the Reformers of the benefits of such a rite. A second possibility is known from Bucer's situation. The Anabaptists challenged that infants should not be baptized because only adults can express faith; for Bucer and the Church at Strasbourg, confirmation provided a convenient means to demonstrate how the profession of faith could be delayed beyond infant baptism to a time after catechesis. From early on in the Reformation, the Reformers defended a middle path between the Catholics and the radical elements represented in the Anabaptists. It is likely that retaining confirmation was one strategy in a wider conflict. A third possibility is that the Reformers actually believed what they wrote, that due to the hallowed origins of their rite (which they clearly misunderstood) it was a profitable ceremony for the Church.

C. Robert Bellarmine (1542-1621)

1. Life

Born at Montepulciano, Italy in 1542, Robert Bellarmine entered a world already divided by the Reformation. Educated by the Society of Jesus, he lectured widely in Europe, and especially at the Roman College in the very program Chemnitz said was founded to halt the Reformation in Germany. From these lectures came Bellarmine's most famous work, *Disputationum de controversiis Christianae fidei adversus hujus temporis haereticos*,[100] originally published in Ingolstadt in 1586, 1588, and 1593. It is the heart of Bellarmine's writing. Pope Clement VIII named the great controversialist a cardinal

---

[100] Milan: Natale Battezzati, 1857-1862.

in 1599 and personally ordained him archbishop in 1602. Bellarmine died in 1621, 100 years after the birth of the Reformation in Germany. He was canonized a saint in the Catholic Church in 1930.

2. Sacraments

In his disputation with "the heretics of this time," Bellamine divides fifteen general controversies among four tomes. The first tome concerns principal elements of the faith: the Word of God, Christ the head of the whole Church, and the Supreme Pontiff. The second tome studies the Church: the Councils and the Church; the members of the Church; the Church in purgatory; and the Church triumphant, or the glory and veneration of the saints. Sacraments are in the third tome: sacraments in general; baptism and confirmation; Eucharist; penance; and finally extreme unction, orders, and matrimony. The final tome considers the realm of grace: the grace of the first human, the loss of grace and the state of sin, the restoration of grace through Jesus Christ our Lord.

The material for the controversy of this dissertation is found in the first two general controversies of the third tome, "Concerning sacraments in general" and "Concerning baptism and confirmation." For the first general controversy, Bellarmine adopts a Thomistic outline – he first presents the opinions of his adversaries, then discusses six points: the name of sacrament, its definition, its causes, the effect of the sacraments, their number and order, and their ceremonies in general.

a. Term and Definition

In the first general controversy the first point considers the already accepted difficulty with the non-scriptural term "sacrament". In the second point Bellarmine seeks the definition of a sacrament: He proposes to summarize from the common statement of all Catholics what constitutes a sacrament of the new law. Bellarmine lists eight criteria: First, a sacrament is a sign. Second, it is a sensible sign. Third, it is given voluntarily, not by nature. Fourth, the sign has some analogy and similarity with the thing it signifies, and is determined by it. Fifth, it represents something sacred, not profane, and carries justification, for sacraments sanctify.[101] Sixth, the sign not only signifies sanctification, but also so signifies it that it happens while

---

[101] This contrasts with Calvin's opinion that justification does not come from sacraments. See *Institutio* 4:14,14 (Chapter II, fn. 19).

the sacrament is applied. Seventh, this happens by the strength of the sacrament itself so that the sacrament is the instrumental cause of sanctification. And eighth, it is a fixed and solemn religious ceremony which consecrates one to God.[102]

Bellarmine continues with the formal definition of sacraments. He says they are defined morally, not physically (chapter 10); he proposes definitions from several sources and accepts that of the catechism of Trent [103] which fulfills all eight criteria (11). He explains how the definition works for sacraments in general and those of the new law in particular (12).

To conclude this point Bellarmine challenges the definitions of his adversaries. He observes that Chemnitz made no mention of the one offered by Trent (13). Bellarmine sees there is no universal definition among the Lutherans. Since Melanchthon often varies his words, whereas "Chemnitz tries to explain all things which pertain to the nature of a sacrament most accurately,"[104] Bellarmine chooses Chemnitz to focus his critique. Chemnitz said a sacrament should be an external matter, a corporeal, visible, tactile sign, and Bellarmine agrees. Second, Chemnitz said this sign must have an express command or divine institution; Bellarmine agrees, but adds that it need not be written in the Scriptures. (This is a major point in the dispute over confirmation.)[105] Third, Chemnitz said the command must be in the New Testament; Bellarmine reiterates his previous point. Fourth, Chemnitz believed a sacrament must not be a temporary institution;

---

[102]   "Prima controversia generalis, De sacramentis in genere, Liber Primus, Controversia II," 9, Battezzati:30-33.

[103] This definition reads, "Sacramentum est res sensibus subjecta, quae ex Dei institutione sanctitatis et justitiae tum significandae, tum efficiendae vim habet," "Controversia II," 11, Battezzati:34. It may be found in "De sacramentis in genere, 11," *Catechismus Romanus ex decreto sacrosancti concilii Tridentini*, ed. Pius V (Rome: Typis Sacrae Congregationis de Propaganda Fide, 1796), p. 139.

[104] "Kemnitius accuratissime conatur explicare omnia, quae ad naturam sacramenti pertinent," 14, Battezzati:36.

[105] Bellarmine explains, "Nam per accidens est ad mandatum, sive institutionem divinam, quod sit scripta, vel non scripta: nam alioqui non fuissent vera sacramenta, Baptismus et Eucharistia, quam Christus et apostoli dabant antequam scriberentur evangelia," 14, Battezzati:38. This argument is actually similar to that proposed by Henry VIII (Chapter I, fn. 40), but if Bellarmine is aware of Henry's support, he does not cite it.

Bellarmine accepts this. Fifth, Chemnitz said a promise is required concerning the grace, effect, or fruit of the sacrament; Bellarmine agrees with reservations, and adds that although Catholics say the promise concerning efficacy is found in the Word of God, it is possible to find it in tradition:

> For Catholics recognize traditions also as the Word of God; the adversaries, however, who accept only the Scriptures, will not easily show that promise concerning grace and the fruit of the sacrament in all the sacraments.[106]

Sixth, Chemnitz held that the promise ought to be conjoined with a sign by divine ordination; this Bellarmine declares false because the words of a sacrament are not promissory, but deprecatory. Seventh, Chemnitz said the promise should be for reconciliation of sins; Bellarmine finds this false as well – he says Chemnitz requires this promise to do away with Orders, and besides, even the Eucharist is not properly for forgiveness but for nourishing charity. And eighth, the general promise is applied and sealed through a sacrament on an individual who uses sacraments with faith; Bellarmine rejects this too, first since if sacraments sealed the promises of God they would be more efficacious than the Word of God; second because the Scriptures do not define sacraments as witnesses of the promises; third they would be superfluous; fourth the baptism of infants who could not profess faith would be in vain; fifth one cannot know when another truly believes.[107]

The result of this lengthy discussion is that there is precious little the two sides agree on concerning the definition of a sacrament. They do agree that a sacrament is an outward sign divinely instituted for perpetuity with a promise of grace. But each side shades the definition according to a wider agenda, and the fundamental differences concern one's interpretation of Scripture and the possibility of accepting revelation in tradition.

Bellarmine has even less in common with Calvin than with

[106] "Catholici enim agnoscunt pro Verbo Dei, etiam traditiones; adversarii autem, qui solas scripturas recipiunt, non facile ostendent promissionem istam de gratia et fructu sacramenti, in omnibus sacramentis," 14, Battezzati:38.

This is a good statement of the Catholic position in the controversy of Scripture and tradition. Because Catholics hold that God's revelation is manifest in tradition as well as in Scripture, they were able to retain confirmation as a sacrament developed and witnessed by the Church, while the Reformers could not.

[107] 14, Battezzati:37-41.

Chemnitz. He says that Calvin's definition in the *Institutio* [108]   is half from Luther (a symbol to seal the promises for sustaining the weakness of faith) and half from Zwingli (a symbol by which we witness before others our piety toward God). He says Calvin's sacraments are witnesses of predestination, "instituted for nourishing that faith by which one firmly believes that he is predestined."[109] Bellarmine divides Calvin's definition into five unacceptable parts:[110] 1) A sacrament is an external symbol (rejected because his symbol works nothing), 2) of God's kindness toward us (rejected because it includes the notion of predestination), 3) by which he seals (rejected as part of the doctrine of Luther and Zwingli),[111] 4) promises (rejected because the promises are of predestination), 5) on our consciences (rejected because it cannot apply to infant baptism).[112]

b. Causes

The third point of this first general controversy concerns the causes of a sacrament: intrinsic, final, and efficient. All agree that the intrinsic causes are the *res* and the words, which function as matter and form, and they especially agree on how these function for two sacraments, baptism and Eucharist.[113] Bellarmine says the final cause of sacraments is for justifying people; they are signs and instrumental causes of the grace of God.[114] Bellarmine's readiness to assign causality to sacraments contrasts with Calvin. Of efficient causes there are three: God, Christ, and the minister. The major question of this disputation is of which sacraments is Christ the efficient cause? Concerning baptism and Eucharist there is agreement, but with the others, Bellarmine says although there is no written text, Christ surely instituted them and James and the Church promulgated them:

[108] 4:14, 1. See Chapter II, fn. 12.

[109]   ". . . ad eam fidem alendam instituta, qua homo certo credit se esse praedestinatum," 16, Battezzati:43.

[110] I have renumbered them for the sake of syntax.

[111] In this point, Bellarmine says he has already refuted Luther's arguments regarding the seal, but actually they are covered in the following chapter.

[112] 16, Battezzati:43-46.

[113] "Controversia III," 18-19, Battezzati:49-56.

[114] 22, Battezzati:62.

"For Chapter 2 of Session 21 of the Council of Trent says the Church has the power of changing and instituting with regard to sacraments, their substance however being intact."[115]

c. Number and Order

A final observation is pertinent from the first controversy. When discussing the fifth point, the number and order of the sacraments, Bellarmine summarizes the preceding work detailing what agreement there is concerning the definition of a sacrament.

> However although we do not agree on explaining the definition of a sacrament (as we have shown above profusely in book 1 in the second controversy), nevertheless we do agree on a certain general definition, namely that sacraments are rites, or external and sensible signs which have a promise of justifying grace added on from divine institution.[116]

He then gives in capsule the proofs for each of the seven sacraments which he will expand in the following general controversies. Throughout this section, Bellarmine followed the Thomistic outline perceived also in Calvin, which will guide his work to completion.

3. Confirmation

The second general controversy contains Bellarmine's arguments for two sacraments, baptism and confirmation. Fundamentally the outlines are the same, but the introductory section on confirmation needs to discuss an area that is not at issue with baptism: Is this a sacrament or not? Then he presents matter, form, effect, the minister, and the ceremonies of confirmation, an outline by now familiar to the reader.

---

[115] "Nam sess. 21. cap. 2. <concilii tridentini> dicit, Ecclesiam habere potestatem mutandi, et instituendi circa sacramenta, salva tamen eorum substantia," 23, Battezzati:65.

[116] "Licet autem non conveniamus in explicanda definitione sacramenti (ut supra fuse ostendimus lib. 1. in secunda controversia) tamen convenimus in definitione quadam generali, nimirum quod sacramenta sint ritus, seu signa externa, et sensibilia, quae ex divina institutione annexam habeant promissionem gratiae justificantis." "Liber Secundus, Controversia V, De numero et ordine sacramentorum," 24, Battezzati:129.

a. Introduction

In the first chapter Bellarmine exposes the problem: The heretics of his time have removed confirmation from the list of the sacraments. Calvin and Chemnitz have followed Luther's model of confirmation, a rite only for catechesis in the Church. Others have joined them, including Ulrich Zwingli, Philipp Melanchthon, and Johannes Brentz. Even before this time, Bellarmine continues, some had denied that confirmation was a sacrament: John Wyclif, the Waldensians, and the Novatians in the early Church. It is also probable that the Donatists and Arians rejected the sacrament. Bellarmine introduces several arguments against the main adversaries, Calvin and Chemnitz, e.g., the testimony of the ancients regarding anointings, the effects of baptism and confirmation, and the accusation that Tertullian and Cyprian were Montanists.[117] These objections to the origin and use of this rite presage the many arguments which follow.

b. That Confirmation Is a Sacrament

In the lengthiest section, chapters two through seven, Bellarmine argues that confirmation is a sacrament with a fivefold attack from the Scriptures, the Popes, the Councils, the Greek Fathers, and the Latin Fathers. In addition he strives to refute his adversaries from these and other sources.

i. Scripture

Before examining Scripture, Bellarmine restates the acceptable criteria for a sacrament. He and his adversaries can at least agree on these points.

> Three things are required for the essence of a Christian sacrament properly called. First, a promise of grace. Second, a sensible sign with a word, which is the means or organ by which the promise may be applied. Third, the divine command, by which it is ordered to be administered. Calvin in book 4 of the *Institutio*, chapter 19, section 5 and Chemnitz in the second part of the *Examen* page 276 <"De Confirmatione" 6> propose these three things for themselves to be shown from the Scriptures in the question concerning confirmation...

---

117   "Secunda controversia generalis, De Baptismo et Confirmatione, Liber Secundus," 1, Battezzati:211-213.

> And they require nothing else; and deservedly: for all things
> are reduced to these; and by the consensus of all, a thing is
> properly called a sacrament, when these three things are
> found.[118]

Here are Bellarmine's clearest criteria for sacraments. They
remarkably resemble the Lutheran tradition and are not entirely
consonant with his earlier distinctions.[119] Here he does not call them
rites, and requires that the sign have a word. In this text he agrees that
the criteria must be shown in Scripture, but earlier he claimed this was
not necessary.[120] He will also redefine the third requirement. Still, he
wants to prove his point from grounds acceptable by both sides.
Bellarmine does not base his theology on Chemnitz's criteria for a
sacrament, but as a controversialist he accepts grounds he and his
adversaries can hold together.

To meet the first criterion, he shows the promise for confirmation in
John 14, 15, and 16, Luke, and Acts, where on various occasions the Lord
promised to send the Holy Spirit.

For the second he says the means by which the promise is applied
is the imposition of hands accompanied by prayer. This sign occurs in
several incidents in Acts: 2, 8, 19, and 11.

It remains for Bellarmine to show the command, which, of course,
he cannot do. Nowhere does Jesus say "Go out and confirm all nations,"
or "Confirm them in memory of me." So instead he shows the execution
of the command which he maintains implies its Christological origin.

> There remains the command. But in place of the command
> we give them the execution of the command. For never would
> the Apostles so ordinarily and assuredly have imposed hands
> on all the baptized that the Holy Spirit might come onto them
> unless the Lord had commanded them this.[121]

---

[118] "Tria requiruntur ad essentiam sacramenti christiani proprie dicti. Primo,
promissio gratiae. Secundo, signum sensibile cum verbo, quod sit medium, seu organum,
quo applicetur promissio. Tertio, mandatum divinum, quo id jubeatur ministrari. Haec
tria postulant sibi ostendi ex Scripturis in quaestione de Confirmatione, Calvinus lib. 4.
Institut. cap. 19. #5. et Kemnitius in 2. part. Exam. pag. 276. . . . Itaque nihil aliud
requirunt; et merito: nam ad haec revocantur omnia; et omnium consensu sacramentum est
proprie dictum, ubi haec tria inveniuntur," 2, Battezzati:213.

[119] See fn. 116 above.

[120] Compare with "Controversia II," 14, Battezzati:38 (fn. 105 above).

[121] "Restat mandatum. Sed pro mandato damus illis mandati exequutionem.
Numquam enim apostoli ita ordinarie, et secure imposuissent omnibus baptizatis manus,
ut veniret super eos Spiritus sanctus, nisi Dominus hoc eis mandasset," 2, Battezzati:214.

Next, Bellarmine responds to the arguments of his adversaries. Calvin said the imposition of hands in Scripture was not a sacrament but an offering of the baptized to God; but Bellarmine observes he has no proof except his own judgment. Second, Calvin and Brentz have said that the visible gifts of the Spirit in Acts have ceased; but Bellarmine says miracles are not the only means of the presence of the Holy Spirit, as Wisdom 1 and Matthew 7 show. Third, Calvin and Chemnitz claimed that the Holy Spirit was given through imposition of hands by an individual privilege for the Apostles not applicable to the later Church. But Bellarmine offers many places in the Scriptures where Jesus' command to the Apostles is really intended for the whole Church. Fourth, Chemnitz objected that the imposition of hands in Acts 8 and 19 is not the Roman practice of anointing. But Bellarmine says the Roman rite includes an imposition of hands as well as an anointing.

ii. Popes

The second proof (chapter III) is from the writings of the Popes and shows not that confirmation is a sacrament, but a ceremony giving grace,

> Now secondly the truth must be proved from the responses of the ancients and of the holy pontiffs. But we shall bring testimonies which indeed may not affirm with eloquent words that confirmation is a sacrament (for neither is it necessary and it could easily be distorted for the signification of a sacrament taken in a broad sense) but we shall bring testimonies which may demonstrate the reality itself; that is, a ceremony giving grace and distinct from baptism.[122]

Bellarmine arranges the testimony in approximately chronological order. Clement of Rome, Urban, and Cornelius begin the list. Miltiades adds that confirmation is greater than baptism because of the minister. Eusebius follows, then Innocent who distinguishes between confirmation and the post-baptismal anointing of the priest. Damasus, Leo, and John III say only the bishop may give the Holy Spirit through imposition of hands and anointing with chrism on the forehead. Gregory and Innocent III conclude the list.

---

[122] "Nunc secundo probanda est veritas ex veterum, et sanctorum pontificum responsis. Adferemus autem testimonia, quae non quidem disertis verbis affirment, Confirmationem esse sacramentum (id enim neque necessarium est, et facile posset detorqueri ad significationem sacramenti largo modo accepti) sed testimonia adferemus, quae rem ipsam demonstrent; idest, caeremoniam dantem gratiam, et a Baptismo distinctam," 3, Battezzati:216.

iii. Councils

Third, he argues through Church councils (chapter IV). Bellarmine gathers his evidence chronologically from Elvira, Arles I, Arles II, Laodicea, Orange, Meaux, Seville II, the council of St. Boniface, Constantinople III, Florence, and Trent.

iv. Greek Fathers

Chapter five contains the testimony from the Greek Fathers. Among them are Dionysius the Areopagite, Clement of Alexandria, Justin, and Origen. Cyril of Jerusalem (whose theology becomes an issue in the controversy) describes the anointing in his baptismal catecheses. Gregory of Nazianzen, Amphilochius, Theodoret, and John Damascene all contribute to the argument.

v. Latin Fathers

Chapter six comprises Latin Fathers. Tertullian and Cyprian are among the earliest. A text of Pseudo-Cyprian follows, along with Eusebius of Emissa, Prudentius, Pacianus, Ambrose, Jerome, Augustine, Bede, Rabanus, Amalarius, Hugh of St. Victor, and Peter Lombard. Stories about chrism come from Optatus, Surius, and Bernard. Taken altogether, Bellarmine's list of sources is an astounding compilation of texts. His facility with an exceptionally broad range of material is unmatched by his adversaries.

Bellarmine presents his adversaries' arguments regarding the foregoing testimony in chapter seven. First there is Calvin, who rejected Jerome and Miltiades as unreliable, but Bellarmine disagrees. Calvin maintained that the Fathers knew only his two sacraments, but Bellarmine cites Miltiades, Eusebius, Cyprian, and Augustine who do call confirmation a sacrament. Chemnitz cited a text of Gratian saying the imposition of hands is not a sacrament, but Bellarmine says the text applies not to confirmation but to reconciliation of heretics. Against Calvin's theory that confirmation was originally only a catechesis for children, Bellarmine charges that neither the Scriptures nor the ancients mention this instruction.

Next Bellarmine responds to five arguments of Chemnitz. To the charge that many sources produced by the Roman Church are apocryphal Bellarmine says even if they are dubious he has others more substantial.

> For even if the cited epistles of Miltiades, Eusebius, and Urban, and also the book of Dionysius the Areopagite, the homilies of Eusebius of Emissa, and the sermons of Cyprian concerning the principal works of Christ are in the sight of some people dubious or even false writings, nevertheless we have many other most certain and most proven authors, and these other ones themselves are most ancient and most excellent, although it is not certain whether they are those whose names they carry.[123]

Chemnitz said other authors are Montanist, and Bellarmine has already challenged this objection. Also, Chemnitz said of the authors who do mention anointing, that they call it a sacrament only in a wide sense, but Bellarmine maintains that the Fathers distinguish confirmation from baptism as sacraments. Chemnitz continued that the ancients never drew away effects from baptism to attribute them to confirmation, and further he questioned the testimony of Cyril. But Bellarmine says each sacrament has its own effects, and there is no reason to doubt the testimony of Cyril. Finally, Chemnitz charged that the more recent authors differed from the Fathers when they abandoned the imposition of hands for anointing, mixed balsam with oil, attributed some effects of baptism to confirmation, and separated the two rites. But Bellarmine responds that the imposition of hands was not abolished, balsam is mentioned by Gregory, the effects may have the same name but they are different in each sacrament, and the Fathers speak of both.

c. Matter

Having presented these many witnesses for confirmation, Bellarmine questions its matter in chapter seven. He supports four propositions with more testimony from the ancients and answers the objections of the Reformers. A preliminary distinction is that the

---

[123] "Nam etiamsi epistolae citatae Melchiadis, Eusebii et Urbani, necnon liber Dionysii areopagitae, homiliae Eusebii emisseni, et sermones Cypriani de operibus cardinalibus Christi, sint apud nonnullos dubiae Scripturae, vel etiam supposititiae: tamen multos habemus alios certissimos, et probatissimos auctores; et isti ipsi sunt antiquissimi, et optimi, licet non sit certum, àn sint illi, quorum nomina praeferunt," 7, Battezzati:221.

remote matter of confirmation is oil mixed with balsam, consecrated by a bishop; the proximate matter is anointing with that oil on the forehead in the sign of a cross.

The first proposition is that chrism is the matter of the sacrament of confirmation. Bellarmine offers proof from councils, Scripture, and the consensus of the Popes and the Fathers, Greek and Latin.

The second proposition is that the matter of confirmation is oil mixed with balsam. He presents testimony from Dionysius, Clement of Rome, Fabian, Cyprian, Gregory of Tours, Gregory the Great, the second Council of Braga, and others.

The third proposition is that chrism must first be consecrated. Although the Reformers call it magic, Bellarmine says that many of his witnesses speak of the blessed oil.

The fourth proposition is that the anointing of chrism in the sign of a cross on the forehead of the baptized is the proximate matter of this sacrament. Again, Bellarmine cites Popes, councils, and the Fathers.

The Reformers' objections to the propositions are in chapter nine together with Bellarmine's responses. Material from Brentz is introduced here for the first time, and another series of objections from Chemnitz.

d. Form

Bellarmine says the words "I sign you with the sign of the cross, and I confirm you with the chrism of salvation in the name of the Father, and of the Son and of the Holy Spirit" are the form of the sacrament (chapter 10). He says they are appropriate because they explain the causes and effect of the sacrament:

> Nor can it be doubted that this is an appropriate form since it clearly explains both the principal cause which is the Holy Trinity, and the ministerial cause, which is the one who pronounces the words themselves, and finally the effect of the sacrament, which is to make a soldier of Christ by signing him with the cross, and to strengthen and to arm by confirming him with chrism.[124]

---

[124] "Neque dubitari potest, quin haec sit conveniens forma, cum aperte explicet, et caussam principalem, quae est sancta Trinitas, et caussam ministerialem, quae est ille, qui verba ipsa profert, et denique effectum sacramenti, qui est facere Christi militem insigniendo illum cruce, et roborare, atque armare confirmando Chrismate," 10, Battezzati:228.

Although the form varies among ancient texts, he says its sense does not change:

> Not all these words and with this order are found among the more ancient authors, nevertheless the same sense is found and this suffices.[125]

Next Bellarmine presents and answers four objections of his adversaries.

e. Effect

Chapter eleven presents two effects of confirmation:

> The effect of this sacrament is twofold. One, that it confers grace making one pleasing <to God> and indeed more so than baptism itself in the direction of strengthening the soul against the attacks of the devil, but less in the direction of remission of sin, because it does not remit the complete penalty as the grace of baptism does. . . .
> The other effect is the character by which we are inscribed into the army of Christ, as through baptism into the family of Christ.[126]

As usual, Bellarmine calls in testimony from Scripture, the Fathers, and councils.

Actually this section is not a "controversy" at all in the same sense as the others. Bellarmine does not present the positions of his adversaries, and his use of other sources is weak. This is especially surprising since Chemnitz held that the main point of the controversy was that confirmation impoverished baptism. Bellarmine leaves unfulfilled the expectation for a response on this issue.

f. Minister

The fifth controversy (chapter 12) is whether the minister of confirmation is the bishop alone. Bellarmine says the heretics who

---

[125] "Apud antiquiores auctores non habentur haec omnia verba, et hoc ordine, tamen habetur idem sensus, et hoc sufficit," Ibid.

[126] "Duplex est sacramenti hujus effectus. Unus, quod gratiam confert gratum <Deo> facientem, et quidem majorem, quam ipse Baptismus, in ordine ad roborandam animam contra diaboli impetus: sed minorem in ordine ad remissionem peccati, quia non remittit totam poenam, ut facit gratia Baptismi. . . .

"Alter effectus est character, quo adscribimur in Christi militiam, sicut per Baptismum in Christi familiam," 11, Battezzati:229-230.

have extracted confirmation from the number of the sacraments (Wyclif, Calvin, and Chemnitz), and even Richard Armachanus (Fitzralph) among the Catholics, also believe that only bishops may administer it.

He then discusses whether a dispensation may be made for the priest to confer the sacrament. Bonaventure, Durandus, and Hadrian say no, but Thomas, Richard, La Palud, and Marsilius teach the contrary. Bellarmine supports the latter position with Fathers and councils. The bishop, he says, is the ordinary minister, as the Scriptures show that the Apostles imposed hands on those baptized by others.

Bellarmine then takes on a series of arguments from Calvin and Chemnitz regarding the proper minister.

g. Ceremonies

Finally, the controversialist presents the two ceremonies regarding this sacrament: the consecration of chrism on Holy Thursday, and the conferral of confirmation by anointing and signing.

Many have written about the first ceremony, Bellarmine says – Isidore, Alcuin, Amalarius, Rabanus, Rupert, and others. There are four parts to it: First are the blessings of oil and balsam through prayers, justified through 1 Timothy. Second are blessings with the sign of the cross, evidenced by many Fathers. Third, the bishop blows on the chrism, as the Lord Himself breathed on His Apostles. Fourth, the clergy greet the chrism, though not in idolatry, Bellarmine adds, as his adversaries accuse.

Bellarmine lists eight particulars of the ceremony of confirmation. First the sponsor presents the one to be confirmed to the bishop. Then the bishop says prayers and imposes hands on the candidates. Third the peace is given. Fourth the bishop strikes each one lightly with his hand. Fifth the forehead is bound to conserve the oil, which signifies grace. Sixth the forehead is not washed for seven days, as at baptism. Seventh confirmation is given at the Easter Vigil and Pentecost. Eighth a fast is enjoined for preparation.

Chemnitz wondered why the Popes preferred superfluous ceremonies over an examination of children, profession of faith, and exhortation. But Bellarmine believes the Church is more faithful to the tradition.[127]

---

[127] Bellarmine needs to tread lightly here. Even the Catechism of the Council of

For we reject nothing of those things, but we want all things to happen in their place and time; nor do we allow to be ripped away from us a sacrament instituted by Christ and ceremonies handed down from the Fathers, on the pretext of a childish examination. And concerning the sacrament of confirmation enough has been said.[128]

4. Summary

Bellarmine seeks the definition of a sacrament not from the Scriptures, as Luther did, nor from the nature of a symbol, as Calvin did, but from what he and the Reformers can agree on together. His purpose differs from the other two – He is not creating a new sacramental theology, he is responding to criticisms to the time-honored beliefs of his own faith. And since his role is a controversialist, he chooses to begin from common ground. However, where Luther turned to Scripture, Bellarmine turned to tradition.

Although Bellarmine's demonstration of the sacramentality of confirmation covers a full range of scholastic argumentation, he devotes most of his effort to extrinsic principles (promise, sign, and command) which he says he has in common with the Reformers. The last of these principles remains unconvincing because he changes the criterion for its application: Instead of showing the command itself Bellarmine shows what he calls the result of the command. He seems more at home with the intrinsic principles of matter and form, and the long history of sacramental confirmation. Still, for Bellarmine's argument to be more convincing, readers need to be able to judge whether the recorded words of Jesus are necessary for a sacrament, and whether there is a distinction between the effects of baptism and confirmation. He helps little with these judgments.

Bellarmine describes two effects of confirmation: It strengthens the soul against attacks of the devil and inscribes one in the army of Christ. But with the Reformers one may still object that these are effects of

---

Trent called for a mature age for confirmation, when the child had the use of reason to understand and defend the faith (*Catechismus* 18, p. 201). Thus, an examination of faith of some kind might be beneficial, but confirmation for the Catholics was more.

[128] "Nos enim nihil horum rejicimus, sed volumus omnia fieri suo loco, et tempore; nec patimur nobis eripi sacramentum a Christo institutum, et caeremonias a Patribus traditas praetextu examinis puerilis. Ac de sacramento Confirmationis satis dictum est," 13, Battezzati:234.

baptism as well. When Bellarmine describes the effects of baptism, he lists three: It takes away all sin, it confers the grace and divine gifts by which one is justified, and it imprints a character by which it cannot be repeated.[129] He attributes no special effects to the post-baptismal anointing with chrism.[130] In confirmation Bellarmine imagines a mature Christian – one who is both subject to increased temptations and renewed in his commitment against evil. It appears that for him the two effects of confirmation are an increase of the effects of baptism, but he does not say so, nor does he explain any other way that the effects of confirmation do not rob baptism of its effects, as the Reformers contend. (Does not strength come with grace, and inscription with initiation?) Since Chemnitz has called this the foundational issue of the debate, Bellarmine's poor explanation of the effects of confirmation is a special weakness in his argument.

By this time, the dispute has become cerebral. It is as much a contest of finding and applying texts as it is a discussion of theology. The outrage which Luther and Calvin expressed for the Church has been replaced by the more pacific and logical mind of Chemnitz. Similarly in the Roman Church, the anger over the division has largely been repressed in the Latin of Bellarmine – terse, but richly illustrated. This generation has grown up a bit, and the fighting is more polite. But the feelings did not go away, the arguments remained unconvincing, and the divisions remained.

---

[129] "Liber Primus, De sacramento baptismi," 12, Battezzati:183.
[130] 27, Battezzati:206.

CHAPTER III:
Sources and Method

The first two chapters have presented the history of the post-Reformation confirmation controversy and the principal positions taken by the protagonists. In addition to meeting the people and the issues of the debate, the reader has been introduced to the method employed in the organization and presentation of each writer's material. This background will facilitate the analysis of contemporary materials in the final chapter to observe the progress of the controversy since the Reformation and the possibilities for furthering its resolution. First, however, this chapter examines the sources and method of the controversy in more detail. This will provide additional insight into specific issues of the controversy as well as a critical apparatus for evaluating the progress of the debate.

To analyze the approach taken by the controversialists this chapter is divided into two sections. The first will be a complete listing of sources quoted by all three protagonists: the second will be a discussion of their method, the use of these texts.

A. Sources

A chart follows, organized primarily for the study of what Calvin, Chemnitz, and Bellarmine said about confirmation. It is a reconstruction of their "dossiers", the material they had on hand to build the arguments for their theology. Under the headings "Calvin", "Chemnitz", and "Bellarmine" a colon separates the chapter and page or column number according to the following editions: *Corpus Reformatorum* for Calvin, Preuss for Chemnitz, and Battezzati for Bellarmine. Column numbers for Calvin's *Antidotum* are distinguished by the addition of the letter "A". (In some entries these numbers occur more than once. For example, at S-16, the chart lists 10:289 twice for

Chemnitz. This means Chemnitz includes two references to Matthew 28 on page 289 of chapter 10.) The headings on the left govern the source cited by the controversialists in the corresponding location. Then a few lines of actual text are reproduced, followed by publication data for editions of the sources cited. The chart, then, is a listing of the "footnotes", grouped so that the reader may compare how the sources are used and by whom.

The assembly of this material provides a ready reference for any student of the history of confirmation, even apart from the controversy examined in this dissertation. For that reason, dates are included for the authors and councils, and an appendix organizes the works chronologically. However, since the first purpose of the chart is for an examination of these three writers, the material is arranged neither chronologically nor thematically, but in the following manner: The complete list appears in eight sections inspired by Bellarmine's own method of presenting the data. Since most of the references are his, and since this does no damage to the arguments of the Reformers but helps organize an examination of their material, this method is useful. The categories are Scripture, Popes, Councils, Greek Fathers, Latin Fathers, Medieval Sources, Reformation Sources, and Secular Sources. Within these categories, the Scripture passages occur in biblical order, the councils in alphabetical order by city, and the other writers first by alphabetical order of their names, then of their works. Therefore to find a patristic reference of Bellarmine, for example, the reader may easily locate his sources in the chart tracing first the proper category, then the alphabetical listing. If further information about the source is needed, the publication data will assist in finding a volume containing the complete work.

The editions cited are generally the most recent ones published. This choice should make the materials more accessible to contemporary students of this matter. Many of the actual sixteenth century editions used by the controversialists are still available for study, but the possibility of their shedding additional light on the controversy beyond what the editorial labors of scholars of the past four hundred years have produced seems slim. In some cases, the sources are available only in sixteenth century editions. These have generally been quoted at more length since they are more rare.

1. SCRIPTURE

PASSAGE	CALVIN	CHEMNITZ	BELLARMINE

S-1: Exodus 20, 7

7:287 18:290

"Non assumes nomen Domini Dei tui in vanum, nec enim habebit insontem Dominus eum, qui assumpserit nomen Domini Dei sui frustra."[1]

S-2: Exodus 29, 4-5. 7

24:294

"Aaron ac filios eius applicabis ad ostium tabernaculi conventus. Cumque laveris patrem cum filiis suis aqua, indues Aaron vestimentis suis. . . et oleum unctionis fundes super caput eius; atque hoc ritu consecrabitur."

S-3: Exodus 30, 22-23. 26. 30

8:223

"Locutusque est Dominus ad Moysen dicens: 'Sume tibi aromata prima myrrhae electae quingentos siclos et cinnamomi boni odoris medium. . . . Et unges ex eo tabernaculum conventus et arcam testamenti. . . . Aaron et filios eius unges sanctificabisque eos, ut sacerdotio fungantur mihi'."

S-4: Deuteronomy 12, 29-31

9:225

"Quando disperdiderit Dominus Deus tuus ante faciem tuam gentes, ad quas ingredieris possidendas, et possederis eas atque habitaveris in terra earum, cave, ne irretiaris per eas, postquam te fuerint introeunte subversae, et requiras caeremonias earum dicens: 'Sicut coluerunt gentes istae deos suos, ita et ego colam'."

---

[1]   All citations in this section are from *Nova Vulgata Bibliorum Sacrorum editio* (Vatican City: Libreria Editrice Vaticana, 1979).

PASSAGE	CALVIN	CHEMNITZ	BELLARMINE

S-5: 2 Kings 13, 16-17

10:229

"Et, cum posuisset ille manum suam, superposuit Eliseus manus suas manibus regis et ait: 'Aperi fenestram orientalem'. Cumque aperuisset, dixit Eliseus: 'Iace sagittam!'. Et iecit. Et ait Eliseus: 'Sagitta salutis Domini, et sagitta salutis contra Syriam. Percuties Syriam in Aphec, donec consumas eam'."

S-6: Psalms 74 (73), 13

24:295

"Tu conscidisti in virtute tua mare, contribulasti capita draconum in aquis."

S-7: Psalms 99 (98), 5

13:233

"Exaltate Dominum Deum nostrum et adorate ad scabellum pedum eius, quoniam sanctus est."

S-8: Psalms 133 (132), 1-2

24:292

"Ecce quam bonum et quam iucundum habitare fratres in unum: sicut unguentum optimum in capite, quod descendit in barbam, barbam Aaron."

S-9: Wisdom 1, 5

2:214

"Spiritus enim sanctus disciplinae effugiet fictum et auferet se a cogitationibus insensatis, et corripietur a superveniente iniquitate."

S-10: Isaiah 25, 6-7

24:294

"Et faciet Dominus exercituum omnibus populis in monte hoc convivium pinguium, convivium vini meri, pinguium medullatorum, vini deliquati. Et praecipitabit in monte isto faciem vinculi colligati super omnes populos et telam, quam orditus est super omnes nationes."

PASSAGE	CALVIN	CHEMNITZ	BELLARMINE

S-11: Daniel 7, 8

4:286

"Considerabam cornua, et ecce cornu aliud parvulum ortum est de medio eorum, et tria de cornibus primis evulsa sunt a facie eius; et ecce oculi quasi oculi hominis erant in cornu isto, et os loquens ingentia."

S-12: Matthew 7, 21

2:214

"Non omnis, qui dicit mihi: 'Domine Domine', intrabit in regnum caelorum, sed qui facit voluntatem Patris mei, qui in caelis est."

S-13: Matthew 10, 20

8:1072

"Non enim vos estis, qui loquimini, sed Spiritus Patris vestri, qui loquitur in vobis."

S-14: Matthew 21, 25-27

5:1069

" 'Baptismum Ioannis unde erat? A caelo an ex hominibus?'. At illi cogitabant inter se dicentes: 'Si dixerimus: 'E caelo', dicet nobis: 'Quare ergo non credidistis illi?'; si autem dixerimus: 'Ex hominibus', timemus turbam; omnes enim habent Ioannem sicut prophetam'. Et respondentes Iesu dixerunt: 'Nescimus'. Ait illis et ipse: 'Nec ego dico vobis, in qua potestate haec facio'."

S-15: Matthew 28, 8-9

13:233

"Et exeuntes cito de monumento cum timore et magno gaudio cucurrerunt nuntiare discipulis eius. Et ecce Iesus occurrit illis dicens: 'Avete'. Illae autem accesserunt et tenuerunt pedes eius et adoraverunt eum."

S-16: Matthew 28, 18-20

10:289 10:289   2:215

"Et accedens Iesus locutus est eis dicens: 'Data est mihi omnis potestas in caelo et in terra. Euntes ergo docete omnes gentes, baptizantes eos in nomine Patris et Filii et Spiritus Sancti, docentes eos servare omnia, quaecumque mandavi vobis. Et ecce ego vobiscum sum omnibus diebus usque ad consummationem saeculi'."

PASSAGE	CALVIN	CHEMNITZ	BELLARMINE

S-17: Mark 7, 32-34

2:216

"Et adducunt ei surdum et mutum et deprecantur eum, ut imponat illi manum. Et apprehendens eum de turba seorsum misit digitos suos in auriculas eius et exspuens tetigit linguam eius et suspiciens in caelum ingemuit et ait illi: 'Effetha', quod est: 'Adaperire'."

S-18: Mark 10, 13. 16

11:289

"Et offerebant illi parvulos, ut tangeret illos. . . . Et complexans eos benedicebat imponens manus super illos."

S-19: Mark 16, 15-18

12:289 19:291   2:215 2:215

"Et dixit eis: 'Euntes in mundum universum praedicate evangelium omni creaturae. Qui crediderit et baptizatus fuerit, salvus erit; qui vero non crediderit, condemnabitur. Signa autem eos, qui crediderint, haec sequentur: in nomine meo daemonia eicient, linguis loquentur novis, serpentes tollent, et, si mortiferum quid biberint, non eos nocebit, super aegrotos manus imponent et bene habebunt'."

S-20: Luke 1, 76-77

10:229

"Et tu, puer, propheta Altissimi vocaberis: praeibis enim ante faciem Domini parare vias eius, ad dandam scientiam salutis plebi eius in remissionem peccatorum eorum."

S-21: Luke 12, 49-50

8:224

"Ignem veni mittere in terram et quid volo? Si iam accensus esset! Baptisma autem habeo baptizari et quomodo coartor, usque dum perficiatur!"

S-22: Luke 22, 19

2:215

"Et accepto pane, gratias egit et fregit et dedit eis dicens: 'Hoc est corpus meum, quod pro vobis datur. Hoc facite in meam commemorationem'."

PASSAGE	CALVIN	CHEMNITZ	BELLARMINE

S-23: Luke 24, 48-49

                                    10:288   2:213 2:214
                                                  7:222

"Vos estis testes horum. Et ecce ego mitto promissum Patris mei in vos; vos autem sedete in civitate, quoadusque induamini virtutem ex alto'."

S-24: John 3, 5

                              19:291 24:292
                                     24:292

"Respondit Iesus: 'Amen, amen dico tibi: Nisi quis natus fuerit ex aqua et Spiritu, non potest introire in regnum Dei."

S-25: John 4, 10

                        6:1070

"Respondit Iesus et dixit ei: 'Si scires donum Dei et quis est, qui dicit tibi: 'Da mihi bibere', tu forsitan petisses ab eo et dedisset tibi aquam vivam'."

S-26: John 6, 48. 51.

                                                  10:229

"Ego sum panis vitae. . . . Ego sum panis vivus, qui de caelo descendi. Si quis manducavit ex hoc pane, vivet in aeternum."

S-27: John 6, 57

                        7:287

"Sicut misit me vivens Pater, et ego vivo propter Patrem, et qui manducat me, et ipse vivet propter me."

S-28: John 7, 37

                        6:1070

"In novissimo autem die magno festivitatis stabat Iesus et clamavit dicens: 'Si quis sitit, veniat ad me et bibat'."

S-29: John 10, 5. 27

                        7:287

"<Oves> alienum autem non sequentur, sed fugient ab eo, quia non noverunt vocem alienorum. . . . Oves meae vocem meam audiunt, et ego cognosco eas, et sequuntur me. "

PASSAGE	CALVIN	CHEMNITZ	BELLARMINE

S-30: John 14, 15-16. 25-26

2:213 2:214

"Si diligitis me, mandata mea servabitis; et ego rogabo Patrem, et alium Paraclitum dabit vobis, ut maneat vobiscum in aeternum. . . . Haec locutus sum vobis apud vos manens. Paraclitus autem, Spiritus Sanctus, quem mittet Pater in nomine meo, ille vos docebit omnia et suggeret vobis omnia, quae dixi vobis."

S-31: John 15, 26-27

2:213 2:214

"Cum autem venerit Paraclitus, quem ego mittam vobis a Patre, Spiritum veritatis, qui a Patre procedit, ille testimonium perhibebit de me; sed et vos testimonium perhibetis, quia ab initio mecum estis."

S-32: John 16, 8-11

2:213 2:214

"Et cum venerit ille <Paraclitus>, arguet mundum de peccato et de iustitia et de iudicio: de peccato quidem, quia non credunt in me; de iustitia vero, quia ad Patrem vado, et iam non videtis me; de iudicio autem, quia princeps mundi huius iudicatus est."

S-33: John 20, 21-22

7:1070   11:289 16:290   2:215 7:222
12:231 13:233

"Dixit ergo eis iterum: 'Pax vobis! Sicut misit me Pater, et ego mitto vos'. Et cum hoc dixisset, insufflavit et dicit eis: 'Accipite Spiritum Sanctum'."

S-34: John 20, 30

8:288

"Multa quidem et alia signa fecit Iesus in conspectu discipulorum suorum, quae non sunt scripta in libro hoc."

PASSAGE	CALVIN	CHEMNITZ	BELLARMINE

S-35: Acts 1, 7-8

	CALVIN	CHEMNITZ	BELLARMINE
	10:288	10:288	2:213 7:222
	10:289	12:289	
	12:289	12:289	
		15:290	

"Dixit autem eis: 'Non est vestrum nosse tempora vel momenta, quae Pater posuit in sua potestate, sed accipietis virtutem superveniente Sancto Spiritu in vos et eritis mihi testes et in Ierusalem et in omni Iudaea et Samaria et usque ad ultimum terrae'."

S-36: Acts 2, 1-4

	CALVIN	CHEMNITZ	BELLARMINE
	8:1072	10:288	2:214 8:223
			9:225 12:233

"Et cum compleretur dies Pentecostes, erant omnes pariter in eodem loco. Et factus est repente de caelo sonus tamquam advenientis spiritus vehementis et replevit totam domum, ubi erant sedentes. Et apparuerunt illis dispertitae linguae tamquam ignis, seditque supra singulos eorum; et repleti sunt omnes Spiritu Sancto et coeperunt loqui aliis linguis, prout Spiritus dabat eloqui illis."

S-37: Acts 2, 14. 16

	CALVIN	CHEMNITZ	BELLARMINE
			2:214 2:215

"Stans autem Petrus cum Undecim levavit vocem suam et locutus est eis: . . . '<Hoc> est, quod dictum est per prophetam Ioel: 'Et erit:' in novissimis diebus, dicit Deus, 'effundam de Spiritu meo super omnem carnem, et prophetabunt filii vestri et filiae vestrae'."

S-38: Acts 2, 38-39[2]

	CALVIN	CHEMNITZ	BELLARMINE
			2:214 2:215
			7:222

"Petrus vero ad illos: 'Paenitentiam, inquit, agite, et baptizetur unusquisque vestrum in nomine Iesu Christi in remissionem peccatorum vestrorum, et accipietis donum Sancti Spiritus; vobis enim est repromissio et filiis vestris et omnibus, qui longe sunt, quoscumque advocaverit Dominus Deus noster'."

---

[2] At 2:215 Bellarmine cites this passage as chapter 3; it is chapter 2.

PASSAGE	CALVIN	CHEMNITZ	BELLARMINE

S-39: Acts 5, 1-2. 10

2:216

"Vir autem quidam nomine Ananias cum Sapphira uxore sua vendidit agrum et subtraxit de pretio, conscia quoque uxore, et afferens partem quamdam ad pedes apostolorum posuit. . . . Confestim cecidit ante pedes eius et exspiravit; intrantes autem iuvenes invenerunt illam mortuam et efferentes sepelierunt ad virum suum."

S-40: Acts 5, 14-16

10:289   2:214 2:215

"<Magis> autem addebantur credentes Domino. . . ut, veniente Petro, saltem umbra illius obumbraret quemquam eorum. Concurrebat autem et multitudo vicinarum civitatum Ierusalem, afferentes aegros et vexatos ab spiritibus immundis, qui curabantur omnes."

S-41: Acts 6, 6

6:1070

"<Elegerunt> quos statuerunt ante conspectum apostolorum, et orantes imposuerunt eis manus."

S-42: Acts 8, 12-13

2:214 2:215

"Cum vero credidissent Philippo evangelizanti de regno Dei et nomine Iesu Christi, baptizabantur viri ac mulieres. Tunc Simon et ipse credidit, et cum baptizatus esset, adhaerebat Philippo; videns etiam signa et virtutes magnas fieri stupens admirabatur."

S-43: Acts 8, 14-17

	CALVIN	CHEMNITZ		BELLARMINE	
	6:1070	10:288	10:288	1:213	2:214
	6:1070	10:289	11:289	2:214	2:214
	8:1072	12:289	12:289	2:214	2:214
		12:289	15:290	2:215	7:221
		16:290	16:290	9:225	9:226
			25:297	10:229	12:230
				12:231	12:231
					12:231

PASSAGE   CALVIN   CHEMNITZ   BELLARMINE

"Cum autem audissent apostoli, qui erant Hierosolymis, quia recepit Samaria verbum Dei, miserunt ad illos Petrum et Ioannem, qui cum descendissent, oraverunt pro ipsis, ut acciperent Spiritum Sanctum; nondum enim super quemquam illorum venerat, sed baptizati tantum erant in nomine Domini Iesu. Tunc imposuerunt manus super illos, et accipiebant Spiritum Sanctum."

S-44: Acts 9, 12

3:502A	10:288	2:215 12:231
10:1073		12:232

"<Et> vidit virum Ananiam nomine introeuntem et imponentem sibi manus, ut visum recipiat."

S-45: Acts 10, 37-38

8:224

"<Petrus dixit:> 'Vos scitis quod factum est verbum per universam Iudaeam incipiens a Galilaea post baptismum, quod praedicavit Ioannes: Iesum a Nazareth, quomodo unxit eum Deus Spiritu Sancto et virtute, qui pertransivit benefaciendo et sanando omnes oppressos a Diabolo, quoniam Deus erat cum illo'."

S-46: Acts 10, 44-48

9:225

"Adhuc loquente Petro verba haec, cecidit Spiritus Sanctus super omnes, qui audiebant verbum. Et obstupuerunt, qui ex circumcisione fideles, qui venerant cum Petro, quia et in nationes gratia Spiritus Sancti effusa est; audiebant enim illos loquentes linguis et magnificantes Deum. Tunc respondit Petrus: 'Numquid aquam quis prohibere potest, ut non baptizentur hi, qui Spiritum Sanctum acceperunt sicut et nos?'. Et iussit eos in nomine Iesu Christi baptizari."

S-47: Acts 11, 15-17

2:214

"<Petrus exponebat:> 'Cum autem coepissem loqui, decidit Spiritus Sanctus super eos sicut et super nos in initio. Recordatus sum autem verbi Domini sicut dicebat: 'Ioannes quidem baptizavit aqua, vos autem baptizabimini in Spiritu Sancto'. Si ergo aequale donum dedit illis

PASSAGE	CALVIN	CHEMNITZ	BELLARMINE

Deus sicut et nobis, qui credidimus in Dominum Iesum Christum, ego quis eram qui possem prohibere Deum?'."

S-48: Acts 11, 20-24. 26

                              10:289 16:290
                                  24:293

"Erant autem quidam ex eis viri Cyprii et Cyrenaei, qui cum introissent Antiochiam, loquebantur et ad Hellenistas evangelizantes Dominum Iesum. Et erat manus Domini cum eis; multusque numerus credentium conversus est ad Dominum. Auditus est autem sermo in auribus ecclesiae, quae erat in Ierusalem, super istis, et miserunt Barnabam usque Antiochiam; qui cum pervenisset et vidisset gratiam Dei, gavisus est et hortabatur omnes proposito cordis permanere in Domino, quia erat vir bonus et plenus Spiritu Sancto et fide. . . . <Et> cognominarentur primum Antiochiae discipuli Christiani."

S-49: Acts 13, 2-3

                      6:1070

"Ministrantibus autem illis Domino et ieiunantibus, dixit Spiritus Sanctus: 'Separate mihi Barnabam et Saulum in opus, ad quod vocavi eos'. Tunc ieiunantes et orantes imponentesque eis manus dimiserunt illos."

S-50: Acts 13, 7-8

                                      2:216

"Hic accitis Barnaba et Saulo, quaesivit audire verbum Dei; resistebat autem illis Elyma, magus, sic enim interpretatur nomen eius, quaerens avertere proconsulem a fide."

S-51: Acts 13, 26

                                      10:229

"Viri fratres, filii generis Abraham et qui in vobis timent Deum, nobis verbum salutis huius missum est."

PASSAGE	CALVIN	CHEMNITZ	BELLARMINE

S-52: Acts 14, 21-22

7:287 10:289
25:297

"Cumque evangelizassent civitati illi et docuissent multos, reversi sunt Lystram et Iconium et Antiochiam confirmantes animas discipulorum, exhortantes, ut permanerent in fide, et quoniam per multas tribulationes oportet nos intrare in regnum Dei."

S-53: Acts 15, 30-32

7:287 25:297

"Illi igitur dimissi descenderunt Antiochiam et congregata multitudine, tradiderunt epistulam; quam cum legissent, gavisi sunt super consolatione. Iudas quoque et Silas, cum et ipsi essent prophetae, verbo plurimo consolati sunt fratres et confirmaverunt."

S-54: Acts 15, 41

10:289

". . . perambulabat autem Syriam et Ciliciam confirmans ecclesias."

S-55: Acts 18, 11

25:297

"Sedit <Paulus> autem annum et sex menses docens apud eos verbum Dei."

S-56: Acts 18, 23

7:287 10:289

"Et facto ibi aliquanto tempore, profectus est perambulans ex ordine Galaticam regionem et Phrygiam, confirmans omnes discipulos."

S-57: Acts 19, 1-6

	6:1070	10:288 10:288	2:214 2:214
		10:289 11:289	2:214 2:214
		12:289 12:289	2:214 7:221
		12:289 15:290	9:225 9:226
		16:290 16:290	12:230
		25:297	

"Factum est autem cum Apollo esset Corinthi, ut Paulus, peragratis

PASSAGE	CALVIN	CHEMNITZ	BELLARMINE

superioribus partibus, veniret Ephesum et inveniret quosdam discipulos, dixitque ad eos: 'Si Spiritum Sanctum accepistis credentes?'. At illi ad eum: 'Sed neque si Spiritus Sanctus est audivimus'. Ille vero ait: 'In quo ergo baptizati estis?'. Qui dixerunt: 'In Ioannis baptismate'. Dixit autem Paulus: 'Ioannes baptizavit baptisma paenitentiae, populo dicens in eum, qui venturus esset post ipsum ut crederent, hoc est in Iesum'. His auditis, baptizati sunt in nomine Domini Iesu; et cum imposuisset illis manus Paulus, venit Spiritus Sanctus super eos, et loquebantur linguis et prophetabant."

S-58: Acts 19, 11-12

2:214 2:215

"Virtutesque non quaslibet Deus faciebat per manus Pauli, ita ut etiam super languidos deferrentur a corpore eius sudaria vel semicinctia, et recederent ab eis languores, et spiritus nequam egrederentur."

S-59: Acts 22, 13-14. 16

12:232

"<Ananias> veniens ad me et astans dixit mihi: 'Saul frater, respice!'. Et ego eadem hora respexi in eum. At ille dixit: '. . . Exsurgens baptizare et ablue peccata tua, invocato nomine ipsius'."

S-60: Romans 5, 5

24:296

". . . spes autem non confundit, quia caritas Dei diffusa est in cordibus nostris per Spiritum Sanctum, qui datus est nobis."

S-61: Romans 6, 3-6

1:501A   19:291
8:1071

"An ignoratis quia, quicumque baptizati sumus in Christo Iesu, in mortem ipsius baptizati sumus? Consepulti ergo sumus cum illo per baptismum in mortem, ut quemadmodum suscitatus est Christus a mortuis per gloriam Patris, ita et nos in novitate vitae ambulemus. Si enim complantati facti sumus similitudini mortis eius, sed et resurrectionis erimus; hoc scientes quia vetus homo noster simul crucifixus est, ut destruatur corpus peccati, ut ultra non serviamus peccato."

PASSAGE	CALVIN	CHEMNITZ	BELLARMINE

S-62: Romans 10, 10

8:1072

"Corde enim creditur ad iustitiam, ore autem confessio fit in salutem."

S-63: Romans 12, 4-5

2:214

"Sicut enim in uno corpore multa membra habemus, omnia autem membra non eundem actum habent, ita multi unum corpus sumus in Christo, singuli autem alter alterius membra."

S-64: 1 Corinthians 5, 7

26:298

"Expurgate vetus fermentum, ut sitis nova consparsio, sicut estis azymi. Etenim Pascha nostrum immolatus est Christus!"

S-65: 1 Corinthians 6, 13

7:1071

"'Esca ventri et venter escis!'. Deus autem et hunc et has destruet."

S-66: 1 Corinthians 7, 31

7:1071

". . . et qui utuntur hoc mundo, tamquam non abutentes; praeterit enim figura huius mundi."

S-67: 1 Corinthians 11, 26-27

10:289   2:216

"Quotiescumque enim manducabitis panem hunc et calicem bibetis, mortem Domini annuntiatis, donec veniat. Itaque, quicumque manducaverit panem vel biberit calicem Domini indigne, reus erit corporis et sanguinis Domini."

S-68: 1 Corinthians 12, 13

10:289 19:291

". . . etenim in uno Spiritu omnes nos in unum corpus baptizati sumus, sive Iudaei sive Graeci sive servi sive liberi, et omnes unum Spiritum potati sumus."

PASSAGE	CALVIN	CHEMNITZ	BELLARMINE

S-69: 1 Corinthians 12, 27. 29. 31

2:214

"Vos autem estis corpus Christi et membra ex parte. . . . Numquid omnes apostoli? Numquid omnes prophetae? Numquid omnes doctores? Numquid omnes virtutes? . . . Aemulamini autem charismata maiora."

S-70: 2 Corinthians 1, 20-22

8:222 9:227
10:229

"Quotquot enim promissiones Dei sunt, in illo 'est'; ideo et per ipsum 'amen' Deo, ad gloriam per nos. Qui autem confirmat nos vobiscum in Christum et qui unxit nos Deus, et qui signavit nos et dedit arrabonem Spiritus in cordibus nostris."

S-71: 2 Corinthians 6, 1-2

10:229

"Adiuvantes autem et exhortamur, ne in vacuum gratiam Dei recipiatis – ait enim: 'Tempore accepto exaudivi te et in die salutis adiuvi te'. Ecce nunc tempus acceptabile, ecce nunc dies salutis."

S-72: Galatians 3, 27

8:1072 19:291

"Quicumque enim in Christo baptizati estis, Christum induistis."

S-73: Galatians 4, 9

7:1071

". . . nunc autem, cum cognoveritis Deum, immo cogniti sitis a Deo, quomodo convertimini iterum ad infirma et egena elementa, quibus rursus ut antea servire vultis?"

S-74: Ephesians 5, 25-27

7:287 19:291   9:227
24:292 24:296

"Viri diligite uxores, sicut et Christus dilexit ecclesiam et seipsum tradidit pro ea, ut illam sanctificaret mundans lavacro aquae in verbo, ut exhiberet ipse sibi gloriosam ecclesiam non habentem maculam aut rugam aut aliquid eiusmodi, sed ut sit sancta et immaculata."

PASSAGE	CALVIN	CHEMNITZ	BELLARMINE

S-75: Colossians 2, 20-22

	7:1071		9:225

"Si mortui estis cum Christo ab elementis mundi, quid tamquam viventes in mundo decretis subicimini: 'Ne tetigeris, neque gustaveris, neque contrectaveris', quae sunt omnia in corruptionem ipso usu secundum praecepta et doctrinas hominum?"

S-76: 1 Timothy 4, 4-5

	18:290		13:233

"Quia omnis creatura Dei bona, et nihil reiciendum, quod cum gratiarum actione percipitur, sanctificatur enim per verbum Dei et orationem."

S-77: 1 Timothy 4, 14

		9:226	12:231

"Noli neglegere donationem, quae in te est, quae data est tibi per prophetiam cum impositione manuum presbyterii. "

S-78: 1 Timothy 5, 19[3]

			12:232

"Adversus presbyterum accusationem noli recipere, nisi sub duobus vel tribus testibus."

S-79: 2 Timothy 1, 6-7

			9:226

"Propter quam causam admoneo te, ut resuscites donationem Dei, quae est in te per impositionem manuum mearum; non enim dedit nobis Deus Spiritum timoris sed virtutis et dilectionis et sobrietatis."

S-80: Titus – [4]

			9:226

". . . et ad Titum semper ordinationem vocat manus impositionem." (as cited by Bellarmine)

---

[3] Bellarmine cites this as chapter 6. It is in chapter 5.

[4] Bellarmine is wrong here. There is no text of Titus that speaks about the imposition of hands.

PASSAGE	CALVIN	CHEMNITZ	BELLARMINE

S-81: Titus 3, 4-7

| | 19:291 24:292 | | 2:214 9:226 |
| | | 24:296 | | 10:229 |

"Cum autem benignitas et humanitas apparuit salvatoris nostri Dei, non ex operibus iustitiae, quae fecimus nos, sed secundum suam misericordiam salvos nos fecit per lavacrum regenerationis et renovationis Spiritus Sancti, quem effudit super nos abunde per Iesum Christum salvatorem nostrum, ut iustificati gratia ipsius heredes simus secundum spem vitae aeternae."

S-82: Hebrews 6, 1-6

| | | 2:214 | 2:214 |
| | | 11:230 | 12:231 |

"Quapropter praetermittentes inchoationis Christi sermonem ad perfectionem feramur, non rursum iacientes fundamentum paenitentiae ab operibus mortuis et fidei ad Deum, baptismatum doctrinae, impositionis quoque manuum, ac resurrectionis mortuorum et iudicii aeterni. Et hoc faciemus siquidem permiserit Deus. Impossibile est enim eos, qui semel sunt illuminati, gustaverunt etiam donum caeleste et participes sunt facti Spiritus Sancti et bonum gustaverunt Dei verbum virtutesque saeculi venturi et prolapsi sunt, renovari rursus ad paenitentiam, rursum crucifigentes sibimetipsis Filium Dei et ostentui habentes."

S-83: Hebrews 10, 35-38

| | | | 2:216 |

"Nolite itaque abicere confidentiam vestram, quae magnam habet remunerationem; patientia enim vobis necessaria est, ut voluntatem Dei facientes reportetis promissionem. Adhuc enim 'modicum quantulum,' qui 'venturus est, veniet et non tardabit. Iustus autem meus ex fide vivet;' quod 'si subtraxerit se, non sibi complacet in eo anima mea.'"

S-84: Hebrews 12, 28-29

| | | | 8:224 |

"Itaque, regnum immobile suscipientes, habeamus gratiam, per quam serviamus placentes Deo cum reverentia et metu; etenim 'Deus' noster 'ignis consumens' est."

PASSAGE	CALVIN	CHEMNITZ	BELLARMINE

S-85: 1 Peter 3, 21

19:291

"Cuius <aquae> antitypum, baptisma, et vos nunc salvos facit, non carnis depositio sordium sed conscientiae bonae rogatio in Deum, per resurrectionem Iesu Christi."

S-86: 1 John 2, 20. 27

24:294   5:217   8:223
8:224   9:227
13:233

"Sed vos unctionem habetis a Sancto et scitis omnes. . . . Et vos unctionem, quam accepistis ab eo, manet in vobis, et non necesse habetis, ut aliquis doceat vos; sed sicut unctio ipsius docet vos de omnibus, et verum est et non est mendacium, et, sicut docuit vos, manetis in eo."

2. POPES

WORK   CALVIN   CHEMNITZ   BELLARMINE

P-1: Adrian VI (1522-1523)[5]
De sacramento confirmationis 4,7

                                                      12:230
"Iam videndum de principali questio. probabilior mihi videtur opinio, quod solus episcopus est conueniens & idoneus minister huius sacramenti. Ita quod simplex sacerdos est ex commissione papae tentando confirmare nihil facit."

Sacrae Theologiae peritissimi, Diuinisque & humani Iuris (quod opus ipsum indicat) Consultissimi, Quaestiones de sacramentis in Quartum Sententiarum librum, summa scientia, maxima pietate, nec minus clariss+ per spicuitate discussae, Vnde uti ex limpidissimo fonte, Christianus quisque salutaria sibi haurire possit, post caeteras impressiones castigatius elegantiusque iterum aeditae. Rome: Marcellus, 1522. Reprint. Ridgewood, NJ: The Gregg Press Incorporated, 1964.

P-2: Aenea Sylvius
Historia Bohemica 35

                                                       1:211
(See Pius II, P-37)

P-3: Clement of Rome (91-101)
Didascalia 3:10,1-3

                                                      3:216
"Αλλ' ουτε λαϊκοις επιτρεπομεν ποιειν τι των ʽιερατικων εργων, ʽοιον θυσιαν η βαπτισμα η χειροθεσιαν η ευλογιαν μικραν η μεγαλην. ʼουχ ʽεαυτῳʼ γαρ ʼτις λαμβανει την τιμην, αλλʼ ʽο καλουμενος ʽυπο του θεουʼ • δια γαρ της επιθεσεως των χειρων του επισκοπου διδοται ʽη τοιαυτη αξια. ʽο δε μη εγχειρισθεις ταυτην, αλλʼ ʽαρπασας αυτην ʽεαυτῳ, την τιμωριαν του Οζια ʽυποστησεται. "

Didascalia et Constitutiones apostolorum. Ed. Francis Xavier Funk. 2 vols. Paderborn: Libraria Ferdinandi Schoeningh, 1905. 1:201.

---

[5] Dates in this section apply to the pontificate of the authors.

WORK　　　　CALVIN　CHEMNITZ　BELLARMINE

P-4: Clement of Rome
Didascalia 3:16,3

3:216

"αλλα μονον εν τη χειροθεσια την κεφαλην αυτης χρισει `ο επισκοπος, `ον τροπον `οι `ιερεις και `οι βασιλεις το προτερον εχριοντο • ουχ `οτι και `οι νυν βαπτιζομενοι `ιερεις χειροτονουνται, αλλ' `ως απο του Χριστου Χριστιανοι, 'βασιλειον `ιερατευμα και εθνος `αγιον, εκκλησια θεου, στυλος και `εδραιωμα' του νυμφωνος, `οι ποτε ου λαος, νυν δε ηγαπημενοι και εκλεκτοι."
Funk, 1:211.

P-5: Clement of Rome
Didascalia 3:17,1-3

3:216

"Εστι τοινυν το μεν βαπτισμα εις τον θανατον του Ιησου διδομενον, το δε `υδωρ αντι ταφης, το ελαιον αντι πνευματος `αγιου, `η σφραγις αντι του σταυρου, το μυρον βεβαιωσις της `ομολογιας • του πατρος `η μνημη `ως αιτιου και αποστολεως, του πνευματος `η συμπαραληψις `ως μαρτυρος • `η καταδυσις το συναποθανειν, `η αναδυσις το συναναστηναι• ... "
Funk, 1:211. 213.

P-6: Clement of Rome
Didascalia 7:42,1-2

8:224

"Και μετα την επαγγελιαν ταυτην κατ' ακολουθιαν ερχεται και εις την του ελαιου χρισιν.　ευλογειται δε τουτο παρα του `ιερεως εις αφεσιν `αμαρτιων και προκατασκευην του βαπτισματος. "
Funk, 1:448.

P-7: Clement of Rome
Didascalia 7:44,1-3

3:216 8:223
8:224 9:226

"Και μετα τουτο 'βαπτισας αυτον εν τα ονοματι του πατρος και του `υιου και του `αγιου πνευματος', χρισατω μυρω επιλεγων•Κυριε `ο θεος `ο

WORK	CALVIN	CHEMNITZ	BELLARMINE

αγεννητος και αδεσποτος, `ο των `ολων κυριος, `ο την οσμην της γνωσεως του ευαγγελιου εν πασι τοις εθνεσιν ευοσμον παρασχομενος • συ και νυν τουτο το μυρον δος ενεργες γενεσθαι επι τω βαπτιζομενω `ωστε βεβαιαν και παγιον εν αυτω την ευωδιαν μειναι του   Χριστου σου, και συναποθανοντα αυτον συναναστηναι και συζησαι αυτω. ταυτα και τα τουτοις ακολουθα λεγετω • `εκαστου γαρ `η δυναμις της χειροθεσιας εστιν `αυτη. εαν γαρ μη εις `εκαστον τουτων επικλησις γενηται παρα του ευσεβους `ιερεως τοιαυτη τις, εις `υδωρ   μονον καταβαινει `ο βαπτιζομενος `ως `οι Ιουδαιοι, και αποτιθεται    μονον τον `ρυπον του σωματος, ου τον `ρυπον της ψυχης."
Funk 1:450.

P-8: Pseudo-Clement
Epistula 4

	3:285 9:288		9:226

(See Pseudo-Isidore, Clement, M-56)

P-9: Cornelius (251-253)

	3:285 24:296		1:212 3:216
	24:296		9:225 9:226

(See Eusebius, G-27)

P-10: Pseudo-Damasus
Epistula 4

	24:295		3:216 8:224
			8:225 9:226
			9:226 12:231

(See Pseudo-Isidore, Damasus, M-57)

P-11: Damasus (366-384)
Vita Sylvestri

	24:295		9:225

"Huius temporibus factum est Concilium cum eius consensu in Nicaea Bithyniae. Et congregati sunt, cccxviij, episcopi catholici, qui exposuerunt fidem integram, sanctam, catholicam, & immaculatam. . . . Et in urbe Roma congregavit ipse cum consilio Augusti episcopos cclxxvij.

WORK	CALVIN	CHEMNITZ	BELLARMINE

... Constituit, & chrisma ab episcopo confici. Et priuilegium episcopis contulit, vt baptizatum consignent, propter haereticam suasionem. Hic & hoc constituit, vt baptizatum lineat presbyter chrismate leuatum de aqua, propter occasionem transitus mortis."
"Decreta Sylvestri Papae Primi." COGP 1:Fo. cxxxvi.

P-12: **Eugene (654-657)**

13:233

"In catecumino, et in baptismo, et in confirmatione unus patrinus fieri potest, si necessitas cogit. Non est tamen consuetudo Romana, sed singuli per singulos suscipiunt."
CIC 1:1394. (Gratian: c. 100, D. 4, de cons.)

P-13: **Pseudo-Eusebius**
Epistola 3

3:216 7:220
7:221

(See Pseudo-Isidore, Eusebius, M-58)

P-14: **Pseudo-Fabian**
Epistula 2,1

9:288 9:288   8:223 8:224
8:224 9:225
9:227

(See Pseudo-Isidore, Fabian, M-59)

P-15: **Gelasius I (492-496)**
Epistula 9 (1),[6]

8:224

"Nec minus etiam presbyteros ultra modum suum tendere prohibemus; nec episcopali fastigio debita sibimet audacter assumere: non conficiendi chrismatis, non consignationis pontificalis adhibendae sibimet arripere facultatem; non praesente quolibet antistite, nisi fortasse jubeantur, vel orationis, vel actionis sacrae supplendae sibi praesumant esse licentiam; neque sub ejus aspectu, nisi jubeantur, aut sedere praesumant, aut veneranda tractare mysteria."
PL 59 (1862):50.

---

[6] What Bellarmine calles epistle one is epistle nine in the PL series

WORK	CALVIN	CHEMNITZ	BELLARMINE

P-16: Gregory (590-604)
Epistula 9, liber 4 [7]

| | | 3:216 | 12:230 |

"Presbiteri baptizatos infantes signare in frontibus sacro cris- mate non presumant. Sed presbiteri baptizatos ungant in pectore, ut episcopi postmodum confirment in fronte."
CIC 1:1399. (Gratian, c. 120, D. 4, de cons.)

P-17: Gregory
Epistula 26, liber 4 [8]

| 10:1073 | 26:298 | 12:230 | 12:232 |

"Peruenit quoque ad nos, quosdam scandalizatos fuisse, quod pres-biteros crismate tangere eos, qui baptizati sunt, prohibuimus. Et nos quidem secundum ueterem usum nostrae ecclesiae fecimus. Sed si omnino hac de re aliqui contristantur, ubi episcopi desunt, ut presbiteri etiam in frontibus baptizatos crismate tangere debeant, concedimus."
CIC 1:331. (Gratian, c. 1, C. 1, q. 95)

P-18: Gregory
Epistula 67, liber 11 (ep. 61, lib. 9)

| 24:295 | | 7:220 | 7:220 |

"Ab antiqua Patrum institutione didicimus, ut qui apud heresim in Trinitatis nomine baptizantur, cum ad sanctam ecclesiam redeunt, aut unctione crismatis, aut inpositione manus, aut sola professione fidei ad sinum matris ecclesiae reuocentur. Unde Arrianos per inpositionem manus occidens, per unctionem uero sancti crismatis ad ingressum catholicae ecclesiae oriens reformat. Monofisitas uero, et alios ex sola confessione recipit, quia sanctum baptisma, quod apud hereticos sunt consecuti, tunc in eis uires emundationis accipit, cum uel illi per inpositionem manus Spiritum sanctum acceperint, uel isti per professionem uerae fidei sanctae et uniuersalis ecclesiae uisceribus fuerint uniti."
CIC 1:1380. (Gratian, c. 44, D. 4, de cons.)

[7] Bellarmine calls this book three in both places. In the PL series, the text is in book four.

[8] Once again, Bellarmine's edition classifies this letter in book three, whereas PL lists it in book four.

WORK	CALVIN	CHEMNITZ	BELLARMINE

P-19: Gregory
Homilia evangelii ascensionis 29,4

2:216

"Nolite ergo, fratres charissimi, amare signa quae possunt cum reprobis haberi communia; sed haec quae modo diximus charitatis atque pietatis miracula amate, quae tanto securiora sunt, quanto et occulta, et de quibus apud Dominum eo major sit retributio, quo apud homines minor est gloria."
Ed. Monks of the Order of St. Benedict from the St. Maur Congregation. PL 76:1216.

P-20: Pseudo-Gregory
Super Cantica Canticorum

3:216 7:222
8:223 8:224
8:225 9:228

(See Bede, Super Cantica, M-14)

P-21: Gregory II (715-731)
Epistula 4 ad Bonifatium

7:220 11:230

"De homine, qui a pontifice confirmatus fuerit, denuo talis iteratio prohibenda est."
CIC 1:1415. (Gratian, c. 9, D. 5, de cons.)

P-22: Gregory IX (1227-1241)
Decretals 1:15,7-8

24:293 26:298   3:216 8:224
9:226 9:227
9:227

"Cum venisset" (See Innocent III, P-26)

P-23: Gregory IX
Decretals 1:16,1

8:223 9:227

"Pastoralis" (See Innocent III, P-27)

WORK	CALVIN	CHEMNITZ	BELLARMINE

P-24: Innocent I (401-417)
Epistula

3:216   7:221
8:224   8:225
9:226 10:229

"De consignandis vero infantibus manifestum est non ab alio quam ab episcopo fieri licere. Nam presbiteri licet sint sacerdotes, pontificatus tamen apicem non habent. Hoc autem pontificibus solis deberi, ut vel consignent, vel paracletum Spiritum tradant non solum consuetudo ecclesiastica demonstrat, verum illa lectio actuum apostolorum quae asserit Petrum et Iohannem esse directos qui iam baptizatis tradant Spiritum sanctum. Nam presbiteris seu extra episcopum sive praesente episcopo cum baptizant, chrismate baptizatos ungere licet, sed quod ab episcopo fuerit consecratum, non tamen frontem ex eodem oleo signare, quod solis debetur episcopis cum tradunt Spiritum paracletum. Verba vero dicere non possum, ne magis prodere videar quam ad consultationem respondere."
La Lettre du Pape Innocent Ier a Décentius de Gubbio (19 Mars 416): Texte critique, traduction et commentaire. Ed. Robert Cabié. BRHE 58 (1973):22, 24.

P-25: Innocent I
Exsuperio Tolosano Episcopo

13:233

"Si quis unus ex coniugio filium aut filiam alterius de sacro fonte susceperit, aut ad crisma tenuerit, uel Christianitatis misterium dederit, ambo, et uxor et uir, conpatres existunt parentibus infantis, quia uir et mulier caro una effecti sunt."
CIC 1:1103. (Gratian, c. 3, C. 30, q. 4)

P-26: Innocent III (1198-1216)
Cum venisset 2. 7-8

24:293 26:298   3:216 8:224
9:226 9:227
9:227

"Ad exhibendum autem exteriorem et visibilem unctionem benedicitur oleum, quod dicitur catechumenorum vel infirmorum, et conficitur

WORK   CALVIN   CHEMNITZ   BELLARMINE

chrisma, quod ex oleo fit et balsamo mystica ratione. . . . Per frontis chrismationem manus impositio designatur, quae alio nomine dicitur confirmatio, quia per eam Spiritus sanctus ad augmentum datur et robur. Unde quum ceteras unctiones simplex sacerdos vel presbyter valeat exhibere, hanc non nisi summus sacerdos, id est episcopus, debet conferre, quia de solis Apostolis legitur, quorum vicarii sunt episcopi, quod per manus impositionem Spiritum sanctum dabant, quemadmodum Actuum Apostolorum lectio manifestat. . . . Verum tamen unctionis sacramentum aliud quidem efficit et figurat tam in novo quam in veteri testamento, unde non iudaizat ecclesia, quum unctionis celebrat sacramentum, sicut antiqui mentiuntur, qui neque scripturas, neque Dei novere virtutem."
CIC 2:132-134. (Gregory IX, Decretal. 1:15,7-8)

P-27: **Innocent III**

                                               8:223 9:227

"Pastoralis. Praeterea nos consulere voluisti, an permitti debeat ministrare qui sine impositione manuum fuerit ad ordinem subdiaconatus assumptus, et si confirmationis sacramentum in eo debeat iterari, qui per errorem fuit non chrismate, sed oleo delinitus. Ad quod fraternitati tuae breviter duximus respondendum, quod in talibus non est aliquid iterandum, sed caute supplendum quod incaute fuerat praetermissum."
CIC 1:134. (Gregory IX, Decretal. 1:16,1)

P-28: **Pseudo-John III (9th c.?)**[9]
Epistula ad episcopos Germaniae 1

                                             3:216 8:224
                                             8:225 9:226

"Perlatum est ad sedem apostolicam emersisse et denuo reviviscere prohibitum et funditus exstirpatum tam a sancto Damaso, quam a sancto Leone, viris apostolicis, atque ab universis synodali auctoritate episcopis, reprehensibilem atque oppido inolitum usum, eo quod quidam chorepiscopi (qui et a praedictorum antecessorum sanctorum

---

[9] Since this letter cites two others from the ninth century, it must be later than the sixth century Pope John III.

WORK	CALVIN	CHEMNITZ	BELLARMINE

apostolicorum patribus et viris apostolicis, et ab ipsis, sive a nobis sunt prohibiti, sicut eorum hactenus testantur decreta) ultra modum suum progredientes (Conc. Parisiense vi. lib. 1 c. 27), donum sancti Spiritus per impositionem manuum tradant, et alia, quae, solum pontificibus debentur, contra fas peragant. . . . Non ergo (ut jam dictum est) aliquem ex septuaginta, licet pauci essent apostoli, ad hoc opus perficiendum direxerunt, sed Petrum et Joannem apostolos per manus impositionem tradere Spiritum sanctum miserunt: quorum vicem episcopi in ecclesia gerunt, et non chorepiscopi (Nicol. I, in epist. ad Rudolphum Bitur. arch.), qui septuaginta discipulorum formam ante prohibitionem eorum gerebant."
PL 72 (1849):13-14.

P-29: **Leo (440-461)**
Epistula 86, alias 88

		3:216	4:217
		8:224	8:225
		9:226	9:226
			12:231

(See Leo III, P-33)

P-30: **Leo**
Epistola 159 (77),7

4:1069	24:295	7:221

"Nam hi qui baptismum ab haereticis acceperunt, cum antea bapti- zati non fuissent, sola invocatione Spiritus Sancti per impositionem manuum confirmandi sunt, quia formam tantum baptismi sine sanctificationis virtute sumpserunt."
Ed. Peter and Jerome Ballerinius. PL 54 (1846): 1138-1139.

P-31: **Leo**
Epistola 166 (35),2

4:1068	7:221

"Quod si ab haereticis baptizatum quempiam fuisse constiterit, erga hunc nullatenus sacramentum regenerationis iteretur; sed hoc tantum quod ibi defuit conferatur, ut per episcopalem manus impositionem virtutem sancti Spiritus consequatur."
PL 54:1194.

WORK	CALVIN	CHEMNITZ	BELLARMINE

P-32: Leo
Sermon 47 (9) de quadragesima

2:215

"Dominus ipse in exhortationibus suis dicit: 'Qui non accipit crucem suam et sequitur me, non est me dignus,' nec dubitare debemus hanc uocem non solum ad discipulos Christi, sed ad cunc- tos fideles totamque Ecclesiam pertinere, quae salutare suum in his qui aderant uniuersaliter audiebat."
Ed. Antonius Chavasse. CChr.SL 138A (1973):274-275.

P-33: Leo III (795-816)
Epistula 86, alias 88[10]

3:216 4:217
8:224 8:225
9:226 9:226
12:231

"Siquidem nec erigere eis altaria, nec ecclesias vel altaria consecrare licet, nec per impositiones manuum fidelibus baptizandis, vel conversis ex haeresi Paracletum Spiritum sanctum tradere, nec chrisma conficere, nec chrismate baptizatorum frontes signare, nec publice quidem in missa quemquam poenitentem reconciliare, nec formatas cuilibet epistolas mittere. Haec enim omnia illicita sunt chorepiscopis, qui ad exemplum et formam septuaginta discipulorum esse noscuntur, vel presbyteris, qui eamdem gestant figuram: quoniam quamquam consecrationem habeant, pontificatus tamen apicem non habent."
Ed. Peter and Jerome Ballerinius. PL 55 (1846):1325. 1327.

P-34: Pseudo-Miltiades
Epistula ad omnes Hispaniae episcopos 2

	5:1069	3:285	1:212 7:221
	8:1071		
	8:1072		
	1:501A		

(See Pseudo-Isidore, Miltiades, M-59)

---

10 Although Bellarmine lists this letter among those of Leo the Great, the editors of this volume of PL argue that Leo III was its author. See "Dissertatio undecima," PL 55:757-764.

WORK	CALVIN	CHEMNITZ	BELLARMINE

P-35: Pseudo-Miltiades
Epistula ad omnes Hispaniae episcopos 2

	10:1073	3:285	3:216 7:220

(See Pseudo-Isidore, Miltiades, M-60)

P-36: Nicholas (858-867)
Rudolpho

13:233

"De his, qui filiastros suos ad confirmationem coram episcopis tenent, id est qui filios uxoris suae de uiro priori, dum crismantur ab episcopis, super se sustinent, si inscientia, sicut asseris, fiat, licet sit peccatum, tamen non usque ad separationem coniugii puniendus est; lugeant tamen, et digna penitencia hoc diluentes Domino dicant: 'Delicta ignorantiae nostrae ne memineris.'"
CIC 1:1098. (Gratian, c. 6, C. 30, q. 1)

P-37: Pius II (Aenea Sylvius Piccolomini) (1458-1464)
Historia Bohemica 35

1:211

"Proruperunt <Hussitae> in blasphemias. . . . Confirmationem, quam chrismate pontifices inducunt, & extremam unctionem inter ecclesiae sacra minime contineri."
Opera quae extant omnia. Basel: Henrichus Petri, 1551. P. 103.

P-38: Pseudo-Urban
Epistola ad omnes christianos 7

	9:1072	3:285	3:216 7:221

(See Pseudo-Isidore, Urban, M-61)

P-39: Vigilius (537-555)
Epistula 1,3

7:220

"Quorum tamen reconciliatio non per illam impositionem manus, quae per invocationem sancti Spiritus fit, operatur, sed per illam qua poenitentiae fructus acquiritur, et sanctae communionis restitutia perficitur."
Ed. J. Garetti. PL 69 (1865):18.

3. COUNCILS

CANON	CALVIN	CHEMNITZ	BELLARMINE

C-1: Arles I (314)
Canon 8

24:295 25:297   4:216 9:226

"De Afris quod propria lege sua utuntur ut rebaptizent, placuit ut si ad ecclesiam aliquis de haeresi uenerit, interrogent eum symbolum, et si peruiderint eum in Patrem et Filium et Spiritum Sanctum esse baptizatum, manus ei tantum imponatur ut accipiat Spiritum (Sanctum); quod si interrogatus non responderit hanc Trinitatem, baptizetur."
Concilia Galliae, A. 314 A. 506. Ed. C. Munier. CChr.SL 148 (1963), pp. 10-11.

C-2: Arles II (442-506)
Canon 17

4:217 9:226

"Bonosiacos autem ex eodem errore uenientes, quos sicut Arrianos baptizare in Trinitatem manifestum est, si interrogati fidem nostram ex toto corde confessi fuerint, cum chrismate et manus impositione in ecclesia recipi sufficit."
Concilia Galliae. CChr.SL 148:117.

C-3: Braga I (563)
Canon 19 (37)[11]

8:224

"Item placuit, si quis presbyter, post hoc interdictum, ausus fuerit chrisma benedicere, aut ecclesiam, aut altarium consecrare, a suo officio deponatur: nam & antiqui hoc canones vetuerunt."
Mansi 9 (1763):779.

---

11   Mansi lists this as canon 19 in a second list of canons for the first Council of Braga. Bellarmine must have worked from an edition that numbered the two lists consecutively and assigned 37 to this text.

CANON	CALVIN	CHEMNITZ	BELLARMINE

C-4: Braga II (572)
Canon 4

8:223

"Placuit, ut modicum balsami, quod benedictum pro baptismi sacramento per ecclesias datur, quia singuli tremisses pro ipso exigi solent, nihil ulterius exigatur: ne forte quod pro salute animarum per invocationem sancti Spiritus consecratur, sicut Simon magus donum Dei pecunia emere, ita non venumdare damnabiliter videamur."
Mansi 9:839.

C-5: Carthage II (390)
Canon 3

8:223 8:224

". . . Ab uniuersis episcopis dictum est; Chrismatis confectio, et puellarum consecratio, a presbyteris non fiat, uel reconciliare quemquam publica missa presbytero non licere, hoc omnibus placet."
Conciliae Africae A. 345 A. 525. Ed. C. Munier. CChr.SL 149 (1974), pp. 13-14.

C-6: Carthage III (c. 398)
Canon 36

8:223 8:224

"Ut presbyter non consulto episcopo uirgines non consecret; chrisma vero nunquam conficiat." CChr.SL 149:335.

C-7: Carthage IV (c. 398)
Canon 36

8:224

"Presbyteri qui per dioeceses ecclesias regunt, non a quibuslibet episcopis, sed a suis, nec per iuniorem clericum, sed aut per ipsos, aut per illum qui sacrarium tenet, ante paschae solemnitatem chrisma petant."
CChr.SL 149:347.

CANON	CALVIN	CHEMNITZ	BELLARMINE

C-8: Constantinople III (680)
Canon 7

4:217

". . . Et nisi quis has duas sententias & memoriter tenuerit, & ex toto corde crediderit, & in oratione saepissime frequentaverit, catholicus esse non poterit. Constitutum namque est a sanctis patribus, ut nullus chrismetur, neque baptizetur, neque a lavacro fontis alium suscipiat, neque coram episcopo ad confirmandum quemlibet teneat, nisi symbolum & orationem dominicam memoriter tenuerit, exceptis his, quod ad loquendum aetas minime perduxit. . . ."
Mansi 11 (1765):1008-1009.

C-9: Elvira (305)
Canon 38 [12]

24:296   4:216

"Peregre navigantes, aut si ecclesia in proximo non fuerit, posse fidelem, qui lavacrum suum integrum habet, nec sit bigamus, baptizare in necessitate infirmitatis positum catechumenum: ita ut si supervixerit, ad episcopum eum perducat, ut per manus impositionem proficere possit." Mansi 2 (1759):12.

C-10: Elvira
Canon 77

4:216

"Si quis diaconus regens plebem, sine episcopo, vel presbytero aliquos baptizaverit, episcopus eos per benedictionem perficere debebit. Quod si ante de saeculo recesserint, sub fide, qua quis credidit, poterit esse justus."
Mansi 2:18.

---

[12] Both the Preuss edition and English translation by Fred Kramer have Chemnitz citing canon 18 of Elvira, which does not apply to the controversy. Surely he means canon 38.

CANON	CALVIN	CHEMNITZ	BELLARMINE

C-11: Florence (1439)
Bulla unionis Armenorum

11:230

"Inter hec sacramenta tria sunt, baptismus, confirmatio et ordo, que caracterem, id est spirituale quoddam signum a ceteris distinctivum imprimunt in anima indelebile. Unde in eadem persona non reiterantur. Reliqua vero quatuor caracterem non imprimunt et reiterationem admittunt." Ed. Georgius Hofmann. CFI 1 (1944):2,128.

C-12: Florence
Bulla unionis Armenorum

	24:294	4:217	8:222
		8:223	8:224
		8:225	9:226
		9:227	9:227
		10:228	12:230

"Secundum sacramentum est confirmatio, cuius materia est crisma confectum ex oleo, quod nitorem significat conscientie, et balsamo, qui odorem significat bone fame, per episcopum benedicto. Forma autem est: signo te signo crucis et confirmo te crismate salutis in nomine patris et filii et spiritus sancti. Ordinarius minister est episcopus. Et cum ceteras unctiones simplex sacerdos valeat exhibere, hanc nonnisi episcopus debet conferre, quia de solis apostolis legitur, quorum vicem tenent episcopi, quod per manus impositionem spiritum sanctum dabant, quemadmodum actuum apostolorum lectio manifestat. Cum enim audissent, inquit, apostoli, qui erant Iherosolimis, quia recepisset Samaria verbum dei, miserunt ad eos Petrum et Iohannem, qui cum venissent, oraverunt pro eis, ut acciperent spiritum sanctum; nondum enim in quenquam illorum venerat, sed baptizati tantum erant in nomine domini Ihesu; tunc imponebant manum super illos, et accipiebant spiritum sanctum. Loco autem illius manus impositionis in ecclesia datur confirmatio. Legitur tamen aliquando per apostolice sedis dispensationem ex rationabili et urgenti admodum causa simplicem sacerdotem crismate per episcopum confecto hoc administrasse confirmationis sacramentum. Effectus autem huius sacramenti est, quia in eo datur spiritus sanctus ad robur, sicut datus est apostolis die penthecostes, ut videlicet christianus audacter Christi confiteatur

CANON   CALVIN   CHEMNITZ   BELLARMINE

nomen. Ideoque in fronte, ubi verecundie sedes est, confirmandus
inungitur, ne Christi nomen confiteri erubescat et precipue crucem eius,
que iudeis est scandalum, gentibus autem stultitia secundum apostolum,
propter quod signo crucis signatur."
CFI 1:2,128-129.

C-13: Laodicea (c. 343-381)
Canon 7

                               24:295 25:297   4:217
"Περι του, τους εκ των ̔αιρεσεων, τουτεστιν Νουατιανων, ητοι
Φωτεινιανων   η   Τεσσαρεσκαιδεκατιων   επιστρεφομενους,   ειτε
{κατηχουμενους}, ειτε πιστους τους παρ' εκεινοις, μη προσδεχεσθαι,
πριν αναθεματισωσι πασαν ̔αιρεσιν, εξαιρετως δε εν ̔η πατειχοντο • και
τοτε λοιπον τους λεγομενους παρ αυτοις πιστους, εκμανθανοντας τα
της πιστεως συμβολα, χρισθεντας τε τω ̔αγιω χρισματι, ̔ουτωκοινωνειν
τω μυστηριω τω ̔αγιω. "
Hefele, Charles Joseph. *Histoire des Conciles.* Trans. a Benedictine.
Paris: Letouzey et Ané, Editeurs, 1907. 1:2,999.

C-14: Laodicea
Canon 48

                               3:285   4:217 8:224
"̔Οτι δει τους φωτιζομενους μετα το βαπτισμα χριεσθαι χρισματι
επουρανιω, και μετοχους ειναι της βασιλειας του Χριστου. "
Hefele 1:2,1021.

C-15: Meaux (845)
Canon 6

                               8:287   4:217 13:233
"Ut episcopi non nisi ieiuni per inpositionem manuum Spiritum sanctum
tradant, exceptis infirmis et morte periclitantibus. Sicut autem duobus
temporibus, Pasca uidelicet et Pentecosten, a ieiunis debet baptismus
celebrari, ita et traditionem Spiritus sancti a ieiunis pontificibus
conuenit celebrari."
CIC 1:1414. (Gratian, c. 7, D., 5, de cons.)

CANON   CALVIN   CHEMNITZ · BELLARMINE

C-16: Milevis (402)
Canon 3
                                                    8:1071
"Placuit, ut quicumque dixerit, gratiam Dei, qua iustificatur homo per
Iesum Christum Dominum nostrum, solam remissionem peccatorum
ualere, que iam conmissa sunt, non etiam ad adiutorium, ut non
conmittantur, anathema sit."
CIC 1:1412. (Gratian, c. 154, D. 4, De cons.)

C-17: Neocaesarea (314-325)
Canon 13
                                                    12:231
"Επιχωριοι πρεσβυτεροι εν τω κυριακω της πολεως προσφερειν ου
δυνανται παροντος επισκοπου η πρεσβυτερων πολεως, ουτε μην αρτον
διδοναι εν ευχη ουδε ποτηριον • εαν δε απωσι και εις ευχην κληθη
μονος, διδωσιν. "
Hefele 1:1,333.

C-18: Nicaea (325)
Canon 31 (Arabic)
                                                    7:220
"Si quis ad fidem orthodoxam convertatur, recipiendus est in ecclesiam
per manus episcopi, vel presbyteri, qui praecipere ei debet, ut
anathematizet cunctos qui contra fidem orthodoxam faciunt, & qui
apostolicae ecclesiae contradicunt. . . . Et postquam haec fecerit,
accipiat eum episcopus, vel sacerdos, ad cujus potestatem pertinet, &
ungat eum unctione chrismatis, & signet ter ungendo, & orando super eum
orationem Dionysii Areopagitae, & fiat oratio ad Deum pro eo devote,
ut recipiat eum. . . ."
Mansi 2:962.

C-19: Nicaea
Canon 69 (Arabic)
                                                    8:224
"Si quis fidelium mulieri infideli morem gerat propter fornicationem,
aut mulier fidelis viro infideli; & ob hanc causam a fide recedant;

CANON	CALVIN	CHEMNITZ	BELLARMINE

poenitentia horum sit, ut spatio trium annorum stent ad januam templi in cilicio & cinere; & peracto hoc tempore intrent in ecclesiam ad orationem; sed ita, ut spatio unius anni stent in angulo ecclesiae ab aliis separati: neque liceat eos salutare, neque cum eis communionem participare: transacto autem anno, debet sacerdos benedicere aquam & oleum, non sicut benedicitur in baptismo, nec ut benedicitur chrisma, sed ut oleum infirmorum, & ut benedicitur aqua ad emundationem immunditiae eorum qui comederunt morticinium: & sic debet eis benedicere sacerdos, & aspergere eos aqua ista; & ipsi etiam debent compungi, & mundabuntur, remitteturque eis peccatum orando pro ipsis: faciendaque est diligens de eis inquisitio, & sic dabitur communio: & qui non paruerit, synodus eum excommunicat."
Mansi 2:976.

C-20: Orange (441)
Canons 1-2

12:230

"1. Haereticos in mortis discrimine positos, si catholici esse desiderant, si desit episcopus, a presbyteris cum chrismate et benedictione consignari placuit.
"2. Nullum ministrorum, qui baptizandi recipit officium, sine chrismate usquam debere progredi, quia inter nos placuit semel chrismari. De eo autem qui in baptismate, quacumque necessitate faciente, non chrismatus fuerit, in confirmatione sacerdos commonebitur. Nam inter quoslibet chrismatis ipsius nonnisi una benedictio est, non ut praeiudicans quidquam, sed ut non necessaria habeatur repetita chrismatio."
CChr.SL 148:78.

C-21: Orleans
Canon 3

| | 9:1072 | 3:286 | 24:295 | 4:217 | 13:233 |
| | 1:501A | | 25:297 | | |

(See Pseudo-Council of Orleans, M-68.)

CANON   CALVIN   CHEMNITZ   BELLARMINE

C-22: Rome (c. 333)
Canon 5

                                                                          8:224

"Constituit etiam voce clara Silvester episcopus urbis Romae, ut nemo
presbyter chrisma conficeret, dicens quoniam Christus a chrismate
vocabitur."
PL 8 (1762):835.

C-23: Seville II (619)
Canon 7   4:217 8:224
                                                                        8:225

". . . Nam quamvis cum episcopis plurima illis ministeriorum communis
sit dispensatio, quaedam novellis & ecclesiasticis regulis sibi prohibita
noverint: sicut presbyterorum, & diaconorum, ac virginum consecratio;
sicut constitutio altaris, benedictio vel unctio: siquidem nec licere eis
ecclesiam, vel altarium consecrare, nec per impositionem manus
fidelibus baptizatis, vel controversis ex haeresi paracletum Spiritum
tradere, nec chrisma conficere, nec chrismate baptizatorum frontem
signare, sed nec publice quidem in missa quemquam poenitentium
reconciliare, nec formatas cuilibet epistolas mittere. . . ."
Mansi 10 (1764):559.

C-24: Terracina (516)
Canon 6

                                                             7:220 11:230

"Dictum est nobis, quod quidam de plebe bis, uel ter, aut eo amplius,
episcopis ignorantibus tamen, ab eisdem episcopis confirmentur. Unde
uisum est nobis, eandem confirmationem, sicut nec baptisma, iterari
minime debere, quia bis, uel amplius baptizatos aut confirmatos non
seculo, sed soli Deo sub habitu regulari uel clericali religiossime
famulari decretum est."
CIC 1:1414. (Gratian, c. 8, D. 5, de cons.)

CANON CALVIN CHEMNITZ BELLARMINE

C-25: Toledo I (398)
Canon 20

26:298 8:224 12:230

"Quamvis pene ubique custodiatur, ut absque episcopo chrisma nemo conficiat; tamen quia in aliquibus locis vel provinciis, presbyteri dicuntur chrisma conficere, placuit ex hac die nullum alium, nisi episcopum chrisma facere, & per dioecesim destinare: ita ut de singulis ecclesiis ad episcopum ante diem paschae diaconi destinentur, aut subdiaconi; ut confectum chrisma ab episcopo destinatum ad diem paschae possit occurrere. Episcopo sane certum est omni tempore licere chrisma conficere: sine conscientia autem episcopi, nihil penitus faciendum. Statutum vero est, diaconum non chrismate, sed presbyterum, absente episcopo; praesente vero, si ab ipso fuerit praeceptum. Hujusmodi constitutionem meminerit semper archidiaconus: vel praesentibus, vel absentibus episcopis suggerendam; ut eam episcopi custodiant; & presbyteri non relinquant."
Mansi 3 (1759):1002.

C-26: Toledo VIII (653)
Canon 7

11:230

". . . Verum sicut sanctum chrisma collatum, & altaris honor, evelli non queunt: ita quoque sanctorum decus honorum, quod his compar habetur & socium, qualibet fuerit occasione perceptum, manebit omnibus modis inconvulsum. . . ."
Mansi 10:1217-1218.

C-27: Tours (461)
Caput 9

3:286

"Praeterea & illud omnimodis observandum est, ut sacrum chrisma, & oleum consecratum semper sub sera sit, ne illud unde Christo incorporamur, & unde omnes fideles sanctificantur, unde reges & sacerdotes inunguntur, aliquis infidelis aut immundus tangat, aut aliquis perfidus ad Dei judicium subvertendum subripiat, quod experimento didicimus."
Mansi 7 (1762):949.

CANON	CALVIN	CHEMNITZ	BELLARMINE

C-28: Trent (1547)
De sacramentis, 9

                                        11:230

"Si quis dixerit, in tribus sacramentis, baptismo scilicet, confirmatione et ordine, non imprimi characterem in anima, hoc est signum quoddam spirituale et indelebile, unde ea iterari non possunt: anathema sit."
CT 5 (1911):995.

C-29: Trent
De confirmatione, 1-3

                        1:284 20:291

(See below for texts.)

C-30: Trent
De confirmatione, 1

            1:501A   25:297   2:213 4:217

"Si quis dixerit, confirmationem baptizatorum otiosam caeremoniam esse et non potius verum et proprium sacramentum, aut olim nihil aliud fuisse, quam catechesim quandam, qua adolescentiae proximi fidei suae rationem coram ecclesia exponebant: anathema sit."
CT 5:996.

C-31: Trent
De confirmatione, 2

            2:502A   26:297   8:222

"Si quis dixerit, iniurios esse Spiritui Sancto eos, qui sacro confirmationis chrismati virtutem aliquam tribuunt: anathema sit."
CT 5:996.

C-32: Trent
De confirmatione, 3

            3:502A   26:298   12:230

"Si quis dixerit, sanctae confirmationis ordinarium ministrum non esse solum episcopum, sed quemvis simplicem sacerdotem: anathema sit."
CT 5:996.

CANON CALVIN CHEMNITZ BELLARMINE

C-33: Vaison-la-Romaine (442)
Canon 3

8:224

"Per singula territoria presbyteri uel ministri, ab episcopis, non prout libitum fuerit, a uicinioribus, sed a suis propriis per annos singulos chrisma petant, adpropinquante solemnitate paschali, nec per quemcumque ecclesiasticum, sed si qua necessitas aut ministrorum occupatio est, per subdiaconum: quia inhonorum est inferioribus summa committi, optimum autem est ut ipse suscipiat qui in tradendo usurus est; si quid obstat, saltem is cujus officii est sacrarium disponere et sacramenta suscipere."
CChr.SL 148:97.

C-34: Verberie
Canon 4

13:233

(See Decretum Compendiense, M-21.)

C-35: Worms (868)
Canon 2

8:224

"Chrisma conficere nullus praeter episcopum praesumat: nam illi soli haec dignitas concessa est."
Mansi 15 (1770):869.

C-36: Worms
Canon 8

8:224

"Igitur presbyteris quamvis cum episcopis plurima mysteriorum communis sit dispensatio, quaedam tamen auctoritate veteris legis, quaedam novellis & ecclesiasticis regulis sibi prohibita noverint. Consecratio ergo virginum, & benedictio vel unctio altaris a presbyteris minime fiat. Similiter non liceat eis ecclesias consecrare, nec per impositionem manus paracletum Spiritum tradere, nec chrisma conficere, nec chrismate baptizatorum frontem signare, sed nec publice quidem in missa quemquam poenitentium reconciliare. Haec enim omnia

CANON	CALVIN	CHEMNITZ	BELLARMINE

illicita esse presbyteris cognoscuntur, quia pontificatus apicem non habent: quae tamen omnia episcopis auctoritate canonum conceduntur." Mansi 15:871.

4. GREEK FATHERS

WORK　　　　　　　CALVIN[13]　CHEMNITZ　BELLARMINE

G-1: Amphilochius (+ c. 394)
In Vitam s. Basilii, 4

　　　　　　　　　　　　　　　　　　　　　　　　5:218

"βαπτισθεις δε `ο Βασιλειος εξηλθε του `υδατος. {και παντας `εις ευχην προετρεψε} θαυμασας δε `ο Μαξιμος του[14] Βασιλειου προς Θεον αγαπην, και επευξαμενος αυτω ενδιδυσκει τα της Χριστου αναστασεως αμφια. `εβαπτισε δε και τον Ευβουλον. και χρισας[15] αυτοις τω 'αγιω μυρω, μετα διδωσι της ζωοποιου κοινωνιας."[16]
Opera Graeco-Latina. Ed. Franciscus Combefis. Paris: Simeon 　Piget, 1644. P. 173.

G-2: Athanasius (295-373)

　　　　　　　　　　　　　　24:296

(See Gratian, c. 58, C. 1, q. 1, M-34.)

G-3: Basil (c. 330-379)
De Spiritu sancto 15,35

　　　　　　　　　　　　24:295　24:295

"Δια τουτο `η μετα σαρκος επιδημια Χριστου • 　`αι των ευαγγελικων πολιτευματων `υποτυπωσεις • τα παθη • `ο σταυρος • `η ταφη • `η αναστασις • `ωστε τον σωζομενον ανθρωπον δια μιμησεως Χριστου, την αρχαιαν εκεινην `υιοθεσιαν απολαβειν. . . . `ουτω και επι της των βιων μεταβολης αναγκαιον εφανη θανατον αμφοτεροις μεσιτευσαι τοις βιοις, περατουντα μεν τα προαγοντα, αρχην δε διδοντα τοις εφεξης. "
Ed. Benoît Pruche. SC 17 bis (1968):364. 366.

13　In Calvin's two brief works on confirmation he never cites a single Greek father to support his argument.

14　In the Combefis text this word is spelled "τυο".

15　In the Combefis text this word is spelled "χροσας".

16　Transliteration by David Hester.

WORK   CHEMNITZ   BELLARMINE

G-4: Basil
De Spiritu sancto 27,66

                              9:288 24:294   8:225 9:227
"Ευλογουμεν δε το τε `υδωρ του βαπτισματος, και το ελαιον της
χρισεως, και προσετι αυτον τον βαπτιζομενον.   Απο ποιων εγγραφων;
Ουκ απο της σιωπωμενης και μυστικης παραδοσεως; Τι δε; αυτην του
ελαιου την χρισιν τις λογος γεγραμμενος εδιδαξε; "
SC 17 bis:480. 482.

G-5: Clement of Alexandria (c. 150-215)
Paidagogos 1:6,26,2

                                    24:295
"Καλειται δε πολλαχως το εργον τουτο, χαρισμα και φωτισμα και
τελειον και λουτρον • λουτρον μεν δι' `ου τας `αμαρτιας
απορρυπτομεθα, χαρισμα δε `ῳ τα επι τοις `αμαρτημασιν επιτιμια
ανειται, φωτισμα δε δι' `ου το `αγιον εκεινο φως το σωτηριον
εποπτευεται, τουτεστιν δι' `ου το θειον οξυωπουμεν, τελειον δε το
απροσδεες φαμεν. "
Ed. Henri-Irénée Marrou. SC 70 (1960):158.

G-6: Clement of Alexandria
Paidagogos 1:6,28,2

                                    24:294
". . . κραμα τουτο αυγης αιδιου το αιδιον φως ιδειν δυναμενης • επει το
`ομοιον τω `ομοιῳ φιλον, φιλον δε το `αγιον τω εξ `ου το `αγιον, `ο δη
κυριως κεκληται φως• . . ."
SC 70:162.

| WORK | CHEMNITZ | BELLARMINE |

G-7: Clement of Alexandria
Stromata 4:7,45,5[17]

           1:213

"και επεκδιηγουμενος επιφερει, `ινα μη `ως Μαρκιων αχαριστως εχδεξηται τις την δημιουργιαν κακην • ..."
Ed. Otto Stählin. GCS 15 (1906):268.

G-8: Clement of Alexandria

         9:288   5:217

(See Eusebius, G-26)

G-9: Cyril of Jerusalem (c. 315-387)
Katêchêsis 2-3

        24:293

(See below.)

G-10: Cyril of Jerusalem
Katêchêsis 2,3

        24:293

". . . `ουτω το επορκιστον τουτο ελαιον επικλησει Θεου και ευχη δυναμιν τηλικαυτην λαμβανει `ως ου μονον καϊον τα ιχνη των `αμαρτηματων αποκαθαιρειν, αλλα και τας αορατους του πονηρου εκδιωκειν δυναμεις."
Ed. Auguste Piédagnel. SC 126 (1966):108.

---

[17]   This text enters the controversy because Chemnitz believes that the anointings of Tertullian and Cyprian place them squarely in the Montanist tradition. Bellarmine cites the *Stromata* to support his argument that the Montanists never anointed in the first place. He builds a good argument, but errs in calling Clement and Eusebius as witnesses, who report on the Marcionist, not the Montanist, heresy in the places Bellarmine notes.

WORK	CHEMNITZ	BELLARMINE

G-11: Cyril of Jerusalem
Katêchêsis 3,3[18]

	24:293	1:212 5:217
		8:225 8:225
		9:228

"Αλλ' `ορα μη `υπονοησης εκεινο το μυρον ψιλον ειναι. `Ωσπερ γαρ `ο αρτος της ευχαριστιας, μετα την επικλησιν του `αγιου Πνευματος, ουκ ετι αρτος λιτος, αλλα σωμα Χριστου, `ουτω και το `αγιον τουτο μυρον ουκ ετι ψιλον, ουδ' `ως αν ειποι τις κοινον μετ' επικλησεως, αλλα Χριστου χαρισμα, και Πνευματος `αγιου παρουσιας της αυτου θεοτητος ενεργητικον γινομενον. `Οπερ συμβολικως επι μετωπου και των αλλων σου χριεται αισθητηριων. Και τω μεν φαινομενω μυρω το σωμα χριεται, τω δε 'αγιω και ζωοποιω Πνευματι `η ψυχη `αγιαζεται. "
SC 126:124.

G-12: Cyril of Jerusalem
Katêchêsis 3,4

	24:294	5:217

"`Ωσπερ γαρ `ο Σωτηρ μετα το βαπτισμα και την του `αγιου Πνευματος επιφοιτησιν εξελθων κατηγωνισατο τον αντικειμενον, `ουτω και `υμεις μετα το `ιερον βαπτισμα και το μυστικον χρισμα ενδεδυμενοι την πανοπλιαν του `αγιου Πνευματος, `ιστασθε προς την αντικειμενην ενεργειαν και ταυτην καταγωνιζεσθε, λεγοντες • 'Παντα ισχυω εν τω ενδυναμουντι με Χριστω.' "
SC 126:126.

---

[18]   At 1:212 Bellarmine says Cyril often refers to chrism. Perhaps he has this text in mind.

WORK　　　　　　　　　　　CHEMNITZ　BELLARMINE

G-13: Cyril of Jerusalem
Katêchêsis 3,5

5:217

"Τουτου του ΄αγιου χρισματος καταξιωθεντες καλεισθε χριστιανοι, επαληθευοντες τη αναγεννησει και το ονομα. Προ γαρ του καταξιωθηναι ΄υμας του βαπτισματος και της του ΄αγιου Πνευματος χαριτος, ουκ ητε κυριως αξιοι, αλλ' ΄οδευοντες προεβαινετε το ειναι χριστιανοι. "
SC 126:128.

G-14: Cyril of Jerusalem
Katêchêsis 3,7

8:223

"Τουτου φυλαξατε ασπιλον • παντων γαρ εσται τουτο διδακτικον, ει εν ΄υμιν μενοι, καθως αρτιως ηκουσατε του μακαριου Ιωαννου λεγοντος και πολλα περι του χρισματος φιλοσοφουντος. Εστι γαρ τουτο το ΄αγιον πνευματικον σωματος φυλακτηριον και ψυχης σωτηριον. "
SC 126:130.

G-15: Pseudo-Dionysius (5th c.)
De ecclesiastica hierarchia 2:2,7

24:295　　　　5:217　7:221
　　　　　　　　　　　　　　7:221

"Παραλαβοντες δε αυτον ΄οι ΄ιερεις, εγχειριζουσι τω της προσαγωγης αναδοχω τε και ΄ηγεμονι • και συν αυτω περιβαλοντες εσθητα τω τελουμενω καταλληλον, επι τον ΄ιεραρχην αυθις απαγουσιν • ΄ο δε τω θεουργικωτατω μυρω τον ανδρα σφραγισαμενος, μετοχον αποφαινει λοιπον της ΄ιεροτελεστικωτατης Ευχαριστιας. "
Ed. Balthasar Corderius. PG 3 (1857):396.

WORK   CHEMNITZ   BELLARMINE

G-16: Pseudo-Dionysius
De ecclesiastica hierarchia 2:3,8

                                                        5:217

"Ἡ δε του μυρου τελειωτικη χρισις ευωδη ποιει τον τετελεσμενον • 'η γαρ 'ιερα της θεογενεσιας τελειωσις 'ενοι τα τελεσθεντα τω θεαρχικω Πνευματι."
PG 3:404.

G-17: Pseudo-Dionysius
De ecclesiastica hierarchia 4:3,2[19]

                                                        9:225

"Τοις γαρ ενθεοις ανδρασιν 'η των πανιερων ακτις, 'ως συγγενεσι του νοητου, καθαρως και αμεσως ελλαμπουσα, και τας νοερας 'αυτων αντιληψεις, απερικαλυπτως 'ευωδιαζουσα, προς το 'υφειμενον ουκετι 'ομοιως προεισιν, αλλ' 'υπ' αυτων 'ως κρυφιων του νοητου θεωρων, ανεκπομπευτως εις το τοις ανομοιος αχραντον, 'υπο πτερωτοις αινιγμασι συγκαλυπτεται • δι' 'ων 'ιερων αινιγματων 'αι των 'υποβεβηκοτων ευκοσμοι ταξεις αναγονται προς την κατ' αυτας 'ιεραν αναλογιαν. "
PG 3:476.

G-18: Pseudo-Dionysius
De ecclesiastica hierarchia 4:3,4

                                                        8:223

"Τελωμεν τοινυν, 'ως 'η του μυρου συνθεσις συναγωγη τις εστιν ευπνοων 'υλων εν 'εαυτη πλουσιως εχουσα ποιοτητας ευοσμους, 'ης 'οι μετασχοντες ευωδιαζονται, κατα την αναλογιαν του ποσου της εγγενομενης αυτοις του ευωδους μεθεξεως."
PG 3:477.

[19] Bellarmine does not give a complete reference here to the text of Dionysius about athletes to which Brenz refers. Perhaps it is this one.

WORK	CHEMNITZ	BELLARMINE

G-19: Pseudo-Dionysius
De ecclesiastica hierarchia 4:3,11

5:217

"Αλλα μην και αυτω τω τελεσθεντι την ῾ιερωτατην της θεογενεσιας τελετην την του θεαρχικου Πνευματος επιφοιτησιν, ῾η του μυρου δωρειται τελειωτικη χρισις, ῾υποτυπουσης, ῾ως οιμαι, της ῾ιερας των συμβολων εικονογραφιας, ῾υπ' αυτου του δι' ῾ημας ανθρωποπρεπως τω θεαρχικω Πνευματι καθαγιασθεντος, αναλλοιωτω της ουσιωδους θεοτητος ῾εξει, το θειοντατον Πνευμα χορηγουμενον."
PG 3:484.

G-20: Pseudo-Dionysius
De ecclesiastica hierarchia 4:3,12

8:224 9:226

" ᾽Οθεν, ῾ως οιμαι, κατα νουν ῾ιεραρχικον θεοπαραδοτως ῾οι θειοι της καθ' ῾ημας ῾ιεραρχιας καθηγεμονες την πανσεμνον ταυτην ῾ιερουργιαν μυρου τελετην εκ του τελουμενου πραγματικως ῾ονομαζουσιν, ῾ως αν τις φαιη Θεου τελετην, ῾εκατερω νῳ την θειαν αυτης τελετουργιαν ῾υμνουντες.' "
PG 3:485.

G-21: Pseudo-Dionysius
De ecclesiastica hierarchia 7:3,10

10:229

"Τας δε τελεστικας επικλησεις ου θεμιτον εν γραφαις αφερμηνευειν, ουδε το μυστικον αυτων, ῾η τας επ' αυταις ενεργουμενας εκ Θεου δυναμεις εκ του κρυφιου προς το κοινον εξαγειν • ..."
PG 3:565.

G-22: Pseudo-Dionysius
De ecclesiastica hierarchia 7:3,11

25:297

"Ουδεν ουν, ῾ως ῾οιμαι, το ατοπον, ει κατα θειαν ῾ο παις αναγωγην αναγεται, καθηγεμονα και αναδοχον ῾ιερον εχων, ῾εξιν αυτω των θειων εμποιουντα, και φυλαττοντα των εναντιων απειρατον. "
PG 3:568.

WORK   CHEMNITZ   BELLARMINE

G-23: Epiphanius (c.315-403)
Panarion 48

1:213

"Κατα των κατα Φρυγας ητοι Μοντανιστων καλουμενων η και
Τασκοδρουγιτων χη, της δε ακολουθιας μη.
Ed. Karl Holl. GCS 31 (1922):219.

G-24: Epiphanius
Panarion 75,3

12:232

" 'τι εστιν επισκοπος προς πρεσβυτερον; ουδεν διαλλαττει 'ουτος
τουτου •   μια γαρ εστι ταξις και μια, φησι, τιμη και 'εν αξιωμα.
χειροθετει, φησιν, επισκοπος, αλλα και 'ο πρεσβυτερος • λουτρον
διδωσιν 'ο επισκοπος, 'ομοιως και 'ο πρεσβυτερος • την λατρειαν της
οικονομιας ποιει 'ο επισκοπος, και 'ο πρεσβυτερος 'ωσαυτως •
καθεζεται 'ο επισκοπος επι του θρονου, καθεζεται και 'ο
πρεσβυτερος'."
Ed. Die Kirchenväter-Commission der Preussischen Akademie der
Wissenschaften. GCS 37 (1933):334.

G-25: Eusebius (c. 263-340)
Ekklesiastike historia 3:16

9:288

"Τουτου δη ουν 'ομολογουμενη μια επιστολη φερεται, μεγαλη τε και
θαυμασια, 'ην 'ως απο της 'Ρωμαιων εκκλησιας τη Κορινθιων
διετυπωσατο, στασεως τηνικαδε κατα την Κορινθον γενομενης. ταυτην
δε και εν πλεισταις εκκλησιαις επι του κοινου δεδημοσιευμενην παλαι
τε και καθ' 'ημας αυτους εγνωμεν."
Ed. Eduard Schwartz and Theodor Mommsen. GCS 9,1 (1903):230.

G-26: Eusebius (Clement)
Ekklesiastike historia 3:23 (17), 8

9:288   5:217

"και μετα τουτο 'υφηκεν της πλειονος επιμελειας και παραφυλακης, 'ως
το τελειον αυτω φυλακτηριον επιστησας, την σφραγιδα κυριου."
GCS 9,1:240.

WORK   CHEMNITZ   BELLARMINE

G-27: Eusebius
Ekklesiastike historia 4:14,7[20]

1:213

"και αυτος δε `ο Πολυκαρπος Μαρχιωνι ποτε εις οψιν αυτω ελθοντι και φησαντι 'επιγνωσκε `ημας' απεκριθη 'επιγνωσκω επιγινωσκω τον πρωτοτοκον του σατανα'."
GCS 9,1:334.

G-28: Eusebius (Cornelius)
Ekklesiastike historia 6:43,14-15[21]

3:285 24:296   1:212 3:216
       24:296   9:225 9:226

" 'ου μην ουδε των λοιπων ετυχεν, διαφυγων την νοσον, `ων χρη μεταλαμβανειν κατα τον της εκκλησιας κανονα, του τε σφραγισθηναι `υπο του επισκοπου • τουτων δε μη τυχων, πως αν του `αγιου πνευματος ετυχεν'; "
Ed. Eduard Schwartz and Theodor Mommsen. GCS 9,2 (1908):620.

G-29: Gregory Nazianzen (c. 330-390)
Oratio 40 (in sanctum baptisma):15

5:217

"Ει δε προκαταλαβοις σεαυτον τη σφραγιδι, και το μελλον ασφαλισαιο τω καλλιστω των βοηθηματων και στερροτατω, σημειωθεις και ψυχην και σωμα, τω χρισματι και τω Πνευματι, `ως `ο Ισραηλ παλαι τω νυκτερινω και φυλακτικω των πρωτοτοκων `αιματι • . . . "
Logoi. PG 36 (1858, reprint 1979):377.

G-30: Gregory Nazianzen
Oratio 42 (ad 150):26

13:233

"Χαιροις, Αναστασια. . . . Συ τε `ο μεγας ναος `ουτος και περιβοητος . . . Χαιρε μοι, `ω χαθεδρα. . . .
PG 36:489.

---

[20] See fn. 17 above.

[21] Chemnitz cites this text as cap. 46 in 3:285, then as cap. 33 in 24:296. The GCS edition marks it 43 with 33 as an alternate.

G-31: Gregory of Nyssa (c. 335-394)
_ 22

24:295

"Baptismus docet, ne vitiorum reliquias sequenti post fidem vitae immisceamus."
(as cited by Chemnitz)

G-32: Hesychius (+ c. 450)
Fragmenta in psalmos 73,13

24:295

"Τουτων τας κεφαλας συνετριψεν ʽο Χριστος εν τω ʽυδατι, αυτος τε βαπτισθεις, και παραδους τοις ανθρωποις βαπτιζεσθαι.   Κεφαλη δε των νοητων δρακοντων ʽη ʽαμαρτια."
PG 93 (1860):1241. 1244.

G-33: John Chrysostom (c. 344-407)
_ 23

12:231

"Presbyterii"

G-34: John Chrysostom
Ad Romanos 6,5

24:295

"Ου γαρ δη τουτο ισχυει το βαπτισμα μονον το τα προτερα αφανισαι πλημμεληματα, αλλα και προς τα μελλοντα ασφαλιζεται."
Ed. Bern. de Monfaucon. PG 60 (1859):483.

G-35: John Chrysostom
Commentarius in S. Matthaeum Evangelium 55,4

13:233

"Καν αναγεννηθηναι δεη, σταυρος παραγινεται • καν τραφηναι την μυστικην εκεινην τροφην, καν χειροτονηθηναι, καν ʽοτιουν ʽετερον ποιησαι, πανταχου το της νιχης ʽημιν παριστατα συμβολον."
Ed. Bern. de Monfaucon. PG 58 (1860):537.

22 Chemnitz does not say which work of Gregory he is quoting. The complete works of Gregory of Nyssa are found in PG 44-46.

23 Bellarmine does not say which work of Chrysostom he is quoting.

| WORK | CHEMNITZ | BELLARMINE |

G-36: John Chrysostom
Homilia de baptismo 2,23 [24]

9:225

"Λοιπον γαρ μαχη και αντιστασις εξ εκεινου προς αυτον γινεται και δια τουτο καθαπερ αθλητας τινας Χριστου ʹουτω δια της αλοιφης εις το σταδιον το πνευματικον εισαγει."

Huit Catéchèses baptismales. Ed. Antoine Wenger. SC 50bis   (1970):147.

G-37: John Chrysostom
In epistolam ad Hebraeos 9,6

11:230

"ʹΩσπερ ουν ουχ ενι δευτερον σταυρωθηναι τον Χριστον • τουτο γαρ παραδειγματισαι αυτον εστιν • ʹουτως ουδε βαπτισθηναι."

Ed. Bern. de Montfaucon. PG 63 (1860):79.

G-38: John Chrysostom
Quod Christus sit Deus 10

13:233

"Τουτο γαρ το του θανατου συμβολον {ου γαρ παυσομαι συνεχως τουτο λεγων} εγενετο ευλογιας ʹυποθεσις πολλης, και παντοδαπης ασφαλειας τειχος διαβολου χαιρια πληγη, δαιμονων χαλινος, χημος της των αντικειμενων δυναμεως • ..."

Ed. Bern. de Monfaucon. PG 48 (1859):827.

G-39: John Damascene (c. 675-749)
De fide Orthodoxae 4,9[25]

24:295   5:218

"Το ελαιον βαπτισματι παραλαμβανεται, μηνυον την χρισιν ʹημων, και χριστους ʹημας εργαζομενον, και τον του Θεου ʹημιν επαγγελλομενον δια

---

[24]   Bellarmine does not say which text of Chrysostom makes this reference to athletes. Although this quote supports Bellarmine's statement, the baptismal homilies were only attributed to Chrysostom in this century.

[25]   Although Bellarmine says cap. 10, his text is found in cap. 9.

WORK	CHEMNITZ	BELLARMINE

του `αγιου Πνευματος ελεον, επει και καρφος ελαιας τοις εκ του
κατακλυσμου περισωθεισιν `η περιστερα κεκομικεν."
Ed. Michaelis Lequien. PG 94 (1864):1125.

G-40: John Damascene
De haeresibus 48

1:213

"ʾΟι Καταφρυγαστων, και Μοντανιστων, και Ασκοδρουγητων • `οιτινες
Παλαιαν και Καινην Διαθηκην δεχονται • `ετερους δε προφητας
παρεισαγονται, Μοντανον τινα αυχουντες, και Πρισκιλλαν."
PG 94:705. 708.

G-41: Justin (+165)
Orthodoxorum 137

5:217

"Επειδη `α ποιει {`η εκκλησια προς} τον ενταφιασμον μετα τον θανατον
αυτου ποιει του ενταφιαζομενου, `η δε μακαρια Μαρια προ του
θανατου εμυρισε τον κυριον. . . ."
Opera quae ferunter omnia. Ed. Ioann. Carol. Theod. eqves de Otto.
CorpAp 5 (1881):220.

G-42: Origen (c. 185-253)
Homilia 8 in Leviticum

5:217 9:226

"Sic ergo conversis a peccato purificatio quidem per illa omnia datur,
quae superius diximus, donum autem gratiae spiritus per 'olei'
imaginem designatur, ut non solum purgationem consequi possit is, qui
convertitur a peccato, sed et Spiritu sancto repleri. . . ."
Ed. W. A. Baehrens. Trans. Rufino. GCS 29 (1920):417.

G-43: Origen
Homilia 9 in Leviticum

5:217

"Omnes enim, quicumque unguento sacri chrismatis delibuti sunt,
sacerdotes effecti sunt, sicut et Petrus ad omnem dicit ecclesiam: 'vos
autem genus electum, regale sacerdotale, gens sancta.' "
GCS 29:436.

WORK   CHEMNITZ   BELLARMINE

G-44: Theodoret (c. 393-466)
Ecclesiasticae historiae 5,9

7:222

"Της δε γε μητρος `απασων των Εκκλησιων της εν `Ιεροσολυμοις, τον αιδεσιμωτατον και θεοφιλεστατον Κυριλλον επισκοπον ειναι γνωριζομεν, κανονιχως τε παρα των της επαρχιας χειροτονηθεντα παλαι, και πλειστα προς τους Αρειανους εν διαφοροις τοποις αθλησαντα."
Ed. Joan. Ludov. Schulze. PG 82 (1864):1217.

G-45: Theodoret
Explanatio in Canticum Canticorum 1,2

5:218

"Ει δε βουλη και μυστιχωτερον νοησαι, αναμνησον σεαυτον πης `ιερας μυσταγωγιας, εν `η `οι τελουμενοι, μετα την αρνησιν του τυραννου, και την του βασιλεως `ομολογιαν, `οιονει σφραγιδα τινα βασιλιχην δεξονται του πνευματιχου μυρου το χρισμα • `ως εν τυπω τω μυρω την αορατον του παναγιου Πνευματος χαριν `υποδεχομενοι. "
Ed. Joan. Ludov. Schulze. PG 81 (1864):60.

G-46: Theodoret
Haereticarum fabularum compendium 3,2

1:213

"Της δε κατα Φρυγας καλουμενης `αιρεσεως ηρξατο Μοντανος, απο κωμης τινος εκει διακειμενης `ορμωμενος, Αρδαβαν καλουμενης."
Ed. Joan. Ludov. Schulze. PG 83 (1859):401.

G-47: Theodoret
Haereticarum fabularum compendium 3,5

1:211

"`Οι δε τουτου διαδοχοι και `ετερα τω δογματι προστεθεικασι • τους γαρ δευτεροις γαμοις `ωμιληκοτας των `ιερων εξελαυνουσι μυστηριων • και παντελως τον της μετανοιας των οικειων συλλογων εξοριζουσι

WORK   CHEMNITZ   BELLARMINE

λογον • και τοις ʽυπο σφων βαπτιζομενοις το παναγιον ου προσφερουσι χρισμα. Δια τοι τουτο και τους εκ τησδε της ʽαιρεσεως τω σωματι της Εκκλησιας συναπτομενους χριειν ʽοι πανευφημοι Πατερες προσεταξαν. Κατα ταυτησι της ʽαιρεσεως πολλας μεν επιστολας ʽο Κορνηλιος εγραψε, πολλας δε Διονυσιος ʽο της Αλεξανδρεων επισκοπος, και ʽετεροι δε πολλοι των τηνικαδε επισκοπων, δι' ʽων καταδηλος ευθυς εγενετο πασιν ʽη του Ναυατου ωμοτης."
PG 83:408.

G-48: Theodoret
Interpretio epistolae ad Corinthios secundae 1,21-22

8:222

" ʽΟ δε βεβαιων ʽημας συν ʽυμιν εις Χριστον, και χρισας ʽημας Θεος. ʽΟ και σφραγισαμενος ʽημας, και δους τον αρραβωνα του Πνευματος εν ταις καρδιαις ʽημων.' ʽΟ Θεος δε τουτων αιτιος των αγαθων • αυτος γαρ και ʽημιν βεβαιαν περι τον Χριστον εδωρησατο πιστιν • αυτος ʽημας εχρισε, και της του παναγιου Πνευματος σφραγιδος ηξιωσεν, οιον τινα αρραβωνα των μελλοντων αγαθων δωρησαμενος ταυτην ημιν την χαριν. "
PG 82:384-385.

G-49: Theodoret
Interpretatio epistolae ad Hebraeos

11:230

"Των αγαν αδυνατων, φησιν, τους τω παναγιω προσεληλυθοτας βαπτισματι, και της του θειου Πνευματος.... Ουχ ʽοιον τε ουν ʽημας παλιν απολαυσαι της του βαπτισματος δωρεας. "
PG 82:717.

WORK	CHEMNITZ	BELLARMINE

G-50: Theophilus Antiochenus (+180)
Ad Autolycum 1,12

8:224 9:225
9:226

"Ειτα αηρ μεν και πασα ʽη ʽυπʼ ουρανον τροπῳ τινι χριεται φωτι και πνευματι. Συ δε ου βουλει χρισθηναι ʽελαιον θεου; Τοιγαρουν ʽημεις τουτον ʽεινεκεν καλουμεθα χριστιανοι ʽοτι χριομεθα ελαιον θεου."
Ed. G. Bardy. SC 20 (1948):84.

5. LATIN FATHERS

WORK	CALVIN	CHEMNITZ	BELLARMINE

L-1: Ambrose (334-397)
Ad Ephesios 4,11-12

12:230

"Denique apud AEgyptum praesbyteri consignant, si praesens non sit episcopus. Sed quia coeperunt sequentes presbyteri indigni inveniri ad primatus tenendos, immutata est ratio, prospiciente concilio, ut non ordo, sed meritum crearet episcopum, multorum sacerdotum judicio constitutum, ne indignus temere usurparet, et esset multis scandalum."
PL 17 (1879):410.

L-2: Ambrose
De mysteriis 6,29

24:294 9:228

"Post haec utique adscendisti ad sacerdotem. Considera quid secutum sit. Nonne illud quod ait Dauid: 'Sicut unguentum in capite quod descendit in barbam barbam Aaron'? Hoc est unguentum de quo et Salomon ait: 'Unguentum exinanitum est nomen tuum, propterea adulescentulae dilexerunt te et adtraxerunt te.'"
Ed. Bernard Botte. SC 25 (1949):117.

L-3: Ambrose
De mysteriis 7,42

13:289 6:219 8:222
9:228 10:229

"Undé repete quia accepisti signaculum spiritale, 'spiritum sapientiae et intellectus, spiritum consilii atque uirtutis, spiritum cognitionis atque pietatis, spiritum sancti timoris,' et serua quod accepisti. Signauit te deus pater, confirmauit te Christus dominus et dedit pignus spiritus in cordibus tuis, sicut apostolica lectione didicisti."
SC 25:121.

| WORK | CALVIN | CHEMNITZ | BELLARMINE |

L-4: Ambrose
De mysteriis 8,43

7:221

"His abluta plebs diues insignibus ad Christi contendit altaria dicens: 'Et introibo ad altare dei, ad deum qui laetificat iuuentutem meam.'"
SC 25:121.

L-5: Ambrose
De sacramentis 1:2,4

9:225

"Unctus es quasi athleta Christi, quasi luctam huius saeculi luctaturus, professus es luctaminis tui certamina."
SC 25:55.

L-6: Ambrose
De sacramentis 2:7,24

10:228

"Ergo mersisti, uenisti ad sacerdotem. Quid tibi dixit? Deus, inquit, pater omnipotens, qui te regenerauit ex aqua et spiritu sancto concessitque tibi peccata tua, ipse te unguet in uitam aeternam. Uide ubi unctus es: in uitam, inquit, aeternam."
SC 25:70.

L-7: Ambrose
De sacramentis 3:2,8

6:219

"Sequitur spiritale signaculum quod audistis hodie legi, quia post fontem superest ut perfectio fiat, quando ad inuocationem sacerdotis spiritus sanctus infunditur, 'spiritus sapientiae et intellectus. . . ' septem quasi uirtutes spiritus."
SC 25:74-75.

L-8: Ambrose
De sacramentis 3:2,11

7:221

"Uenire habes ad altare. . . . Hoc est mysterium quod legisti in euangelio. . . ."
SC 25:75.

WORK	CALVIN	CHEMNITZ	BELLARMINE
L-9: Augustine (354-430) _26			
			9:225
"athleta"			
L-10: Augustine De baptismo 3:16,21			
	12:1074	24:294 24:296 24:296 24:297	2:215 6:219 7:220 7:220 7:220 7:220 7:220

". . . neque enim temporalibus et sensibilibus miraculis adtestantibus per manus inpositionem modo datur spiritus sanctus, sicut antea dabatur ad commendationem rudis fidei et ecclesiae primordia dilatanda. quis enim nunc hoc expectat, ut hi, quibus manus ad accipiendum sanctum spiritum inponitur, repente incipiant linguis loqui? sed inuisibiliter et latenter intellegitur. . . . cum ergo aliud sit sacramentum, quod habere etiam Simon magus potuit, aliud operatio spiritus, quae in malis etiam hominibus fieri solet, sicut Saul habuit prophetiam, aliud operatio eiusdem spiritus, quam nisi boni habere non possunt, sicut est finis praecepti caritas de corde puro et conscientia bona et fide non ficta, quodlibet haeretici et schismatici accipiant, caritas quae cooperit multitudinem peccatorum proprium donum est catholicae unitatis et pacis nec eius in omnibus, quia nec omnes sunt eius, sicut suo loco uidebimus. praeter ipsam tamen esse illa caritas non potest, sine qua cetera, etiamsi agnosci et adprobari possunt, prodesse tamen et liberare non possunt. manus autem inpositio non sicut baptismus repeti non potest. quid est enim aliud nisi oratio super hominem?"
Ed. M. Petschenig. CSEL 51 (1908):212-213.

---

26 Bellarmine gives no further information here about the location of the text to which he refers.

| WORK | CALVIN | CHEMNITZ | BELLARMINE |

L-11: Augustine
De baptismo 5:1,1

6:218

"Ecclesiae catholicae consuetudinem pristinam nunc teneri, cum ab haereticis uel schismaticis uenientes, si euangelicis uerbis consecratum baptismum perceperunt, denuo non baptizantur, beato Cypriano teste utimur."
CSEL 51:261.

L-12: Augustine
De baptismo 5:20[27]

1:212 7:220
8:225

". . . cur autem ad uerba quae procedunt ex ore homicidae possit tamen deus oleum sanctificare et in altari quod haeretici posuerunt non possit nescio, nisi forte quem cor hominis fallaciter conuersum intus non inpedit, lignum fallaciter positum inpedit foris, quominus sacramentis suis adesse dignetur nullis hominum falsitatibus inpeditus. si ergo ad hoc ualet quod dictum est in euangelio: 'deus peccatorem non audit,' ut per peccatorem sacramenta non celebrentur, quomodo exaudit homicidam deprecantem uel super aquam baptismi uel super oleum uel super eucharistiam uel super capita eorum quibus manus inponitur?"
CSEL 51:285-286.

L-13: Augustine
De baptismo 5:23,33

12:1075   24:296   7:220 7:221

". . . manus autem inpositio si non adhiberetur ab haeresi uenienti, tamquam extra omnem culpam esse iudicaretur. propter caritatis autem copulationem, quod est maximum donum spiritus sancti, sine quo non ualent ad salutem quaecumque alia sancta in homine fuerint, manus haereticis correctis inponitur."
CSEL 51:290.

---

[27] Bellarmine says at 7:220 that Augustine teaches "passim" about chrism in works he has already cited. Here is one example, though he speaks of oil, not specifically chrism.

WORK	CALVIN	CHEMNITZ	BELLARMINE

L-14: Augustine
De baptismo 7:20,39

         24:294

". . . bene tamen quod totiens meminerunt etiam primum apostolorum Petrum potuisse aliter sapere quam ueritas postulabat. quod accidisse etiam Cypriano sine ulla eius contumelia credimus quicumque diligimus Cyprianum, quia non eum fas est diligi maiore caritate quam Petrum."
CSEL 51:355-356.

L-15: Augustine
De bono vidvitatis 1,2

         22:291

". . . quid ego amplius te doceam quam id quod apud apostolum legimus? sancta enim scriptura nostrae doctrinae regulam figit, ne audeamus 'sapere plus quam oportet sapere,' sed sapiamus, ut ipse ait, 'ad temperantiam, sicut unicuique deus partitus est mensuram fidei.' "
Ed. Iosephus Zycha. CSEL 41 (1900):306.

L-16: Augustine
De correptione et gratia[28] 12,38

         6:287

"Subventum est igitur infirmitati voluntatis humanae, ut divina gratia indeclinabiliter et inseparabiliter ageretur...."
Ed. Monks of the Order of St. Benedict from the Congregation of St. Maur. PL 44 (1861):940.

L-17: Augustine
Contra Cresconium 2:32,40

         24:294

". . . ego huius epistulae auctoritate non teneor, quia litteras Cypriani non ut canonicas habeo, sed eas ex canonicis considero, et quod in eis diuinarum scripturarum auctoritati congruit cum laude eius accipio, quod autem non congruit cum pace eius respuo."
Ed. M. Petschenig. CSEL 52 (1909):399-400.

---

[28] It is not clear which text Chemnitz has in mind. Perhaps it is this passage.

WORK	CALVIN	CHEMNITZ	BELLARMINE

L-18: Augustine
Enarrationes in psalmos 26:2,2

6:219

"Vnctio ista perficiet nos spiritaliter in illa uita, quae nobis promittitur. . . . Vngimur enim modo in sacramento, et sacramento ipso praefiguratur quiddam quod futuri sumus."
Ed. Eligivs Dekkers, Iohannes Fraipont. CChr.SL 38 (1956):155.

L-19: Augustine
Enarrationes in psalmos 44,32

12:231

"Quid est: 'Pro patribus tuis nati sunt tibi filii?' Patres missi sunt apostoli, pro apostolis filii nati sunt tibi, constituti sunt episcopi."
CChr.SL 38:516.

L-20: Augustine
Enarrationes in psalmos 65,17

24:292

"Propterea et in sacramentis, et in catechizando, et in exorcizando, adhibetur prius ignis. . . . Post ignem autem exorcismi uenitur ad baptismum, ut ab igne ad aquam, ab aqua in refrigerium."
Ed. Eligivs Dekkers, Iohannes Fraipont. CChr.SL 39 (1956):851.

L-21: Augustine
Enarrationes in psalmos 141,9

8:225

"Vsque adeo de cruce non erubesco, ut non in occulto loco habeam crucem Christi, sed in fronte portem. Multa sacramenta aliter atque aliter accipimus: quaedam, sicut nostris, ore accipimus, quaedam per totum corpus accipimus."
CChr.SL 38:2052.

L-22: Augustine
Epistula 43 (162):5,16

1:212

"et tamen qualis ipsius beati Melchiadis ultima est prolata sententia!

WORK	CALVIN	CHEMNITZ	BELLARMINE

quam innocens, quam integra, quam prouida atque pacifica! . . . o uirum optimum! o filium Christianae pacis et patrem Christianae plebis!"
Ed. Al. Goldbacher. CSEL 34,2 (1898):98.

L-23: Augustine
Epistula 82 (19):1,3

	24:293	24:294	
		24:294	

"alios autem ita lego, ut, quanta libet sanctitate doctrinaque praepolleant, non ideo uerum putem, quia ipsi ita senserunt, sed quia mihi uel per illos auctores canonicos uel probabili ratione, quod a uero non abhorreat, persuadere potuerunt."
CSEL 34,2:354.

L-24: Augustine
Epistula 148[29] (111):4,15

		24:294	

"neque enim quorumlibet disputationes quamuis catholicorum et laudatorum hominum uelut scripturas canonicas habere debemus, ut nobis non liceat salua honorificentia, quae illis debetur hominibus, aliquid in eorum scriptis inprobare atque respuere, si forte inuenerimus, quod aliter senserint, quam ueritas habet diuino adiutorio uel ab aliis intellecta uel a nobis. talis ego sum in scriptis aliorum, tales uolo esse intellectores meorum."
Ed. Al. Goldbacher. CSEL 44 (1904):344-345.

L-25: Augustine
De fide et operibus 9,14

			9:226

"si enim spado cum respondisset: 'credo filium dei esse Iesum Christum,' hoc ei sufficere uisum est, ut continuo baptizatus abscederet, cur non id sequimur? cur non imitamur atque auferimus cetera, quae necesse

---

[29] Preuss records this as epistle "III", a misprint for letter 111. Following the CSEL numbering of the letters of Augustine, it is 148.

WORK	CALVIN	CHEMNITZ	BELLARMINE

habemus, etiam cum ad baptizandum temporis urget angustia, exprimere interrogando, ut baptizandus ad cuncta respondeat, etiamsi ea memoriae mandare non uacuit?"
CSEL 41:51.

L-26: Augustine
De haeresibus 26

1:213

"Cataphryges sunt quorum auctores fuerunt Montanus tamquam paracletus et duae prophetissae ipsius, Prisca et Maximilla."
Ed. R. Vander Plaetse-C. Beukers. CChr.SL 46 (1969):302.

L-27: Augustine
De haeresibus 53

12:232

"Aeriani ab Aerio quodam sunt qui, cum esset presbyter, doluisse fertur quod episcopus non potuit ordinari. . . . Dicebat etiam presbyterum ab episcopo nulla differentia debere discerni."
CChr.SL 46:323-324.

L-28: Augustine
In Iohannis evangelium 80,3

5:1069

"Detrahe uerbum, et quid est aqua nisi aqua? Accedit uerbum ad elementum, et fit sacramentum, etiam ipsum tamquam uisibile uerbum."
Ed. Radbodvs Willems. CChr.SL 36 (1954):529.

L-29: Augustine
In Iohannis evangelium 118,5

8:225 13:233

"Quod signum nisi adhibeatur siue frontibus credentium, siue ipsi aquae ex qua regenerantur, siue oleo quo chrismate unguuntur, siue sacrificio quo aluntur, nihil eorum rite perficitur."
CChr.SL 36:657.

WORK	CALVIN	CHEMNITZ	BELLARMINE

L-30: Augustine
In epistolam Ioannis ad Parthos 3,5

			8:223

"Unctio spiritalis ipse Spiritus Sanctus est, cujus sacramentum est in unctione visibili."
Ed. Paul Agaësse. SC 75 (1961):194.

L-31: Augustine
In epistolam Ioannis 6,10

			6:219

"Oportet enim ita significari in omnibus linguis Spiritum Sanctum, quia Evangelium Dei per omnes linguas cursurum erat toto orbe terrarum. Significatum est illud, et transiit. Numquid modo quibus imponitur manus ut accipiant Spiritum Sanctum, hoc exspectatur, ut linguis loquantur? . . . Interroget cor suum: si diligit fratrem, manet Spiritus Dei in illo."
SC 75:298.

L-32: Augustine
Contra litteras Petiliani 2:104,239[30]

	24:292	6:219	7:220
		7:220	7:221
		7:222	11:230

". . . in hoc unguento sacramentum chrismatis uultis interpretari, quod quidem in genere uisibilium signaculorum sacrosanctum est sicut ipse baptismus, sed potest esse et in hominibus pessimis in operibus carnis uitam consumentibus et regnum caelorum non possessuris et ideo nec ad barbam Aaron nec ad oram uestimenti eius nec ad ullam contextionem uestis sacerdotalis pertinentibus? in bonis et in malis potest, illis ad praemium illis ad iudicium, ab inuisibili unctione caritatis, quae propria bonorum est."
CSEL 52:154-155.

---

[30] At 7:220 Bellarmine refers in general to a passage where Augustine calls anointing a sacrament. Here is an example.

WORK   CALVIN   CHEMNITZ   BELLARMINE

L-33: Augustine
Contra litteras Petiliani 3:6,7

                                22:291

"Proinde siue de Christo siue de eius ecclesia siue de quacumque alia re, quae pertinet ad fidem uitamque uestram, non dicam nos nequaquam comparandi ei qui dixit: 'licet si nos,' sed omnino quod secutus adiecit: 'si angelus de caelo uobis annuntiauerit praeterquam quod' in scripturis legitimis et euangelicis 'accepistis, anathema sit.'"
CSEL 52:168.

L-34: Augustine
De moribus ecclesiae 1:35,80

                                24:295

"Et illo sacrosancto lavacro inchoatur innovatio novi hominis, ut proficiendo perficiatur, in aliis citius, in aliis tardius."
Ed. Monks of the Order of St. Benedict from the Congregation of St. Maur. PL 32 (1877):1344.

L-35: Augustine
De symbolo ad catechumenos (De tempore) 1:3,9

                                13:233

"De cruce ipsius quid loquar? quid dicam? Extremum genus mortis elegit, ne aliquod genus mortis ejus martyres formidarent."
Ed. Monks of the Order of St. Benedict from the Congregation of St. Maur. PL 40 (1861):632.

L-36: Augustine
De symbolo ad catechumenos 4:1,1

                                24:292

"Omnia sacramenta quae acta sunt et aguntur in vobis per ministerium servorum Dei, exorcismis, orationibus, canticis spiritualibus, insufflationibus, cilicio, inclinatione cervicum, humilitate pedum, pavor ipse omni securitate appetendus; haec omnia, ut dixi, escae sunt, quae vos reficiunt in utero, ut renatos ex Baptismo hilares vos mater exhibeat Christo."
PL 40:660-661.

WORK	CALVIN	CHEMNITZ	BELLARMINE

L-37: Augustine
De Trinitate 15:26,46

	24:292	6:219 7:221
		9:226

"Neque enim aliquis discipulorum eius dedit spiritum sanctum. Orabant quippe ut ueniret in eos quibus manum imponebant, non ipsi eum dabant. Quem morem in suis praepositis etiam nunc seruat ecclesia. . . . Et manifestius de illo scriptum est in actibus apostolorum: 'Quoniam unxit eum deus spiritu sancto,' non utique oleo uisibili sed dono gratiae quod uisibili significatur unguento quo baptizatos ungit ecclesia."
Ed. W. J. Mountain, Fr. Glorie. CChr.SL 50A (1968):526.

L-38: Augustine
Epistula ad catholicos (De unitate ecclesiae) 3,6

22:291

". . . si autem Christi ecclesia canonicarum scripturarum diuinis et certissimis testimoniis in omnibus gentibus designata est, quidquid attulerint et undecumque recitauerint qui dicunt: 'ecce hic est Christus, ecce illic,' audiamus potius, si oues eius sumus, uocem pastoris nostri dicentis: 'nolite credere.' illae quippe singulae in multis gentibus ubi ista est non inueniuntur, haec autem quae ubique est etiam ubi illae sunt inuenitur. ergo in scripturis sanctis canonicis eam requiramus."
CSEL 52:237.

L-39: Augustine
De natura et origine animae (Ad Victorem) 2:13,18

24:294

". . . illum ego turbinem atque illa saxa deuitans nauem illis committere nolui et de hac re ita scripsi, ut rationem potius cunctationis meae quam temeritatem praesumptionis ostenderem. quod opusculum meum cum apud te inuenisset, inrisit seque illis cautibus animosiore impetu quam consultiore commisit."
Ed. Carolus F. Urba, Iosephus Zycha. CSEL 60 (1913):353-354.

WORK	CALVIN	CHEMNITZ	BELLARMINE

L-40: Cyprian (200-258)
Epistula 69,16 (lib. 4, ep. 7)[31]

24:295

". . . ut manifestum sit diabolum in baptismo fide credentis excludi, si fides postmodum defecerit regredi."
Ed. Guilemus Hartel. CSEL 3,2 (1871):765.

L-41: Cyprian
Epistula 70,2 (lib. 1, ep.12)[32]

		3:285 24:292	1:212 6:218
		24:293 24:295	8:224 9:225
			9:226 9:226

". . . itaque qui haereticos adserunt, aut interrogationem mutent aut uindicent ueritatem, nisi si eis et ecclesiam tribuunt quos baptisma habere contendunt. ungi quoque necesse est eum qui baptizatus est, ut accepto chrismate id est unctione esse unctus Dei et habere in se gratiam Christi possit. porro autem eucharistia est unde baptizati unguntur oleum in altari sanctificatum."
CSEL 3,2:768.

L-42: Cyprian
Epistula 72,1 (lib. 2, ep. 1)[33]

| | | 3:285 24:292 | 6:218 7:220 |
| | | 24:296 | 9:226 |

". . . eos qui sunt foris extra ecclesiam tincti et apud haereticos et schismaticos profanae aquae labe maculati, quando ad nos adque ad ecclesiam quae est una uenerint, baptizari oportere, eo quod parum sit eis manum inponere ad accipiendum spiritum sanctum, nisi accipiant et ecclesiae baptismum. tunc enim demum plene sanctificari et esse filii Dei posunt, si sacramento utroque nascantur."
CSEL 3,2:775.

---

[31] Numbers in parentheses show how Bellarmine and Chemnitz refer to the letters of Cyprian. Hans Freihen von Soden's *Die Cyprianische Briefsammlung Geschichte Ihrer Entstehung und überlieferung*, TU 10,3 (1904) was helpful in determining the numbering of these epistles.

[32] See fn. 31 above. Bellarmine says at 1:212 that Cyprian mentions chrism; perhaps he means this text.

[33] See fn. 31 above.

WORK	CALVIN	CHEMNITZ	BELLARMINE

L-43: Cyprian
Epistula ad Jubajanum 9[34]

1:213 6:218
9:226 9:226

"Quod nunc quoque apud nos geritur, ut qui in Ecclesia baptizantur, praepositis Ecclesiae offerantur, et per nostram orationem ac manus impositionem, Spiritum sanctum consequantur et signaculo Dominico consummentur."
PL 3 (1865):1160.

L-44: Cyprian
De lapsis 9,25

7:221

". . . ac ne quid deesset ad criminis cumulum, infantes quoque parentum manibus inpositi uel adtracti amiserunt paruuli quod in primo statim natiuitatis exordio fuerant consecuti. nonne illi, cum iudicii dies uenerit, dicent: 'nos nihil fecimus nec derelicto cibo et poculo Domini ad profana contagia sponte properauimus.'"
Ed. Guilelmus Hartel. CSEL 3,1 (1868):243.

L-45: Eusebius Gallicanus (7th c.)
De pentecoste 1-2

6:218 7:221

"Aduertamus summae diuitias bonitatis. Quod in confirmandis neophytis manus impositio tribuit singulis, hoc tunc spiritus sancti descensio in credentium populo donauit uniuersis. . . . Ergo spiritus sanctus, qui super aquas baptismi salutifero descendit illapsu; in fonte plenitudinem tribuit ad innocentiam; in confirmatione augmentum praestat ad gratiam, quia in hoc mundo tota aetate uicturis inter inuisibiles hostes et pericula gradiendum est. In baptismo regeneramur ad uitam, post baptismum confirmamur ad pugnam; in baptismo abluimur, post baptismum roboramur."
Ed. Fr. Glorie. CChr.SL 101 (1970):337-338.

---

34 Bellarmine gives no citation at 1:213; perhaps it is this text.

WORK	CALVIN	CHEMNITZ	BELLARMINE

L-46: Filastrius (+ c. 397)
Catalogus 49,2

1:213

". . . quosdam autem suos prophetas, id est Montanum nomine, et Priscillam et Maximillam adnuntiant, quos neque prophetae neque Christus nuntiauit."
Ed. F. Heylon. CChr.SL 9 (1957):238.

L-47: Gelasius (6th c.)
Decretum 5:7,9 (dist. 15)

9:288

"Cetera quae ab hereticis sive scismaticis conscripta vel praedicata sunt, nullatenus recipit catholica et apostolica Romana ecclesia; e quibus pauca, quae ad memoriam venerunt et a catholicis vitanda sunt, credidimus esse subdenda: . . . opuscula alterius Clementis Alexandrini, apocrypha."
Das Decretum Gelasianum de libris recipiendis et non recipiendis. Ed. Ernst von Dobschütz. Leipzig: J. C. Hinrichs'sche Buchhandlung, 1912. TU 38,4:11-12.

L-48: Gennadius (+ c. 492)
Liber ecclesiasticorum dogmatum 21 (52)[35]

7:221

". . . et si consentiunt credere uel adquiescunt confiteri, purgati iam fidei integritate confirmentur manus inpositione: si uero paruuli sunt uel hebetes qui doctrinam non capiant, respondeant pro illis qui eos offerunt iuxta morem baptizandi, et sic manus inpositione et chrismate communiti eucharistiae mysteriis admittantur."
Ed. C. H. Turner. JThS 7,25 (1905):93-94.

L-49: Gregory of Tours (538-594)
De gloria martyrum 41 (40)[36]

8:223

"Require nunc, sacratissime Auguste, quis astet, qui ablutus balsamo

---

[35] Bellarmine's reference to number 52 matches 21 in the JThS edition.
[36] PL lists as section 41 what Bellarmine cites from 40.

WORK	CALVIN	CHEMNITZ	BELLARMINE

unctus, et abscedat protinus, ut accedant dii quos invocamus. . . . Quis est hic numinibus nostris contrarius, ac religionis Christianae socius, qui frontem chrismatis inscriptione signatam ferat, lignumque crucis adoret?"
PL 71 (1879):742.

L-50: Hilary of Poitiers (315-367)
Contra Arianos[37]

24:295

"Sacramento baptismi, vere Filius Dei unusquisque perficitur."
(as cited by Chemnitz)

L-51: Isidore (560-636)
De ecclesiasticiis officiis 1:29 (28),2[38]

8:225 13:233

"Quo die proinde etiam sanctum chrisma conficitur, quia ante biduum paschae Maria caput ac pedes Domini unguente perfudisse perhibetur."
Ed. Faustinus Arevalus. PL 83 (1862):764.

L-52: Jerome (331-419)
Epistula 41 ad Marcellam 3

1:213 12:231

". . . illi Sabelli dogma sectantes trinitatem in unius personae angustias cogunt. . . . apud nos apostolorum locum episcopi tenent; apud eos episcopus tertius est."
Ed. Isidore Hilberg. CSEL 54 (1910):313.

L-53: Jerome
Epistula 108,10 (De obitu Paulae)

13:233

". . . mixtisque gaudio lacrimis loquebatur: 'salue, Bethlem, domus panis, in qua natus est ille panis, qui de caelo descendit. salue, Ephrata, regio uberrima atque karpophoros, cuius fertilitas deus est.'"
Ed. Isidore Hilberg. CSEL 55 (1912):316.

---

[37]   I was unable to find the passage Chemnitz quotes here. The complete text of Hilary's work is PL 10:9-472.

[38]   Bellarmine's text reads chapter 28, but the reference is in 29 in PL.

WORK   CALVIN   CHEMNITZ   BELLARMINE

L-54: Jerome
In Hiezechielem 8:27,17

                                                                9:228

"Dicitur autem quibus terra Iudaea, quae nunc appellatur Palaestina, abundet copiis frumento, balsamo, melle et oleo et resina, quae a Iuda et Israel ad Tyri nundinas deferuntur."
Ed. Franciscus Glorie. CChr.SL 75 (1964):371.

L-55: Jerome
Contra Luciferianos 6-7. 9

                        4:1069   24:292   1:213

"Neque enim aqua lavat animam, sed prius ipsa lavatur a Spiritu, ut alios lavare spiritualiter possit. . . . Si ergo baptizati sunt vero et legitimo Ecclesiae baptismate, et ita postea Spiritum sanctum consecuti sunt: et tu apostolorum sequere auctoritatem, et baptiza eos qui Christi non habent baptisma, et poteris invocare Spiritum sanctum. . . . Quod si hoc loco quaeris quare in Ecclesia baptizatus, nisi per manus episcopi, non accipiat Spiritum sanctum, quem nos asserimus in vero baptismate tribui, disce hanc observationem ex ea auctoritate descendere, quod post ascensum Domini Spiritus sanctus ad apostolos descendit."
Ed. Joannes Martinaeus. PL 23 (1865):169. 171-173.

L-56: Jerome
Contra Luciferianos 8

                                        6:219 7:221

"Exigis ubi scriptum sit? In Actibus apostolorum. Etiam si Scripturae auctoritas non subesset, totius orbis in hanc partem consensus instar praecepti obtineret. Nam et multa alia quae per traditionem in Ecclesiis observantur, auctoritatem sibi scriptae legis usurpaverunt. . . ."
PL 23:172.

L-57: Jerome
Contra Luciferianos 9

                    4:1069   24:294 24:296   12:232
                              24:296 26:298

"Et multis in locis idem factitatum reperimus, ad honorem potius sacerdotii quam ad legem necessitatis. Alioqui si ad episcopi tantum

| WORK | CALVIN | CHEMNITZ | BELLARMINE |

imprecationem Spiritus sanctus defluit, legendi sunt qui in villulis, aut in castellis, aut in remotionibus locis per presbyteros et diaconos baptizati ante dormierunt, quam ab episcopis inviserentur. . . . Ut enim accipit quis, ita et dare potest; nisi forte eunuchus a Philippo diacono baptizatus, sine Spiritu sancto fuisse credendus est. . . ."
PL 23:173.

L-58: Jerome
De viris illustribus, 112

24:293

"Cyrillus Hierosolymae episcopus, saepe pulsus Ecclesia, et receptus, ad extremum sub Theodosio principe octo annis inconcussum episcopatum tenuit. Exstant ejus *katêchêseis*, quas in adolescentia composuit."
PL 23:705-706.

L-59: **Liber de ecclesiasticis dogmatibus**

7:221

(See Gennadius, L-48.)

L-60: **Martin of Braga (515-580)**
Capitula ex synodis 52

12:230

"Presbyter, praesente episcopo, non signet infantes, nisi forte ab episcopo fuerit illi praeceptum."
Ed. Claude W. Barlow. PMAAR 12 (1950):137.

L-61: **Optatus (fl. 365)**
Contra Parmenianum 2,19

1:212 6:219
8:225

"Et quod uobis leue uidetur, facinus inmane commissum est, ut omnia sacrosancta supra memorati uestri episcopi uiolarent. iusserunt eucharistiam canibus fundi, non sine signo diuini iudicii. . . . ampullam quoque chrismatis per fenestram, ut frangerent, iactauerunt, et cum casum adiuuaret abiectio, non defuit manus angelica, quae ampullam spiritali subuectione deduceret."
Ed. Carolus Ziwsa. CSEL 26 (1893):53-54.

WORK	CALVIN	CHEMNITZ	BELLARMINE

L-62: Pacianus (+ c. 392)
De baptismo 6

6:219

"Haec autem compleri alias nequeunt, nisi lavacri et chrismatis et antistitis sacramento. Lavacro enim peccata purgantur; chrismate sanctus Spiritus superfunditur; utraque vero ista, manu et ore antistitis impetramus: atque ita totus homo renascitur et innovatur in Christo."
PL 13 (1845):1093.

L-63: Pacianus
Epistula 1,6

6:219

"Sed poenitere non licuit. . . . Si ergo et lavacri et chrismatis potestas, majorum et longe charismatum ad episcopos inde descendit; et ligandi quoque jus adfuit atque solvendi."
PL 13:1057.

L-64: Pacianus
Epistula 3,3[39]

6:219

"Vestrae plebi unde Spiritum; quam non consignat unctus sacerdos? Unde aquam, quae a matrice dicessit?"
PL 13:1065.

L-65: Prudentius (348-405)
Hymnum ante somnum 125-128

6:219

"Cultor dei, memento
te fontis et lauacri
rorem subisse sanctum,
te chrismate innotatum."
Carmina. Ed. Mauricius P. Cunningham. CChr.SL 126 (1966), p. 33.

WORK   CALVIN   CHEMNITZ   BELLARMINE

L-66: Prudentius
Psychomachia 360-361

                                                    6:218 8:225
". . . post inscripta oleo frontis signacula per quae unguentum regale
datum est et chrisma perenne. . . ."
CChr.SL 126:163.

L-67: Rufinus (345-410)
— 40

                                        24:293

"Cyrillus"

L-68: Tertullian (155-220)
De baptismo⁴¹

                                        24:295   13:233
"Ex ea die qua baptizati sumus lavacro quotidiano per totam
hebdomadem abstinemus."
(as cited by Chemnitz)

L-69: Tertullian
De baptismo 7-8⁴²

                            9:288 24:292   1:212 1:213
                            24:293 24:294   6:218 8:224
                                    24:296   9:225 9:226
                                               9:226 9:227
"Exinde egressi de lauacro perungimur benedicta unctione de pristina
disciplina qua ungui oleo de cornu in sacerdotium solebant ex quo Aaron
a Moyse unctus est. . . . Sic et in nobis carnaliter currit unctio sed

---

    ³⁹ Bellarmine says letter 2; the text is in letter 3 of this edition.

    ⁴⁰ I was unable to locate the passage Chemnitz wants here, a reference of Rufinus to
Cyril.

    ⁴¹ Both Chemnitz and Bellarmine refer to the practice of abstaining from the daily
bath for a week after baptism, but I have not found the text in Tertullian.

    ⁴² Bellarmine may have this text in mind when at 1:212 he says Tertullian often
refers to chrism, although the text uses a more generic term, oil.

WORK CALVIN CHEMNITZ BELLARMINE

spiritaliter proficit, quomodo et ipsius baptismi carnalis actus quod in aqua mergimur, spiritalis effectus quod delictis liberamur.
"Dehinc manus inponitur per benedictionem aduocans et inuitans spiritum sanctum. . . . <Quemadmodum> enim post aquas diluuii quibus iniquitas antiqua purgata est, post baptismum ut ita dixerim mundi, pacem caelestis irae praeco columba terris adnuntiauit dimissa ex arca et cum olea reuersa. . . ."
Ed. Carolus Halm. CSEL 1 (1866):282-283.

L-70: Tertullian
Contra Marcionem 1:14,3

1:212 6:218
9:226

"Sed ille quidem usque nunc nec aquam reprobauit creatoris, qua suos abluit, nec oleum, quo suos ungit, nec mellis et lactis societatem, qua suos infantat, nec panem, quo ipsum corpus suum repraesentat, etiam in sacramentis propriis egens mendicitatibus creatoris."
CSEL 1:455.

L-71: Tertullian
De praescriptione haereticorum 30,1[43]

1:213

"Vbi tunc Marcion, Ponticus nauclerus, Stoicae studiosus?"
CSEL 1:210.

L-72: Tertullian
De praescriptione haereticorum 36,4-5

6:218

". . . uideamus quid didicerit, quid docuerit: . . . eam aqua signat, sancto spiritu uestit, eucharistia pascit, martyrium exhorbatur et ita aduersus hanc institutionem neminem recipit."
CSEL 1:217.

---

[43] As in fn. 17 above, Bellarmine confuses the Montanists with the Marcionists.

WORK	CALVIN	CHEMNITZ	BELLARMINE

L-73: Tertullian
De praescriptione haereticorum 40,4

8:225 9:226

". . . et, si adhuc memini Mithrae, signat illic in frontibus milites suos. Celebrat et panis oblationem et imaginem resurrectionis inducit et sub gladio redimit coronam."
CSEL 1:220.

L-74: Tertullian
De resurrectione carnis 8,3

6:218 9:226

"Sed et caro abluitur, ut anima emaculetur; caro unguitur, ut anima consecretur; caro signatur, ut et anima muniatur; caro manus inpositione adumbratur, ut et anima spiritu inluminetur; caro corpore et sanguine Christi uescitur, ut et anima de deo saginetur. Non possunt ergo separari in mercede quas opera coniungit."
Ed. Carolus Halm. CSEL 2 (1867):931.

6. MEDIEVAL SOURCES

WORK   CALVIN   CHEMNITZ   BELLARMINE

M-1: Alcuin (735-804)
De divinis officiis 16-17

                                            8:225 13:233

"Hodie chrisma conficitur vel consecratur. Unde Christus, id est, unctus, a chrismate appellatur."
PL 101 (1863):1205.

M-2: Alcuin
De divinis officiis 19

                                10:228 10:228

"Et postquam induti fuerint, dat pontifex super eos orationem, imposita scilicet manu super capita eorum, cum invocatione septiformis gratiae Spiritus sancti. Oratio: 'Omnipotens sempiterne Deus, qui regenerare.' Hac finita, facit crucem de chrismate cum pollice in singulorum frontibus, ita dicendo: 'In nomine Patris, et Filii, et Spiritus sancti, pax tibi.'"
PL 101:1220.

M-3: Alexander of Hales (c. 1186-1245)
Glossa in quatuor libros Sententiarum 4:7,6

                          26:298

"Unde convenit ut minister ad hanc gratiam a Domino tribuendam sit superior in Ecclesia eo per quem datur prima. Cum ergo ad sacerdotes pertineat dare sacramenta Poenitentiae et Baptismi, quae sunt apud debiles, convenit summis sacerdotibus dare sacramentum Confirmationis et Ordinis."
Ed. PP. Collegium S. Bonaventurae. *Bibliotheca Franciscana Scholastica Medii Aevi* 15. Quaracchi, Florence: Typographia Colegii S. Bonaventurae, 1957. P. 131.

M-4: Alexander of Hales
Glossa in quatuor libros Sententiarum 4:24,1

                          8:287

"Praeterea, dicitur quod forma illa verborum quae est in Confirmatione,

WORK	CALVIN	CHEMNITZ	BELLARMINE

eo quod non est expressa a Domino vel ab Apostolis, non est de substantia sacramenti Confirmationis, sed tantum inunctio chrismatis in fronte; multo fortius ergo forma horum verborum non erit de substantia sacramenti Ordinis."
Collegium S. Bonaventurae. 15:421.

M-5: Amalarius (c. 780-850)
Liber officialis 1:12, 26.28

8:225 13:233
13:233

"Quando a populis offertur, simplex liquor est; per benedictionem sacerdotum transfertur in sacramentum. Haec administratio significat debere adesse terrenam administrationem spirituali. . . . Libet primo dicere de hoc quod dicit: 'Halat ter in ampullam'. Halitus ab interioribus et secretis procedit ad publicum, et vocatur spiritus."
Ed. Johannes Hanssens, StT 139 (1948):75-76.

M-6: Amalarius
Liber officialis 1:27,3.5

6:219 10:228
10:228 11:230

"Unde unus eorum, doctor egregius, Beda dicit in tractatu super Actus apostolorum: 'Nam presbyteris, sive extra episcopum, seu praesente episcopo, cum baptizant, chrismate baptizatos ungere licet, sed quod ab episcopo fuerit consecratum; non tamen frontem ex eodem oleo signare, quod solis debetur episcopis, cum tradunt Spiritum paraclitum baptizatis'. . . . Episcopus vero transilit verba: 'Ipse te linit chrismate salutis,' quasi ditior, non solum ut salvare possit, sed etiam ditare. . . ."
StT 139:139.

M-7: Pseudo-Anselm
In epistolam II ad Corinthios 1

8:222

(See Herveus, M-52.)

WORK	CALVIN	CHEMNITZ	BELLARMINE

M-8: Armachanus, Richard

	26:298	12:230	12:230
			12:231

(See Richard Armachanus, M-76.)

M-9: Arnaldus of Bonnevaux (Pseudo-Cyprian) (+ c. 1156)
De ablutione pedum[44]

	9:288	9:227	11:230

"Nam baptismum repeti ecclesiasticae prohibent regulae; et semel sanctificatis nulla deinceps manus iterum consecrans praesumit accedere. Nemo sacros ordines semel datos iterum renovat, nemo sacro oleo lita iterum linit aut consecrat, nemo impositioni manuum vel ministerio derogat sacerdotum, quia contemelia esset Spiritus sancti, si evacuari posset quod ille sanctificatio emendaret, quod ille semel statuit et confirmat. Ipse summus sacerdos sui est sacramenti institutor et auctor. . . ."
PL 189 (1854):1650.

M-10: Arnaldus of Bonnevaux
De unctione chrismatis et aliis sacramentis

	3:285 9:288		6:218 7:221
	24:292		8:223 8:223
			8:225 9:227

"Hodie in Ecclesia cum caeteris untionibus ad populum acquisitionis sanctificandum, in participationem dignitatis et nominis, sacrum chrisma conficitur, in quo mistum oleo balsamum, regiae et sacerdotalis gloriae exprimit unitatem, quibus dignitatibus initiandis divinitus est unctio instituta. . . . totus templi decor ad Assyrios est translatus. Neque enim decebat ut Christiana religio ornamentis visibilibus occupata, in manufactis delectaretur, sed ipsa tabernaculi consumptio et templi ruina, et sancta in rapinam exposita, excellentioris gloriae intimarent stabilitatem, et manentia in perpetuum sacramenta cultores suos ad intuitum invisibilium informarent. . . . Non haec medendis corporibus est unctio instituta, quia sanctificatis elementis jam non propria natura

---

[44] Bellarmine is not alone in attributing this work to Cyprian. Maldonatus does too, according to Joseph Huby, "Une Exégèse faussement attribuée à Saint Cyprien," Biblica 14 (1933):96. But Arnaldus is its author.

WORK	CALVIN	CHEMNITZ	BELLARMINE

praebet effectum, sed virtus divina potentius operatur, sed adest veritas signo, et spiritus sacramento. . . . Ex hujus unctionis beneficio et sapientia nobis et intellectus divinitus datur, consilium et fortitudo coelitus illabatur, scientia et pietas, et timor inspirationibus supernis infunditur. Hoc oleo uncti cum spiritalibus nequitiis colluctamur. . . ."
PL 189:1653-1655.

M-11: Bede (c. 673-735)
Expositio Actuum Apostolorum 8,14

8:225

"Notandum autem quod Philippus qui Samariae euangelizabat unus de septem fuerit; si enim apostolus esset, ipse utique manum imponere potuisset ut acciperent spiritum sanctum. 'Hoc enim solis pontificibus debetur.' <Innocentius ad Decentium>."
Ed. M. L. W. Laistner. CChr.SL 121 (1983):39.

M-12: Bede
In Lucae Evangelium expositio 6:22,39

6:219

"Et pulchre sui corporis et sanguinis mysteriis imbutos in montem oliuarum discipulos educit ut omnes in morte sua baptizatos altissimo sancti spiritus chrismate confirmandos esse designet qui dicere possint cum psalmista: 'Signatum est super nos lumen uultus tui domine."
Ed. D. Hurst. CChr.SL 120 (1960):385.

M-13: Bede
Super Mattheum 16

21:291

"Nec sufficere ad salutem nobis arbitremur, si turbis negligentium uel quorumlibet indoctorum fide uel actibus adequemur, quibus sacris litteris unica est credendi pariter et uiuendi regula prescripta."
CIC 1:597. (Gratian, c. 24, C. 8, q.1)

WORK   CALVIN   CHEMNITZ   BELLARMINE

M-14: Bede (Gregory)
Super Cantica Canticorum[45]

                                        3:216 7:222
                                        8:223 8:224
                                        8:225 9:228

"In Engaddi balsamum gignitur, quod cum oleo, pontificali benedictione chrisma efficitur, quo dona sancti Spiritus exprimuntur."
Ed. Monks of the Order of St. Benedict from the St. Maur Congregation. PL 79 (1862):493n.

M-15: Bernard (1090-1153)
Vita sancti Malachiae 4,8

                                               6:219

"Puerum mente captum ex his, quos lunaticos vocant, inter confirmandum sacra unctione sanavit. Hoc ita notum certumque fuit, ut illum mox constituerit ostiarium domus suae, vixeritque idem puer incolumis in eo officii usque ad virilem aetatem."
Ed. J. LeClercq and H. M. Rochais. Rome: Editiones Cistercienses, 1963. 3:317.

M-16: Bonaventure (c. 1217-1274)
Sententiae 4:7,2

                              8:287

"Institutum est igitur hoc elementum, Spiritu Sancto dictante, ab ipsis Ecclesiae rectoribus; et quia Christus non instituerat nec vim ei dederat, secundum quod ipse contactu mundissimae carnis dederat aquis, et ut ipse, conficiendo corpus suum, instituit elementum sive materiam Eucharistiae, ut panem vel vinum: ideo episcopi non valentes se ipsis materias consecrare, consecrari per benedictionem instituerunt. Et ideo materia huius sacramenti debet esse consecrata."
Ed. Collegium S. Bonaventurae. Editio minor. Quaracchi-Florence: Ad Claras Aquas, 1949. 4:154.

---

[45] Although Bellarmine assigns this text to Gregory, it appears with him in only some manuscripts, and seems to be taken from the following passage of Bede:
"Qui bene etiam in uineis Engaddi esse memoratur; namque in uineis Engaddi ut praefati sumus balsamum gignitur quod in chrismae confectione liquori oliuae admisceri ac pontificali benedictione solet consecrari quatenus fideles omnes cum impositione

WORK	CALVIN	CHEMNITZ	BELLARMINE

M-17: Bonaventure
Sententiae 4:7,3

                                                                    12:230

"Dicendum quod illud sacramentum nec potest nec debet per alios
dispensari, et si alii praesumunt, nihil faciunt."
Collegium S. Bonaventurae. 4:155.

M-18: Compendium Theologiae

                                   3:286

(See Ripelin, Hugues, M-77.)

M-19: Pseudo-Cyprian
De ablutione pedum

                                   9:288   9:227 11:230

(See Arnaldus of Bonnevaux, M-9.)

M-20: Pseudo-Cyprian
De unctione chrismatis et aliis sacramentis

                         3:285   9:288   6:218 7:221
                                 24:292   8:223 8:223
                                                       8:225

(See Arnaldus of Bonnevaux, M-10)

M-21: Decretum Compendiense (757)
Concilium apud Vermeriam

                                                                    13:233

"Si quis filiastrum uel filiastram suam ante episcopum tenuerit ad
confirmationem, separetur ab uxore sua, et aliam numquam accipiat.
Similiter et mulier."
CIC 1:1096. (Gratian, c. 2, C. 30, q. 1)

---

manus sacerdotalis qua spiritus sanctus accipitur hac unctione signentur qua etiam altare
dominicum cum dedicatur et cetera quae sacrosancta esse debent perunguuntur." Ed. D.
Hurst, *In Cantica Canticorum*, CChr.SL 119B (1983):206.

WORK	CALVIN	CHEMNITZ	BELLARMINE

M-22: Durandus Saint-Pourcain (c. 1275-1334)
In Petri Lombardi Sententias theologicas commentarium libri IIII
4:7,4,9

12:230

"Ad sciendum autem ueritatis contineat praedicta opinio, advertendum est, quòd supposito quòd confirmatio sit uerum sacramentum à Christo institutum, & minister eius sit omnis sacerdos quantum ` est ex institutione Christi, licet ex prohibitione ecclesiae reseruata sit eius collatio solum episcopis, tunc facilè est dicere, quod ex commissione Papae simplex sacerdos possit confirmare, quia prohibitio ecclesiae solum facit, quod non liceat simplici sacerdoti confirmare, cui tamen liceret si non esset prohibitio ecclesiae."
Venice: Guerraea, 1571. Republ. Ridgewood, NJ: The Gregg Press Incorporated, 1964. 2:308.

M-23: Duranti, William (c. 1230-1296)
De confirmatione

3:286 12:289
24:293 24:295

"Sane aliquo crismato in fronte, caput illius alba vitta linea circumligetur, ne recens unctio defluat aut deleatur; que septem diebus portari deberet, propter septem Spirituo Sancti dona, qui in hoc recipitur sacramento, sed quoniam periculosum esset tanto tempore crisma in fronte portari, dispensative permittimus ut sacerdotes tertia die vittas solvant et super fontes eas comburant et frontes lavent, vel ex ipsis vittis candele fiant et ad altare offerantur. Posset tamen ex vitta una caput circumligari alterius confirmandi."
Instructions et constitutions de Guillaume Durand le spéculateur d'après le manuscrit de Cessenon. Ed. Jos. Berthelé, M. Valmary. Archives du Départment de l'Hérault: Documents et Inventaires complémentaires. Montpellier: Imprimerie Delord-Boehm et Martial, 1900. P. 16.

M-24: Duranti, William
De crismandis in fronte pueris 1:1,2-4

| | 5:1069 | 2:285 3:285 | 2:216 10:228 |
| | 7:1071 | 10:288 13:289 | 13:233 |

2. "Et tunc, elevatis et super confirmandos extensis manibus, dicit:

WORK	CALVIN	CHEMNITZ	BELLARMINE

'Omnipotens sempiterne Deus qui regenerare dignatus es hos famulos et famulas tuas ex aqua et spiritu sancto, quique dedisti eis remissionem omnium peccatorum, emitte in eos septiformem spiritum sanctum tuum paraclitum de caelis, spiritum sapientiae et intellectus, spiritum consilii et fortitudinis, spiritum scientiae et pietatis, adimple eos spiritu timoris tui et consigna eos signo crucis Christi in vitam propitiatus aeternam. Per.' Resp.: 'Amen.'

3. "Tunc sedens super faldistorium coram altari vel alibi paratum, inquisito sigillatim nomine cuiuslibet consignandi sibi per patrinum vel matrinam flexis genibus presentati, et summitate pollicis dextre manus crismate intincta, pontifex facit crucem in fronte illius dicens: 'Iohannes,' vel 'Maria,' vel quovis alio nomine, 'Signo te signo crucis et confirmo te crismate salutis. In nomine + patris et + filii et spiritus + sancti, ut replearis eodem spiritu sancto et habeas vitam eternam.' Resp.: 'Amen.' Et dicendo: 'In nomine patris et filii et spiritus sancti,' producit signum crucis ante faciem illius.

4. "Et deinde dat sibi leviter alapam super genam, dicens: 'Pax tecum.'"
Le Pontifical Romain au Moyen-Age.

Ed. Michel Andrieu. StT 88   (1940):333-334.

"Ordo L," *Le Pontifical Romano-Germanique du Dixième Siècle* 2.   StT 227 (1963):109.

M-25: **Duranti, William**
Ordo in quinta feria cene domini 3:2,75-82. 84

4:286 12:289
15:290 18:290

"75. Alia benedictio quam quidam dicunt. 'Creaturam omnium, domine, procreator, qui per Moysen famulum tuum, permixtis herbis aromatum, fieri precepisti sanctificationem unguenti, clementiam tuam suppliciter deposcimus, ut huic unguento, quod radix produxit stirpea, spiritualem gratiam largiendo, plenitudinem sanctificationis infundas. Sit nobis, domine, fidei hilaritate conditum; sit sacerdotalis unguenti crisma perpetuum; sit ad celeste vexillum impressione dignissimum, ut quicumque, baptismate sacro renati, isto fuerint liquore peruncti, corporum atque animarum bene + dictionem plenissimam consequantur et illi beate fidei collato munere perhenniter amplientur. Per.' Resp.: 'Amen.'

WORK   CALVIN   CHEMNITZ   BELLARMINE

"76. Deinde misceat et conficiat super patenam vel in aliquo parvo vasculo balsamum cum modico olei de ampulla sumpti, dicens in ipsa commixtione:

"77. 'Oremus Deum nostrum omnipotentem, qui incomprehensibilem filii sui sibique coeterni divinitatem mirabili dispositione vere humanitati inseparabiliter coniunxit et, cooperante gratia spiritus sancti, oleo exultationis pre participibus suis linivit, ut homo, fraude diaboli perditus, gemina et singulari constans materia, perhenni redderetur de qua exciderat hereditati, quatenus hos ex diversis creaturarum speciebus liquores creatos sancte trinitatis perfectione bene + dicat et benedicendo sancti + ficet, concedatque ut simul permixti unum fiant et, quicumque exterius inde perunctus fuerit, ita interius liniatur, quod omnibus sordibus corporalis materie carens, se participem regni celestis effici gratuletur. Per eumdem. In unitate.' Resp.: 'Amen.'

"78. Nunc, que prius in parvo vasculo mixta fuerant, commisceantur cum oleo, quod est in ampulla, ad crisma parato, dicente pontifice: 'Hec commixtio liquorum fiat omnibus ex ea perunctis propiciatio et custodia salutaris in secula seculorum. Amen.'

"79. Deinde, priusquam crisma benedicatur, pontifex alet plane ter in modum crucis super os ipsius ampulle involute. Et similiter alent omnes sacerdotes successive, quibus per ordinem per archidiaconum ipsa deferatur ampulla.

"80. Quo facto, ampulla ipsa super mensam reposita, pontifex stans, lenta voce, quasi lectionem legens, incipit absolute hunc exorcismum crismalem: Exorcismus olei crismalis. 'Exorcizo te, creatura olei, per Deum patrem omnipotentem, qui fecit celum et terram. . . Iesu Christi filii eius domini nostri. Qui cum eo vivit et regnat Deus in unitate spiritus sancti.'

"81. Deinde dicit, media voce, iunctis manibus ante pectus: 'Per omnia secula seculorum. . . ' Prephatio. 'Vere dignum. . . . Te igitur precamur, domine, sancte pater, omnipotens, aeterne Deus, per eundem Iesum Christum filium tuum dominum nostrum ut huius creaturae pinguedinem sancti + ficare tua benedictione digneris et sancti spiritus ei admiscere virtutem, cooperante potentia Christi tui, a cuius sancto nomine chrisma nomen accepit, unde unxisti sacerdotes reges, prophetas et martires, ut spiritalis lavachri baptismo renovandis creaturam chrismatis in sacramentum perfectae salutis vitaeque confirmes, ut sanctificatione

WORK   CALVIN   CHEMNITZ   BELLARMINE

unctionis infusa corruptione primae nativitatis absorta, secundum uniuscuiusque templum acceptabilis vitae innocens odore redolescat, ut secundum constitutionis tuae sacramentum regio et sacerdotali propheticoque honore perfusi, vestimento incorrupti muneris induantur, ut sit his qui renati fuerint ex aqua et spiritu sancto chrisma salutis eosque aeternae vitae participes et caelestis gloriae facias esse consortes. Per eundem dominum. . . . Amen.

"82.Prephatione finita, pontifex salutat ter crisma nudum sive ampullam absque velamine, dicens ter, semper inclinando illi: 'Ave sanctum crisma.' Et ultimo deosculetur ampullam. Similiter et duodecim sacerdotes, qui iuxta eum sunt, faciunt successive, ad quos per ordinem per archidiaconum deferatur ampulla, velata tamen ut a nemine eorum videatur. Quo peracto, ampulla in uno mense latere collocetur. . . .

"84. Exorcismus olei catechumenorum[46], qui dicitur lenta voce quasi legendo: 'Exorcizo te, creatura olei, in nomine Dei patris omnipotentis et in nomine Iesu Christi et spiritus sancti, ut in hac invocatione trinae potestatis atque unius virtute deitatis. . . ut fiat haec unctio divinis sacramentis purificata in adoptionem carnis et spiritus eis qui ex eo ungui debent in remissionem omnium peccatorum, ut efficiantur eorum corpora ad omnem gratiam spiritalem accipiendam sanctificata. . . ."

StT 88:577-579.

StT 227:74-75.

M-26: Duranti, William
Ordo in sabbato sancti 3:4,18

20:291

". . . pontifex baptizet illos hoc modo. Primo enim interrogat offerentem: 'Quis vocaris?' Et prosequitur formam solitam baptizandi. "Ut autem surrexerint a fonte, illi qui eos suscipiunt, levantes ipsos infantes in manibus suis, offerunt eos uni presbitero. Ipse vero presbiter facit de chrismate crucem cum pollice in vertice eorum ita dicendo: 'Deus omnipotens, pater domini nostri Iesu Christi, qui te regeneravit ex aqua et spiritu sancto, quique dedit tibi remissionem omnium peccatorum, ipse te linit chrismate salutis in Christo Iesu domino nostro in vitam aeternam.' Resp. 'Amen.'"

StT 88:591.

StT 227:106-107.

---

[46] Chemnitz applies this text to his comments on chrism, but it is part of the rite for blessing the oil of catechumens.

| WORK | CALVIN | CHEMNITZ | BELLARMINE |

M-27: Gabriel Biel (c. 1420-1495)
4:7,1 "De confirmationis sacramento"

8:288

"Dubitatur secundo: cur unctio chrismatis in capite facta a ` sacerdote post baptismum non est sacramentum: sicut illa, quae sit in fronte ab episcopo: non enim annumeratur illa in uertice inter ecclesiae sacramenta. Respondetur, quod aliae unctiones in pectore, inter scapulas oleo catechuminorum, & in uertice chrismate non sunt sacramenta proprie: sed sacramentalia: quia non ` sunt a christo instituta tanquam gratiae efficacia signa: sed ab ecclesia ad disponendum ad gratiam baptismatis suscipiendam, uel significandam: & non principaliter ad conferendum gratiam: sic enim ecclesia instituere non potuit."
Commentarius in qvartvm librvm sententiarvm. Brescia: Thomas Bozola, 1574. P. 162.

M-28: Gabriel Biel
4:7,1 "De confirmationis sacramento"

13:290   10:229

"Dicitur certa uerba proferentis: ubi tangitur forma huius sacramenti, quae est. Signo te signo crucis. Confirmo te chrismate salutis, in nomine patris, & filij, & spiritussancti, amen. . . . Verum quidam loco uerbi signo, dicunt consigno, (ut Pet. de pal. & alij) & loco dictionis salutis, dicunt sanctificationis. Et non refert: quia illa uerba eundem sensum habent."
Bozola:157.

M-29: Gerson, Jean (1363-1429)
_ 47

3:286

"Quid prodest, si per Baptismum a lapsu erigeris, nisi etiam per confirmationem ad standum confirmeris?"
(as cited by Chemnitz)

---

47 I do not find this reference to Hugo in Gerson's work.

WORK	CALVIN	CHEMNITZ	BELLARMINE

M-30: Gerson, Jean
De sacramento confirmationis

	13:290	24:293	10:229

"Forma est talis signo te signo crucis, confirmo te chrismate salutis. In nomine Patris, & Filii, & Spiritussancti."
Summa theologica et canonica in sex libros digesta. Venice: Dominicus Nicolinus, 1587. Fol. 127.

M-31: Gratian (12th c.)
Decreti prima pars c. 1, C. 1, q. 95, "Peruenit"

	10:1073		26:298	12:230	12:232
					12:232

(See Gregory, Epistula 26, liber 4, P-17.)

M-32: Gratian
Decreti secunda pars c. 53, C. 1, q. 1

		24:296	

"Alii formam ecclesiae in baptizando seruant. Sed dum ab eis baptizantur, qui in heresi uel scismate eis communicant, sacramentum quidem baptismi ab eis accipiunt, uirtutem uero non consecuntur, quam sine fide nullus consequi potest. Unde de Domino dicitur, quod in patria sua non poterat facere signum propter incredulitatem eorum."
CIC 1:379.

M-33: Gratian (Athanasius)
c. 58, C. 1, q. 1

		24:296	

"Ecce quando ab hereticis baptisma cum sua uirtute accipitur, cuius tam necessaria amministracio est, ut nec etiam a paganis datum possit reiterari. . . . Illi rei ordinem pandunt, baptizatos a se esse quosdam cathecuminos confitentur per Athanasium puerum, qui illis fuerat episcopus simulatus. . . . (Statuit) iterari baptismum non debere, sed adinpleri ea, que sacerdotibus est mos."
CIC 1:380.

WORK	CALVIN	CHEMNITZ	BELLARMINE

M-34: Gratian
c. 73, C. 1, q. 1 gloss

| | | 24:297 | 7:221 |

"Ex eo autem, quod manus inpositio iterari precipitur, sacramentum non esse ostenditur."
CIC 1:384.

M-35: Gratian
c. 24, C. 8, q. 1 "Nec sufficere"

| | | 21:291 | |

(See Bede, Super Mattheum 16, M-13.)

M-36: Gratian
c. 2, C. 30, q. 1, "Si quis filiastrum"

| | | | 13:233 |

(See Decretum Compendiense, M-21.)

M-37: Gratian
c. 6, C. 30, q. 1, "De his, qui"

| | | | 13:233 |

(See Nicholas, Rudolfo, P-36.)

M-38: Gratian
c. 3, C. 30, q. 4, "Si quis unus"

| | | | 13:233 |

(See Innocent I, Exsuperio Tolosano Episcopo, P-25.)

M-39: Gratian
c. 44, D. 4, de cons., "Ab antiqua"

| | | 24:295 | 7:220 7:220 |

(See Gregory, Epistula 67, liber 11, P-18.)

M-40: Gratian
c. 100, D. 4, de cons., "In catecumino"

| | | | 13:233 |

(See Eugene, P-12.)

WORK	CALVIN	CHEMNITZ	BELLARMINE
M-41: Gratian De cons. 4,120, "Presbiteri" (See Gregory, Epistula 9, liber 4, P-16.)			3:216 12:230
M-42: Gratian c. 154, D. 4, de cons., "Placuit ut" 8:1071 (See Milevis, Canon 3, C-16.)	8:1071		
M-43: Gratian c. 1, D. 5, de cons., "Omnes fideles" 9:1072 (See Pseudo-Isidore, Urban, M-61.)	9:1072	3:285	3:216 7:221
M-44: Gratian c. 2, D. 5, de cons., "Spiritus sanctus" 5:1069 8:1071 8:1072 1:501A (See Pseudo-Isidore, Miltiades, M-59.)	5:1069 8:1071 8:1072 1:501A	3:285	1:212 7:221
M-45: Gratian c. 3, D. 5, de cons., "De his uero" 10:1073 (See Pseudo-Isidore, Miltiades, M-60.)	10:1073	3:285	3:216 7:220
M-46: Gratian c. 4, D. 5, de cons., "Manus quoque" (See Pseudo-Isidore, Eusebius, M-57.)			3:216 7:220 7:221

WORK	CALVIN	CHEMNITZ	BELLARMINE

M-47: Gratian
c. 5, D. 5, de cons., "Nouissime"

	11:1074	3:286	6:219 8:225
			11:230

(See Rabanus Maurus, De clericorum institutione 1,30, M-74.)

M-48: Gratian
c. 6, D. 5, de cons., "Ut ieiuni"

	9:1072	3:286 24:295	4:217 13:233
	1:501A	25:297	

(See Pseudo-Council of Orleans, M-68.)

M-49: Gratian
c. 7, D. 5, de cons., "Ut episcopi"

		8:287	4:217 13:233

(See Meaux, Canon 6, C-15.)

M-50: Gratian
c. 8, D. 5, de cons., "Dictum est"

			7:220 11:230

(See Terracina, Canon 6, C-24.)

M-51: Gratian
c. 9, D. 5, de cons., "De homine"

			7:220 11:230

(See Gregory II, Epistula 4 ad Bonifatium, P-21.)

M-52: Herveus (Pseudo-Anselm) (+ c. 1150)
In epistolam II ad Corinthios 1

			8:222

"Unxit nos in reges et sacerdotes, quia reges et sacerdotes ungebantur dum constituerentur, 'et qui signavit nos,' id est discrevit nos ab infidelibus signo crucis, quod nostris frontibus imposuit, 'et dedit in cordibus nostris pignus spiritus,' quando per impositionem manuum accepimus Spiritum sanctum in pignus futurae beatitudinis."
PL 181 (1854):1011.

WORK   CALVIN   CHEMNITZ   BELLARMINE

M-53: Hugh of St. Victor (+ 1142)
De sacramentis 2:7,2

                                                    2:216 6:219
                                                           9:226

"Manus impositio quae usitato nomine confirmatio vocatur, qua
Christianus unctione chrismatis per impositionem manus in fronte
signatur; solis episcopis apostolorum vicariis debetur, ut Christianum
consignent, et spiritum Paracletum tradant; sicut in primitiva Ecclesia
Spiritum sanctum per impositionem manuum dandi soli apostoli
potestatem habuisse leguntur."
Ed. Canons Regular of the Royal Abbey of St. Victor in Paris. PL 176
(1854):459-460.

M-54: Hugh of St. Victor
De sacramentis 2:7,6

                                                           13:233

"Solent quidam quaerere quando tempore debeant unctionem chrismatis
observare in capite ut scilicet capita non lavent qui accipiunt manus
impositionem, absque tempore baptisterii. Quibus responderi potest
conveniens esse, ut tanto tempore adventus Spiritus sancti apud
unumquemque qui eum accepit celebretur, quanto tempore generaliter ab
Ecclesia celebratur adventus Spiritus sancti super apostolos, hoc est
septem diebus. Et merito; quia septem sunt dona Spiritus sancti; et in
septem comitibus ad hospitem suum Spiritus sanctus venit."
PL 176:462.

M-55: Pseudo-Isidore (847-852)[48]
Clement, Epistula 4: cap. 79-80

                                     3:285 9:288   9:226

"Omnibus ergo festinandum est sine mora renasci deo et demum
consignari ab episcopo, id est septiformem gratiam spiritus sancti

---

[48]   Although many had expressed doubts about the False Decretals even before the
time of Bellarmine, he persists in ascribing these works to the Popes in question. It is
surprising that Cicognani lists Bellarmine among those who held doubts about the
Decretals since he uses them to support his argument throughout this controversy. See
Amleto Giovanni Cicognani, *Canon Law*,   Second, Revised Edition (Philadelphia: The
Dolphin Press, 1935), p. 242.

WORK	CALVIN	CHEMNITZ	BELLARMINE

percipere, quia incertus est uniuscuiusque exitus vitae. Cum autem regeneratus fuerit per aquam et postmodum septiformis spiritus gratia ab episcopo, ut memoratum est, confirmatus, quia aliter perfectus esse christianus nequaquam poterit, nec sedem habere inter perfectos si non necessitate, sed incuria aut voluntate remanserit, ut a beato Petro apostolo accepimus ut caeteri sancti apostoli praecipiente domino ducuerunt, et demum ex operibus bonis ostendat in se similitudinem eius, qui eum genuit patris. Post haec vero agnoscat deum honorare. . . ."
Decretales Pseudo-Isidorianae et capitula Angilramni. Ed. Paulus Hinschius. Leipzig: Bernhard Tauchnitz, 1863. Pp. 63-64.

M-56: Pseudo-Isidore
Damasus, De vana superstitione corepiscoporum vitanda. XIX. (Epistula 4)[49]

3:216   8:224
8:225   9:226
9:226 12:231

"Quod vero eis non liceat sacerdotes consecrare nec diaconos nec subdiaconos nec virgines, nec altare erigere, nec unguere aut sacrare, nec ecclesias dedicare, nec crisma conficere, nec chrismate baptizatorum frontes signare, nec publice quidem in missa quemquam in penitentiam reconciliare, nec formatas epistolas mittere, nec populum benedicere, nec ante episcopum in baptisterio aut in sacrario introire, nec presente episcopo infantem tinguere aut signare, nec penitentem sine praeceptione episcopi sui reconciliare. . . . Quod autem solis apostolis eorumque successoribus proprii sit officii tradere spiritum sanctum, liber actuum apostolorum docet: praesertim cum nullus ex septuaginta discipulis, quorum isti in aecclesia speciem gerunt, legatur donum sancti spiritus per manus inpositionem, ut praedictum est, tradidisse."
Hinschius:513.

---

[49] This is listed as Epistula 3 in PL 13 (1845):431.

WORK	CALVIN	CHEMNITZ	BELLARMINE

M-57: Pseudo-Isidore
Eusebius, Epistula 3

		3:216	7:220
			7:221

"Manus quoque impositionis sacramentum, magna veneratione tenendum est, quod ab aliis perfici non potest, nisi a summis sacerdotibus."
CIC 1:1413-1414 (Gratian, c. 4, D. 5, de cons.).

M-58: Pseudo-Isidore
Fabian, Decreta: Epistola cuius supra ad omnes horientales episcopos (Epistula 2) 9-10

	9:288 9:288	8:223 8:224
		8:224 9:225
		9:227

"In illa die dominus Iesus, postquam coenavit cum discipulis suis et pedes eorum lavit, sicut a sanctis apostolis praedecessores nostri acceperunt nobisque reliquerunt, crisma conficere docuit; ipsa enim lavatio pedum nostrorum significat baptismum, quando sancti crismatis unctione perficitur atque confirmatur. Nam sicut ipsius diei solempnitas per singulos annos est celebranda, ita ipsius sancti chrismatis confectio per singulos annos est agenda et de anno in anno renovanda et fidelibus tradenda...."
Hinschius:160-161.

M-59: Pseudo-Isidore
Miltiades, Epistula ad omnes Hispaniae episcopos 2

	5:1069	3:285	1:212 7:221
	8:1071		
	8:1072		
	1:501A		

"Spiritus sanctus, qui super aquas baptismi salutifero descendit lapsu, in fonte plenitudinem tribuit ad innocentiam, in confirmatione augmentum prestat ad gratiam. Et quia in hoc mundo tota etate uicturis inter inuisibiles hostes et pericula gradiendum est, in baptismo regeneramur ad uitam, post baptismum confirmamur ad pugnam; in baptismo abluimur, post baptismum roboramur. Et quamuis continuo transituris sufficiant regenerationis beneficia, uicturis tamen necessaria

WORK	CALVIN	CHEMNITZ	BELLARMINE

sunt confirmationis auxilia. Regeneratio per se saluat mox in pace beati seculi recipiendos; confirmatio armat et instruit ad agones mundi huius et prelia reseruandos. Qui autem post baptismum cum acquisita innocentia inmaculatus ad mortem peruenit, confirmatur morte, quia iam non potest peccare post mortem."
CIC 1:1413. (Gratian, c. 2, D. 5, de cons.)

M-60: Pseudo-Isidore
Miltiades, Epistula ad omnes Hispaniae episcopos 2

	10:1073	3:285	3:216 7:220

"De his uero, super quibus rogastis uos informari, id est: utrum maius sit sacramentum manus inpositionis episcoporum, aut baptismus? scitote, utrumque magnum esse sacramentum, et, sicut unum maioribus, id est summis pontificibus est accomodatum, quod a minoribus perfici non potest, ita et maiori ueneratione uenerandum et tenendum est. Sed ita coniuncta sunt hec duo sacramenta, ut ab inuicem nisi morte preueniente nullatenus possint segregari, et unum sine altero perfici non potest."
CIC 1:1413. (Gratian, c. 3, D. 5, de cons.)

M-61: Pseudo-Isidore
Urban, Epistola ad omnes christianos 7

	9:1072	3:285	3:216 7:221

"Omnes fideles per manus inpositiones episcoporum Spiritum sanctum post baptismum accipere debent, ut pleni Christiani inueniantur, quia, cum Spiritus sanctus infunditur, cor fidele ad prudentiam et constantiam dilatatur."
CIC 1:1413. (Gratian, c. 1, D. 5, de cons.)

M-62: Marsilius of Inghen (1330-1396)
Questiones super sententiam 4:5,3

			12:230

"Tertia conclusio: quod papa potest committere simplici sacerdoti potestatem confirmandi. sed hoc priuilegio speciali. probatur quia potest ex priuilegio concedere: vt conferat ordines. ergo vt confirmet: concedere potest."
Argentine: Martinus, 1501. Reprint. Frankfurt/Main: Minerva GmbH, 1966. Fo. cccccviii.

WORK	CALVIN	CHEMNITZ	BELLARMINE

M-63: Netter, Thomas (Waldensis) (c. 1377-1430)[50]
De sacramentis 2:113,1. 4

1:211   9:226

"Vult Wicleffus ad nihilum deducere omnes gentes in unctionibus christianis, non in sacramento Confirmationis solum, sed Baptismi, & Ordinis: quia Christus non fuit sic in sua persona chrismatus. . . . Ecce Apostoli ipsi inspirati ad hoc a Deo, vocaverunt hoc sacramentum 'unguenti perfectionem.' Nemo igitur dicat qui vult esse fidelis, quod sacramentum Confirmationis fiebat sine unctione per solam manus impositionem a Christo & Apostolis. Non enim minus manum imponit qui ungendo imponit."

Doctrinale Antiquitatum Fidei Catholicae Ecclesiae. Ed. Bonaventura Blanciotti. Venice: Antonius Bassanesius, 1757. 2:657. 660.

M-64: Netter, Thomas (Waldensis)
De sacramentis 2:114,1

12:230

"Deinceps autem contentionem solvendam puto, quam Wicleffus contra Antistitum potestatem instaurat, quia ipsis solis facultas adjacet confirmandi sacramento tenus fideles. . . . Hinc devotus frater & magister Guillelmus in libro suo contra Trialogum edito, dicit eum hunc errorem, sicut & multos alios, ab Armachano emunxisse Richardo, libro suo xi, de quaestionibus Armenorum, cap. iv. ubi eum sustinere videtur, 'quantum est ad Evangelica,' & 'Apostolica dicta,' inquit. Qualiter autem dicant Romana decreta, non quaerit."

Blanciotti 2:664.

M-65: Nicholas of Clairvaux (fl. 1145-1151) (Pseudo-Peter Damian)[51]
Sermo 1 de dedicatione (69)

8:223   8:225
8:225

---

50 Netter was a Carmelite from Walden in Britain, not a Waldensian on the side on the Reform.

51 The "Introdvctio" of Sancti Petri Damiani Sermones, ed. Ioannis Lucchesi, CChr.SM 57:xii attributes this letter to Nicholas.

WORK	CALVIN	CHEMNITZ	BELLARMINE

"In baptismate Spiritus datur ad veniam, hic ad pugnam; ibi mundamur ab iniquitatibus, hic virtutibus praemunimur. Nonne in superliminari fronte domus nostrae terrestris consecrata manus sacri Chrismatis imprimit unctionem? . . . Sextum est sacramentum dedicationis ecclesiae. . . . Tunc benedicit aquam sale, cinere, vino hyssopoque conspersam, alphabetum ex transverso quadrangula ratione conscribit, altare septies ex eadem aqua respergit, cruces chrismate, altare vero mistura chrismatis, oleique perungit, ad quatuor altaris cornua incensum incendit, altare tersum novis velaminibus operit, aliaque multa, quae sermonis brevitas non permittit inserere."
Ed. Domni Constantini Cajetani. PL 144 (1867):898. 900.

M-66: Nicholas of Cusa (1401-1464)
De concordantia catholica 3,2

24:292

"Etiam antiqua decreta non habent textum nisi usque ad SS Item decreta Romanorum pontificum inclusive, et sic non invenitur in illis libris iste SS de historia Silvestri." Opera omnia.
Ed. Gerhardus Kallen. Hamburg: Felix Meiner, 1959. P. 333.

M-67: Ordo Romanus (10th c.)
Item ordo de sabbato sancto in die. XCIX, 385. 387

7:221   10:228

"385. Pontifex vero veniens ad infantes, tenente archidiacono chrisma involutis scapulis et brachiis ex panno lineo, elevata et imposita manu super capita omnium, dat orationem super eos cum invocatione septiformis gratiae spiritus sancti. . . .
"387.Oratione expleta, interrogantibus diaconibus nomina singulorum, pontifex, tincto pollice in chrismate, faciat crucem in singulorum frontibus ita dicendo: 'Confirmo et consigno te in nomine patris et filii et spiritus sancti.' Resp. 'Amen.'"
StT 227:109.

WORK	CALVIN	CHEMNITZ	BELLARMINE

M-68: Pseudo-Council of Orleans (9th c.?)[52]
Canon 3[53]

	9:1072	3:286 24:295	4:217 13:233
	1:501A	25:297	

"Ut ieiuni ad confirmationem ueniant perfectae etatis, ut moneantur confessionem facere prius, ut mundi donum Spiritus S. ualeant accipere, et quia numquam erit Christianus, nisi in confirmatione episcopali fuerit crismatus."
CIC 1:1414. (Gratian, c. 6, D. 5, de cons.)

M-69: Palud, Pierre La (1277-1342)
Quartus sententiarum 4:7,4

			12:230

"Seconda, conclusio est, quod simplex sacerdos ex commissione pape potest confirmare: et minores ordines conferre: quoniam papa consecratus sit non autem maiores."
Paris: Johannes Petit, 1518. Fo. xxx.

M-70: Pseudo-Peter Damian
Sermo 1 de dedicatione (69)

		8:223 8:225	
		8:225	

(See Nicholas of Clairvaux, M-65.)

---

52 Chapter IV will present the problem of dating this canon.

53 Fred Kramer's translation of 25:297 reads as follows: "And for this resaon a canon of a Council of Orleans requires a ripe age in the confirmand." He explains in a footnote, "A number of councils were held at Orleans. We have been unable to identify either the particular council or the precise canon, and have therefore used the indefinite article (2:213)." Kramer's difficulty would have been lessened by a comparison with other references to the canon in this same chapter of Chemnitz and throughout the controversy; surely, Chemnitz refers to the canon cited by Gratian.

WORK   CALVIN   CHEMNITZ   BELLARMINE

M-71: Peter Lombard (c. 1100-1160)
Liber sententiarum 4:7,1

                                      6:219 9:227
                                            10:229

"Nunc de sacramento confirmationis addendum est, de cuius virtute quaeri solet. Forma enim aperta est, scilicet verba quae dicit episcopus, cum baptizatos in frontibus sacro signat chrismate."
SpicBon 5 (1981):276.

M-72: Peter Lombard
Liber sententiarum 4:7,2. 4

                     10:1073   1:212
                     11:1074

"Quod 'sacramentum ab aliis perfici non potest nisi a summis sacerdotibus; nec tempore Apostolorum ab aliis quam ab ipsis Apostolis legitur peractum; nec ab aliis quam qui locum eorum tenent perfici potest aut debet. Nam si aliter praesumptum fuerit, irritum habeatur et vacuum, nec inter ecclesiastica reputabitur sacramenta.' (Gregorius). Licet autem 'presbyteris baptizatos tangere in pectore,' sed 'non chrismate signare in fronte.'
"(Melchiades) 'Scitote utrumque magnum esse sacramentum, sed unum maiori veneratione tenendum, sicut a maioribus datur.' Ecce maius dicit sacramentum confirmationis. – Forte non ob maiorem virtutem vel utilitatem quam conferat, sed quia a dignioribus datur, et in digniori parte corporis fit, id est in fronte. – Vel forte quia maius virtutum augmentum praestat, licet baptismus ad remissionem plus valeat. Quod videtur innuere Rabanus, dicens in unctione baptismi 'Spiritum Sanctum descendere ad habitationem Deo consecrandam,' in hac vero 'eiusdem septiformem gratiam cum omni plenitudine sanctitatis et virtutis venire in hominem.'
"Hoc sacramentum tantum a ieiunis et ieiunis tradi debet, sicut et baptismus, nisi aliter cogat necessitas."
SpicBon 5:277-279.

WORK	CALVIN	CHEMNITZ	BELLARMINE

M-73: Peter Lombard
Liber sententiarum 4:7,3

6:219

"Virtus vero huius sacramenti est donatio Spiritus Sancti ad robur, qui in baptismo datus est ad remissionem. Unde Rabanus. . . . Item (Urbanus). . . ."
SpicBon 5:278.

M-74: Rabanus Maurus (776 or 784-856)
De clericorum institutione 1,30

11:1074   3:286   6:219 8:225
                                            11:230

"Nouissime a summo sacerdote per manus inpositionem Paraclitus traditur baptizato, ut roboretur per Spiritum sanctum ad predicandum aliis idem donum, quod in baptismate consecutus est per gratiam uitae donatus eternae. Signatur enim baptizatus cum crismate per sacerdotem in capitis summitate; per pontificem uero in fronte, ut in priore unctione significetur super ipsum Spiritus sancti descensio ad habitationem Deo consecrandam: in secunda quoque, ut eiusdem Spiritus sancti septiformis gratia cum omni plenitudine sanctitatis, et scientiae, et uirtutis uenire in hominem declaretur."
CIC 1:1414. (Gratian, c. 5, D. 5, de cons.)

M-75: Rabanus Maurus
De clericorum institutione 2,36 (26)[54]

24:293 24:295   8:225 13:233

"Quo die proinde etiam sanctum chrisma conficitur, quia ante biduum Paschae, Maria caput ac pedes Domini unguento perfudisse perhibetur."

PL 107 (1851):347.

---

[54] The Battezzati edition indicates cap. 26. The actual text is in 36.

WORK	CALVIN	CHEMNITZ	BELLARMINE

M-76: Richard Armachanus (Fitzralph) (1300-1360)
Armenicae 11,4

26:298   12:230 12:230
                    12:231

"non querimus qualia sunt decreta romane ecclesie sed quid potest ex sacra scriptura euangelica et apostolica apparere certe enim sicut legitur actuum 7 quod apostoli imponebant manus hominibus baptizatis ita potes legere .1. ad thy. 4. sic noli negligere gratiam que est in te que data est tibi per prophetam cum impositione manus presbyteri quod videtur ad hoc dictum vt ostendatur iste actus scilicet impositio manus vt detur spiritussanctus ad potestatem presbyteri que una est cum potestate sacerdocij pertinere haec enim nomina apud nos s. presbyter et sacerdos eiusdem sunt sensus vbi nisi velis de tuo sensu contra rationem et preter testimonium scripture sacre exponere solos episcopos nomine presbyteri ibi debere intelligi aut in alijs dictis consimilibus satis ex hoc dicto poterit apparere hunc actum non solum ad apostolos sed etiam ad omnes presbyteros pertinere."
Summa Domini Armacani in questionibus Armenorum. Noviter impressa. Ed. Johannes Sudoris. Paris: Jehan Petit, 1512. Fo. lxxxiii.

M-77: Ripelin, Hugues (13-14th c.)
De confirmatione, 2

3:286

"Animam & corpus armat. Animam quidem per impressionem characteris contra pusillanimitatis vitium: corpus vero per clypeum cru` cis contra insultus daemonum. Contra verecundiam & timorem in confessione nominis Christi audaciam praestat. . . . Pugnantem coronat: quod notatur in vitta, quae circa caput confirmati ligatur."
Hugo Argentinensis. *Compendium totius theologicae veritatis, vii. libris digestum.* Ed. Ioannes de Combis. Lyons: Gulielmus Rouillius, 1579. P. 520.

M-78: Rupert of Deutz (c. 1075-1129)
Liber de divinis officiis 5,17-18

8:225 13:233

"Et si quaeras, cur non ipsa quoque chrismatis consecratio dilata est, ideo scilicet, quod ab hac feria quinta usque in uesperam sabbati qua

WORK   CALVIN   CHEMNITZ   BELLARMINE

hora utendum est chrismate, uacamus a missarum solemniis. Ipsa autem chrisma nonnisi inter missarum solemnia eo loco, quo pacem accipimus, fas est consecrari. . . . 'Huius vero chrismatis olei consecratio,' quae 'dicitur principalis, quia ad eius unctionem principalis tribuitur Spiritus, id est septiformis Paracletus, habet officium per se.'"
Ed. Hrabanvs Haacke. CChr.SM 7 (1967):171-172.

M-79: Theophylactus (c. 1050-1108)
Expositio in epistulo ad Hebraeos 6

11:230

"Ουχ αρα δει αναβαπτιζειν `υμας, αλλα μενειν επι του προτερου βαπτισματος."
Ed. Fr. J. F. Mariua Bern. de Rubeis. PG 125 (1864):252.

M-80: Thomas Aquinas (c. 1225-1274)
Summa theologiae 3:72,2

8:223 9:226

"Respondeo dicendum quod chrisma est conveniens materia huius sacramenti. . . . et ideo oleum competit materiae huius sacramenti. admiscetur autem balsamum propter fragrantiam odoris, quae redundat ad alios."
Ed. Roberto Busa. Stuttgart-Bad Cannstatt: Friedrich Frommann Verlag Günther Holzboog KG, 1980. 2:885.

M-81: Thomas Aquinas
Summa theologiae 3:72,4

8:287   10:228

"ag1: Ad quartum sic proceditur. videtur quod haec non sit conveniens forma huius sacramenti, consigno te signo crucis, confirmo te chrismate salutis, in nomine patris et filii et spiritus sancti, amen. usus enim sacramentorum a christo et ab apostolis derivatur. sed neque christus hanc formam instituit, nec apostoli ea usi leguntur. ergo haec non est conveniens forma huius sacramenti.
"ra1: Ad primum ergo dicendum quod, sicut supra dictum est, per ministerium apostolorum quandoque dabatur effectus huius sacramenti, scilicet plenitudo spiritus sancti, quibusdam visibilibus signis miraculose a deo confectis, qui potest effectum sacramenti sine

WORK   CALVIN   CHEMNITZ   BELLARMINE

sacramento conferre, et tunc non erat necessaria nec materia nec forma huius sacramenti. quandoque autem tanquam ministri sacramentorum hoc sacramentum praehebant, et tunc, sicut materia, ita et forma ex mandato christi utebantur. multa enim servabant apostoli in sacramentorum collatione quae in scripturis communiter propositis non sunt tradita."
Busa 2:886.

M-82: Thomas Aquinas
Summa theologiae 3:72,11

                        26:298   12:230 12:230

"Ad primum ergo dicendum quod papa in ecclesia habet plenitudinem potestatis, ex qua potest quaedam quae sunt superiorum ordinum, committere inferioribus quibusdam, sicut presbyteris concedit conferre minores ordines, quod pertinet ad potestatem episcopalem. et ex hac plenitudine potestatis concessit beatus gregorius papa quod simplices sacerdotes conferrent hoc sacramentum, quandiu scandalum tolleretur."
Busa 2:888.

M-83: Waldensis, Thomas (Netter)
De sacramentis 2:113,1. 4

                                1:211 9:226

(See Netter, Thomas, M-63.)

M-84: Waldensis, Thomas (Netter)
De sacramentis 2:114,1

                                      12:230

(See Netter, Thomas, M-64.)

M-85: Wyclif, John (c. 1330-1384)
Trialogus 4,14

                            1:211 12:230
                          12:231 12:231

"Alithia: . . . Sed nimis levis videtur esse haec confirmatio, quia dici posset probabiliter, quod licet baptisatio in nomine Jesu Christi fuit ad tempus valida, quousque nomen istud fuerat sufficienter publicatum, tamen publicatione hac facta fuit ad formam verborum evangelii

WORK	CALVIN	CHEMNITZ	BELLARMINE

redeundum, et sic nomine tenus baptisati in Samaria fuerunt legitime baptisandi, sicut baptisati baptismo Johannis vel alio baptismo illegitimo sunt sine periculo iterum baptisandi. . . .

"Phronesis: <Nec> adhuc video contradictionem claram ex ratione vivaci vel scriptura, quomodo contradicerem verbis tuis. . . . Non tamen video, quod generaliter sit hoc sacramentum de necessitate salutis fidelium, nec quod praetendentes se confirmare pueros regulariter hos confirmant, nec quod hoc sacramentum sit specialiter episcopis Caesariis reservatum. Et ulterius videtur mihi quod foret plus religiosum et conformius modo loquendi scripturae, negare quod nostri episcopi dant Spiritum Sanctum vel confirmant ulterius Sancti Spiritus dationem, quia glossata quantumcunque locutione tali a doctoribus nostris concessa, adhuc stat mali intellectus periculum, et modi loquendi deficit fundamentum. Unde quibusdam videtur, quod ista levis et brevis episcoporum confirmatio cum adjectis ritibus tantum solemnisatis est ideo motione diaboli introducta, ut populus in fide ecclesiae illudatur et episcoporum solemnitas aut necessitas plus credatur."

Ed. Gotthardus Lechler. Oxford: Clarendon Press, 1869. Pp. 292-294.

7. REFORMATION SOURCES

WORK   CALVIN   CHEMNITZ   BELLARMINE

R-1: Andrada, Diego (1528-1578)
Orthodoxarum explicationum

5:286 7:287

"Cùm enim diuinae sapientiae leges imponere, infinitam ipsius bonitatem certis quibusdam terminis circunscribere, abditissima illius consilia suo iudicio tanquàm norma quadam metiri uolunt, sit, ut ea solùm Christo beneficia accepta referant, quae sibi necessaria fuisse arbitrantur; quae uerò non percipiunt, nefariè abiiciant, aspernentur, conculcent. Quod quidem in coelesti hoc plane'que diuino confirmationis sacramento apertè cernitur. Nam cùm salutis nostrae principium atque fundamentum in fide, Christi'que cognitione ponatur, quae & ad felicitatem nobis à Christo promissam aditum aperit, & ad omne officii genus ueluti stimulis quibusdam excitat; tanta'que sit humanae naturae infirmitas, ut ' praesentis mortis metus nos facilè de fide deiicere, atque deturbare possit Christus Iesus, qui humani generis necessitatibus prouidentissimè inuigilauit, & suos tanquàm oues inter lupos constituit, diuinum hoc sacramentum instituit, illique sanguinis sui uim & potentiam impressit, ut fidem nobis in sacro lauacro collatam firmaret, perficeret, atque ueluti altissimis radicibus defigeret, quò mentes tanta hac Spiritus sancti uirtute confirmatas & roboratas, neque periculi tempestas, neque honoris aura posset à fidei cursu spe, aut metu dimouere."

Orthodoxarvm explicationvm libri decem, In quibus omnia ferè de religione capita, quae his temporibus ab haereticis in controuersiam vocantur, apertè & dilucidè explicantur; Praesertim contra Martini Kemnicij petulantem audaciam, qui Coloniensem Censuram, quam à uiris societatis Iesu compositam esse ait, unà cum eiusdem sanctissimae societatis uitae ratione, temerè calumniandam suscepit. Venice: Iordanus Ziletus, 1564. Fol. 275.

R-2: Antididagma (1544)
De administratione sacramenti Baptismi

24:295

"Forsan cogitabit quispiam secum, quare vngat presbyter baptizatum

WORK   CALVIN   CHEMNITZ   BELLARMINE

Chrismate: quum postea in confirmatione illiniat Episcopus Chrisma
fronti? Responsio. Apostolicorum Episcoporum gesta referunt, beatum
Siluestrum constituisse, vt presbyter baptizatum chrismate liniret
subleuatum de aqua propter occasionem transitus mortis inexpectatae,
ne baptizati (propter absentiam Episcopi, quem fortè conquirere
difficile esset) sine manuum impositione de hac vita migrarent. Idcirco
Siluester quantum in se erat volens praeuenire talem casum, ordinauit,
vt absente Episcopo, baptizati à Presbytero vngerentur: Si autem
praesens esset Episcopus, vngerentur ab ipso & communicarentur, &c.
Voluit tamen nihilominus beatus ille Siluester, vt post vnctionem quam
presbyter facit in vertice, praeueniendi discriminis causa, confirmaretur
baptizatus etiam postmodum ab Episcopo chrismate, sed in fronte. Quod
autem de communione commemoratur hoc loco, durauit etiam Augustini
temporibus. Postmodum tamen talis communio paruulorum per Ecclesiam
(non sine magnis causis) sublata est, &c."

Antididagma, seu Christianae et Catholicae religionis, per Reuer. &
illustriss. Dominos Canonicos metropolitanae ecclesiae Coloniensis
propugnatio, aduersus librum quendam uniuersis ordinibus, seu statibus
dioecesis eiusdem, nuper bonae titulo Reformationis exhibitum, ac
postea, mutatis quibusdam Consultoriae deliberationis nomine
impressum. Paris: Ioannes Roigny, 1549. Fol. 60.

R-3: Bellarmine, Robert (1542-1621)
De sacramentis in genere 2,18

11:230

"Sequitur tertia quaestio de effectu sacramentorum, quae est de
charactere; An scilicet sacramenta aliqua imprimant in anima
indelebilem characterem."
Battezzati 3:120.

R-4: Bellarmine, Robert
De sacramentis in genere 2,19

11:230

"'Character indelebilis est.' Haec habetur in conciliis notatis, et ab
omnibus conceditur. Ratio a posteriori est, quia constat, sacramenta quae
imprimunt characterem, non posse repeti."
Battezzati 3:121.

WORK	CALVIN	CHEMNITZ	BELLARMINE

R-5: Bellarmine, Robert
De sacramentis in genere 2,23

7:220

"Controversia V. quae est de numero sacramentorum, quatuor habebit partes."
Battezzati 3:127.

R-6: Bellarmine, Robert
De sacramento baptismi 25

1:213

"Unguntur enim catechumeni oleo benedicto ante Baptismum, in pectore et scapulis, ungendi postea Chrismate post Baptismum. Meminit hujus unctionis Clemens lib. 3. recognitionum. . . Chrysostomus hom. 6. in cap. 2. epist. ad Coloss. . . . Ambros. quoque utriusque unctionis meminit. . . . Cyrillus utriusque etiam meminit. . . . Utriusque etiam meminit Augustinus serm. 206. de tempore."
Battezzati 3:205.

R-7: Bellarmine, Robert
De sacramento baptismi 26

13:233

"Quinta est, tempus paschale et pentecostes. Etsi enim quovis tempore dari possit Baptismus, si necessitas urgeat: tamen veteres diligentissime servabant hanc caeremoniam, ut solum in sabbathis, paschae et pentecostes ordinarie baptizarent."
Battezzati 3:206.

R-8: Bellarmine, Robert
De sacramento baptismi 27

1:213

"Secunda est, unctio Chrismatis in vertice; quae quidem introducta videtur, quia non semper adest episcopus, qui possit continuo dare post Baptismum sacramentum Confirmationis. Ideo enim interim ungitur a presbytero baptizatus, non quidem in fronte, sed in vertice, Chrismate ab episcopo consecrato. Meminit hujus caeremoniae Damasus in vita Sylvestri. Innocentius I. epist. 1. cap. 3. Ambros. lib. 3. de sacramentis cap. 1. et Hieronymus in dialogo contra Luciferianos, ubi dicit,

WORK	CALVIN	CHEMNITZ	BELLARMINE

presbyteris non licere sine Chrismate baptizare."
Battezzati 3:206.

R-9: Bellarmine, Robert
De sacramento confirmationis 1

7:219

"Idem Calvinus ibidem canon. 3. tridentinos Patres, asinos et porcos vocat, cum tamen modestissimus videri velit. . . . Ibidem de Melchiade papa et martyre, cujus verba proxime citaverat, ita loquitur: 'Os sacrilegum. . . .'"
Battezzati 3:212.

R-10: Bellarmine, Robert
De sacramento confirmationis 1

7:221

"Jam vero Martinus Kemnitius multa similiter habet, et mendacia, et convicta; sed uno tantum loco ero contentus. Igitur in 2. par. Exam. pag. 298. tria simul mendacia conglutinat. Primum est, quod unctio Chrismatis ex schola Montani prodierit. Secundum, quod Tertullianus et Cyprianus in hac re Montanistae fuerint. Tertium, quod Hieronymus hanc sententiam refutet in Dialogo contra Luciferianos."
Battezzati 3:213.

R-11: Bellarmine, Robert
De sacramento confirmationis 2

12:231

"Quinque argumentis probandum est, Confirmationem esse sacramentum vere ac proprie dictum, ut concilium tridentinum docet sess. 7. canon. 1. de Confirmatione. Primo, ex Scripturis. Secundo, ex traditione, et testimoniis summorum pontificum. Tertio, ex testimoniis conciliorum. Quarto, ex testimoniis Patrum graecorum. Quinto, ex testimoniis Latinorum."
Battezzati 3:213.

WORK   CALVIN   CHEMNITZ   BELLARMINE

R-12: Bellarmine, Robert
De sacramento confirmationis 2

7:219

"Tria requiruntur ad essentiam sacramenti christiani proprie dicti. Primo, promissio gratiae. Secundo, signum sensibile cum verbo, quod sit medium, seu organum, quo applicetur promissio. Tertio, mandatum divinum, quo id jubeatur ministrari. Haec tria postulant sibi ostendi ex Scripturis in quaestione de Confirmatione, Calvinus. . . et Kemnitius. . . et merito."
Battezzati 3:213.

R-13: Bellarmine, Robert
De sacramento confirmationis 2

7:222

"Nam ut omittam quae infra de Chrismate dicenda sunt, falsum est rejectam esse manus impositionem. Bis enim episcopus manus imponit confirmandis, ut ex pontificali Romano intelligi potest, semel cum super eos manus extendit, atque orat: et rursum cum signat in fronte, atque ungit; ipsa enim unctio, et signatio cum manu fiat, manus impositio rectissime dicitur, ut docet Hugo lib. 2. de sacramentis part. 7. cap. 2."
Battezzati 3:216.

R-14: Bellarmine, Robert
De sacramento confirmationis 3

7:221 7:221
7:222 8:223

"Nunc secundo probanda est veritas ex veterum, et sanctorum pontificum responsis. Adferemus autem testimonia, quae non quidem disertis verbis affirment, Confirmationem esse sacramentum (id enim neque necessarium est, et facile posset detorqueri ad significationem sacramenti largo modo accepti) sed testimonia adferemus, quae rem ipsam demonstrent; idest, caeremoniam dantem gratiam, et a Baptismo distinctam."
Battezzati 3:216.

WORK	CALVIN	CHEMNITZ	BELLARMINE

R-15: Bellarmine, Robert
De sacramento confirmationis 8

1:213

"Igitur materiam hujus sacramenti remotam catholici communi consensu esse docent, oleum balsamo admixtum, atque ab episcopo consecratum."
Battezzati 3:222.

R-16: Bellarmine, Robert
De sacramento confirmationis 8

9:228

"Tertia propositio: 'Chrisma, quod est materia sacramenti Confirmationis, prius consecratum, ac benedictum esse debet.' In hac etiam catholici omnes conveniunt. Et quia Calvinus, et Kemnitius hanc benedictionem superstitiosam, et magicam vocant. . . probanda est haec veritas testimoniis veterum, sanctorum pontificum, conciliorum, Patrum."
Battezzati 3:224.

R-17: Bellarmine, Robert
De sacramento confirmationis 10

10:229

"Forma hujus sacramenti sunt haec verba: 'Signo te signo crucis, et confirmo te Chrismate salutis in nomine Patris, et Filii et Spiritus sancti.' . . . Apud antiquiores auctores non habentur haec omnia verba, et hoc ordine, tamen habetur idem sensus, et hoc sufficit."
Battezzati 3:228.

R-18: Bellarmine, Robert
De sacramento confirmationis 13

9:228

"Tertio, halat episcopus aliquoties super ampullam Chrismatis. Et quidem haec caeremonia ridicula, et magica videtur haereticis."
Battezzati 3:233.

WORK   CALVIN   CHEMNITZ   BELLARMINE

R-19: Bellarmine, Robert
De sacramento ordinis 1

                                                              12:230
"De sacramento Ordinis, quae ad hunc locum pertinent, sunt hae questiones."
Battezzati 3:763.

R-20: Brenz, Johannes (1499-1570)
De sacramentis: De baptismo

                                        9:225 9:225
                                               9:225
"Deinde, docemus eum qui baptizatur in nomine Patris & Filij & Spiritus Sancti, vngi spirituali chrismate, hoc est, fieri membrum Christi per fidem, & donari Spiritu Sancto, vt ad percipienda coelestia aures mentis eius aperiantur, & oculi cordis illustrentur. . . . Et vsus externi Chrismatis pertinet ad elementa mundi. . . . Et Dionysius, quem Areopagitam vocant, & quem putant descipsisse ritus Ecclesiae ab Apostolis traditos, significat quidem externum Chrisma fuisse in Ecclesia vsitatum, sed significat etiam haud obscurè, hunc ritum partim ab athleticis vnctionibus Ethnicorum, partim ex lege Mosaica sumptum esse. . . . Praeterea, quomodo confectio seu ritus externi Chrismatis, ab Apostolis ipsis traditus esse, vt Fabianus scribit verè affirmari posset, cùm Acta Conciliorum testentur, hunc ritum institutum esse à Sylvestro?"
"Confessio illustrissimi Principis ac Domini, D. Christophori Ducis Wirtembergensis, & Theccensis, Comitis Montebeligardi, &c (1561)." *Corpus et Syntagma Confessionum Fidei quae in diversis regnis et nationibus, ecclesiarum nomine fuerunt authenticè editae: in celeberrimis Conuentibus exhibitae, publicáque auctoritate comprobatae.* Editio Nova. Geneva: Petri Chovet, 1654. " 2:109.

R-21: Brenz, Johannes
De sacramentis: De confirmatione

                                        1:211 2:214
                                               2:214
"Nomen *Sacramenti*, sicut & nomen *Mysterii* (quod Interpretes *Sacramentum* exponunt) latissimè patet. Sed quia visum est quibusdam

WORK	CALVIN	CHEMNITZ	BELLARMINE

numerum Sacramentorum in septem contrahere, percurremus singula, vt ostendamus quid in doctrina quorundam Scriptorum desideremus, & quid cum sententia verè Catholicae & Orthodoxae Ecclesiae pugnare videatur. . . . Et sentimus vtilissimum esse, vt pueri & adolescentes à Pastoribus Ecclesiae suae in Cathechismo examinentur, & siquidem piè ac rectè fuerint eruditi, approbentur: si verò prauè, emendentur. Sed ex personali & temporali facto Apostolorum non est absque certo mandato Dei generale & perpetuum Sacramentum in Ecclesia statuendum."
Corpus et Syntagma Confessionum Fidei. 2:108. 110.

R-22: Cajetan (1469-1534)
Summa 3:72,2

9:227

"Vnde intelligimus mixtum ex oleo & balsamo (quod chrisma consueuimus vocare) esse regularem materiam confirmationis de necessitate praecepti, & non de necessitate sacramenti."
Tertia Pars Summae Sacrae Theologiae Sancti Thomae Aquinatis, Doctoris Angelici. Lyons: Haeredes Iacobi Iuntae, 1558. 4:333.

R-23: Calvin, John (1509-1564)
Antidotum 7,2

1:212

"Quaestio est an ab hominum arbitrio novam et arcanam spiritus virtutem oleum accipiat, simul atque illis placuerit vocari chrisma. Olei enim qui faciat mentionem, nemo est ex veteribus, imo nec ex media illa aetate, quae iam multis vitiis abundabat. Crepent igitur licet, nihil proficient negando, se in spiritum Dei esse contumeliosos, eius virtutem dum ad putidum oleum transferunt."
CR 35 (1868):502.

R-24: Calvin, John
Antidotum 7,3

1:212 2:215
12:232

"Et certe digni sunt cornuti infulatique asini tali praerogativa. Quid enim agerent, quando ad obeundum munus episcopale nihilo sunt aptiores, quam ad canendum porci? . . . Nam si ex scriptura petatur

WORK   CALVIN   CHEMNITZ   BELLARMINE

ratio, nullum illic est, omnium confessione, presbyteri et episcopi
discrimen. Deinde manuum impositionem iubetur Paulus ab Anania
recipere, qui unus erat ex discipulis (Act. 9, 17). . . . Denique vel Dei lege
sancitum est quod volunt, vel humano placito."
CR 35:502.

R-25: Calvin, John
Institutio 4:15,20

                                                               1:212
"Neque enim aut mulieribus aut hominibus quibuslibet mandavit
Christus ut baptizarent; sed quos apostolos constituerat, iis mandatum
hoc dedit."
CR 30 (1864):974.

R-26: Calvin, John
Institutio 4:18,20

                       11:1074
". . . et re vera ad plenum manifestavit, quantum nostra interest, dum
nunc per speculum eum conspicimus (1 Cor. 13, 12). Iam vero, ut hoc
hominibus ablatum est, ne nova sacramenta in ecclesia Dei condere
possint, ita optandum esset, iis ipsis, quae a Deo sunt, quam minimum
humanae inventionis admisceri."
CR 30:1065.

R-27: Calvin, John
Institutio 4:19,4

                                                       1:211 7:219
                                                              7:221
"Qui ergo baptismo initiati erant infantes, quia fidei confessione apud
ecclesiam tunc defuncti non erant, sub finem pueritiae, aut ineunte
adolescentia, repraesentabantur iterum a parentibus, ab episcopo
examinabantur secundum formulam catechismi, quam tunc habebant
certam ac communem. . . . Leo Papa: si quis ab haereticis redit, ne iterum
baptizetur; sed quod illic ei defuit, per episcopalem manuum
impositionem virtus spiritus ei conferatur: . . . Meminit et Hieronymus
contra Luciferianos. Quanquam autem non infitior, in eo nonnihil
hallucinari Hieronymum, quod apostolicam esse observationem dicit,

WORK	CALVIN	CHEMNITZ	BELLARMINE

longissime tamen ab istorum ineptiis abest. . . . Talem ergo manuum impositionem, quae simpliciter loco benedictionis fiat, laudo et restitutam hodie in purum usum velim."
CR 30:1068-69.

R-28: **Calvin, John**
Institutio 4:19,5

2:213 2:214
10:229

"Sed ubi Dei verbum quod spiritus sancti praesentiam hic promittat? Ne iota quidem obtendere possunt. Unde ergo nos certiores facient, chrisma suum esse vas spiritus sancti? . . . Haec prima ministri lex est ne quid sine mandato obeat. Age, mandatum huius ministerii aliquod producant, et verbum non addam."
CR 30:1069.

R-29: **Calvin, John**
Institutio 4:19,6

2:214 2:214
2:214 2:215
2:215

"Tuentur se quidem apostolorum exemplo, quos nihil temere fecisse existimant. Recte id sane: nec a nobis reprehenderentur si se apostolorum imitatores ostenderent. . . . Huic autem impositioni manuum non altius subesse mysterium cogito; sed huiusmodi caeremoniam adhibitam ab illis interpretor, ut ipso gestu significarent, se Deo commendare et velut offerre eum cui manus imponebant. . . . Sed cessarunt illa virtutum miracula et manifestae operationes, quae per manuum impositionem distribuebantur, nec nisi ad tempus esse debuerunt."
CR 30:1069-70.

R-30: **Calvin, John**
Institutio 4:19,7

10:229

". . . unde tamen oleum, quod vocant salutis? Quis eos in oleo salutem quaerere docuit? . . . Hoc vero non a me, sed a Domino audacter

WORK	CALVIN	CHEMNITZ	BELLARMINE

pronuntio: qui oleum vocant oleum salutis, salutem quae in Christo est abiurant, Christum abnegant, partem in regno Dei non habent. Oleum enim ventri, et venter oleo; utrumque Dominus destruet. . . . <In> sacramentis divinitus traditis duo spectanda esse: substantiam rei corporeae quae nobis proponitur, et formam quae illi a verbo Dei impressa est, in qua tota vis iacet."
CR 30:1071.

R-31: Calvin, John
Institutio 4:19,8

1:212 7:219
8:224

"Dei verbum est: omnes, qui in Christo baptizati sunt, Christum induisse eum suis donis (Gal. 3, 27). Verbum unctorum: nullam promissionem in baptismo percepisse, qua in agonibus instruantur. Illa vox est veritatis, hanc mendacii esse oportet. Verius ergo definire hanc confirmationem possum quam ipsi hactenus definierint: nempe insignem esse baptismi contumeliam, quae usum ipsius obscurat, imo abolet; falsam esse diaboli pollicitationem, quae nos a veritate Dei abstrahit. Aut, si mavis, oleum diaboli mendacio pollutum, quod velut offusis tenebris simplicium mentes fallit."
CR 30:1072.

R-32: Calvin, John
Institutio 4:19,10

1:212 1:212
2:215 7:219
12:230 12:231
12:231 12:231
12:231 13:233

"Postremo constituunt, sacram hanc unctionem maiori in veneratione habendam esse quam baptismum, quod illa summorum pontificum manibus peculiariter administratur, baptismus ab omnibus vulgariter sacerdotibus distribuitur. . . . Os sacrilegum, tune pinguedinem foetore duntaxat anhelitus tui inquinatam, et verborum murmure incantatam, audes Christi sacramento opponere, et conferre cum aqua verbo Dei sanctificata? . . . Verum prima ratione nonne se Donatistas produnt, qui

WORK   CALVIN   CHEMNITZ   BELLARMINE

vim sacramenti a ministri dignitate aestimant? Faxo tamen, vocetur
dignior confirmatio a dignitate episcopalis manus. . . . An soli episcopi
apostoli? . . . cur non eodem argumento contendunt, solis episcopis
sacramentum sanguinis in coena Domini attingendum esse? . . . Postremo
non erat apostolus Ananias, ad quem tamen Paulus missus est ut visum
reciperet, baptizaretur, et impleretur spiritu sancto (Act. 9, 17)."
CR 30:1073.

R-33: **Calvin, John**
Institutio 4:19,11

                                                      1:212 1:212
                                                             1:213

"Ecce praeterita aqua, et nullo numero habita, unum oleum in baptismo
magnifaciunt. Nos ergo contra dicimus, in baptismo quoque frontem aqua
tingi. Prae hac, vestrum oleum non unius stercoris facimus, sive in
baptismo, sive in confirmatione."
CR 30:1074.

R-34: **Calvin, John**
Institutio 4:19,12

                                                      7:219 7:219
                                                      7:220 7:220

"Iam vero quum verbo Dei et probabili ratione defici se vident,
praetexunt quod solent, vetustissimam esse hanc observationem, et
multorum saeculorum consensu firmatam. Etiamsi id verum esset, nihil
tamen efficiunt: non e terra est sacramentum, sed e coelo; non ex
hominibus, sed ab uno Deo. . . . Sed quid vetustatem obiectant, quum
veteres, dum proprie loqui volunt, nusquam plura duobus sacramentis
recenseant? . . . De manuum impositione loquuntur veteres; sed an
sacramentum vocant? Augustinus aperte affirmat, nihil aliud esse quam
orationem. Neque hic mihi putidis suis distincitonibus obganniant, non
ad confirmatoriam Augustinum illud retulisse, sed curatoriam vel
reconciliatoriam. Exstat liber et in hominum manibus versatur. . . .
Loquitur enim de iis qui a schismate ad ecclesiae unitatem redibant. Eos
iteratione baptismi opus habere negat; sufficere enim manuum
impositionem, ut per vinculum pacis spiritum sanctum illis Dominus
largiatur."
CR 30:1074-75.

WORK	CALVIN	CHEMNITZ	BELLARMINE

R-35: Calvin, John
Institutio 4:19,13

7:221

"Utinam vero morem retineremus quem apud veteres fuisse admonui, priusquam abortiva haec sacramenti larva nasceretur; non ut esset confirmatio talis qualem isti fingunt, quae sine baptismi iniuria nec nominari potest; sed catechesis, qua pueri aut adolescentiae proximi fidei suae rationem coram ecclesia exponerent."
CR 30:1075.

R-36: Calvin, John
Institutio 4:19,21

13:233

"Isti oleum non dignantur nisi ab episcopo consecratum, hoc est, multo halitu calefactum, multo murmure incantatum, et novies flexo genu salutatum: ter, ave sanctum oleum: ter, ave sanctum chrisma: ter, ave sanctum balsamum."
CR 30:1081.

R-37: Calvin, John
Institutio 4:19,31

10:229

"Superest impositio manuum, quam ut in veris legitimisque ordinationibus sacramentum esse concedo, ita nego locum habere in hac fabula, ubi nec Christi mandato obtemperant, nec finem respiciunt quo nos ducere debet promissio."
CR 30:1088.

R-38: Chemnitz, Martin (1522-1586)
Examen Pars 1, Locus 2: Sectio 6,5

23:292

"Sed profitemur et hoc quod non ex nobis finximus, sed ab ipsis Patribus didicimus, quod scilicet inquiramus et allegemus testimonia Patrum, non ideo, quasi ea, quae ex perspicuis Scripturae testimoniis ostenduntur et probantur, per se nec certa, nec firma satis sint, aut non satis habeant ex se roboris et autoritatis, nisi accedat Patrum etiam consensus."
Preuss:82.

WORK	CALVIN	CHEMNITZ	BELLARMINE

R-39: Chemnitz, Martin
Examen Pars 1, Locus 2:8,10

24:292

"Adscribam igitur tantum Nicolai Cusani judicium, quod ut a Cardinale profectum, repudiare non poterunt."
Preuss:97.

R-40: Chemnitz, Martin
Examen Pars 2, Locus 1:1,1,2,12

24:292

"Augustinus enim primus ferme coepit vocabulum sacramenti, in hac quidem materia extendere, et latius usurpare quam antiquitas fecerat, Epistola enim 5. ad Marcell. de signis loquens, inquit: Quae cum ad res divinas pertinent, sacramenta appellantur. Et de civitate Dei, lib. 10. cap. 5. inquit: Sacramentum sacrum signum est."
Preuss:230.

R-41: Chemnitz, Martin
De confirmatione 6 (pag. 276)[55]

2:213

"In hac igitur quaestione, quae sint illa media, per quae credendum sit, Spiritum sanctum velle efficacem esse, ante omnia petimus ex verbo Dei nobis monstari expressum mandatum et promissionem divinam. Quando enim illa habemus, tunc scimus mediis illis, utpote divinitus institutis, reverenter esse utendum, scimus etiam quid illis tribuendum sit."
Preuss:287.

R-42: Chemnitz, Martin
De confirmatione 9

9:227

"Tertullianus enim de baptismo dicit, unctionem non ex Christi institutione, sed ex pristina disciplina Veteris Testamenti sumptam esse. Sermo de ablutione pedum, qui Cypriano tribuitur, chrisma

---

[55]   This pagination is used by Bellarmine, who is working from the original 1566 edition.

WORK   CALVIN   CHEMNITZ   BELLARMINE

numerat inter ea, quae non Christus ipse, sed Apostoli per Spiritum
sanctum instituisse existimentur. Et in sermone de chrismate affirmat,
unctionem chrismatis ex ceremoniis Veteris Testamenti reliquam
mansisse. Basilius etiam dicit, nullam exstare *logon gegrammenon*, de
unctione chrismatis. Ignoravit igi tur illam Fabiani Epistolam."
Preuss:288.

R-43: Chemnitz, Martin
De confirmatione 11 (pag. 285)

13:233

"Quod enim Pontifex inhalando in chrismatis pinguedinem, fingit se
imitari illud, cum Christus insufflando dixit: Accipite Spiritum
Sanctum, non tantum ridiculum, sed magicum, superstitiosum et
blasphemum est."
Preuss:289.

R-44: Chemnitz, Martin
De confirmatione 12 (pag. 286)

8:223 8:224
9:225

"Sed jam arrige aures optime lector: magnum enim et insigne audies
acumen. Act. 1 externum elementum est ignis, in specie dissectarum
linguarum. Act. 8 et 19 est impositio manuum. Usque adeo vero idem est
elementum seu eadem materia, etiam in pontificiorum confirmatione, ut
in illis historiis, dicatur fundamentum institutionis habere. Quomodo
vero illud? Miraberis scio, ubi audieris: igni in Pentecoste, respondet in
Pontificia confirmatione, oleum. Qua ratione? Quis oleum nutrit ignem.
Sed idem facit etiam baculus quercinus, fumo bene induratus. Speciei
linguarum respondet balsamum, quia est odoriferum."
Preuss:289.

R-45: Chemnitz, Martin
De confirmatione 12 (pag. 287)

8:224 9:228

"Et talis quidem est materiae confirmationis probatio ex scriptura
Consecrationem vero, seu potius excantationem chrismatis, qualis in

WORK	CALVIN	CHEMNITZ	BELLARMINE

Pontificali describitur, ne ulla quidem syllaba ex scriptura probare conantur, quia ne in speciem quidem illud facere possunt."
Preuss:289.

R-46: Chemnitz, Martin
De confirmatione 13 (pag. 288)

                                                    10:229 10:229

"Quid vero de forma confirmationis. Signo te, etc. Nunquid ex scriptura probari potest, vel Christum instituisse, vel Apostolos usurpasse illam formam verborum? . . . Et inde fit, quod in ipsis Pontificalibus non eadem est illa forma. Gabriel enim recitat, quosdam pro chrismate salutis, dicere chrisma sanctificationis. Gerson habet hanc formam: Firmo te signo crucis, et chrismate, etc."
Preuss:289-290.

R-47: Chemnitz, Martin
De confirmatione 15 (pag. 289)

                                                            13:233

"Et his recensitis statim attexunt: Quicunque cum Pontificali non exclamaverit: Ave sanctum chrisma: illum omnes illas promissiones convellere, et proculcare."
Preuss:290.

R-48: Chemnitz, Martin
De confirmatione 16 (pag. 290-291)

                                                    2:215 2:215

                                                    2:215 2:216

"Apostoli enim multa habuerunt peculiaria privilegia, reliquis Ecclesiae ministris non imitanda. . . . Sed Apostoli illo ritu visibilia dona spiritus, ut donum linguarum, contulerunt: quae miracula jam in Ecclesia desiise, manifestum est. Et si maxime ritus ille Apostolorum esset (quod tamen non est) sacramentum universale, qua autoritate Pontificii, abolita Apostolica impostione manuum, delibutionem incantati chrismatis substituere potuerunt, et ad illam allegare promissiones? Chrismatis enim institutio in Novo Testamento, ex scriptura ostendi et probari non potest. Num vero nulla plane sunt media, per quae Deus conferre velit dona confirmationis et perseverantiae? Sunt omnino divinitus ordinata, certa, sive organa,

WORK   CALVIN   CHEMNITZ   BELLARMINE

sive media, per quae Spiritus sanctus dona illa vult conferre, confirmare, augere et conservare verbum, scilicet Eucharistia, fides, oratio, lucta, exercitium acceptorum donorum mentis. Inter haec vero, crucifactionem Pontificii chrismatis non legimus."
Preuss:290.

R-49: Chemnitz, Martin
De confirmatione 24 (pag. 297)

                                              7:221

"Primo enim praecipuae sententiae, quae de Chrismatione allegantur, sumptae sunt ex scriptis, quae partim ab ipsa Ecclesia Romana, inter apocrypha relata sunt: partim verae antiquitati prorsus sunt ignota, supposititia igitur, et commentitia esse non est dubium. . . ."
Preuss:292.

R-50: Chemnitz, Martin
De confirmatione 24,2 (pag. 298)

                             1:213   1:213
                             1:213   1:213
                                     7:221

"Quaedam sententiae de unctione chrismatis, ex schola Montanici patacleti prodierunt. Ex professo enim Montanicum est, quod Tertullianus de baptismo inquit, eos qui baptizantur in aquis, non consequi spiritum sanctum sed in aqua mundatos, sub Angelis tantum praeparari Spiritui sancto: qui demum postquam egressi sint de lavacro, per benedictam unctionem et impositionem manus advocetur, et invitetur. Hanc sententiam Hieronymus multis verbis ex scriptura refutat, in Dialogo adversus Luciferianos. . . . Ex Tertulliano vero magistro suo Cyprianus hausit quod lib. 2, Epist. 1 ita discerpit sententiam Christi, Joh. 3. Nisi quia renatus fuerit ex aqua et spiritu, quod baptismo tantum aquam tribuit, Spiritum sanctum vero tribuit unctioni et impostioni manuum."
Preuss:292.

WORK	CALVIN	CHEMNITZ	BELLARMINE

R-51: Chemnitz, Martin
De confirmatione 24,3

7:221

"Unctionem vero adhibuerunt, quia in Orientalibus praesertim locis, multus et varius erat usus olei, unguenti, et unctionis. . . ."
Preuss:292.

R-52: Chemnitz, Martin
De confirmatione 24,4 (pag. 305)[56]

1:212 7:222
8:224

". . . hoc tamen affirmare non dubito, in vera et puriori antiquitate non posse ostendi, Pontificiam illam antithesin, inter baptismum et chrismationem, quae praecipuos effectus baptismo adimit et derogat, et chrismationi tribuit. . . . De Cyrillo vero Hierosolymitano, cujus catecheses nuper editae sunt, quaedam breviter dicenda sunt, ille enim praecipuus jam cogitur esse Pontificii chrismatis patronus. . . . Et Hieronymus dicit, Cyrillum hunc in adolescentia conscripsisse *katêchêseis*. Rufinus addit, ipsum aliquando in fide, saepius in confessione variasse. . . . Neque enim Antiochiae primum appellati fuerunt Christiani, inde quod externa aliqua oleae pinguedine deliniti et delibuti fuerint."
Preuss:293-294.

R-53: Chemnitz, Martin
De confirmatione 24,5 (pag. 309)

7:222 7:222
7:222 9:227
9:227 9:228
9:228

"Magna est dissimilitudo et diversitas, inter chrisma de quo veteres loquuntur, et inter confirmationem, sicut illa apud Pontificios servatur . . . . Primo enim quod ad materiam, sicut loquuntur, vel ad externum

---

[56]   Bellarmine says at 1:212 that Chemnitz calls chrism "Cyrillum" here, but it does not occur in this passage.

| WORK | CALVIN | CHEMNITZ | BELLARMINE |

signum attinet, veteribus usurpata fuit impositio manuum. . . . Sed Pontificii contendunt, si oleum non sit Balsamo mixtum, non esse verum sacramentum. Et licet ex scholasticis quidam disputent, solum oleum esse de necessitate: concilium tamen Florentinum decernit, materiam confirmationis debere esse chrisma, ex oleo et balsamo confectum. . . . Nativum certe balsamum una cum ipsis arboribus jam defecisse constat. Periit igitur ex rerum natura, ipsa materia confirmationis, quam Pontificii requirunt. . . . Cyrillus baptizatos post baptismum chrismate inungit, primum in fronte, secundo, in auribus, tertio, in naribus, quarto, in pectore. Ambrosius de his, qui initiantur, cap. 6, baptizato post baptismum inungit caput, ut inde defluat unguentum. . . . <Secundo, sed> sicut varias habuerunt caeremonias, antecedentes intinctionem Baptismi: ita etiam varias habuerunt ceremonias post tinctionem, connexas tamen et conjunctas ipsi actionis Baptismi. . . . Tertio, effectus quos Pontificii hodie suae confirmationi tribuunt, illos veteres ipsi Baptismo adscribunt."
Preuss:294-295.

R-54: Chemnitz, Martin
De confirmatione 24,6 (pag. 317)

1:213

"Sed et ex hac consuetudine, et ex more recipiendi eos qui ab haeresi ad Ecclesiam revertebantur, jam tum Hieronymi tempore, imo longe ante, non vulgus tantum, sed et Episcopi quidam finxerant hanc opinionem, quasi Baptisma ipsum esset sine Spiritu sancto: qui tunc primum daretur et acciperetur, quando Episcopus ad invocationem Spiritus sancti, manus baptizatis imponeret. Hanc vero opinionem, quae tamen est Tertulliani prebyteri, Cornelii Papae, et Cypriani Episcopi, Hieronymus serio et graviter refutat."
Preuss:296.

R-55: Chemnitz, Martin
De confirmatione 24,6 (pag. 319)

7:220 7:221

"Expresse autem loquitur de haereticis et schismaticis revertentibus. Quomodo vero per manus impositionem charitas inspiratur, respondet Augustinus: Manus impositio quid aliud est, quam oratio super

WORK	CALVIN	CHEMNITZ	BELLARMINE

hominem: ergo non sicut baptismus, repeti non potest. Et Gratianus de illa Augustini sententia 1 quaest. 1 cap. Arianos, inquit: Ex eo quod manus impositio iterari praecipitur, Sacramentum non esse ostenditur." Preuss:297.

R-56: Chemnitz, Martin
De confirmatione 25 (pag. 320)

1:211

"Nostri saepe ostenderunt, ritum Confirmationis. . . hoc modo posse usurpari, ut scilicet illi qui in infantia baptizati sunt (talis enim nunc est Ecclesiae status) cum ad annos discretionis pervenissent, diligenter in certa et simplici catechesi doctrinae Ecclesiae instituerentur. Et cum initia mediocriter percepisse viderentur, postea Episcopo et Ecclesiae offerrentur: atque ibi puer in infantia baptizatus, primo brevi et simplici commonefactione admoneretur de suo Baptismo: quo scilicet sit baptizatus, quomodo quare et in quid sit baptizatus, quid in illo Baptismo tota Trinitas ipsi contulerit et obsignarit, foedus scilicet pacis, et pactum gratiae: quomodo ibi facta sit abrenuntiatio Satanae, professio fidei, et promissio obedientiae. Secundo, puer ipse coram Ecclesia ederet propria et publicam professionem hujus doctrinae et fidei. Tertio, interrogaretur de praecipuis Christianae religions capitibus, ad singula responderet: aut si quid minus intelligeret, rectius erudiretur. Quarto, admoneretur, et hac professione ostenderet, se dissentire ab omnibus ethnicis, haereticis, fanaticis et prophanis opinionibus. Quinto, adderetur gravis et seria exhortatio ex verbo Dei, ut in pacto Baptismi, et in illa doctrina et fide perseveraret, et proficiendo subinde confirmaretur. Sexto, fieret publica precatio pro illis pueris, ut Deus Spirtu suo sancto illos in hac professione gubernare, conservare et confirmare dignaretur. Ad quam precationem, sine superstitione adhiberi posset impositio manuum. Nec inanis esset ea precatio: nititur enim promissionibus de dono perseverantiae, et gratia confirmationis."
Preuss:297.

WORK   CALVIN   CHEMNITZ   BELLARMINE

R-57: Chemnitz, Martin
De confirmatione 25 (pag. 323)

                                                                    13:234

"Miretur autem aliquis, quare Pontificii in sua confirmatione illa tolerare nolint. Sed ratio est quia hoc modo confirmatio nihil aliud esset, quam commonefactio de suscepto Baptismo: et esset corroboratio in gratia, quae in Baptismo collata est. Illud vero Pontificii nolunt, sicut, supra ostensum est: atque propterea haec quae diximus, ex sua confirmatione exterminant, licet valde insidiose posita sint verba Canonis, 'Non tantum esse catechesin et professionem fidei' cum tamen plerunque talem aetatem in confirmatione deligant, ubi plane nullus potest locus esse catechesi, explorationi, professioni et exhortationi. Usque adeo nullam, vel manifestissime utilem emendationem homines isti vel tolerare possunt, vel admittere cogitant."
Preuss:297.

R-58: Chemnitz, Martin
De confirmatione 26 (pag. 324-325)[57]

                                                        8:222   12:230
                                                       12:230   12:232
                                                       12:232   12:232
                                                                12:232

"Sicut Viennae quondam Faber Episcopus clamitavit, fundamenta orbis tantum non collapsura, cum minister deferens ampullam Chrismatis, calceos aestu in itinere torrefactos, pinguedine ex ampullae orificio exundante et superfluente, ex simplicitate quadam perunxisset.
"Tertius Canon illinitionem Chrismatis in Confirmatione, solis Episcopis sub anathematis interminatione vindicat. . . . Scriptura ignorat discrimen Episcopi et Presbyteri. Hieronymus dicit: Quicquid hujus fit, magis ad honorem sacerdotii, quam ad legis necessitatem fieri. . . . Nec ignorant, quomodo Canonistae, quomodo Alexander, Thomas, Richardus, hanc quaestionem ex illo Canone disputent. . . . Anathema igitur erit etiam omnis Episcopus, qui oves suas non ipse Chrismate confirmarit."
Preuss:298.

---

[57]   At 12:230 the Battezzati edition refers to pag. 225, but it matches the material equal to pag. 325.

WORK	CALVIN	CHEMNITZ	BELLARMINE

R-59: Colloquy of Ratisbon (1540)
De confirmatione

25:297

"Et quia nunc infantes omnes baptizantur et ad baptisma fidei professionem per se non edunt, conveniet, ut pueri, postquam catechizati et de religione Christi instituti ad confirmationis sacramentum percipiendum adducantur, fidem Christi et oboedientiam ecclesiae suo etiam ore profiteantur, quemadmodum in concilio Aurelianensi can. 3. (qui habetur De consecratione dist. V cap. 6 Ut ieiuni) constitutum est, ut tamen hinc aliarum ecclesiarum mos hactenus observatus non damnetur, donec concilio generali super eo statuatur."
"Das Regensburger Buch aus 1540/1541." Ed. Georg Pfeilschifter. ARCEG 6 (1974):68.

R-60: Eck, John (1486-1543)
De sacramento confirmationis

25:297

"Appendicem illam totam reijcerem, nisi in fine autor seipsum inclinaret: quia puer baptisatus & confirmatus habet maiorem gratiam, quam baptisatus tantum. Sequitur puerum baptisatum & confirmatum: morientem premiari maiori gloria beatitudinis: cuius unus gradus excellit omnes diuitias mundi: Ideo acceleranda est confirmatio infantis inquit Holcot & Maioris, necque oportet expectare usum rationis ait Gerson: Quod citat concilium Aurelianensis c. 3. Sic etiam citauit Gratianus: sic Ivo. in Panormia: attamen in impresso Concilio Aurelianensis non reperitur: quod si etiam inuenitur, liquet canonem loqui de adultis, qui sunt perfectae aetatis, debent uenire ieiuni ad confirmationem, facta prius peccatorum confessione."
Apologia pro reverendis. et illustris. principibus Catholicis. ac alijs ordinibus Imperij aduersus mucores & calumnias Buceri, super actis Comitiorum Ratisponae. Ingolstadt: 1542. Fol. xxxxv.

WORK	CALVIN	CHEMNITZ	BELLARMINE

R-61: Faber, Johannes (1478-1541)
—58

26:298

"ampullam Chrismatis"

R-62: Gropper, Johannes (1503-1559)
De sacramento confirmationis

3:286 5:287
7:287

"Qui enim post baptismum cum acquisita innocentia immaculatus peruenit ad mortem, ipsa morte cofirmatur, quod non poßit peccare post mortem. Iam vero quum nos post transitum mare rubrum uastum huius mundi desertum ingredi, ac cum hostibus & internis & externis, priusquam ad terram repromißionis perueniamus, sine intermißione dimicare oporteat, nempe carne, mundo, & diabolo, quorum impetus tantus est, ut nemo secure glorietur se in hoc corpore peccati, sine peccato esse posse, quod humanae cupiditates & ueteris peccati reliquiae in sinu nostro latentes, rebellionem aduersus spiritum mouere nunquam cessant. Mundus quoque nos adhuc mortali corpore onustos, omnibus machinis oppugnat. Denique diabolus mille artifex tanquam leo rugiens, semper circuit quaerens quem deuoret, ut merito quis hanc initurus luctam grauiter terreatur, nisi interim agnoscat Christum redemptorem (qui carnem domuit, mundum uicit, ac diabolum mundi principem foras eiecit) aduersus hosce insultus alia parata remedia, quibus luctanctibus nobis subueniret, reliquisse, ut non in uirtutibus nostris, sed in eo faciamus uirtutem. . . . In baptismo, filij dei renascimur, & coelestis haereditatis promißionem accipimus, sed ut hanc retineamus, pupillis tutore est opus. Quare non satis uisum est Christo, in baptismo nobis impartiri spiritum innouantem, nisi & per confirmationis sacramentum largiretur spiritum tuentem ac defendentem, qui tamen non alius, sed idem est spiritus in baptismo datus, alius tantum atque alius secundum diuersas gratiarum donationes & charismata. Nam quatenus in confirmatione datur, paracletus est, qui regenerati in Christo, & custos,

---

[58] It is not clear among the works of Fabri which one Chemnitz refers to here, a story of the scandalous use of chrism on a hot day to repair shoes.

WORK   CALVIN   CHEMNITZ   BELLARMINE

& consolator, & tutor est."
Enchiridion christianae institutionis in Concilio Prouinciali Coloniensi editum, opus omnibus uerae pietatis cultoribus longe utilißimum. Venice: Ioannes Francesius, 1543. Fol. 59.

R-63: Hesshusen, Tilemann (1527-1588)
De erroribus pontificiorum 22,26

                                                                    13:233
"Chrisma tantùm non adorandum esse: siquidem haec verba dici iubent Pontificij, Ave sanctum Chrisma. Pontificale. . . . <Antidota:> Tota doctrina Pontificiorum de Confirmatione est merum figmentum cerebri humani sine omni testimonio Sacrae scripturae. . . . Idolatria & incantatio quae in magica consecratione Chrismatis exercetur, damnatur in primo & 2. praeceptis. Non habebis DEOS alienos coram me. Et non assumes nomen Domini DEI tui inuanum."
Sexcenti errores pleni blasphemiis in Deum quos Romana Pontificia Ecclesia contra Dei verbum furenter defendit. Frankfurt am Mainz: Georgius Coruinus, 1572. Fo. 111.

R-64: Hubmaier, Balthasar (1485-1528)
Schriften[59]

                                                                    11:289
"Christus infantibus, qui sibi adducebantur, benedictionem conferabat, non Baptismo, sed imositione manuum, Marc. 10."
(as cited by Chemnitz)

R-65: Leipzig Interim (1548)
Firmung

                                                                     1:211
"Daß die Firmung gelehrt und gehalten werde, und sonderlich die Jugend, die erwachsen, von ihren Bischoffen, oder weme es dieselbigen befehlen, verhdret werden ihres Glaubens, daß sie denen bekennen, und die Zusage, die ihre Pathen in der Taufe für sie gethan, und dem Teufel abgesagt haben, bekräftigen, und also in ihrem Glauben vermittelst

---

[59] I could not locate this text in Hubmaier. His complete works are in the following volume: Ed. Gunnar Westin, Torsten Bergsten, QFRG 29 (Gütersloher Verlagshaus: Gerd Mohn, 1962).

WORK CALVIN CHEMNITZ BELLARMINE

göttlicher Gnade confirmirt und bestätigt werden, mit Auflegung der Hände und christlichen Gebethen und Ceremonien."
CR 7 (1840):261. 217.

R-66: Luther, Martin (1483-1546)
De confirmatione

26:298

"Ita, quales sunt sacerdotes, tale habeant ministerium et offitium."
De captivitate Babylonica ecclesiae praeludium. 1520. WA 6 (1888):550.

R-67: Luther, Martin
De confirmatione

1:211

"Quare satis est pro ritu quodam Ecclesiastico seu cerimonia sacramentali confirmationem habere, similem caeteris cerimoniis consecrandae aquae aliarumque rerum."
WA 6:550.

R-68: Melanchthon, Philipp (1497-1560)
Loci theologici

1:211

"Olim fuit exploratio doctrinae, in qua singuli recitabant summam doctrinae et ostendebant se dissentire ab Ethnicis et Haereticis, et erat mos ad erudiendos homines, item ad discernendos profanos et pios admodum utilis. Postea fiebat publica precatio, et Apostoli imponebant eius manus. Ita donabantur manifestis donis Spiritus sancti. Sed nunc ritus Confirmationis, quem retinent Episcopi, est prorsus otiosa ceremonia. Utile autem esset, explorationem et professionem doctrinae fieri et publicam precationem pro piis, nec ea precatio esset inanis."
CR 21 (1854):853.

R-69: Nausea, Friedrich (1490-1552)
De confirmatione 3,29

12:289

"Quem deinde sic confirmatum, idem episcopus in maxillam percutit, ob nonnullas nec contemnendas causas. . . . Tertia, ut hac percussione

WORK   CALVIN   CHEMNITZ   BELLARMINE

repraesentet manuum impositionem, qua apostoli in confirmando usi
sint: nec aliud nunc fieri conferrique per episcopum, quod per apostolos
olim."
Catholicus catechismus. Cologne: Quentelianus, 1543. Fo. xxx.

R-70: Dominic Soto (1495-1560)
De sacramento confirmationis 4:7,1,2

                                                           9:227

"At uerò Caietan. in hoc articulo ait, quòd licèt balsamum sit
necessarium necessitate praecepti, non tamen necessitate sacramenti.
Itaque qui illud non apponeret, peccaret quidem mortaliter, nihilominus
sacramentum conficeret. Et quanuis vbique uerear communi me obijcere
opinioni, tamen quia contrarium non est hactenus ab ecclesia tanquam
catholicum definitum, fateor hanc mihi opinionem semper placuisse,
neque modò displicere posse."
Commentariorvm Fratris Dominici Soto in qvartum sententiarvm. Ed.
Caesarea Maiestatus. Venice: Hieronymus Zenarius, & Fratres, 1584.
1:359.

R-71: Surius (1522-1578)
3, Vita Bonifacii[60]

                                                    4:217 8:224

"concilium"

R-72: Surius
1, Vita Remberti

                                                           6:219

"Fertur vero etiam, priscorum more sanctorum, quaedam fecisse
miracula, nempe cum in Svediam proficisceretur, non raro maris
tempestatem suis orationibus sedasse, caeci cujusdam oculos illuminasse,
idque cum   pontificali   more   illum   sacro   adhibito   chrismate
confirmaret."
Historiae seu vitae sanctorum. Turin: Eq. Petri Marietti, 1875. 2:104.

---

[60] I have been unable to locate the reference to a council of Boniface in Surius's work.
See R-72 for publication data.

WORK	CALVIN	CHEMNITZ	BELLARMINE

R-73: Franciscus Victoria (c. 1485-1546)
De sacramento confirmationis

9:227

"Balsamum autem necessarium est in materia confirmationis necessitate praecepit. . . . Et ex ritu ecclesiae. Non est autem necessarium necessitate sacramenti, nam balsamum est in sola Syria terra paganorum, & difficulter potest inueniri. & non videtur, quod materiam tam arduam vuoluerit Deus esse materiam sacramenti. non est ergo necessarium de essentia sacramenti, sicut nec aqua in consecratione sanguinis."
Summa sacramentorum ecclesiae. Ed. Marcus Antonius. Venice: Ioannes de Albertis, 1609. Fol. 31.

R-74: Zwingli, Ulrich (1484-1531)
De vera et falsa religione

1:211

"Reliqua sacramenta ceremoniae potius sunt; nihil enim initiant in ecclesia dei. Unde non immerito loco moventur; non enim a deo institutae sunt, ut aliquid eis in ecclesia initiemus. . . . Confirmatio tunc sumpsit exordium, qum vulgo coeptum est infantes tingi, qum apud priscos ii modo tingerentur, qui in vitae dimicatione constituti essent. Quamquam quid hoc erat? Num mortis discrimen doctiores rerum Christianarum faciebat? Sed imbibitus erat error, qui baptismum existimabat post fidem peccata abluere; qui deinde, ut adsolet atrocius grassatus, ausus fuit infantibus etiam salutem negare, quasi vero crudelior sit Christus quam Moses, sub quo inter filios Israel censebantur, qui circumcisi essent, aut oblationibus initiati; etiamsi Abraham fide nondum imitarentur, nec enim poterant."
CR 90 (1911): 761-762. 823.

---

8. SECULAR SOURCES

WORK　　　　　　　CALVIN　　CHEMNITZ　　BELLARMINE

X-1: Pliny the Younger (61-114)
Historia naturalis 5:12,54 (25)

9:227 9:228

"Sed omnibus odoribus praefertur balsamum, uni terrarum Iudaeae concessum, quondam in duobus tantum hortis, utroque regio, altero iugerum viginti non amplius, altero pauciorum. ostendere arborum hanc urbi imperatores Vespasiani, clarumque dictu, a Pompeio Magno in triumpho arbores quoque duximus. servit nunc haec, ac tributa pendit cum sua gente, in totum alia natura quam nostri externique prodiderant; quippe viti similior est quam myrto: malleolis seri didicit nuper, vincta ut vitis; et inplet colles vinearum modo. quae sine adminiculis se ipsa sustinet tondetur similiter fruticans; ac rastris nitescit properatque nasci, intra tertium annum fructifera. folium proximum tuberi, perpetua coma. saeviere in eam Iudaei sicut in vitam quoque suam; contra defendere Romani et dimicatum pro frutice est; seritque nunc eum fiscus; nec unquam fuit numerosior; proceritas intra bina cubita subsistit."

Rackham, H. *Pliny: Natural History with an English Translation in Ten Volumes*, 4. Cambridge: Harvard University Press, 1945.

X-2: Virgil (70-19 BC)
The Aeneid 7

13:233

"Continuo, Salve fatis mihi debita Tellus,
Vosque, ait, o fidi Troiae salvete Penates!
Hic domus, haec patria est. Genitor mihi talia (namque
Nunc repeto) Anchises fatorum arcana reliquit:
Quum te, nate, fames ignota ad litora vectum
Adcisis coget dapibus consumere mensas,
Tum sperare domos defessus ibique memento
Prima locare manu molirique aggere tecta.
Haec erat illa fames; haec nos suprema manebat.
Exitiis positura modum.
Quare agite et primo laeti cum lumine solis,
Quae loca quive habeant homines, ubi moenia gentis,

matter, form, effect, minister, and ceremonies.[62] Each time Bellarmine quotes a source to support his position, he fits it into this structure. This allows him to use effectively those authors who support this method, as in the question among medieval theologians regarding the proper minister for confirmation.[63] However this technique brings Bellarmine to the anachronism of imposing his framework on earlier authors. For example, he calls in a host of ancient witnesses to show that chrism is the matter for confirmation;[64] yet, these pre scholastics presented oil as a symbolic element in the rite, not as part of a hylomorphic theory of sacramental theology.

Calvin arranges his material in a fashion similar to Bellarmine. He proposes thescholastic sacramental elements to show confirmation is not a sacrament. He often introduces these sections with a citation from Gratian and then gives his opposition to its theology.[65] He draws on the support of the Scriptures and – to a limited extent – patristics to underline his position. For example, concerning the effect of confirmation, Calvin turns to Gratian's quote of Pseudo-Miltiades for the Catholic position: In baptism the Holy Spirit is given for innocence, and in confirmation for an increase of grace; in baptism one is regenerated for life and in confirmation one is prepared for battle.[66] But Calvin counters this position with Romans 6 to show that baptism alone comprises these powers.[67] He adds Romans 10, Matthew 10 and Galatians 3 for support.[68] In the same argument Calvin makes a rare use of a conciliar text, a decree from Milevis,[69] to show that the grace of God at baptism does not simply remit sins but also fortifies against sinning again. As will be shown below, Calvin can be careless in the use

---

[62] See Chapter II, fn. 27 above.

[63] See below, fn. 153-155.

[64] See below, fn. 183-184.

[65] References to the chart in this chapter will be numbered according to their appearance in the sections abbreviated as follows: S=Scripture, P=Popes, C=Councils, G=Greek Fathers, L=Latin Fathers, M=Medieval Sources, R=Reformation Sources, X=Secular Sources. For texts of Gratian refer to M-44 and M-42 for section 8 (effect), M-43 and M-48 for section 9 (effect), M-45 for section 10 (minister), M-47 for section 11 (ceremonies).

[66] M-59.

[67] S-61.

[68] S-62, S-13, and S-72.

[69] C-16.

of his sources; he imposes his conclusions on them as easily as
Bellarmine does. He follows the thomistic outline. He draws more from
the Scriptures than from patristics. He uses the Scriptures to contrast
them with the Catholic position.

Chemnitz himself explains to the reader how he intends to use the
materials at his disposal.

> So that the entire dispute concerning confirmation
> might be explained in a brief and more suitable order, first
> we will recount what is the doctrine of the Papists and what
> they say about confirmation. Second we will show how that
> doctrine and statement of the Papists either agrees with
> Scripture or contradicts it. Third we will say certain things
> concerning the statements which are quoted from the
> writings of the ancients on behalf of confirmation. Finally we
> shall examine the canons and ask again how our churches
> judge that the rite of confirmation is able to be observed and
> used in the Church piously and with fruitfulness for
> edification.[70]

Chemnitz takes a different approach in organization: His
material is outlined not according to Thomas, but as a response to the
canons of the Council of Trent. This technique was used earlier by
Calvin in his *Antidotum*, though Chemnitz expands on the form. He
presents the Roman Church's position and contrasts it with Scripture
and tradition, to enhance the examination of the canons. So far is
Chemnitz from following the method of his adversaries, that
Bellarmine must skip around the *Examen* to find the elements which
correspond to his own outline.[71] It is Chemnitz then whose presentation
of the material shows more creativity.[72]

In contrasting the Catholics with Scripture and tradition
Chemnitz calls on a far greater assembly of witnesses for his argument

---

[70]   "Ut tota disputatio de Confirmatione, brevi et commodiori ordine explicari
possit, Primo recitabimus, quae sit Pontificiorum doctrina, et sententia de
Confirmatione. Secundo, Ostendemus quomodo illa Pontificiorum doctrina et sententia,
Scripturae vel consentiat, vel repugnet. Tertio, Dicemus quaedam de sententiis, quae ex
veterum scriptis pro Confirmatione allegantur. Postremo Canones examinabimus, et
repetemus, quomodo Ecclesiae nostrae judicent ritum Confirmationis pie, et cum fructu ad
aedificationem posse in Ecclesia observari et usurpari." 1, Preuss:284.

[71]   Observe the seemingly haphazard order of Bellarmine's use of Chemnitz texts
in R-41 through R-58.

[72]   For sheer creativity it is difficult to surpass the work of Luther. His approach
to the sacraments through the Scriptures was a unique contribution to the field.

than does Calvin. He both exposes information and comments on it. He usually quotes an entire passage, but sometimes paraphrases[73] or gives only a citation. In general, his use of sources is selective: A comparison of his and Bellarmine's use of the writings of Augustine show how one author's corpus may support either side.[74]

Therefore, while the method of Chemnitz's outline is unique in the controversy, his use of sources is similar to Calvin's: He relies primarily on Scripture and uses the other fonts as they substantiate his position. He chooses selectively and organizes the sources according to his own system. Of the three controversialists he is the least dependent on Thomas's order of presentation, but shares the reliance of scholasticism on historical research and interpretation.

2. Treatment of Sources

This section will examine three groups of sources – Scripture, patristics, and liturgical fonts – to see in general the differences and similarities in their use by the controversialists.

a. Scripture

The Reformers call on the Scriptures to amplify their understanding of baptism, to contrast the apostolic events with those of the Roman Church, and to pose minor applications.

Calvin's presentation never refers to the Old Testament, and almost each part cites from the New. His theology of confirmation is tempered by his theology of baptism, developed from many Scripture texts, mostly Pauline, which for him set the events of Acts in relief.[75] He uses Scripture to defuse the arguments of his opponents. He contrasts the Catholic rite of confirmation with the apostolic practice in Acts. In doing so, however, he adopts the thomistic method, and seeks matter and form from the Scriptures.[76] He observes the formula is not in Scripture and that the miraculous gifts accompanying the first imposition of hands no longer happen.[77] In these instances he uses Scripture to contrast with the reality he sees in the Roman Church.

[73] He paraphrases even Luther, for example, at 26:298 (see R-56) and inverts the order of Cyril's sentences from the second mystagogical catechesis (see G-10).

[74] See L-9 through L-39.

[75] See the example in fn. 67 and 68 above.

[76] 7, CR 30:1071.

[77] R-28 and R-30, R-29.

Calvin turns to the Scriptures for other purposes: He uses Matthew 21[78] about John the Baptist's dialogue with the Pharisees to deliver a pejorative homily, asking his opponents to prove that confirmation comes from heaven. In two instances he interprets the Scriptures especially freely: He believes the imposition of hands in Acts 8 records an offering of the baptized and that Ananias's imposition of hands on Paul is another expression of the apostolic rite.[79] Still, his primary purpose is to contrast Scripture with the theology and results of Catholic confirmation.

Chemnitz uses Scripture in similar ways. He employs a broad range of New Testament texts which analyze the events of Acts against a theology of baptism. His many references include Ephesians 5, Mark 16, Romans 6, 1 Corinthians 12, John 3, Titus 3, and 1 Peter 3.[80] Like Calvin, he also shows the difference between the events of Acts and the practice of the Roman Church. He admits that miraculous events accompanied the imposition of hands in Acts 8 and 19, the cure by Ananias in Acts 9, and the prayers of the Apostles in Acts 5,[81] but this conflicts with the results of confirmation in the Roman Church. Chemnitz argues that, in fact, "confirmation" (strengthening) occurs by the Word alone without the imposition of hands or any semblance of a sacrament in Acts 14, 15, and 18.[82] He believes that if confirmation were a sacrament, a command would have been given for all time. The Scriptures do not call for the universal application of confirmation, whereas they do for baptism and Eucharist – in Matthew 28, 1 Corinthians 11, and 1 Corinthians 12.[83] He takes the silence of Scripture to mean that the presumed divine command given to the Apostles was of a temporary nature.[84]

Chemnitz, like Calvin, cites Scripture for lesser arguments: He uses Daniel 7 and 1 Corinthians 5[85] to make reproachful descriptions of the Roman Church. He misapplies Acts 19 to support his theory that

[78] S-14.

[79] S-43 and R-29; S-44.

[80] S-74, S-19, S-61, S-68, S-24, S-81, and S-85.

[81] S-43 and S-57, S-44, and S-40.

[82] S-16, S-67, and S-68.

[83] S-52, S-54, and S-56.

[84] 16, Preuss 290.

[85] S-11 and S-64.

confirmation was originally an examination of faith.[86]

Both Reformers, then, use Scripture as the backbone of their argument. The absence of scriptural evidence regarding confirmation is actually their strongest argument, and the wealth of texts describing the theology of baptism is a formidable contrast with the Roman Church's theology of the effects of confirmation. They also cite other examples of God's grace in the New Testament which share effects of confirmation but are not regarded as sacraments. Some texts are misapplications or weak supports.

Bellarmine wants to prove from the Scriptures that confirmation is a sacrament, since that is precisely what his adversaries say is not possible. He argues from Acts 8 and 19, from John 14, 15, and 16, and the last chapter of Luke,[87] that the sign for the sacrament, its promise of divine grace, and evidence of its divine command are all in the Bible. His success is incomplete: There is no written divine command, so he argues from the good character of the Apostles who he says would not have imposed hands without instructions from God. Bellarmine takes the passages, especially the principal one from Acts 8,[88] and applies them to every field of his thomistic schema. Contrary to the approach of Luther who looked to the Scriptures for a definition of a sacrament (beginning from the concept of testament),[89] Bellarmine's approach accepts a traditional definition of sacrament and shows how for him the Scriptures fulfill it.

He is less inclined to turn the Scriptures against the person of his adversary as the previous generation of controversialists would, although he does not resist using a favorite quote of the Reformers (Hebrews 10 on the necessity of faith)[90] to support his own position that faith needs to be cultivated, a task he says imposition of hands accomplished in the apostolic era.

However, Bellarmine does not reply to the Reformers' use of Scripture to amplify their understanding of baptism in contrast to confirmation. Bellarmine has another controversy on baptism, but he does not present material here to show how from his point of view the

[86] S-57.

[87] S-43 and S-57; S-30, S-31, and S-32; and S-23.

[88] S-43.

[89] See Chapter I, fn. 5.

[90] S-83.

theology of confirmation is not contrary to that of baptism in the Scriptures. He does respond, however, to the objection of his adversaries that there is no connection between the miraculous events in Acts and the Roman rite of confirmation. But to do so he turns to tradition: the Pseudo-Isidorian letter of Fabian and the decree from the Council of Florence.[91]

Thus, Bellarmine uses the Scriptures to argue that confirmation is a sacrament, to document his thomistic schema, and as a reference point for the sacramental practice of the later Church.

In none of the controversialists is there an analysis of Scripture passages according to historical-critical methods. Influenced by the scholastic methods of their own age, they isolated scriptural events and passages which supported the logic of their theological positions. Their hermeneutical standpoint favors not the Scriptures themselves, but the theology of their positions, even though the use of Scripture to support a theological theory was against the Spirit of the Reform. Even the historical-critical hermeneutic does not provide all the answers, but it would have added a measure of objectivity to the research. Luther, searching the Scriptures for the foundation of his theology, was probably truer to the idea of a scriptural hermeneutic than later generations were, who increasingly used passages not for their own integrity, but as weapons against the other side. It is also noteworthy that a good part of the Reformers' position is based on what the Scriptures do not say, and Bellarmine's attempt to fill this silence weakens his argument, although neither side can argue well from material that is simply not there.

b. Patristics

The second group of sources considered in this general analysis of method is the Fathers of the Church. All three controversialists rely on their testimony of ecclesial practice and scriptural interpretation.

The Reformers draw on the Fathers to support their explanations about the theology of confirmation, its history, and even the correct interpretation of other patristic texts.

Calvin uses patristic sources rarely; his argument is drawn primarily from the Scriptures. Still, he turns to other fonts when he sees their usefulness. However, he does not always apply them accurately. Concerning his belief that there are only two sacraments,

[91] M-58 and C-12.

for example, he cites Augustine[92] and claims that all the ancients agreed.[93] But Augustine never considered the question of number, and Calvin's report on other fonts is too general. Calvin commits another generalization in the *Antidotum* when he claims that none of the ancients mention oil.[94] Another inaccuracy is his criticism of a certain text from Gratian[95] which does not represent well the Catholic position. In addition, he simply misapplies some texts: He says Leo and Jerome describe confirmation as an examination of faith, but the references have nothing to do with his point.[96] He lifts lines from the Council of Milevis, Gregory the Great, and Augustine which support his argument,[97] but they lend it comparatively little help. In this controversy, Calvin's use of patristics betrays his unfamiliarity with the sources and carelessness in using them. He is best when he simply quotes from Gratian, and even in those instances his record is spotty.

Chemnitz uses patristic texts to demonstrate that even in the Catholic tradition there are different opinions about the institution of confirmation and its proper minister.[98] Having built his theology of baptism from Scripture he shows that the ancient writers who mention anointing did not assign to it the effects of baptism, especially Clement, Cyprian, Hilary, Basil, Gregory of Nyssa, John Chrysostom, Augustine, and Hesychius.[99]

In addition, Chemnitz uses the Fathers in a polemic against other Fathers quoted by the Catholics: Jerome and Rufinus[100] speak about Cyril; Eusebius and Gelasius[101] challenge the canonicity of works by Clement; the tradition of Ambrose is pitted against the pontifical of Duranti;[102] and Jerome is used to show Tertullian montanizes.[103]

---

[92] L-28 and L-10.

[93] R-34.

[94] R-23.

[95] C-21. This text will be analyzed in chapter IV

[96] P-31 and P-30, L-55 and L-57.

[97] C-16, P-17, and L-10.

[98] See below, fn. 144-148.

[99] G-5, L-40, L-50, G-3, G-31, G-34, L-34, and G-32.

[100] L-58 and L-67.

[101] G-25 and L-47.

[102] L-3 and M-24.

[103] L-55 and L-69.

Further, Chemnitz has the Fathers provide testimony to the history of the development of confirmation. He reveals the use of the imposition of hands, the separation of the bishop's role, and the practice of delaying confirmation through the Council of Elvira, Eusebius, Athanasius, Jerome,[104] and others. As he showed that the Roman anointing differed from the Scriptural events, he demonstrates it differs from the early patristic anointings of Ambrose, Dionysius and John Damascene.[105] The tradition of imposing hands for reconciling heretics is presented by Cyprian, the Council of Laodicea, the Council of Arles, and Leo the Great, while Gregory distinguishes the Eastern and Western customs of imposing hands.[106]

Besides citing the Fathers favorably to support his argument, Chemnitz also cites them critically to show where they have erred. He justifies this dual approach to patristics by keeping Scripture as the norm.[107] Predictably, much criticism concerns the interpretation of Scripture. Chemnitz reviles Thomas's use of John 20[108] and corrects Cyril, Clement, and Cyprian[109] in their interpretation of pertinent passages. In addition, Chemnitz criticizes the theology of confirmation raised by Pseudo-Urban, Clement, Cyprian, the Council of Laodicea, Eusebius, Pseudo-Miltiades among the ancients, and the ritual of Duranti.[110] He denies the reliability of Fabian's letter and regards Tertullian and Cyprian as Montanists.[111] He gives little credence to more recent witnesses, such as Rabanus, Gerson, and the Council of Florence,[112] and scoffs at his contemporaries Andrada, Gropper, and Nausea.[113]

Chemnitz invites the reader to consider how the Papists, "proud of their own opinion search out from wherever whatever supports."[114]

---

[104] C-9, G-28, G-2, and L-57.

[105] L-2, G-15, and G-39.

[106] L-41, C-13, C-1, P-30, and P-18.

[107] See for example 22:291.

[108] M-81 and S-34.

[109] G-11, P-7, L-42.

[110] M-61, P-7, L-41 and L-42, C-14, G-28, M-59, and M-24.

[111] M-58, L-69, and L-41.

[112] M-75, M-30, and C-12.

[113] R-1, R-62, and R-69.

[114] ". . . praesumptae suae opinionis, undecunque conquirant qualiacunque suffragia." 10:288.

Actually, all parties are guilty of seeking votes for their preconceived opinions. Whereas Chemnitz is generally faithful to his sources, he sometimes adapts the material. His interpretation of the imposition of hands in Augustine's *De baptismo* as a personal acceptance of baptismal faith betrays his Lutheran training.[115] He also reinterprets material from Cyril to fit his distinctions between baptism and confirmation, and broadly interprets the Councils of Laodicea and Arles and the work of Dionysius[116] to describe confirmation as examination of faith before a bishop. Sometimes his evidence is unstable: Like Calvin, Chemnitz cites a text and gloss from Gratian which are not representative of Catholic theology in general.[117]

In summary, Chemnitz cites from the patristics to show divisions both among Catholics and within the sources themselves, which betray a diversity in the celebration and theology of confirmation in history. He corrects the Fathers against the norm of the Scriptures, but sometimes forces the interpretation to fit his position.

Bellarmine – uniquely in this controversy – uses the patristic texts as companions to Scripture for building his argument. Where the Reformers would criticize the Fathers according to norms of Scripture, Bellarmine lets them speak with full voice. Where the Reformers support their case primarily from corroborating Scripture texts, Bellarmine looks to corroborating patristic texts. An examination of the first controversy on the sacramentality of confirmation will serve as an example, where he divides his witnesses into five groups: Scripture, Popes, Councils, Greek Fathers, and Latin Fathers – each sharing the burden of proof.

As an example of how Bellarmine uses a variety of texts for his argument one may examine the controversy over balsam.[118] He stretches the question of the matter of confirmation over two chapters, one to present his position, the other to respond to the objections of the Reformers. In the midst of the first section Bellarmine proposes that chrism is made of a mixture of oil and balsam.[119] He supports this not

---

[115] This interpretation of L-10 will be explained in the next chapter.

[116] G-10 and G-11, C-13, C-1, and G-22.

[117] C-21.

[118] The complete disputation on confirmation is too vast to analyze here – Bellarmine refers to his sources over 800 times; since he repeats his method, one section is indicative of the others.

[119] 8:223.

from the Scriptures (where it cannot be found) but from tradition: Dionysius, Clement, the Pseudo-Isidorian letter of Fabian, Pseudo-Cyprian, Gregory of Tours, Pseudo-Gregory (Bede), the Second Council of Braga, and the Council of Florence.[120] In reality Clement's reference is obscure and the pseudonymous sources are later than Bellarmine thinks, but still his method is to present an army of witnesses to show the affirmation of history behind his argument. Among the objections of the Reformers is a complaint from Chemnitz that in spite of what the Catholics would like to use, true balsam doesn't exist any more, so it is impossible to make chrism anyway.[121] Chemnitz is supported by a text of Pliny the Younger,[122] one of two secular sources in the controversy, who records that the Romans destroyed all the native balsam in Palestine. Bellarmine charges that Pliny was unaware of native Indian balsam and summons Jerome and Pseudo-Gregory[123] to give early testimony to its presence in Israel. This is one example of how Bellarmine uses his sources to add historical support to his position.

In other citations, Bellarmine openly exposes the division of opinion among Catholics. A section below will demonstrate this in regard to the proper minister of confirmation. Another example is found again in the balsam dispute where Bellarmine acknowledges that some theologians believed the addition of balsam was not essential to the sacrament. Innocent III and those who comment on the Sentences[124] teach that balsam is required by necessity of the sacrament, but Cajetan, Dominic Soto, and Francis Victoria,[125] hold the contrary. Not all the texts, then, directly support Bellarmine's argument. Even though he sides with the latter group, he presents the opposite opinion to show that others disagree.

Finally, there are instances where Bellarmine uses his sources inaccurately. His tendency towards using sources anachronistically has already been shown, how he applies an ancient text to fit the framework of scholasticism developed centuries later.[126] He sometimes misapplies texts, as will be shown below concerning the reconciliation

120 G-18, P-7, M-58, M-9, L-49, M-14, C-4, and C-12.

121 R-53.

122 X-1.

123 L-54 and M-14.

124 P-27; M-71, M-72, and M-73.

125 R-22, R-70, and R-73.

126 See fn. 64 above.

of heretics.[127] But perhaps a greater difficulty is his use of pseudonymous sources. Bellarmine is not alone in this -- the practice used by preceding controversialists was already attacked by Chemnitz:

> For first, the foremost statements which are brought forward concerning chrismation have been taken up from writings which partly have been relegated among the apocrypha by the Roman Church herself; partly they were totally unknown to true antiquity, and therefore there is no doubt that they are forged and counterfeit.[128]

Bellarmine stated that even if some people regard various writings as dubious, he has others which are more certain.[129] This is true, but Bellarmine continued to use these pseudonymous sources to illustrate his points as if they were genuine, or at least comparable in value to authentic ones, and since he was aware that their authority was questionable, they weaken his arguments. Further, writing after Chemnitz's accusation makes Bellarmine's dependence on these sources even more deleterious to his argument. A more profitable position would admit the later dating and less prestigious authorship of these works for the contribution they still make toward an understanding of the history of confirmation. The work of Pseudo-Cyprian, for example, which Bellarmine acknowledges is not really Cyprian,[130] he still calls an ancient source, presumably because it is found in some manuscripts together with the works of that Latin Father. But in fact it is by Arnaldus of Bonnevaux, who post-dates Cyprian by almost a thousand years.[131]

The Reformers are not caught in the web of these historical inaccuracies. Chemnitz does criticize a pseudonymous letter of Clement as if it were authentic,[132] but the problems are much more related to the Roman Church because of its dependence on tradition.

This discrimination of sources never reaches the Scriptures. In the entire argument, Bellarmine quotes from the Protestant apocrypha

[127] See fn. 197 below.

[128] See R-49 for original.

[129] Chapter II, fn. 123.

[130] M-8 and M-9; see 3:285.

[131] See Joseph Huby, "Une Exégèse faussement attribuée à Saint Cyprien," *Biblica* 14 (1933):96.

[132] M-55.

once, a minor reference to the book of Wisdom,[133] strung together with many other examples. Presumably, the disputed texts were not needed for supporting this particular controversy.

In summary, Bellarmine relies on patristic sources as foundational to his argument together with the Scriptures, to refute the adversary and to support his own theology. This is the most unique feature of his method compared with that of the Reformers. He openly shows divisions in Catholic theology to resolve them for his readers. He misapplies some texts and misuses pseudonymous sources to build his case.

All the controversialists draw on the patristics to lend support for their own position and criticism against the other. They note the historical divisions that preceded this dispute. In their zeal they comment more from the hermeneutic of the post- Reformation than from that of the texts themselves. This loss of balance in their approach causes them to misuse and misapply some texts. Calvin uses the sources sparingly, and poorly. Chemnitz, who is unique in his outline of the material, still presents his sources in the style of the others. For Bellarmine, the patristic texts form an integral part of his argument with the Scriptures. He uses the greatest volume of references, but the number can obscure that he avoids some controversies introduced by the Reformers.

c. Liturgical Sources

The final group of sources in this general analysis is liturgical. These texts play a minor role in the controversy. They arise primarily in the context of the question of the form of confirmation. The discussion over Duranti's rite of confirmation follows in the next chapter, but some comments are made here regarding the method of using these texts.

Calvin's entire argument builds on Scripture and some testimony of the ancients. He never turns to a liturgical text to prove his own theology, but only to challenge that of the Roman Church. In fact, he so roots his own position in Scripture that his own position in Scripture that he chides the Church for using a liturgical source at all as a font of theology. [134]

Chemnitz, however, lays open the ritual texts of baptism, confirmation and the blessing of oils to present the Roman   Church's

---

133 S-9.
134 R-30.

position on the sacraments. [135] He shows that the scriptural gesture of imposing hands was replaced in the liturgy by anointing with chrism,[136] and criticizes the many rituals not found in the Bible which have been added to the rite.[137] He recognizes that the liturgy is a font of theology, but criticizes it as a poor and even errant source when compared to the Scriptures.

Among the many fonts Bellarmine calls upon to help his argument, he rarely turns to the liturgy. It is the greatest lacuna in his research. Even when he does cite Duranti or the Roman Ordo,[138] Bellarmine finds them a practical guide for carrying out the rubrics of confirmation as much as a theological one for understanding its meaning. Yet through the history of the Church, East and West, there is a great wealth of pontificals and rituals which could have been tapped for their theological contribution to the controversy. For all his knowledge of the Church's tradition, Bellarmine sparingly cited the pontificals as primary sources for theology. Of course, in this controversy the addition of liturgical texts to Bellarmine's argument would achieve little in convincing his adversaries of the rightness of his opinion since they have scorned the value of such sources, but it would have improved the integral unity and completeness of his otherwise scholarly historical research.

Of all these groups of sources, then, the liturgical texts receive the least attention in the controversy. Calvin spurns them, Chemnitz sees their value and criticizes them, and Bellarmine ignores a great part of his own tradition.

3. Examples

To analyze these methods in depth two examples will be taken from among the arguments in the controversy. The introduction to this entire study observed that throughout the tradition there has been some instability in the areas of who is the minister and what is the matter of confirmation. This section takes up these two concerns to evaluate how the protagonists of this controversy analyzed the sources at their disposal to support their positions. To proceed, a theological question is posed, then Calvin, Chemnitz, and Bellarmine respond. For

[135] M-26, M-24, and M-25.
[136] See 2:285.
[137] M-24.
[138] M-24 and M-67.

each response the method will be analyzed and evaluated on its own, then contrasted with the other writers. A third example is not specifically a controversy, but an analysis of how the controversialists handle the material concerning the reconciliation of heretics.

a. Minister: Priest or Bishop?
i. Calvin
a'. Analysis

Calvin takes up the controversy over the minister in both the *Institutio* and the *Antidotum*.[139] In the *Institutio* it is one of several sections which begin by posing a quote from Gratian to which Calvin formulates his response. Here the canon is attributed to Miltiades from the Pseudo-Isidorian collection.[140] It holds that confirmation should be held in greater veneration than baptism since it is administered by a bishop, not a priest. Calvin comments on the irony of setting a human invention over a divine institution, and enchanted oil over sanctified water.

He says some moderate this position. (He does not specify who.) They say confirmation has no greater power than baptism, but a worthier minister confers it. Against this opinion Calvin says its supporters reveal themselves as Donatists who evaluate a sacrament on the worthiness of the minister. He admits that bishops add dignity to confirmation, but denies that they inherited this ministry from the Apostles for several reasons: First, it is not bishops who succeed the Apostles: If priests were not their successors as well, even the Eucharist would have to be reserved to bishops. Second, imposition of hands was not reserved to the Apostles: The Scriptures record that Ananias, who was not an Apostle, imposed hands on Paul so that he might receive the Holy Spirit.[141] Finally, he says the office does not belong to bishops by divine right; if it did, they would need to explain how Gregory could have transferred it to priests.[142]

Calvin treats the material in the *Antidotum* in a similar way. The position of his adversary is represented by canon 3 of Trent on confirmation. He comments by insulting the bishops of the Roman

---

[139] R-32 and R-24.
[140] M-60.
[141] S-44.
[142] P-17.

Church, then says there is nothing in Scripture to support the difference between bishop and priest or that this ministry belongs to the bishop. Again he cites the case of Ananias and argues from Gregory that even priests can confirm.

Calvin's method then is this: Twice in the *Institutio* and once in the *Antidotum* he proposes the argument of his adversary (Gratian, an unknown source, and Trent) and then responds by showing the error in its logic when compared to evidence from Scripture (Ananias), lack of evidence from Scripture (that bishops succeed Apostles), and the testimony of the Fathers (Gregory).

b'. Evaluation

Calvin faithfully presents the viewpoint of Pseudo-Miltiades and then reduces it to absurdity. He gives a similar treatment to the position that bishops are successors to Apostles. In a way he pushes too hard because even he admits that a bishop adds dignity to confirmation. His argument from the silence of Scripture on this issue has value since the ecclesiastical distinctions of bishop, priest, and Apostle were not made by Luke: One cannot successfully argue episcopal succession from Acts alone. His citation of Gregory is a good one for his argument – in point of fact, it is not bishops alone who confirm.

The weakness of his argument is his use of the Ananias story. True, Ananias imposed hands for the reception of the Holy Spirit and he was not an Apostle, but there is no Scriptural evidence that the case is similar to Acts 8 and 19, and far less that it is related to Pentecost.

ii. Chemnitz
a'. Analysis

Chemnitz takes up the question of the minister in direct response to the third canon of Trent at the very end of his section. Similar to Calvin's approach in the *Antidotum*, he begins by complaining about bishops: he cites Luther and a Pauline text.[143]

Then he invites the reader to examine the anathema of Trent against several witnesses: Scripture offers no distinction between priest and bishop. Jerome said confirmation pertained more to the honor of priesthood than to the necessity of law.[144] The Council of Toledo, citing

[143] R-66 and S-64.
[144] L-57.

historical precedents, said a priest   may administer chrism in the absence of a bishop.[145] Gregory dispensed priests to anoint the foreheads of the baptized with chrism.[146] Among more recent authors, Alexander of Hales, Thomas   Aquinas, and Richard Armachanus[147] held that a priest might administer confirmation by dispensation; Chemnitz presents their opinion in opposition to the canon of Trent which simply states the sacrament is administered by a bishop.[148]

Chemnitz concludes the discussion by ridiculing the practice of suffragan bishops administering confirmation. He interprets Trent to say that the bishop of a region himself must confirm, and draws on Innocent III for support.[149]

Chemnitz's method is to contrast the canon of Trent with a broad range of material which teaches the contrary. As Calvin did, he argues from the silence of Scripture and from historical sources that a priest can anoint. Chemnitz is opposed to Trent's bald statement that anointing belongs to the bishop.

b'. Evaluation

Chemnitz collects many texts which give solid witness to the practiceof priests anointing with chrism. His choice of Jerome is, however, weak. Jerome uses the word "sacerdotium", which has the meaning of either priest or bishop, and the rest of the passage speaks of the "episcopus", or bishop. It seems unlikely that Jerome's subtle change in terms would indicate a change in the meaning of the complete passage. Still, the permission for a priest to anoint is well documented here and in other passages throughout the chart.[150]

Although the documentation is fundamentally sound, the strength of the argument for Chemnitz as well as for Calvin depends on the opposition of these passages to Trent. First, Chemnitz proves only that priests may confirm; he does not prove that they may always confirm. Second, Trent was hardly trying to establish a new tradition that would abrogate the permission given to priests; rather, it was responding to the contrary opinion that any priest can confirm. The

---

[145] C-25.

[146] P-17.

[147] M-3, M-82. and M-76.

[148] C-32.

[149] P-26.

[150] See fn. 154 and 155 below. This passage from Jerome reappears at fn. 169 below.

canon does not explain how the dispensation works, and for this reason Chemnitz says it is opposed to the tradition, but it is an argument from silence. Still, he does reveal the weakness in Trent's canon.[151]

iii. Bellarmine
a'. Analysis

Faithful to Thomas's schema, Bellarmine discusses who is the proper minister of confirmation near the end of his presentation. First he presents the differing opinions, then offers texts from Scripture, and responds to the objections of his adversaries.

In the introduction Bellarmine presents the various sides of the controversy. First, his adversaries Wyclif, Calvin, and Chemnitz[152] say that any priest may confirm. Even among Catholics some took this side: Richard Armachanus and Thomas (Waldensis) Netter.[153] Then, within the Catholic Church some say a priest may never confirm (Bonaventure, Durandus, and Adrian)[154] while others say there are occasions when he can (Thomas Aquinas, Richard Armachanus, Pierre La Palud, Marsilius, and Gregory).[155]

Bellarmine then reconstructs the influences on the Council of Trent. He cites Ambrose, Gregory, Gratian, Thomas, Martin of Braga, and the Councils of Orange, Toledo, and Florence.[156] All speak of the role of the bishop in confirming and of the dispensation afforded to some priests.[157] Bellarmine concludes that Trent is faithful to this history and that Chemnitz is wrong to say Trent is opposed to it.

Next he offers proofs from the Scriptures. For biblical evidence he turns to the classic texts of Acts 8 and 19 where Peter, John, and Paul are called in to impose hands for Christian communities.[158] Bellarmine argues that there is no other reason why Apostles were called in except

---

[151] C-32.

[152] M-85, R-32, and R-58.

[153] M-76 and M-64.

[154] M-17, M-22, and P-1.

[155] M-82, M-76, M-69, M-62, and P-17.

[156] L-1, P-17, M-31, M-82, L-60, C-20, C-25, and C-12.

[157] Bellarmine is in error at 4:216. Quoting the councils which support the sacramentality of confirmation, he says Arles I (C-1) permits the return of heretics not by a second baptism, but by imposition of hands "ab episcopo." In fact, the canon does not mention the bishop.

[158] S-43 and S-57.

that this ministry pertains to the first ecclesiastical rank, and hence to bishops, their successors.

Responding to his adversaries, he finds absurd Wyclif's suggestion that perhaps Philipp had not baptized legitimately and the Apostles were now doing it right. Then he takes on Calvin's contention that if priests did not properly succeed the Apostles the Eucharist would have to be celebrated by bishops alone. Here Bellarmine begins a digression on the levels of ecclesiastical powers. Citing no sources, he explains that the Apostles held full ecclesial power on four levels: as Christians, priests, bishops, and universal rulers (a level shared in ordinarily by Peter, extraordinarily by the others). That bishops succeed Apostles is shown in the testimony of the Council of Neocasearea, Pseudo-Damasus, Jerome, Leo, and Augustine.[159] Since the Apostles shared power on so many levels, the question is how one can know that confirmation belongs to the episcopal ministry of the Apostles.

In response, Bellarmine offers proofs from Scripture, tradition, and reason: From the Scriptures he observes that confirmation is never attributed to anyone in another ministerial level – There are examples of deacons preaching, but only Apostles imposed hands. Then he proposes Hebrews 6 which lists imposition of hands as part of the Church's ministry;[160] this implies that it was not a ministry which ceased with the Apostles, but one which was continued by the Church. He deduces from these Scripture texts that imposition of hands was proper to the Apostles as bishops, and carried out by their successors. From tradition, Bellarmine says that all who cite Acts 8 as evidence for confirmation claim it is reserved to bishops by the same text. Finally, Bellarmine argues from reason: Confirmation is the perfection of baptism, and should be administered by one of higher rank. As the militia inscribes in the presence of a duke or emperor, inscription into the army of Christ, he says, is in the presence of a bishop.

Finally, Bellarmine responds to a series of arguments from his principal adversaries Calvin and Chemnitz, many of which have already been seen. Against Calvin's accusation that reserving confirmation to bishops is Donatist, Bellarmine argues from reason that the Donatist controversy was over moral worthiness, not ecclesiastical rank; even Calvin reserved the administration of baptism and

[159] C-17, M-56, L-52, P-33, and L-19.
[160] S-82.

Eucharist to priests.[161] Second, Calvin argued that priests, not bishops succeed the Apostles. Bellarmine deduces from his previous discussion on the many ministries of the Apostles that priests do succeed them but not in all ways. He also states from John 20 that the Apostles were priests before the ressurection and bishops afterwards.[162] The third argument is from Richard Armachanus,[163] that not only bishops imposed hands in the New Testament: in 1 Timothy 4 it is presbyters and in Acts 9 Ananias does. Bellarmine argues from Chrysostom's use of the word that the ordination in 1 Timothy is by the *presbyterum*, an assembly of bishops, and that Ananias imposed hands as a cure, not as confirmation.[164] Paul had not been baptized yet, and Bellarmine guesses he received confirmation from God as the other Apostles did at some unrecorded moment of his life. Fourth, Calvin asks how Gregory could have dispensed priests to confirm if bishops did it by divine law.[165] Bellarmine responds with an extended legal argument. His point is that bishops are the ordinary ministers of confirmation by divine law and priests may confirm by an extraordinary concession; the same phenomenon happens with preaching.

Bellarmine inserts into the discussion here a question among Catholics if bishops confirm by order or by jurisdiction. It seems that if it is by order there can be no dispensation, as a deacon cannot celebrate the Eucharist. If by jurisdiction it seems that a non-consecrated bishop who enjoys the jurisdiction of a bishop but the order of priesthood may confirm. Bellarmine responds that bishops confirm by order, which is in priests inchoatively. He explains that the bishop's character is an absolute, perfect, and independent power for conferring confirmation and orders, whereas the priestly character is an absolute, perfect, and independent power for baptism and Eucharist, but inchoate, imperfect, and dependent on the will of the superior for confirmation. Without the perfection of a dispensation, the priest does nothing by confirming and if perfected he confirms by his own character. The character, Bellarmine continues, is not a physical power (or how could it be perfected?) but a sign of the divine pact by which God produces the sacramental effect with the one who has it. The bishop's character is a

---

[161] R-25.

[162] S-33.

[163] M-76.

[164] G-33, S-77, and S-44.

[165] P-17.

sign of an absolute pact, the priest's is conditional. Throughout this presentation, Bellarmine gives no sources for the controversy among Catholics nor for his response.

Bellarmine resumes the controversy with his adversaries and concludes by responding to several arguments of Chemnitz. Chemnitz says the Scriptures do not know a distinction between priest and bishop; Bellarmine says they do, and cites 1 Timothy 5 to show the difference between "presbyterum" and "testores".[166] He accuses Chemnitz of accepting an argument from Arianism as recorded by Epiphanius and Augustine.[167] Chemnitz cited Jerome in arguing that priests could confirm. Bellarmine says the complete text reserves the practice to bishops and that Jerome's reference to the absence of a law pertains not to the law that bishops confirm but to a succeeding argument in Jerome's text that confirmation is not neccesary for salvation. Finally, Chemnitz counters that in practice it is suffragans who confirm in Germany, not the ordinary bishops themselves. Bellarmine says that the suffragans confirm validly because they are ordained bishops and have jurisdiction although they lack the possession of the diocese. He uses few resources through these responses and relies largely on deductive reasoning, the success of which varies with the strength of the starting principles or assumptions.

b'. Evaluation

Bellarmine uses many methods in citing his sources. He faithfully presents material from his adversaries and from different camps within the Catholic Church. He applies many of the same texts from tradition to support his argument that the Reformers use to support theirs, but his position is not what the Reformers think it is: For Bellarmine, the issue is not that bishops can confirm and priests cannot (a point the Reformers were able to refute with fonts of dispensations), but that bishops are ordinary ministers and priests confirm by concession. He says Trent is in keeping with this tradition, but the information in canon 3 is incomplete.[168]

In quoting Scripture, Bellarmine often twists the texts to agree with his position. Acts 8 and 19 give no reason for calling in the Apostles to impose hands; Bellarmine argues from silence that the

---

[166] S-78.

[167] G-24 and L-27.

[168] C-32.

ministry was proper to their office. But in reality other possibilities exist – a sign of unity with the Church, for example. Similarly he says the ministry is carried out only by Apostles. But that does not prove that no one else exercised it. In fact, the argument from Hebrews 6 gives favorable testimony that the practice of imposing hands endured beyond the apostolic age and the minister is unknown. Of course, it is difficult to know from the text if that imposition is the same as in Acts 8 and 19, but the text's other references to ablutions and catechism make an initiatory context possible. Bellarmine more accurately interprets Ananias's imposition of hands than does Calvin, but then, leaving the text, he inserts his own theory that Paul received confirmation directly from God. The application of Chrysostom's text to 1 Timothy 4 is an anachronism, the distinction between priest and bishop in 1 Timothy 5 is obscure, and the statement that the Apostles became bishops after the resurrection is a fantasy.

There are whole sections here where Bellarmine spins his theology without any supports. Especially in the discussion concerning the episcopal character Bellarmine leaves the controversy with "the heretics of his time" and turns to instruct his Catholic readers about a fine point of theology. But he gives no sources for this section, preferring to argue from reason and tradition – and not the earliest tradition. The argument comparing confirmation to enlisting in the militia chooses an image that was developed after the rite split from baptism.

Among the many witnesses Bellarmine cites most are represented fairly, but two bear special attention: Gregory the Great and Jerome. In Jerome's *Dialogue against the Luciferians* he says many who live in large towns or far from the bishop receive his imposition of hands for the coming of the Holy Spirit long after baptism. Jerome says the practice is found in many places "ad honorem potius sacerdotii, quam ad legem necessitatis."[169] Then he explains that baptism by priests and deacons suffices for those who die without this imposition. Chemnitz lists this text to show that priests may confirm ("ad honorem sacerdotii"). Bellarmine however is right that throughout the rest of the text, Jerome assigns this ministry to the bishop; it is likely that Jerome is not changing his mind here, but simply explaining that imposition of hands is an honor of clergy. Oddly enough, Bellarmine does not offer the obvious argument that "sacerdotium" has two meanings, priest and bishop. Rather, he applies the following phrase

[169] L-57.

("ad legem necessitatis," or as his edition has it "non ob legis necessitatem") to the next sentence of Jerome's text. He is trying to avoid the interpretation that it is not necessary for the bishop to impose hands (and hence that priests may) and proposes this as a solution: the non-neccesity pertains to receiving confirmation, not to its episcopal administration. It is a far-fetched solution, and not a necessary one, given the full context of the passage. Calvin mentions this text of Jerome, too, but in saying that it supports the early practice of examining children with confirmation, he completely misses the point of the controversy concerning the passage.

The other text from the ancients figuring into each side of the dispute is a letter of Gregory the Great recorded by Gratian.[170] Chemnitz quotes the letter to show that the bishop is not the only minister of confirmation since priests have received permission for it in history. Bellarmine agrees, but with the nuance that the bishop is the ordinary minister of the sacrament, which a priest administers by dispensation. Bellarmine takes a more liberal view than those who held that only bishops are the minister. His adversary becomes not Chemnitz, who says all priests may confirm, but others who say only bishops may.[171] To support his position, he cites an earlier letter of Gregory[172] which had prohibited the practice which the latter letter then allowed: Permission presumes prohibition. Gratian and Thomas, he says, cited the correct version of the text.[173] Bellarmine's interpretation seems more accurate than Chemnitz's, but the two are arguing different points.

In summary, Bellarmine has accumulated many references on this point; some support better than others. His Scripture sources are weak because later ministerial distinctions were unknown to Luke. To propose

---

[170] P-17.

[171] Bellarmine examines the edition of Gregory because it has been corrupted, he surmises, by people who held the other opinion, that only bishops are the ministers. He says some editions record Gregory gave permission for priests to anoint with chrism the "baptizandos", not the "baptizatos". Those versions would lead one to conclude that priests could give only the pre-baptismal anointing with chrism.

This is not the only instance in the controversy where Bellarmine comments on the edition of the text. At 5:217, he cites Clement of Alexandria, as found in Eusebius (G-26), and he informs the reader that he is using the Latin translation of Christophorson, which most favors his interpretation.

[172] P-16.

[173] PM-31 and M-82.

his theology of ministerial rank and power he abandons the scholastic method of amassing sources and speaks on his own. But the bare theology seems completely unsupported by Scripture and tradition as a result. In general, his patristic references are sound, but he may force them to agree with his position, even to the point of re-editing a text.

Concerning the proper minister of confirmation, all the controversialists show merit in their use of sources, but they also prejudice their testimony. Some texts are ambiguous enough to support either side, but rather than seek their true meaning, the controversialists simply interpret the ambiguity to their own benefit. Calvin and Chemnitz miss the point of Trent's canon 3, but it is not entirely their fault: The canon does not include the nuance that priests may confirm by dispensation, so they argue that tradition is contrary. Bellarmine digresses from the controversy to resolve tangential questions among Catholics. He misses Chemnitz's point in the controversy over Jerome's text. All show a fear of losing the controversy, rather than a hunger for discerning the truth of the historical fonts.

b. Matter: Anointing vs. Imposition of Hands

The controversy over anointing was waged in the field of the matter of confirmation. The Reformers from Luther on complained that the Church had abandoned the apostolic imposition of hands in favor of anointing with chrism. The Catholics maintained anointing was part of a continuous tradition from the time of the Apostles.

i. Calvin
a'. Analysis

When Calvin speaks in his response to the *Acts of Regensburg* about the kind of confirmation he would accept in his own tradition he allows a non-sacramental imposition of hands which he thinks is in keeping with the ancient tradition.[174] But in the *Institutio* he evaluates both imposition of hands and anointing negatively.[175] The imposition of hands in Acts, he says, was not to be repeated. Simple observation shows him that when one does impose hands, the effects are different now from what they were then. The practice of anointing has no scriptural evidence for it. He summons the letters to the Galatians, Colossians, and 1 Corinthians to show Paul's opposition to the elements

---

174 See Chapter II, fn. 59.
175 R-28 and R-29.

of this world,[176] and implies the Roman Church's oil would be scorned by the Apostle.

In the *Antidotum* Calvin again rejects the use of oil, this time since it is not found in the writings of the ancients. It is an argument from the silence of the Fathers, though throughout this controversy his primary dependence on Scripture is evident.

As in the controversy concerning the minister, Calvin's method is to contrast the theology of the Catholics with evidence from Scripture.

b'. Evaluation

On this issue Calvin is carried away by the emotion of the argument. His statement in the *Antidotum* that no ancient writer speaks of oil is carelessly false. His application of the Pauline texts to the Roman Church's use of oil is far-fetched. Even baptism and Eucharist use the elements of this world.

He supports his argument (that the use of imposition of hands was peculiar to the Apostles) by the empirical evidence that the results from the action in his day were not as dramatic as those in Acts. It is a good argument if one accepts that the purpose of the imposition of hands was to bring about those miraculous events, but that is debatable.

His strongest objection is the non-scriptural origin of the use of oil. Here the argument from the silence of Scripture works to his favor. Anointing for confirmation is a practice which developed in the early centuries of the Church, but did not enjoy apostolic usage. His insight here is perhaps too easily overlooked by the Roman Church with its long tradition of anointing.

ii. Chemnitz
a'. Analysis

Chemnitz considers the Roman Church's matter for confirmation in section 12.[177] He says her position is that she is faithful to the scriptural tradition of Acts 1, 8, and 19.[178] But Chemnitz observes this is obscure since they use neither fire (for Pentecost) nor imposition of hands in their rite, just chrism. He believes this historical development was divinely inspired so that all might know its

---

[176] S-73, S-75, S-66, and S-65.

[177] R-44.

[178] S-35, S-43, and S-57.

waywardness. He ridicules the Roman Church's allegories comparing the fire of Pentecost with oil and imposition of hands with the slap on the cheek. So by referring to the ritual itself, he shows its incongruity with the Scriptures.

In an earlier section he uses patristic sources to criticize the institution of anointing. He says Tertullian records that the anointing came from the Old Testament, not from Christ; that Pseudo-Cyprian says the anointing was instituted not by Christ but by the Apostles and stems from the Old Testament; and that Basil says there is no written word concerning anointing with chrism.[179]

Chemntz's method is to launch a twofold argument against the Roman Church's practice of anointing: its disparity with Scripture and with patristic testimony.

b'. Evaluation

Chemnitz's strongest argument is the comparison of Scripture with the ritual. He shows the disparity between the central place of imposition of hands in Acts 8 and 19 with the symbol of oil. Concerning his use of the Fathers, Tertullian simply says the anointing has Old Testament roots; he does not discuss sacramental institution by Christ at all. Similarly, Pseudo-Cyprian does not present institution as such nor presume that a rite inspired by the Old Testament cannot be the foundation for a sacrament in the New. But Chemnitz is right that Basil says there is no written word concerning anointing with chrism.

Thus, in general, Chemnitz more accurately treats scriptural and liturgical texts than patristic ones in this matter.

iii. Bellarmine
a'. Analysis

Considering the matter of confirmation, Bellarmine first presents his position and then responds to the objections of his adversaries.[180] He proposes that oil is the matter for confirmation, and defends his position from the Councils of Florence and Trent.[181] He supports them in turn with testimony from the Scriptures and tradition.

There are two Scripture passages Bellarmine says prove the

---

[179] L-69, M-9, and G-4.
[180] R-15.
[181] C-12 and C-31.

proposition by their mention or allusion to this anointing: 2 Corinthians 1 and 1 John 2.[182] He presents the interpretations of Ambrose, Pseudo-Anselm (Herveus), and Theodoret for the first passage[183] and Cyril and Augustine for the second.[184] He says that the consensus of the Popes, councils, and Fathers given in a previous controversy support this position. He concludes with a principle, that the authority of the Church takes on more importance where evidence is lacking from the Scriptures.

Then in a later section[185] he responds to two objections of Chemnitz. The Reformer says that the texts of Acts make no mention of anointing.[186] Bellarmine offers two possible solutions: One is that the Apostles may have switched from imposing hands to anointing when they received some unwritten command from Christ to do so. Thomas Aquinas, the Council of Florence, and Innocent III explain that chrism replaced imposition of hands for the Church.[187] The other possibility is that imposition of hands actually meant the same thing as anointing. Since Dionysius, Clement, Theophylus, Tertullian, Cyprian, Cornelius, and Origen give evidence to the early usage of anointings, he argues this is a preferable proposal.[188] According to this theory, the Apostles anointed with chrism when they imposed hands, but Luke simply abbreviated the rite in his text. To prove this point, Bellarmine first accepts the witness of those who wrote that the Holy Spirit comes with anointing.[189] Since Acts says the Holy Spirit was given by the Apostles, he concludes it is likely they anointed to achieve that effect. Second he recalls that many Fathers link the role of the bishop to the testimony of Acts 8.[190] If the Fathers made this connection, surely the Apostles must have anointed in the same way bishops do, Bellarmine argues. Finally he proposes other examples of Scripture where the text is surely abbreviated from the reality.[191] He concludes resolving an

---

[182] S-70 and S-86.

[183] L-3, M-53, and G-48.

[184] G-14 and L-30.

[185] 9:225-228.

[186] S-43 and S-57.

[187] M-80, C-12 and P-26.

[188] G-20, P-7, G-50, L-69 and L-70, L-41, G-28, and G-42.

[189] 9:226.

[190] P-24, M-56, P-33, L-43, and L-37.

[191] S-77, S-79, and S-80 regarding ordination, for example.

apparent disparity between the texts of Innocent III and the Council of Florence.[192]

Bellarmine challenges Chemnitz's second objection, which is from the Fathers. The Reformer says Tertullian, Cyprian and Basil maintain that the institution of chrism was a post-apostolic development.[193] Bellarmine says the texts are not so evident, and restates his position that the Christological institution comes from a non-written tradition, but a most certain one nonetheless.[194]

Bellarmine customarily cites the historical fonts both to support his theology and to refute that of the adversaries. Here he quotes Scripture not for its own viewpoint but to support the hylomorphic theory of scholastic sacramental theology.

b'. Evaluation

In the question of anointing, Bellarmine's use of sources is generally poor. He is faithful to presenting the opinions of Florence and Trent against those of Chemnitz, but his use of supporting texts is sloppy. The Scripture texts and the Fathers who commented on them address the mystery of the Holy Spirit, but it is inaccurate to apply them to confirmation. His principle that the Church supplies what Scripture omits is an honest expression of his position, but it lacks the nuance the Reformers argue: Even the silence of Scripture can tell the Church something about God. His responses to Chemnitz's objections are riddled with guesses about the apostolic practice. His suggestion that the Apostles anointed with chrism when they imposed hands in Acts 8 and 19 is ludicrous. To accuse Luke of abbreviation at this point is to grasp at air. His best work is in refuting the use of Chemnitz's three patristic sources. He is more accurate than the Reformer in relating how Tertullian uses Old Testament imagery, how Pseudo-Cyprian describes institution, and the unharmful implication of Basil's remark that there is no written word about chrism.

---

[192] P-26 and C-12.

[193] See above, fn. 179.

[194] Successors to the dispute rebuked this position. Hamon L'Estrange wrote, "But that it <confirmation> is so <a sacrament> in true propriety of speech our adversaries shall never obtain from us, until they can find *verbum et elementum*, and both of Christ's institution, to meet in it; neither of which, as they confess, are yet to be found, their great Cardinal <Bellarmine> putting us off for both to 'tradition unwritten,'" *The Alliance of Divine Offices*, Library of Anglo-Catholic Theology, fourth edition (Oxford: John Henry Parker, 1846), pp. 389-90.

c. Reconciliation of Heretics

Throughout the controversy all three writers cite texts from the early Church concerning the rites of initiation and the reconciliation of heretics. These rites enjoyed some variation and shared similar elements. Specifically, there are instances when the reconciliatory gesture of imposing hands was accompanied by an anointing with chrism. The rite thus resembled confirmation and caused some confusion in the application of these texts by all the controversialists.

For Bellarmine, if reconciliation of heretics included an anointing with chrism, he regarded the entire rite as confirmation, not reconciliation. This is evident from his use of Gregory's Epistle 67, the First and Second Councils of Arles, the Council of Laodicea, the Council of Orange, and Epistle 72 of Cyprian.[195] If the return of heretics was by simple imposition of hands, Bellarmine presumes confirmation is not involved, as in Leo's Epistles 159 and 166, Pope Vigilius, the Council of Nicaea canons 31 and 69, and Augustine's De baptismo.[196] This causes a problem when he analyzes Cyprian's Epistle to Jubajanus.[197] There Cyprian, who elsewhere mentions anointing as part of the rite, makes no reference to oil. Bellarmine believes he omitted it here in writing, but in fact it was Cyprian's practice to anoint.

For Chemnitz, the mention of chrism in rites of reconciliation strengthens his position that anointing was simply a rite which had been separated from baptism. He regards reconciliations with anointing as reconcilation, not confirmation. This causes him trouble when he states that history shows confirmation was an examination of the faith of a candidate because he uses as references the First Council of Arles and the Council of Laodicea, both of which he discounted earlier as rites of reconciliation.[198] He too faces problems with Cyprian, who describes rites of receiving heretics in Epistle 70.[199] Cyprian, who favors admission by baptism for those baptized outside the Church, describes a post-baptismal anointing for those candidates. Chemnitz circumvents the testimony by accusing Cyprian of Montanism, an accusation Bellarmine rightly argues is unique in history.

---

[195] P-18, C-1, C-2, C-14, C-20, and L-42.

[196] P-30, P-31, P-39, C-18, C-19, and L-10.

[197] L-43.

[198] C-1 and C-13.

[199] L-41.

Calvin makes a good argument that Augustine's *De baptismo* passage[200] concerns reconciliation of heretics, but not without some difficulties.[201]

Bellarmine presumes that if the anointing of heretics was not given in reconciliation it either must have preceded or was to follow at a later occasion ("as we do with the Lutherans," he sneers).[202] But the records are not that clear. All parties are trying to force rites of the early Fathers into the sixteenth century patterns. They do not analyze a text from its own perspective. The arguments of all are weakened by a superficial treatment of the history and meaning of reconciliation, and a too-quick presumption to associate its theology with that of confirmation.

4. Conclusions

The method of the controversy is heavily influenced by scholasticism. The technique of gathering sources to prove a theological position was brought to full use by the protagonists of this study. For Bellarmine, it meant continuing the tradition of his predecessors, and for the Reformers this was also largely true. Already in the first generation after Luther, they are concerned with proving the principles of the Reform, using Scripture in much the same fashion as Catholics used a full range of sources from tradition. Thus the Reformers were already drifting from the original ideals of Luther – letting the Scriptures dictate one's theology – to having the Scriptures support the already-formed ideas of the movement.

Besides scholasticism, the other influence in the debate is the concept of controversy. Texts were cited not only to prove a theological opinion, but to disprove the opinion of an adversary. These citations are sometimes accurate, sometimes careless. The controversialists cite ambiguous texts with the same authority as clear ones. Calvin's applications are the most superficial. Chemnitz's methodical presentation veils the hermeneutic weakness he shares with the others. Bellarmine builds assumptions into structural elements.

The division resulting from the Reformation is less surprising when one sees the theologians at work: Each side had become so sure of its own righteousness it could only see the weaknesses in the opposing

---

200 L-10.

201 See treatment of this source in next chapter.

202 ". . . ut modo facimus cum Lutheranis." 7:220.

side. It was not so much the logical integrity of the subjective side (the success of which went unperceived by the opponents), but the rational weaknesses perceived in the opposing side which solidified membership, and hence the divisions of the post-Reformation. Since the acceptance of logical deductions was a subjective process, the winning of converts may be attributable not so much to keenness of logic (and logical acuity is foundational to post-scholastic controversies), but to an emotional conviction that one side is right and the other wrong.

CHAPTER IV:
Controversies

To celebrate confirmation with understanding requires some knowledge of its history. Before offering a reflection on the contemporary celebration of this rite, the study of the sixteenth century controversy concludes with an analysis of historical sources cited in the debate. This will both illustrate the earlier process of interpreting sources and provide a foundation for constructing a modern theology of confirmation.

The previous chapter analyzed the method of the controversialists in their general use of sources. This chapter critically examines specific sources in the controversy. Since the complete list of sources is clearly too extensive to cover in detail, this chapter selects five of them to observe how each party interpreted their common material. As the previous chapter examined specific issues of the controversy to reveal its method; this chapter examines the sources themselves and how they are cited to support a number of issues. The texts for this chapter have been chosen because of the frequency with which they are cited and the insight they provide into the content of the controversy.

This chapter, then, moves from method to controversy. It enters the debate on confirmation to weigh both sides of the issues by means of sources. With this chapter the dissertation repositions the debate into a historical-critical hermeneutic. It examines the sources themselves as well as what the disputants said about them. This will conclude the examination of the controversy at the early years after the Reformation and prepare for an analysis of its modern status in the final chapter.

A. Scripture: Acts 8, 16-17
1. Introduction
The most important text of the controversy is from the Bible, Acts 8, 16-17. It concerns the following event: The Apostles in Jerusalem heard

that the Samaritans had accepted the Word of God, so they sent Peter
and John to pray for them, that they might receive the Holy Spirit.

> For <the Holy Spirit> had not yet come onto any one of them,
> but they had only been baptized in the name of the Lord
> Jesus. Then they imposed hands on them and they were
> receiving the Holy Spirit.[1]

This text is the most important because it appears most often of all the
texts in the controversy–not just of those from Scripture–and because it
concerns a pivotal question raised by the Reformers: Do the Scriptures
substantiate confirmation as a sacrament? The controversialists often
link this text with Acts 19, 6, where Paul imposes hands on the
baptized in Ephesus. The passages are parallel because in each instance
an Apostle imposes hands on those who have been baptized, who then
receive the Holy Spirit. Several questions figure in the discussion: Did
the Apostles receive a command for this ministry? Was it a universal
command for the entire Church to imitate for all ages? Since only
Apostles imposed hands, were they acting as episcopal ministers,
distinct from the presbyteral ministry?

2. Usage
a. Bellarmine

Bellarmine cites Acts 8 fourteen times in his section on
confirmation to illustrate eight different arguments.[2] For him, this text
remarkably illustrates almost each one of his controversial points:

"That confirmation is a sacrament:"
1) The imposition of hands imparts the Holy Spirit (1:213, 2:214,
   2:214, and 2:214).[3]
2) Scripture authorizes the *sign* of confirmation:
   prayer and the imposition of hands (2:214).
3) The Apostles would not have imposed hands without a
   command (2:214).

---

[1] See chart entry S-43 in Chapter III for text in Latin.

[2] The citation from Bellarmine at 9:225 indicated on the chart entry simply
establishes Chemnitz's position. There is another reference at 9:226 where Bellarmine
argues from the Fathers that the Apostles must have used chrism in Acts 8 since the
Fathers say they were acting as bishops. The primary argument is from the Fathers, not
from Acts 8, so it is omitted here.

[3] Numbers cite chapter and page of the Battezzati edition.

4) Imposition of hands is the *means* for the promise of the Holy Spirit (2:215).

5) Confirmation is not an examination of children (7:221).

"The Matter of Confirmation:"
6) The absence of chrism is due to Luke's abridgment (9:226).

"The Form of Confirmation:"
7) The Apostles prayed some unwritten form (10:229).

"The Minister of Confirmation:"
8) The bishop is the minister of confirmation (12:230, 12:231, 12:231, and 12:231).

Bellarmine cites Acts 19 only in conjunction with Acts 8, to support all the arguments numbered above except 4) and 7), and part of 8). Whereas Acts 19 would have supported argument 4), it does not work for argument 7) since the text does not say that Paul prayed when he imposed hands. Nor does Acts 19 support one of the points in argument 8) (viz., the first reference at 12:231). There Bellarmine challenges Wyclif's suggestion that Peter and John acted not as bishops, but as ordinary ministers to correct the false baptism administered by Philip. The problem is that Acts 19 concerns Ephesians who had received John's baptism and, after Paul's arrival, received another baptism and the imposition of hands. The ambiguity over the validity of the first baptism could have supported Wyclif's opinion. Thus for Bellarmine, Acts 8 remains the primary text for illustrating his position.

To clarify Bellarmine's interpretation of these texts it helps to examine another incident in Acts. The story concerns Peter and the Gentile community at Caesarea, as related in Acts 10, 44-48 and again in Acts 11, 15-17.[4] Some of the Caesareans came to Joppa at the request of Cornelius to bring Peter back with them. When Peter instructed their community, the Holy Spirit fell on these Gentiles (Peter says "as on us in the beginning"–i.e., at the Pentecost event related in Acts 2), and they were baptized. Bellarmine uses this incident twice in his argument to show a contrast; namely, that this was not confirmation as Acts 8 and 19 were. He reasons that since a sacrament must have a sign in Scripture, what happened at Caesarea (as at Jerusalem in the beginning) was not a sacrament, but a special reception of the Holy Spirit without the mediation of a sign.

4 S-46 and S-47

Regarding Acts 2 and 10, the Holy Spirit was not given in those places by the ministry of the sacraments, but with a singular privilege the effect of the sacrament was given by God without the sacrament.[5]

Compared with Acts 8 and 19, according to Bellarmine,

. . . the Scripture never mentions another means or sensible sign by which that gift might be given except the imposition of hands with a prayer.[6]

So for Bellarmine, the imposition of hands and prayer of Peter and John in Acts 8 is the quintessential text for showing confirmation as a sacrament.

b. Calvin

John Calvin uses the same Scripture passage to show that confirmation is not a sacrament. In general, the *Institutio*'s section on confirmation quotes Scripture much less than Bellarmine, partly because of Bellarmine's style (his unmatched ability to assemble texts), and partly because it is Calvin's position that confirmation as a sacrament is not in Scripture at all.

Calvin refers to Acts 8 twice in this section. In the first instance he answers the defense of the Roman Church that she follows the good example of the Apostles. Calvin agrees that the Apostles imposed hands as a faithful exercise of their ministry, but he raises two objections: that they did so only as a gesture of offering, and that the purpose of imposing hands no longer exists for the Church.

I hear what the Apostles did: namely, they carried out their ministry faithfully. . . . However I think that no deeper mystery is behind this imposition of hands, but I understand that a ceremony of this kind was used by them so that they might signify by the gesture itself that they were commending to God and as it were offering the one on whom they were imposing hands. If this ministry which the Apostles were then

---

[5] "Quod attinet ad cap. 2. et 10. Actor. non fuisse in his locis ministerio sacramentorum datum Spiritum sanctum, sed singulari privilegio datum a Deo effectum sacramenti sine sacramento," 9, Battezzati:225-226. Bellarmine refers to non-sacramental since unmediated confirmation also at 8:223, 12:232, and 12:233.

[6] ". . . Scriptura nusquam meminit alterius medii, seu signi sensibilis, quo daretur donum illud, nisi manus impositionis cum oratione," 2:214.

discharging would be remaining in the Church until now, the imposition of hands would also have to be preserved; but where that grace has ceased to be conferred, what purpose does the imposition of hands serve?[7]

Calvin further explains that the signs which accompanied this imposition of hands illumined the new preaching of the Gospel to help the early Church build a foundation of faith.

Calvin's other reference to Acts 8 illustrates that the Roman Church's interpretation of confirmation detracts from the meaning of baptism. Here Calvin faces a problem with the Scripture text, which states that the Holy Spirit had not yet come on those who were baptized until Peter and John imposed hands on them. This would seem to imply that the imposition of hands does bring about an effect that baptism does not; namely, the coming of the Holy Spirit. But Calvin knows from another Scripture text that the Spirit comes to those who confess Jesus, so he says Luke must have been referring to a special manifestation of the Spirit, evident here in a unique example distinct from baptism:

> But what Luke says in the passage we have cited (that people had been baptized in the name of Jesus Christ who had not received the Holy Spirit) does not simply deny that they were endowed with a single gift of the Spirit who were believing in Christ with their heart and confessing Him with their mouth <Rom 10, 10>; but he understands a reception of the Spirit by which manifest powers and visible graces were being received.[8]

Thus Calvin interprets this same text to show its unreliability in supporting the Roman position. He argues from two points: the purpose of the imposition of hands (an offering of the baptized which shows

---

[7] "Audio quid apostoli fecerint: nempe suum ministerium fideliter exsequuti sunt. . . . Huic autem impositioni manuum non altius subesse mysterium cogito; sed huiusmodi caeremoniam adhibitam ab illis interpretor, ut ipso gestu significarent, se Deo commendare et velut offerre eum cui manus imponebant. Hoc ministerium quo tunc apostoli fungebantur, si adhuc in ecclesia maneret, manuum quoque impositionem oporteret servari; sed ubi gratia illa conferri desiit, quorsum pertinet manuum impositio?" 4:19, 6, CR 30:1070.

[8] "Quod autem Lucas, eo quem citavimus loco, dicit baptizatos in nomine Iesu Christi fuisse, qui non accepissent spiritum sanctum: non simpliciter negat, uno spiritus dono praeditos, qui in Christum corde crederent et ipsum ore confiterentur; sed acceptionem spiritus intelligit, qua manifestae virtutes et visibiles gratiae percipiebantur," 8, CR 30:1072.

miraculous signs illuminating the early preaching of the Church), and the integrity of baptism (the sacrament in which the Holy Spirit is received).

c. Chemnitz

Martin Chemnitz uses the same passage at several places in his argument, primarily to demonstrate the inappropriateness of taking what was a command for the Apostles only and applying it to the universal Church. He sets forth Acts 8 and 19 as the texts adduced by the Roman Church to justify confirmation. With irony he criticizes the logic of his adversaries, who imitate apostolic imposition by anointing.

> Also, the Apostles imposed hands on the baptized who thus received the Holy Spirit (Acts 8 and 19). As a result now in the Church the forehead of the baptized must be smeared with chrism consecrated as it is described in the Pontifical, with that form of words which was described above, and the effects recounted above will follow.[9]

Similarly in a later text, he mocks the Roman Church's position that the slap on the cheek after anointing is equivalent to the imposition of hands before the coming of the Holy Spirit.

> For since in the papist Church to follow is the same thing as to precede, the bishop striking the one confirmed on the cheek after confirmation therefore repeats the imposition of hands in Acts, which then preceded the presenting of the Spirit. But what do I hear? Is imposing hands then beating someone with blows on the face? So when Christ says "They will impose hands over the sick" <Mark 16:18>, the meaning will be: "They will beat the bedridden well with blows, and then they will be worse."[10]

[9]   "Apostoli etiam baptizatis manus imposuerunt, qui ita acceperunt Spiritum Sanctum. Act. 8 et 19. Ergo nunc in Ecclesia chrismate, sicut in Pontificali describitur, consecrato, linienda est frons baptizatorum, cum forma illa verborum, quae supra descripta est, et sequentur effectus supra recitati," 10, Preuss:288.

[10]   "Quia enim in Pontificia Ecclesia sequi idem est quod praecedere, ideo Episcopus percutiens confirmatum in maxillam post confirmationem, repraesentat impositionem manuum in Actis, quae tunc praecessit donationem spiritus. Quid vero audio? Est ne igitur manus imponere, alapis aliquem in faciem caedere? Quando igitur Christus dicit, super aegrotos manus imponent, sensus erit: Decumbentes alapis bene caedent, et tunc pejus habebunt," 12, Preuss:289.

Chemnitz admits that the early Church must have had a promise offering visible gifts of the Spirit, but since the gifts no longer exist, the promise must have been temporary, not for the universal Church.

> I hear and read what was written (Acts 1, 8, and 19). However I find that visible gifts of the Spirit – like the miracle of tongues and others – were conferred on the baptized in the primitive Church through the imposition of hands. . . . Therefore the Apostles possessed both a command and a promise of what they were doing. And if the outpouring of those sensible gifts were to endure in the Church up to now, rightly would the imposition of hands be used, which was accustomed to be used for prayers, and especially when miracles were happening through the hands of the Apostles (Acts 5). But it is beyond controversy that those miracles ceased in the Church long ago. Therefore that which is written concerning the Apostles was temporary, not universal and perpetual (Acts 1, 8, and 19).[11]

Later Chemnitz responds again to the argument that the Apostles would have imposed hands only if they had received a divine command and promise. He maintains that the command was only for their activity, not for all time:

> . . . therefore we also demand in this place that a general command be shown to us that what the Apostles did in Acts 8 and 19, that must be done always by all ministers in the Church.[12]

Chemnitz's understanding of the apostolic imposition of hands is that its promise concerned outward manifestations of the gift of the Spirit. Seeing these promises fulfilled no longer in the Church, he cannot justify the practice of imposing hands.

11 "Audio et lego quod scriptum est, Act. 1, 8 et 19. Invenio autem visibilia dona spiritus: ut miraculum linguarum, et alia, in prima Ecclesia baptizatis collata fuisse per impositionem manuum. . . . Habuerunt igitur Apostoli ejus, quod faciebant, et mandatum, et promissionem. Et si effusio illorum sensibilium donorum adhuc in Ecclesia duraret, recte adhiberetur etiam impositio manuum, quae ad orationes adhiberi solebat: et praecipue quando per manus Apostolorum fiebant miracula, Act. 5. Sed miracula illa jamdudum desiisse in Ecclesia, extra controversiam est. Temporarium igitur non universale et perpetuum fuit illud, quod de Apostolis scribitur. Act. 1, 8 et 19," 10, Preuss:288-289.

12 ". . . ergo et hoc loco requirimus, ut ostendatur nobis mandatum generale, omnibus temporibus, ab omnibus ministris in Ecclesia illud faciendum esse, quod Apostoli Act. 8 et 19 fecerunt," 16, Preuss:290.

Therefore, when Chemnitz calls for a command to continue the apostolic practice and for a promise concerning its efficacy, he is looking for miraculous manifestations of the Spirit, and he finds no result resembling them from the liturgical practice of the Roman Church:

> Therefore this proof rests on the Papists, that they show a command of God that that deed of the Apostles in Acts 8 and 19 ought to be imitated, used, and repeated in the Church up to the consummation of the age, until Christ comes for judgment. . . . Also a promise concerning efficacy must be shown if we are to have imitated that which the Apostles did then. But neither can be shown or proven.[13]

Then, similar to Calvin, Chemnitz argues that the effects assigned to confirmation detract from those of baptism. He knows the position of his adversaries:

> For they say that although those sensible and miraculous gifts of the Spirit (Acts 1, 8, and 19) have already ceased, universal and perpetual nevertheless are the promises concerning the grace of confirmation, concerning the gift of perseverance, concerning the conservation and increase of spiritual gifts, concerning strengthening through the Spirit against the flesh, the world, and the devil, etc.[14]

But for Chemnitz, who believes the scriptural effects of imposing hands are visible manifestations of the Spirit (speaking in tongues, for example), the Roman Church commits a double error regarding the effects of confirmation: they ignore the scriptural effects and assign new ones stolen from baptism.

> But we embrace with our whole heart those most sweet promises concerning the necessary gifts and helps of the Spirit after baptism, and by the assurance of those things we fight against spiritual enemies and invoke God. But the question in this place is not concerning those promises which it is certain exist in the Word of God: but the question is whether God wants those promises to have been bound to the

---

[13]   "Incumbit igitur Pontificiis haec probatio, ut ostendant mandatum Dei, quod illud Apostolorum factum, Act. 8 et 19 usque ad consummationem seculi, donec Christus ad judicium veniat, in Ecclesia imitandum, usurpandum et frequentandam sit. . . . Monstranda etiam est promissio de efficacia, si illud quod Apostoli tunc fecerunt, imitati fuerimus. Neutrum vero ostendi et probari potest," 11, Preuss:289.

[14]   "Dicunt enim, licet sensibilia et miraculosa illa dona spiritus, Act. 1, 8 et 19 jam desierunt, universales tamen et perpetuae sunt promissiones, de gratia confirmationis, de dono perseverantiae, de conservatione et augmento donorum spiritualium, de corroboratione per spiritum adversus carnem, mundum, et Diabolum, etc.," 15, Preuss:290.

smearing of Papist chrism so that then and through that
medium that efficacy of the Spirit is given, when the bishop
anoints the forehead with the episcopally enchanted chrism
after certain words have been added, and with one good
slap.[15]

When Chemnitz concludes his argument, he suggests that Acts 8
and 19 support the Reformers' belief that the original purpose of
confirmation was as an examination of children. He says that Acts 19, 1-
7 records a questioning of doctrine and a profession of faith, where Paul
asks certain disciples of Ephesus if they have received the Holy Spirit
and into what were they baptized. He cites Acts 8 to support his
position since it adds a reference to public prayer.[16]

Chemnitz then sees the action of the Apostles in Acts as a
fulfillment of their ministry according to a command of God to bring
visible manifestations of the Spirit on those who were baptized. He
sees no command or promise, however, concerning the universal
application of the Apostles' ministry here. In fact, since the visible
manifestations of the Spirit are no longer evident, the Roman Church is
wrong to claim it continues the apostolic practice. Moreover, by
attributing the effects of baptism to their confirmation, they further
misrepresent the intention of the text. Finally, he sees in both Acts 8
and 19 a support for his thesis that imposition of hands may be
continued in the Church today not as a sacrament, but as an examination
of children before the pastor.

3. Analysis
a. Bellarmine

The starting point for Bellarmine's argument is the faith and
tradition of the Church that confirmation is a sacrament. Through the
use of Acts 8 and 19 he tries to convince the Reformers that the
Scriptures verify his position, according to the definition of a
sacrament he has already presented.

---

15   "Nos vero dulcissimas illas promissiones, de necessariis donis et subsidiis
spiritus, post baptismum, toto pectore amplectimur, et earum fiducia cum hostibus
spiritualibus luctamur, et Deum invocamus. Hoc vero loco quaestio est, non de ipsis
promissionibus, quas in verbo Dei exstare certum est: sed quaestio est, an illas
promissiones Deus velit, ad delibutionem Pontificii chrismatis alligatas esse, ita ut tunc
et per illud medium efficacia illa spiritus detur, quando Episcopus chrismate
pontificaliter excantato, frontem, additis certis verbis, et una bona alapa inungit," 15,
Preuss:290.

16   25, Preuss:297.

There are several strong points to Bellarmine's argument. The Scripture texts do make a distinction between the event of baptism and a later pouring out of the Spirit. In fact, the Scriptures indicate that the imposition of hands actually imparts the Holy Spirit. His texts also support the calling of an apostolic minister for the gift. And they distinguish the divinely originated Pentecost events in Jerusalem and Caesarea (Acts 2 and 10) from the ecclesially administered gifts in Samaria and Ephesus (Acts 8 and 19).

However, his argument suffers from weaknesses. Not least is that Bellarmine changes the grounds for determining a sacrament after he has entered the argument. Instead of showing the divine command, he shows the results of the command, not a criterion originally accepted by both sides. Although he defines a sacrament by matter and form, the Scriptures mention neither the anointing nor the formula used when the sacrament is administered in the Church. Regarding matter, Bellarmine's argument that Luke abridged the text and simply omitted the apostolic practice of anointing is preposterous. Thus he does not satisfactorily account for the surprising historical leap from imposition of hands to anointing. Regarding form, as there is no expressed dominical command in Scripture for confirmation, there is no expressed form. Regarding the minister of the sacrament, although the texts state an Apostle imposed hands in each case, the application of this apostolic ministry to bishops is not Lucan. Bishops are not mentioned till the Pastoral Epistles, and their relationship to Apostles is not clear.

b. The Reformers

The Reformers begin from the conviction in their young tradition that confirmation is not a sacrament. They set out to prove from criteria which are essentially Luther's that the Scriptures do not support calling the rite a sacrament, but do support its use as an examination of faith in the Church.

The strength of their argument lies in the interpretation of this text through their knowledge of baptism gained by other Scripture texts; e.g. Romans 10, 10; Romans 5, 5; 6, 3-6; 1 Corinthians 12, 13; Galatians 3, 27; Ephesians 5, 25-27; and Titus 3, 4-7. With this information, they know of the bond between the Holy Spirit and baptism, and challenge the attribution of the effects of baptism to confirmation. Their position is further strengthened by the historical development of the rite, which moved from imposition of hands to anointing and emphasized the distance between the apostolic and Roman practices. The Reformers also observed the absence of the once evident visible gifts of the Spirit, and posed a critical question for the controversy: What is the real effect of confirmation? Finally, their argument gains strength from the weaknesses of the Catholic position.

However, their position also has weaknesses. Calvin limply proposes the textually unsupportable argument–surprising in a Reformer–that the imposition of hands in Acts was an offering to God. He says the argument is his own, and Bellarmine concurs. Chemnitz's explanation that the texts describe an examination of faith is also unlikely, although he at least derives his interpretation from the passage itself. In another development, Chemnitz backs down on the need for a command in the text and tacitly gives approval to Bellarmine's method of showing the results of the command: He opens Pandora's box by admitting that some command and promise must have been given the Apostles, since men of such character would never have imposed hands without it. Then he vigorously tries to close it by insisting both that the command would have to have been universal, and that there are no *results* to assure it was; i.e., the visible manifestations of the Spirit have ceased–manifestations which Calvin says were important for the early Church to nourish its young faith. But Chemnitz's argument implies that if outward manifestations had continued in the Church, no command would have been necessary, since the results would have interpreted universally the unwritten command the Apostles must have received. And if Chemnitz is wrong about the primary results of confirmation–if those results are not visible manifestations, but rather the internal increase of spiritual gifts and the proclamation of the Gospel–he loses his foundational argument. His interpretation of these primary results is weakened by the text itself which speaks of the Apostles' mission in a general way (that the believers might receive the Holy Spirit), and not specifically to impart miraculous gifts.

c. Conclusions

Bellarmine and the Reformers, coming from two different definitions of sacrament and two different faith traditions about confirmation, logically end with two opposing interpretations of this text. Yet, in examining Acts itself, neither the Catholic ceremony with anointing in the central place, nor the reformed ceremony with its examination of faith in the same place wins support. In this sense, the arguments of both parties fall apart. Nor do they discuss an issue first raised by Calvin: What is the difference between the gifts of the Spirit at baptism and the gifts at confirmation? Bellarmine, who argues his case from a separate outpouring of the Spirit in the events of Acts, is silent on this point. In addition, the reader is frustrated that the key which would unlock the answer to the controversy (a command and promise from Christ) cannot be found. And whether that key is lost, or whether it never existed, cannot be determined through silence.

B. Gratian: Council of Orleans
1. Introduction

Gratian's reference to a canon from the Council of Orleans provides another key to understanding the controversy. Though not pivotal to the discussion, it is a canon which all three controversialists comment on, and which illustrates their usage of conciliar sources. Its part in the confirmation controversy can be traced back to John Eck.[17]

Whenever the text is quoted in the controversy, it is identified more as Gratian's than as a canon of Orleans. The text runs as follows:

> C. VI. Let only those fasting come to confirmation. Also from the Council of Orleans, c. 3.
> That those fasting come to confirmation at a mature age, that they be admonished to make a confession first, that being upright they may be worthy to receive the gift of the Holy Spirit, and because one will never be a Christian unless he will have been chrismated with episcopal confirmation.[18]

This canon is part of "De consecratione distinctio 5," concerning confirmation. The preceding canons, taken primarily from the False Decretals, construct a theology of confirmation from medieval sources. In addition, certain requirements are explained from conciliar sources concerning fasting, and the single reception of the sacrament.

However, contrary to Gratian, the Council of Orleans is not the source of this text. Canon 3 of the Council of 511 is about slaves, not confirmation. The first half of this canon appears in the Carolingian *Herardi Turonensis Capitula* (858) as cap. 75.[19] The end of the canon,

---

17 See pg. 26 above.

18   "C. VI. Ad confirmationem non nisi ieiuni ueniant. "Item ex Concilio Aurelianensi, c. 3." CIC 1:1414. For full text, see chart entry M-68.

19 PL 121 (1852):769.

which makes confirmation constitutive of being a Christian, is added
several centuries later in *Ivonis Carnotensis Decretum* (1117), 1:254,[20]
where the canon is attributed to the Council of Orleans. Its theology is
possibly dependent on the Pseudo-Isidorian letter of Clement from the
ninth century.[21] Nevertheless, the controversialists refer to the canon
as from the Council of Orleans, as cited by Gratian.

2. Usage
a. Calvin

Rarely does Calvin cite a conciliar text at all. Except for Trent
itself, he mentions only two, both taken from Gratian. Drawing from
"De consecratione distinctio 5," he combines his single reference to
Orleans with a statement attributed to Pope Urban from the Pseudo-
Isidorian collection to criticize the Catholics' theology of confirmation.

> Further they add that all faithful ought to receive the
> Holy Spirit through the imposition of hands after baptism
> that they be found full Christians; because there will never be
> a Christian except the one who will have been chrismated by
> episcopal confirmation. They say these things to the letter.
> But I thought that all things whichever pertain to Christianity
> had been written in full and included in the Scriptures! Now I
> see that the true form of religion has to be sought and
> learned from another place than the Scriptures. Therefore
> the wisdom of God, heavenly truth, the whole doctrine of
> Christ only begins Christians: oil perfects them.[22]

Calvin thus seizes the second part of Gratian's canon to make his
point that not only the rite of confirmation, but the Catholics' theology
of it comes from a source outside the Scriptures. Appealing to the
foundational role of the Word of God for instruction, Calvin uses this
text against his adversaries to disprove the sacramentality of
confirmation.

---

[20] PL 161 (1855):120.

[21] M-55.

[22] "Addunt praeterea, fideles omnes spiritum sanctum per manuum impositionem,
accipere debere post baptismum, ut pleni christiani inveniantur; quia nunquam erit
christianus nisi qui confirmatione episcopali fuerit chrismatus. Haec illi ad verbum.
Atqui putabam, quaecunque ad christianismum pertinent, omnia scripturis perscripta ac
comprehensa esse. Nunc, ut video, aliunde quam ex scripturis, vera religionis forma
petenda discendaque est. Dei ergo sapientia, coelestis veritas, tota Christi doctrina,
christianos duntaxat inchoat: oleum perficit." 9, CR 30:1072.

He ridicules the same canon in the *Antidotum* for its bold claims.[23]

b. Chemnitz

Of the seven occurences of this text in the entire controversy three belong to Chemnitz. With this canon he stresses his primary point: Catholic theology robs baptism of efficacy and applies it to confirmation. He knows a gloss to the text which supports his position:

> But let the reader always remember that there is an antithesis between baptism and confirmation. The Council of Orleans, "De consecratione distinctio 5": "One will never be a Christian unless he will have been chrismated in episcopal confirmation." And the gloss says: "A child baptized but not chrismated will have a lesser glory than one who will have been confirmed;" and adds, "this then has to be conceded in any event, if it is assumed that grace is conferred to the child in baptism." And let the reader observe well, namely that grace can be entirely withdrawn from baptism and referred to chrism.[24]

Like Calvin, Chemnitz stresses the latter half of the canonical text.

In his two other citations, Chemnitz returns to a phrase in the first part of the canon, that confirmation be received at a mature age. Here he changes his approach and gives a positive assessment of the canon to support his theory that confirmation should be received in maturity by a child baptized in infancy:

> Also this narration shows that chrismation had once been joined and connected to the action of baptism itself. Afterwards, that the number of sacraments might be increased, they turned it away from the action of baptism; and that it might become from that point a special sacrament, they wanted some space of time to intervene between baptism and smearing, namely 12 or 25 years, as the gloss conveys in "De consecratione distinctio 5," capitula ut Jejun.[25]

---

[23] Chapter II, fn. 51.

[24] "Semper autem meminerit Lector, antithesin esse inter Baptismum et Confirmationem. Concilium Aurelianense, de Consecratio. distinct. 5. Nunquam erit Christianus, nisi in confirmatione Episcopali fuerit chrismatus. Et glossa dicit: parvulum baptizatum, et non chrismatum, habiturum minorem gloriam quam qui etiam confirmatus fuerit: et addit, hoc tunc saltem concedendum esse si ponatur, parvulo in Baptismo conferri gratiam. Et hoc Lector bene abservet, posse scilicet gratiam in universo detrahi baptismo, et referri ad chrisma." 3, Preuss:286.

[25] "Ostendit et haec narratio, Chrismationem olim fuisse conjunctam et connexam

With this text, Chemnitz thus strengthens his statement that chrismation, once connected with the action of baptism, was removed by the Roman Church to make an independent sacrament.

Similarly, in describing the rite of confirmation he prefers, an examination of children's faith, Chemnitz finds support from Gratian's canon, which added to the apostolic practice a mature age for confirmation.

> For in the apostolic imposition of hands, history manifestly witnesses that an exploration of doctrine and profession of faith were made (Acts 19). . . . And therefore the canon of Orleans requires a mature age in the one to be confirmed.[26]

In summary, Chemnitz uses both parts of Gratian's canon to make two separate points: that the Roman Church transfers the grace of baptism to confirmation, and that the mature age required for confirmation indicates it is only an examination of faith.

c. Bellarmine

Twice Bellarmine uses this canon: first as part of his fundamental argument that confirmation is a sacrament, illustrated from many different authorities – in this case, councils;[27] second in describing the importance of fasting to prepare for confirmation.[28]

The canon represents one of the instances in which Bellarmine gives the reader not only the the council and canon number in the first citation, but also the text of the canon itself. This is significant because he provides only the first half of the canon, describing a worthy preparation for receiving confirmation, and does not include the clause added to the canon late in its history about the necessity of receiving confirmation. He ignores the part of the canon the Reformers used to challenge the sacramental nature and effects of confirmation, and quotes the part which relates to its history.

---

ipsi actioni Baptismi. Postea ut numerus Sacramentorum augeretur, avulserunt eam ab actione Baptismi: atque ut fieret inde peculiare Sacramentum voluerunt inter-baptismum et delibutionem, intercedere spatium aliquod temporis, annos scilicet 12 vel 25, sicut tradit glossa de Consecrat. dist. 5 cap. ut Jejun." 24:5, Preuss:295.

[26] "In Apostolica enim impositione manuum, factam fuisse explorationem doctrinae et professionem fidei, manifeste testatur historia, Act. 19. . . Atque ideo canon Aurelianensis perfectam aetatem requirit in confirmando." 25, Preuss:297.

[27] 4, Battezzati:217.

[28] 13, Battezzati:233.

For Bellarmine, then, the canon describes the Church's use of confirmation at a moment in history. The canon explains aspects of the ritual, and its antiquity enhances the dignity of confirmation as a sacrament.

3. Analysis
a. The Reformers

The Reformers argue a position traceable to Luther, that confirmation is not a sacrament because it lacks scriptural support, but that it is a praiseworthy ceremony for making a confession of faith before the community. Therefore they rally to the first part of Gratian's canon requiring a mature age, and scoff at the second which makes confirmation constitutive of Christianity. Once again, their reflection on baptismal theology gleaned from many New Testament texts keeps them from attributing the strength of baptism to confirmation.

The argument is strong in many ways: It observes that not only do the form and matter for the rite originate outside of Scripture, but its theology does too. Their objection to the theology of the second part of the canon is in keeping with the broader Christian tradition: Baptism makes one Christian, not confirmation. Moreover, the mature age specified by a canon of the post-patristic Church is indeed an indication that the anointing originally administered at baptism received its own identity later in history.

Yet the argument has weaknesses: The second part of this canon is not truly representative of the Roman Church's theology of confirmation. Whereas the Reformers have uncovered a point of questionable theological merit, it is so out of keeping with mainstream confirmation theology that Bellarmine omits the text from his argument. Regarding the question of age, Chemnitz is aware that the separation of the rites is a later development. But his prejudice toward profession of faith at a later age is so strong he does not reflect here on the sacramental theology of the early Church which anointed at baptism.

b. Bellarmine

Bellarmine argues from the tradition of the Church that confirmation is a sacrament. For him, its historical development represents continuity, not creativity, and lends support to the sacramentality of the rite.

The strength of his argument is in the Church's classical application of tradition: Not just the Scriptures, but the very history of the Church is a font of divine revelation. Although his second argument is somewhat insignificant in the great scope of the controversy (that one should fast before being confirmed), it is perhaps the most faithful use of Gratian's canon. This canon seeks to help the believer make preparation for a holy ceremony. Bellarmine uses the canon exactly that way.

His argument is weakened because of the late dating of the canon. Although it certainly still forms part of the Church's tradition, it carries less force dating from some years after Gratian's placement of it. Another weakness is a point perhaps so obvious that the Reformers never comment on it: Nowhere does the canon call confirmation a sacrament. Read through the eyes of the sixteenth century, this renders the text ambiguous.

c. Conclusions

The first half of Gratian's canon intends to help one make a worthy reception of confirmation. It witnesses the historical development placing confirmation at a point in one's life later than baptism. By not specifically calling confirmation a sacrament, the text retains an ambiguity which allows both sides to claim its support, albeit unsatisfactory. The second half of the canon is not representative enough of Roman theology to merit a weighty consideration. It is an example of a text which makes minor contributions to the debate, but does not carry the force the disputants are inclined to assign it.

C. Cyril: *The Jerusalem Catecheses*
1. Introduction

The collection of catechetical instructions under the name of Cyril of Jerusalem has preserved for generations the rites of initiation from an early Church community. The first two parts are pre-catechesis and catechetical instructions addressed to candidates for baptism in Jerusalem, largely explaining the elements of the creed. The final part is a set of five mystagogical catecheses addressed to the newly-baptized during the Easter Octave, explaining the rites of initiation. Of these five, the first two treat baptism, the third anointing, the fourth Eucharist, and the fifth the liturgy of the Mass. All the passages from Cyril cited in this post-Reformation controversy are from these mystagogia.

In the second mystagogical catechesis Cyril presents elements of the rite of baptism. Part of the preparation is an anointing from head to toe with exorcised oil, which Cyril calls a symbol of participation in the richness of Christ:

> <This> oil, exorcised by the invocation of God and by prayer, receives such power that it not only purifies by burning away the traces of sins, but even drives out the unseen[29] powers of evil.[30]

Cyril's presentation of postbaptismal anointing with chrism first gives its spiritual significance, then a description of the rite, and finally scriptural quotations which prefigure the rite. Here, from the first section, he explains the meaning of anointing with chrism:

> Christ has been chrismated with the spiritual oil of gladness, that is to say the Holy Spirit, called the oil of gladness because He is the Author of spiritual gladness; and you, you have been chrismated with perfume, having become companions and participants of Christ. . . . But take care not to regard this as simple perfume. For just as the bread of the Eucharist after the epiclesis of the Holy Spirit is no longer mere bread but rather the Body of Christ, by the same token this holy chrism is no longer mere perfume—one might say, common—after the epiclesis, but it has rather become a gift[31] of Christ, and the effector of His own divinity by the coming of the Holy Spirit. It is this chrism that has been symbolically anointed upon your forehead and the other senses. And while the body is anointed by visible chrism, the soul is sanctified by the holy and life-creating Spirit.[32]

This passage receives the greatest attention from the controversialists.

---

[29] When Chemnitz quotes this passage the Preuss edition uses the word with the opposite meaning here, "visibiles". 24:4, Preuss:293.

[30] See chart entry G-10 for text. Trans. Jack Custer.

[31]   There is a textual variation here. SC accepts "χαρισμα", both Bellarmine and Chemnitz use editions which have "χρισμα". The mention of chrism here would seem to make the text even more important for the controversy, but – presuming SC is correct – the absence of the word is no great loss here since the text elsewhere speaks of "μυρον", which is essentially the same.

[32] G-11. Trans. Custer.

2. Usage
a. Calvin

Calvin's brief treatment of confirmation never cites Cyril's text. In fact, throughout the controversy he refers to no Greek Fathers at all either to support his position or criticize his adversaries.

b. Chemnitz

Not till near the end of his work does Chemnitz examine the *Catecheses*. Having criticized the Roman Church's theology of confirmation, he studies the writings of the ancients to determine what they said and how reliable they are. Here he claims many texts were forgeries or influenced by Montanism. In this context he turns to Cyril for an extended examination of his authority and theology.[33]

Chemnitz begins by calling Cyril "the patron of papal chrism."[34] Citing other Fathers, he questions the reliability and the orthodoxy of the *Catecheses*.

> The papists nevertheless will not snatch away from us that freedom which in examining and judging the writings of all the Fathers Augustine often presses, that it has been given to the Church namely that they be examined according to the norm of Scripture. And Jerome says that this Cyril composed the *Catecheses* in adolescence. Rufinus adds that he wavered one time in faith, often in confession. The authority of this writer is not therefore canonical.[35]

He thus begins his attack on Cyril against his character.

Chemnitz makes these remarks about Cyril's theology of the pre-baptismal anointing from the second mystagogical catechesis:

> But Cyril anoints those needing to be baptized with this oil before baptism. If therefore before baptism both sins and the very vestiges of sins have already been expurgated through oil, how does he then say that baptism is absolution of sins, that it produces adoption and the gift of the Holy Spirit? But he explains himself when he says, "That oil is a

---

[33] 24:4, Preuss:293-294.

[34] "Pontificii chrismatis patronus." 24:4, Preuss:293.

[35] "Illam tamen libertatem nobis Pontificii non eripient, quam in examinandis et dijudicandis omnium patrum scriptis, Augustinus saepius inculcat, Ecclesiae datam esse, ut scilicet ad normam scripturae exigantur. Et Hieronymus dicit, Cyrillum hunc in adolescentia conscripsisse katêchêseis. Rufinus addit ipsum aliquando in fide, saepius in confessione variasse. Non igitur Canonica est scriptoris hujus autoritas." 24:4, Preuss:293.

symbol of the abundance of Christ communicated to us, and that the diabolic work may be destroyed in us," namely in baptism and through baptism, of which efficacy of baptism oil is the symbol and sign.[36]

The oil under discussion is not chrism, but the prebaptismal anointing. Still, with this passage Chemnitz expresses the dangers of attributing the effects of baptism to another part of the rite. If Cyril does not intend to make oil a symbol of the real power which baptism holds, Chemnitz continues, his work is at odds internally and with Scripture.

The third mystagogical catechesis troubles Chemnitz because it could suggest that chrism possesses the powers of baptism:

How therefore does that Cyril then attribute to chrism those things which he himself affirms, with Scripture as a witness, are properties of baptism, namely the cleansing of sins, the sanctification of the Spirit, and participation in Christ? I interpret simply in this way, that he understands chrism to be a symbol, signifying and suggesting what is the power and efficacy of baptism, not that he wants either to take away that power from baptism or to share it between baptism and chrism.[37]

He concludes this section differing with Cyril's statement that once judged worthy of chrismation, one is called Christian.

For we are made and exist as Christians not by some external smearing of grease, but by Christ our Lord, whom we put on in baptism, whom we understand in the Word, that by faith he may dwell in our hearts. For neither at Antioch were they first called Christians because they had been anointed and smeared with some external fatness of an olive tree.[38]

[36] "Atqui hoc oleo Cyrillus ungit baptizandos ante baptismum. Si igitur ante baptismum et peccata, et ipsa peccatorum vestigia per oleum jam expurgata sunt: quomodo mox dicit, baptismum esse peccatorum absolutionem, conciliare adoptionem, et donum Spiritus sancti? Sed explicat se, cum inquit: Illud oleum, symbolum est pinguedinis Christi nobis communicatae, et quod diabolica operatio in nobis deleta sit, scilicet in baptismo et per baptismum: cujus efficaciae baptismi, symbolum et significatio est oleum." 24:4, Preuss:293.

[37] "Quomodo igitur ea quae ipse etiam teste scriptura affirmat, baptismi propria esse, purgationem scilicet peccatorum, sanctificationem spiritus, et participationem Christi, Cyrillus ille mox Chrismati tribuit? Ego simpiciter ita interpretor, quod intelligat chrisma esse Symbolum, significans et admonens, quae sit baptismi virtus et efficacia: non quod illam virtutem velit, vel baptismo detrahere, vel eam partiri inter baptisma et inter chrisma." 24:4, Preuss:293.

[38] "Christiani enim efficimur et sumus, non ab externa aliqua pinguedinis delibutione, sed a Christo Domino nostro, quem in baptismo induimus, quem in verbo

Chemnitz continues, comparing Cyril's text against the Scriptures. Cyril sees chrismation prefigured in the anointing of Moses, and as a fulfillment of 1 John 2, "He will teach you all things for he dwells in you," where John uses oil as an image of the Spirit. But Chemnitz rejects both applications:

> For it is most certain that John speaks not concerning some external pouring of grease, but concerning the spiritual, interior, and invisible anointing of the Spirit. And because in the New Testament we have the truth itself, one must not go back to the figures of the Old Testament, without the command of Christ.[39]

Cyril's scriptural applications conclude with Isaiah 25, but Chemnitz says the original version does not include a reference to oil, and that the text is allegorical. He rejects Cyril's applications as "cold," "constrained," "contorted," and "strange."[40]

In a later argument, Chemnitz criticizes the diversity of the rites of anointing. For him this indicates that its tradition has not been consistent. He uses Cyril as an example of this diversity since Cyril anointed the baptized not just on the forehead, but on the ears, the nose, and the breast as well.[41]

In summary, Chemnitz questions the reliability of young, irresolute Cyril. He corrects the theology of anointing found in the *Cateches* according to Cyril's other statements about baptism. He finds Cyril's treatment of the Scriptures superficial. And he declares this tradition at variance with other traditions of anointing.

c. Bellarmine

By comparison with his treatment of the other sources, Bellarmine's rebuttal against Chemnitz's depreciation of Cyril is lengthy. Bellarmine strives to re-establish Cyril's reliability, then

---

apprehendimus, ut fide in cordibus nostris habitet. Neque enim Antiochae primum appellati fuerunt Christiani, inde quod externa aliqua oleae pinguedine deliniti et delibuti fuerint." 24:4, Preuss:293-294.

[39] "Certissimum enim est, Johannem loqui non de externa aliqua pinguedinis delibatione, sed de spirituali, interiori et invisibili unctione spiritus. Et quia in Novo Testamento, ipsam veritatem habemus, non est redeundum ad figuras Veteris Testamenti, sine mandato Christi." 24:4, Preuss:294.

[40] "frigidae," "coactae," "contortae," "peregrinae." 24:4, Preuss:294.

[41] 24:5, Preuss:294.

draws on his support for his own analysis of what makes confirmation a sacrament.

Bellarmine lists Cyril among the Greek Fathers who witness the sacramentality of confirmation. He argues that by framing anointing between baptism and Eucharist, Cyril regards it as a sacrament. His comments on its power and efficacy say the same.

> Cyril of Jerusalem out of five mystagogical catecheses wrote 1 and 2 concerning baptism, 3 concerning confirmation, 4 and 5 concerning Eucharist, which are the three sacraments which are received on the same day by neophytes. Hence it is apparent that Cyril not only regarded confirmation as a sacrament, but even as a sacrament most properly called, because he places it in number with baptism and Eucharist. . . . Note at this place first that chrism is also conferred here with Eucharist; which is an argument that each, equally, is properly a sacrament. Second, note that the consecrated oil has the power of sanctifying, which is a property of true sacraments, which are instruments of sanctification.[42] Third, that they not only have the power of sanctifying but also the soul is really truly sanctified by the Holy Spirit when the forehead is anointed with chrism. Fourth, note that this author has spoken cautiously when he says that the bread of the Eucharist after consecration is the Body of Christ; he did not say however that the anointing after consecration is the Holy Spirit, lest we think there is imagined by Cyril a similar transubstantiation of oil such as happens in bread; but he said it is not bare oil, but the chrism of Christ having power of sanctifying from the Holy Spirit.[43]

[42]   This is one of the criteria for sacramentality established by Bellarmine through his study of the Catechism of Trent. See Chapter II, fn. 103 above.

[43]   "Cyrillus hierosolymitanus ex quinque catechesibus mystagogicis, 1. et 2. scripsit de Baptismo, 3. de sacramento Confirmationis, 4. et 5. de Eucharistia, quae sunt tria sacramenta, quae eodem die percipiuntur a neophytis. Unde apparet Cyrillum non tantum habuisse Confirmationem pro sacramento, sed etiam pro sacramento propriissime dicto, quandoquidem illud in numero ponit cum Baptismo et Eucharistia. . . . Nota ad hunc locum primo conferri hic etiam Chrisma cum Eucharistia; quod est argumentum utrumque esse aeque proprie sacramentum. Secundo nota, unguentum consecratum vim habere sanctificandi, quod est proprium verorum sacramentorum, quae sunt instrumenta sanctificationis. Tertio, non solum vim habere sanctificandi, sed etiam reipsa vere animam sancto Spiritu sanctificari, cum frons Chrismate perungitur. Quarto nota, hunc auctorem caute loquutum, cum ait, panem Eucharistiae post consecrationem esse corpus Christi; unguentum autem post consecrationem non dixit esse Spiritum sanctum, ne putaremus a Cyrillo fingi similem transubstantiationem unguenti, qualis fit in pane: sed dixit, non esse nudum unguentum, sed Chrisma Christi habens energiam sanctificandi a Spiritu sancto." 5, Battezzati:217.

Bellarmine regards the witness of Cyril worthy of a lengthy reflection. Commenting on the same catechesis, he compares moments in the life of Christ with Christian initiation:

> In the same text Cyril teaches the same thing, how first Christ received baptism, second the dove descended upon him, third temptation befell him, so it also happens with us who first are baptized, then receive the Holy Spirit through chrism, and thus at length descend to battle with the devil.[44]

And he upholds Cyril's application of the name Christian to those who are anointed:

> In the same place he also says that a Christian is properly called so by chrism. For since a Christian is called as it were "anointed", one does not seem worthy of this name who has not been anointed by this oil by which Christians are perfected.[45]

For Bellarmine all these references support his position that confirmation is a sacrament.

In all other references to this source Bellarmine builds his argument concerning the matter of confirmation. He says there is a remote matter (chrism) and proximate matter (anointing), and that Cyril supports the existence of both.

To prove the remote matter is chrism Bellarmine uses texts from Scripture, including 1 John 2, 27, which Cyril himself cites.[46] He also argues that chrism must be consecrated, using Cyril's reference to the epiclesis as one of many sources describing this rite.[47]

Cyril also alludes to what Bellarmine calls the proximate matter, signing the forehead with the sign of the cross. Although Chemnitz argued that the multiple signings called for in the *Catecheses* weakened the effective use of this source, Bellarmine says Cyril emphasizes anointing the forehead, and there is no objection to

---

[44] "Idem Cyrillus ibidem docet, quemadmodum Christus primo Baptismum accepit; secundo descendit in eum columba: tertio excepit eum tentatio: ita nobiscum etiam fieri, qui primo baptizamur deinde per Chrisma recipimus Spiritum sanctum et sic tandem ad praelium descendimus cum diabolo." 5, Battezzati:217.

[45] "Ibidem etiam dicit, Christianum proprie denominari a Chrismate. Cum enim Christianus dicatur quasi unctus, non videtur dignus hoc nomine qui non est unctus hoc unguento, quo Christiani perficiuntur." 5, Battezzati:217.

[46] G-14. This is the same passage Chemnitz criticizes; see fn. 39 above.

[47] 8, Battezzati:225.

anointing other senses:

> I respond <to Chemnitz> that Cyril in the place cited
> especially wants the forehead to be anointed, as he expressly
> says, then other senses; which indeed is not against us:
> because we assert this alone, that there is no sacrament
> unless chrism is applied on the forehead, we nevertheless do
> not deny that afterwards some other part of the body can also
> be anointed, according to the various customs of the
> Church.[48]

For Bellarmine then the witness of Cyril supports both his general argument that confirmation is a sacrament and the specific description of its matter. One senses the respect Bellarmine holds for this theologian in his dependence on Cyril, especially in the lengthy opening exposition at 5:217.

3. Analysis
a. Chemnitz

Chemnitz takes many approaches to patristic texts. He sometimes questions the authenticity or reliability of the source. He most often judges a patristic text against its conformity with the Bible since his own argument is rooted in Scripture. In meeting Cyril, he faces a formidable witness (the "patron of papal chrism") for the Roman Church and delivers a studied analysis of the *Catecheses* from both these perspectives.

Chemnitz's argument is sound; he himself holds Scripture as the norm, and his patristic sources do the same; they even encourage self-criticism by the norm of Scripture. Chemnitz's interpretation of Cyril's second and third mystagogical catecheses is creditable, where he declares that oil has no power, but is a symbol of Christ's power. Not even Bellarmine criticizes this emphasis on oil as a symbol. Also, Chemnitz's criticisms of Cyril's use of Scripture have merit. There is no question that the Apostles were called Christians for the first time at Antioch, even though they were not anointed—a passage Cyril ignored

---

[48] "Respondeo <Kemnitio>: Cyrillum loco citato, praecipue velle frontem inungi, ut ipse expresse ait, deinde alios sensus; quod quidem non est contra nos: siquidem id solum asserimus, nisi in fronte adhibeatur Chrisma, sacramentum nullum esse; non tamen negamus, quin deinde possit juxta varios Ecclesiae mores inungi etiam alia aliqua corporis pars." 9, Battezzati:228.

when describing an effect of chrism as making a person a Christian. Although he praises Cyril's knowledge of baptismal texts in Scripture, Chemnitz disapproves of the allegorical interpretation of passages for confirmation, e.g. 1 John 2, 27 and Isaiah 25, 6-7. The warning about allegory is important since there is no straightforward Scripture text regarding the anointing in confirmation.

But Chemnitz's argument also has weaknesses. Quite simply, Cyril's *Catecheses* have been treated as a reliable source for early Christian initiation from the time of their composition all though the Church's history. Together with Ambrose, Tertullian, John Chrysostom, Theodore of Mopsuestia, Egeria,[49] and others they present almost indisputable evidence that from the Church's earliest days post-baptismal, pre-Eucharistic anointing with chrism constituted an accepted part of Christian initiation. In addition, Chemnitz's attempts to discredit the testimony of Cyril with character witnesses–Jerome who said he was young, Rufinus who said he wavered in faith–are not persuasive, in view of the influence the *Catecheses* had on subsequent writers.[50]

b. Bellarmine

Bellarmine has two goals in mind as he presents the material from Cyril. He wishes to fit the *Catecheses* into the framework of his own argument, and to respond to the challenge mounted by Chemnitz.

The argument has strengths. First Bellarmine is dealing with a reliable text that forms a solid witness for his position. Although the scholastic category "matter" was unknown to Cyril (and its application to the argument could hence be regarded as a weakness), the text is important for observing the historical development of what came to be known as the matter of confirmation, so it does help Bellarmine's argument. Cyril's comparison of the baptism of Christ, descent of the dove, and temptation of Christ to the life of the Christian is taken up

---

[49] In fairness to Chemnitz, Egeria's diary was unknown at the time of the Reformation.

[50] "Saint Cyrille de Jérusalem n'est pas un inconnu pour les auteurs ecclésiastiques. Ils connaissent son activité pastorale et littéraire et utilisent ses écrits pour donner plus d'autorité à leurs propres idées, soit en s'inspirant simplement de ses productions, soit en reproduisant des parties de ses ouvrages." W. J. Swaans, "A propos des 'Catéchèses Mystagogiques' attribuées à S. Cyrille de Jerusalem," *Le Muséon: Revue d'Etudes Orientales* (Louvain), 55 (1942):17. Swaans continues with a presentation of many fathers who drew on the texts of Cyril. See pp. 17-23.

by Bellarmine as an early example of how the anointing was an event separate from baptism in ritual, theology, and spirituality.

A weakness is Bellarmine's application to Cyril's text of terms that developed only much later. Cyril anoints with "myron", which may be translated as "chrism", and Bellarmine's enthusiastic mistranslation of "charisma" as "chrism" is forgivable because of the textual variation.[51] But Cyril does not call the anointing confirmation. Nor does he call this nor baptism nor Eucharist a sacrament. Bellarmine's reason for calling it a sacrament fulfills his own criteria in 5:217, but these are later clarifications imposed on the text. It is thus an exaggeration for Bellarmine to say "Cyril regards confirmation as a sacrament most properly called."[52] It would have been better to say he regarded anointing with chrism integral to Christian initiation. In addition, Bellarmine calls chrism the oil by which Christians are perfected,[53] a superlative Cyril avoids.

c. Conclusions

At the risk of adding more fuel to the fire, in the years following this controversy many writers–and especially Protestants–questioned the genuine authorship of the mystagogical catecheses. In 1574 Josias Simmler published his theory, based on the new discovery of some manuscripts, that the whole collection of catecheses was pseudonymous.[54] This began a debate which has never been fully resolved.[55] Coincidentally, the publication of Simmler's book occurred between the publication of Chemnitz's *Examen* and Bellarmine's

---

[51]   Fred Kramer's English translation of Chemnitz includes this note: "The Preuss edition has changed 'charisma' of the 1574 edition to 'chrisma', but erroneously. According to Migne, op. cit., Tom. 33, col. 1091, the author of the *Catecheses* wrote 'charisma', which the Latin text renders 'donarium', i.e., a votive offering or gift (p. 203, n. 7)." But Bellarmine, working from the original 1566 edition of Chemnitz also quotes Cyril's text with "chrisma". It may rather be that the textual variant was not recognized till after Chemnitz's time.

[52]   See fn. 43 above.

[53]   "... est unctus hoc unguento, quo Christiani perficiuntur." 5, Battezzati:217.

[54]   Iosias Simler, *Bibliotheca institvta et collecta primvm a   Conrado Gesnero, Deinde in Epitomen redacta et nouorum Librorum accessione locupletata, iam vero postremo recognita, et in duplum post priores editiones aucta, per Iosiam Simlerum Tigurinum,* (Zürich: Christophor Froschover, 1574), p. 153.

[55]   Swaans, pp. 3-10. For a more complete bibliography on this question see Johannes Quasten, *Patrologia,* trans. Nello Beghin (Casale: Marietti, 1983) 2:370.

response. Bellarmine makes no mention of this other question–whether or not Cyril wrote the *Catecheses* at all–but it is plausible to think a man of his erudition would be aware of the new question, and this could account in part for his vigorous defense of Cyril at this time.

A point both parties miss is the meaning of the difference between Cyril's description of anointing and the developed confirmation of the Reformation age. In the later age the rite had been separated from baptism and had received its own interpretation. For Cyril, though, it was initiation, whereas for the later Church it was more a rite of maturity. Thus, Cyril's description of the gift of the Holy Spirit in the anointing does not threaten the theology of baptism as Chemnitz fears since the rites were administered together and initiation was a unit. The Roman Church's theology of confirmation as arming the matured Christian for the struggle of life would have been unknown to Cyril's community who were anointed in the baptismal ceremony itself. The Reformers' preference for an examination of faith with imposition of hands would be difficult to justify from Cyril's text: The examination took place before baptism, and– surprisingly–there is no imposition of hands described in the mystagogical catecheses, just an anointing.[56] Thus the weight of recent liturgical history and the newfound but consistent tradition among Reformers calling for an examination of faith create as it were a screen through which the controversialists interpreted the texts of Cyril.

D. Augustine: *De baptismo*
1. Introduction

Of Augustine's many works against the Donatists, *De baptismo* takes up one issue in earnest: rebaptism. The Donatists believed that only their baptism was valid. Consequently they would rebaptize one joining the faith who had been baptized by a heretic. For this they drew support from the writings of St. Cyprian. Augustine, however, denounced their position in *De baptismo* and supported the necessity of baptizing once only.

In the confirmation controversy several passages are cited from

---

[56] Among the pre-baptismal catecheses, Cyril says that as Peter gave the Spirit through the imposition of hands, so will the neophytes receive it when they are baptized (Cat. 16, 26), and although he promises a further treatment, the mystagogical catecheses never take up the theme. See PG 33 (1857):955-956.

this work. The one used most frequently is from book three, where Augustine discusses the imposition of hands. Since baptism happens once only, Augustine does not rebaptize a reconciled heretic, he imposes hands. By comparing this rite with the one in Acts, he discusses the resultant activity of the Spirit in good and evil people.

> But that the Holy Spirit is said to be given in the catholic church alone through the imposition of hands, doubtless our elders wanted this to be understood which the Apostle said, "Because the charity of God has been poured out in our hearts through the Holy Spirit Who has been given to us." For that is the charity which they do not have who were cut off from communion of the catholic church, and through this, even if they may speak with the tongues of humans and angels, if they may know all sacraments and all wisdom and if they may have all prophecy and all faith so that they would move mountains and distribute all their possessions to the poor and hand over their body so that they burn, it profits them nothing. But one does not have the charity of God who does not love the unity of the Church, and through this the Holy Spirit is understood rightly to be said that He is not received except in the catholic church. For neither is the Holy Spirit given only through the imposition of hands when temporal and sensible miracles attest to this, as earlier He was given for the support of inexperienced faith and for extending the beginnings of the Church. For who expects this now, that those on whom hands are imposed for receiving the Holy Spirit suddenly begin to speak in tongues? But invisibly and secretly divine charity is understood to be inspired in their hearts because of the bond of peace that they may be able to say, "Because the charity of God has been poured out in our hearts through the Holy Spirit Who has been given to us." But many are the operations of the Holy Spirit which the same Apostle had mentioned in a certain text when he judged how much they imbued, so he concluded, "But one and the same Spirit works all these things, dividing the properties for each one just as he wills." Since then the sacrament is one thing, which even Simon the magician was able to have; the operation of the Spirit is another thing, which is accustomed to happen even in evil people, as Saul possessed prophecy;[57] the operation of the same Spirit which only the good are able to have is yet another thing, since just as charity is the end of the law concerning a pure heart and good conscience and a faith not feigned; whichever the heretics and schismatics may receive, the charity which covers a multitude of sins is a proper gift of catholic unity and

---

[57] This line is echoed in the Augsburg Confession, article 8. See Chapter I, fn. 56.

peace, nor of that in all people, because neither do all belong to it, as we will see in its place. Outside of it, nevertheless, that charity is not able to exist, without which other things, even if they can be recognized and proved, nevertheless are not able to be useful and liberate. But the imposition of hands is not like baptism, which cannot be repeated.[58] For what else is it but a prayer over a person?[59]

Both sides of the controversy cite this text in support of their positions. To the Catholics it showed many uses for the imposition of hands, to the Reformers it revealed confirmation as a prayer, not a sacrament.

2. Usage
a. Calvin

Scripture remains the primary storehouse for Calvin, and he admits patristic texts pale by comparison since sacraments are proved not by human writers, but by God.[60] Nonetheless, Calvin cannot resist

---

[58] Oddly, none of the controversialists comment on Augustine's grammar. I have had to mistranslate this phrase to preserve the sense of Augustine's argument. He could not possibly have intended what he wrote here, that baptism can be repeated. It would completely overturn his argument against the Donatists. I believe Augustine would not be displeased with my solution. He himself altered the text of Psalm 36 and explained, "Quid ad nos quid grammatici uelint? Melius in barbarismo nostro uos intellegitis, quam in nostra disertitudine uos deserti eritis." CChr.SL 38:371.

[59] "Spiritus autem sanctus quod in sola catholica per manus inpositionem dari dicitur, nimirum hoc intellegi maiores nostri uoluerunt quod apostolus ait: 'quoniam caritas dei diffusa est in cordibus nostris per spiritum sanctum qui datus est nobis.' ipsa est enim caritas, quam non habent qui ab ecclesiae catholicae communione praecisi sunt, ac per hoc, etiamsi linguis hominum et angelorum loquantur, si sciant omnia sacramenta et omnem scientiam et si habeant omnem prophetiam et omnem fidem ita ut montes transferant et distribuant omnia sua pauperibus et tradant corpus suum ut ardeant, nihil eis prodest. non autem habet dei caritatem, qui ecclesiae non diligit unitatem, ac per hoc recte intellegitur dici non accipi nisi in catholica spiritus sanctus. neque enim temporalibus et sensibilibus miraculis adtestantibus per manus inpositionem modo datur spiritus sanctus, sicut antea dabatur ad commendationem rudis fidei et ecclesiae primordia dilatanda. quis enim nunc hoc expectat, ut hi, quibus manus ad accipiendum sanctum spiritum inponitur, repente incipiant linguis loqui? sed inuisibiliter et latenter intellegitur propter uinculum pacis eorum cordibus diuina caritas inspirari, ut possint dicere: 'quoniam caritas dei diffusa est in cordibus nostris per spiritum sanctum qui datus est nobis. multae autem sunt operationes spiritus sancti, quas idem apostolus cum quodam loco quantum sufficere arbitratus est commemorasset, ita conclusit: 'omnia autem haec operatur unus atque idem spiritus, diuidens propria unicuique prout uult.' cum ergo. . . " The remainder of this text is in the chart, L-10. De baptismo 3:16,21, ed. M. Petschenig, CSEL 51 (1908):212-213.

[60] 12, CR 30:1074. See Chapter II, fn. 55.

claiming Augustine for his argument that confirmation is not a sacrament.[61] He cites this passage but once when disputing confirmation in the *Institutio.*

At the end of his thomistic analysis of confirmation, Calvin discusses the Roman Church's use of sources. He says the ancient writers counted only two sacraments, and although they mention imposition of hands they never number it among them.

> The ancients speak concerning the imposition of hands, but do they ever call it a sacrament? Augustine openly affirms that it is nothing else but a prayer.[62]

Calvin is aware there is a difficulty here. The context of Augustine's statement concerns reconciliation of heretics. Calvin knows he will be accused of applying the gesture of imposition to the wrong controversy.

> For <Augustine> speaks concerning those who were returning to the unity of the Church from schism. He denies they have the need of a repetition of baptism, for the imposition of hands suffices that the Lord may bestow the Holy Spirit to them through the bond of peace.[63]

But here Calvin shows that the imposition of hands in this text–because it is repeatable–is already a repetition in the reconciliation of heretics, having once been given in the rite of baptism:

> But because it might seem absurd that the imposition of hands be repeated rather than baptism, he shows the difference. For what else, he says, is the imposition of hands than a prayer over a person? And that this is the sense is apparent from another place, where he says because of the bond of charity, which is the greatest gift of the Holy Spirit, without which whatever other holy things will have been in a person are not efficacious for salvation, the hand was imposed on reformed heretics.[64]

---

[61] In fact, Calvin used the passage in a similar way in his 1544 response to the faculty of theology at Paris. See chapter II, fn. 40.

[62] "De manuum impositione loquuntur veteres; sed an sacramentum vocant? Augustinus aperte affirmat, nihil aliud esse quam orationem." 12, CR 30:1074.

[63] "Loquitur enim <Augustinus> de iis qui a schismate ad ecclesiae unitatem redibant. Eos iteratione baptismi opus habere negat; sufficere enim manuum impositionem, ut per vinculum pacis spiritum sanctum illis Dominus largiatur." 12, CR 30:1074-75.

[64] "Quoniam autem absurdum videri poterat manuum impositionem repeti potius quam baptismum, discrimen ostendit. Quid enim, inquit, aliud est manuum impositio,

Thus for Calvin, the imposition of hands from the rite of initiation was repeated in the reconciliation of heretics. Baptism is not repeatable, imposition is. And this imposition of hands on heretics, which is the same as the Roman Church's confirmation after baptism, is not a sacrament, but a prayer.

b. Chemnitz

As with his comments on Cyril of Jerusalem, Chemnitz reviews this text of Augustine near the end of his work when examining the reliability and interpretation of patristic sources. Here he describes the discontinuity he sees between the anointing in the writings of the ancients and that observed in the Roman Church.

One difference he perceives is matter: Whereas the early Church observed this rite with imposition of hands, the Roman Church does so now with oil. Chemnitz takes Augustine as an example. Although *De baptismo* is specifically cited only later in this section, it is likely he has it in mind here.

> For first, what pertains to matter, as they call it, or to the external sign, the imposition of hands was used by the ancients, which was in use up to the age of Jerome and Augustine. But now with the Papists, the imposition of hands has been utterly abolished in confirmation.[65]

Later Chemnitz observes another difference: The rite of confirmation was once joined to baptism, but now they are separated. He gives several reasons. First is that to reconcile heretics, the Church chose the rite of imposition of hands. To explain how someone could receive baptism and then, having fallen away, be sanctified through the imposition of hands, Chemnitz says that baptism must be received by faith. If it is not, as was surely the case with these heretics, the imposition of hands at their conversion indicates the moment in which they received the sanctification offered in baptism.

---

quam oratio super hominem? Atque hunc esse sensum ex altero loco apparet, ubi dicit, propter caritatis copulationem, quod est maximum donum spiritus sancti, sine quo non valent ad salutem quaecunque alia sancta in homine fuerint, manus haereticis correctis imponitur." 12, CR 30:1075.

[65] "Primo enim quod ad materiam, sicut loquuntur, vel ad externum signum attinet, veteribus usurpata fuit impositio manuum, quae adhuc Hieronymi et Augustini aetate in usu fuit. Jam vero apud Pontificios, impositio manuum in confirmatione prorsus abolita est." 24:5, Preuss:294.

But the one who was baptized, not having true faith, was not able to receive the Holy Spirit and the sanctification of baptism; for those things we receive by faith. But when afterwards he was converted to true faith, then finally, rightly, and profitably he was obtaining the promise of baptism; and so he was receiving with true faith for the first time the sanctification of baptism, having been offered indeed before, but not received; and the Holy Spirit was being invoked over him that this might happen; the symbol of the imposition of hands was being applied to this invocation, as Augustine says that the imposition of hands is nothing else than a prayer over a person, in book 3 against the Donatists, chapter 16.[66]

For Chemnitz, then, Augustine's text presents as it were a later completion of initiation and conversion, marked by the imposition of hands.

The final citation of this passage is where Chemnitz explains why the imposition of hands was separated from baptism: It was the custom for bishops to impose hands on those baptized by presbyters and deacons, but gradually this custom degenerated and new rites and opinions were added until the original purpose was obscured. As an example of this, Chemnitz shows how Augustine explains the purpose of the imposition of hands in terms different from the sixteenth century Roman Church.

For also Augustine against the Donatists, in book 3, chapter 16 asks why the Holy Spirit is said to be given in only the catholic Church through the imposition of the hand. And he responds not from those things which the Papists attribute to their confirmation, but he says, "Our ancestors wanted that which the Apostle said to be understood, 'Charity has been poured forth in our hearts through the Holy Spirit.' For that is the charity which they do not have who have been cut off from the communion of the catholic Church."[67]

---

[66] "Sed qui baptizatus fuit, non habens veram fidem, non potuit accipere Spiritum sanctum, et sanctificationem Baptismi: illa enim fide accipimus. Sed quando postea ad veram fidem convertebatur, tunc demum recte et salutariter apprehendebat promissionem Baptismi: atque ita sanctificationem Baptismi, antea oblatam quidem, sed non acceptam, tunc primum fide vera accipiebat: idque ut fieret, invocabatur super eum Spiritus sanctus: cui invocationi adhibebatur Symbolum impositionis manuum, sicut Augustinus inquit, nihil aliud esse manuum impositionem, quam orationem super hominem, lib. 3 contra Donatistas cap. 16." 24:6, Preuss:296.

[67] "Nam et Augustinus contra Donatistas lib. 3, cap. 16 quaerit, quare Spiritus sanctus in sola catholica, per manus impositionem dari dicatur? Et respondet, non de illis quae Pontificii suae confirmationi tribuunt, sed inquit: Hoc intelligi majores nostri voluerunt, quod Apostolus ait: Charitas diffusa est in cordibus nostris per Spiritum

He continues, explaining that the manner of this imposition is not as a sacrament, but a repeatable prayer.

> However he speaks expressly about returning heretics and schismatics. But how through the imposition of hands charity is inspired, Augustine responds, "What else is the imposition of the hand than a prayer over a person; therefore it is not like baptism which cannot be repeated."[68]

In summary, with this text of Augustine Chemnitz shows the dissimilarity between its imposition of hands and Roman confirmation. The matter of the ritual is different, so is the purpose. He sees Augustine's rite for returning heretics as a reception of the grace promised in baptism, which pours love into the heart and authenticates membership in the Church.

c. Bellarmine

Bellarmine thoroughly treats this text in several places, both in response to the Reformers and to build his own argument.

First it is a key text in response to the Reformers' position that the miraculous results of apostolic imposition of hands have ceased. Bellarmine argues they were necessary only for the early Church:

> There was however a reasonable cause why <the Holy Spirit> was being given visibly then, now only invisibly; because at the beginning of the Church miracles of this kind were necessary for planting and nourishing the faith. Hence Augustine in book 3 of *De baptismo*, chapter 16. . . .[69]

He also lists the text among those by Latin Fathers which illustrate that confirmation is a sacrament.[70] Then he specifically challenges Calvin's interpretation.

---

sanctum. Ipsa enim est charitas, quam non habent qui ab Ecclesiae catholicae communione praecisi sunt." 24:6, Preuss:296.

[68] "Expresse autem loquitur de haereticis et schismaticis revertentibus. Quomodo vero per manus impositionem charitas inspiratur, respondet Augustinus: Manus impositio quid aliud est, quam oratio super hominem: ergo non sicut baptismus, repeti non potest." 24:6, Preuss:297. See fn. 58 above.

[69] "Fuit autem caussa rationabilis, quare tunc daretur visibiliter, nunc solum invisibiliter; quia initio Ecclesiae ad fidem plantandam et nutriendam, ejusmodi miracula necessaria erant. Unde Augustinus lib. 3. de Baptismo cap. 16. . . ." 2, Battezzati:215.

[70] 6, Battezzati:219.

Bellarmine cannot agree with Calvin that the Fathers name only two sacraments, excluding confirmation. To begin with, Bellarmine argues that the text cited by Calvin, in spite of Calvin's insistence, concerns reconciliation, not confirmation:

> I respond to the place cited <by Calvin> from Augustine, that Augustine is speaking about the simple imposition of the hand which was happening in the reconciliation of penitents, not about the imposition of the hand with chrism which is properly the sacrament of confirmation.[71]

Bellarmine continues against Calvin, saying that just because Augustine says this imposition of hands is not repeatable, it does not mean it is not a sacrament:

> If these things were to prove anything they would prove only that confirmation is a repeatable sacrament. They would not prove however that it is not a sacrament properly called, which had to be proved by Calvin. . . . Where Augustine from the fact that the imposition of the hand is a prayer does not conclude that it is not a sacrament, but that it is not such a sacrament that cannot be repeated; in other respects it is proved manifestly to be a sacrament. For here is sensible matter, the imposition of hands; there is form, the prayer; there is effect, the grace of the Holy Spirit, as Calvin himself contends. Why therefore is it not a sacrament? And neither from this can it be proved that confirmation is a repeatable sacrament. For (as I have said) confirmation is not treated here, but the reconciliation of penitents.[72]

Bellarmine continues against Calvin saying that had Augustine intended this passage to refer to confirmation, he would have mentioned chrism:

[71] "Ad locum ex Augustino citatum <a Calvino> Respondeo, Augustinum loqui de simplici manus impositione; quae fiebat in reconciliatione poenitentium, non de manus impositione cum Chrismate, quae est proprie sacramentum Confirmationis." 7, Battezzati:220.

[72] "Haec omnia si quid probarent, probarent solum Confirmationem esse sacramentum iterabile; Non autem probarent, non esse sacramentum proprie dictum, quod Calvino probandum erat. . . . Ubi Augustinus ex eo quod manus impositio est oratio, non colligit non esse sacramentum, sed non esse sacramentum tale, ut repeti non possit. Alioqui sacramentum esse manifeste probatur. Nam hic est materia sensibilis, impositio manuum: est forma, oratio; est effectus, gratia Spiritus sancti, ut ipse Calvinus contendit. Cur ergo non est sacramentum? At neque ex hoc probari potest Confirmationem esse sacramentum iterabile. Nam (ut dixi) non agitur hic de Confirmatione, sed de reconciliatione poenitentium." 7, Battezzati:220.

Augustine teaches at different places that confirmation happens with chrism, as is evident from places recounted above. Here however he not only does not mention chrism, but he openly indicates that he is speaking about an imposition of hands without chrism; otherwise he would not say, "What else is it but a prayer?" for it could be answered it is a consecration and a marking through the anointing of chrism.[73]

He argues from other sources that confirmation given once cannot be repeated, and that the reconciliatory imposition of hands is different from the confirmatory imposition, especially in the Western Church.[74]

There is a problem in his response to Calvin which Bellarmine recognizes: He has already cited this same text not as reconciliation, but to prove that imposition of hands is the sacrament of confirmation.

... Augustine in book 3 of *De baptismo*, chapter 16, i.e., in that very chapter where he says the imposition of hands is nothing but a prayer, says also through that imposition of hands it is not expected now that people speak in tongues as was happening at the time of the Apostles, but that it is enough if the Holy Spirit is poured out invisibly, which text we have cited above in favor of the sacrament of confirmation. Therefore Augustine is speaking about the confirmatory imposition of the hand, or certainly he takes equivocally the imposition of the hand in one and the same chapter, which seems absurd.[75]

Responding to his own objection, Bellarmine argues that Augustine refers to two different uses of the same gesture–the one confirmatory, the other reconciliatory.

---

[73] "Augustinus passim docet Confirmationem fieri Chrismate, ut patet ex locis supra allegatis. Hic autem non solum non meminit Chrismatis, sed aperte indicat se loqui de impositione manuum sine Chrismate; alioqui non diceret: 'Quid est aliud, nisi oratio?' posset enim responderi, est consecratio, et consignatio per Chrismatis unctionem." 7, Battezzati:220.

[74] 7, Battezzati:220.

[75] ". . . Augustinus lib. 3. de Baptismo, cap. 16. id est, in illo ipso capite, ubi dicit, impositionem manuum nihil esse, nisi orationem, dicit etiam per eam manuum impositionem nunc non exspectari, ut homines loquantur linguis, ut fiebat tempore apostolorum, sed satis esse si infundatur Spiritus sanctus invisibiliter: quem locum nos supra citavimus pro sacramento Confirmationis. Ergo Augustinus loquitur de manus impositione confirmatoria; vel certe aequivoce accipit in uno et eodem capite manus impositionem; quod videtur absurdum." 7, Battezzati:220.

I respond. . . that Augustine takes the imposition of the hand in that chapter in a varying way, but without any fallacy. For his purpose was to get around the argument of St. Cyprian, who was concluding from the fact that only in the catholic Church is the Holy Spirit able to be given and received, that the sacraments of the heretics were not true and valid. To lessen the force of this argument Augustine explains at the beginning of the chapter what ought to be understood by the Holy Spirit, when it is said that He cannot be given or received except in the catholic Church through the imposition of the hand; and he says that the gift of charity is understood; for only the good are able to have this and therefore only those in the catholic Church; because outside it none are good. But in this place Augustine takes the imposition of the hand in general, whether it be confirmatory or reconciliatory or (to put it this way) ordinatory; for always through it is given grace and charity, unless an obstacle is opposed.[76]

He explains how these impositions differ.

Then Augustine wants to show that through the imposition of the hand the gift of charity is truly given, and he declares it by the example of the confirmatory imposition of the hand when he says that now it is not expected that they speak in tongues on whom the hand is imposed, but charity is poured out on them secretly. Therefore he interprets there the imposition of the hand more in the strict sense (that is, as confirmatory alone), nor yet is it a faulty equivocation, because what pertains to the whole genus rightly is declared by the example of one species.[77]

[76] "Respondeo. . . Vario modo accipere Augustinum in eo capite manus impositionem, sed sine ullo vitio. Nam propositum ejus erat solvere argumentum s. Cypriani, qui ex eo, quod in sola Ecclesia catholica dari potest, et accipi Spiritus sanctus, colligebat sacramenta haereticorum non esse vera et rata. Ad hoc argumentum diluendum Augustinus initio capitis explicat, quid intelligi debeat per Spiritum sanctum, cum dicitur non posse dari, vel accipi, nisi in Ecclesia catholica per manus impositionem: ac dicit intelligi donum charitatis; hoc enim non possunt habere nisi boni, et ideo non nisi in Ecclesia catholica; quia extra illam nulli sunt boni. Hoc autem loco accipit Augustinus manus impositionem in genere, sive sit confirmatoria, sive reconciliatoria, sive (ut sic loquar) ordinatoria: semper enim per eam datur gratia et charitas, nisi ponatur obex." 7, Battezzati:220-221.

[77] "Deinde vult Augustinus ostendere per manus impositionem dari revera donum charitatis; et declarat exemplo manus impositionis confirmatoriae, cum dicit, nunc non expectari, ut loquantur linguis, quibus manus imponitur, sed latenter eis infundi charitatem. Itaque ibi accipit manus impositionem magis stricte (idest, pro sola confirmatoria), nec tamen est vitiosa aequivocatio; quia quod convenit toti generi, recte declaratur exemplo unius speciei." 7, Battezzati:221.

He concludes by reflecting on three distinctions Augustine makes about the operation of the Spirit.

> Afterwards he returns to the argument of Cyprian and distinguishes three things: the sacrament; the freely given gift of the Holy Spirit, as prophecy; and the gift making <one> pleasing, that is, charity; and he says that the first two things are able to exist outside the Church, or in evil people; not however the third; and therefore they ought to go back to the Church so that they might receive it in her through the reconciliatory imposition of hands. And because anyone could suspect that this imposition of the hand was not able to be repeated, as neither baptism nor confirmation nor orders may be repeated, Augustine therefore subjoins that the imposition of the hand can be repeated, that is, the reconciliatory one, because it is nothing else but a prayer over a person, that is, it is not any consecration, which remains and imprints a character, because of which it cannot be repeated, but it is only a ceremony supporting prayer.[78]

For Bellarmine, then, this passage shows that confirmation is a sacrament in the apostolic tradition of Acts. It is distinct from reconciliation, which also uses an imposition of hands which can be repeated, and which Augustine refers to here as a prayer, while not denying its sacramentality.

3. Analysis
a. The Reformers

Radically devoted to the Scriptures, the Reformers approach patristics with caution. Instead of strengthening their own case with positive patristic witness, they weaken the case of the Roman Church by criticizing their use of that witness. Their purpose here is to show that Augustine does not support the Roman Church as she says he does because of the dissimilarity of content and meaning between his

---

[78] "Postea redit ad argumentum Cypriani, et distinguit tria: Sacramentum, donum Spiritus sancti gratis datum, ut prophetiam; et donum gratum faciens, idest, charitatem; ac dicit extra Ecclesiam, vel in malis hominibus esse posse duo priora, non tamen tertium; et idcirco debere ad Ecclesiam redire, ut in ea per manus impositionem reconciliatoriam illud accipiant. Et quia poterat aliquis suspicari, non posse repeti hanc manus impositionem, sicut non potest repeti Baptismus, nec Confirmatio, nec Ordinatio, ideo Augustinus subjungit, posse repeti manus impositionem, idest, reconciliatoriam, quia nihil est aliud, nisi oratio super hominem, idest, non est consecratio aliqua; quae maneat, et characterem imprimat, unde repeti non possit, sed est tantum caeremonia adjuvans orationem." 7, Battezzati:221.

imposition and her confirmation.

The argument has strength if one accepts the disputed point that the reconciliation of heretics was a confirmatory gesture. It examines well the differences between the Roman rite and the descriptions of Augustine: the use of oil versus the imposition of hands, a theology of strengthening versus a theology of charity. Chemnitz presents a point clearly rooted in the Lutheran tradition when he distinguishes baptism and reconciliation of heretics as sanctification offered and sanctification received: The individual who finally accepts the grace of baptism in the imposition of hands has made a personal expression of faith–a constitutive element for baptism in the Lutheran tradition. Understandable as this interpretation is for a follower of Luther, Chemnitz comes perilously close to attributing to reconciliation the powers of baptism, as he accuses the Catholics of attributing those powers to confirmation.

The weakness of the argument is in the real nature of the imposition of hands in this passage. The ambiguity is twofold: Imposition of hands was used both for initiating Christians and for reconciling heretics; confirmation in both the Roman and Reformed Churches evolved into a ritual temporally distinct from baptismal initiation. So reconciliation of heretics falls into neither category neatly–confirmation of the sixteenth century nor initiation of the fourth. The Reformers argue that Augustine's confirmatory imposition of hands was a repeatable rite, yet they do not speak of repetition in their own tradition.

b. Bellarmine

Bellarmine tries to reconcile the differences between Augustine's description of imposition and the sacrament of confirmation as it developed in the Church. He also distinguishes the various uses of imposition of hands. While discoursing on Augustine's interpretation of Cyprian, he seizes the opportunity to stress to the Church in the age of the Reformation the need for unity in faith.

His argument is strong in its attempt at carefully interpreting Augustine. He is honest enough to examine the ambiguity in his own use of the text–he uses it first to show confirmation is a sacrament, then to show that the text is not about confirmation at all. He shows insight into the historical situation of Cyprian, Augustine, and the Donatists.

There are weaknesses, however. Although Bellarmine distinguishes two applications of the gesture in this passage, it is not clear if Augustine had this in mind. Where Augustine refers to Acts–the place Bellarmine says he discusses confirmation–he simply explains the gesture used to reconcile heretics. Its meaning is that imposition of hands imparts the Holy Spirit. It seems less plausible that Augustine is interpreting the action of the Apostles as confirmation than that he is explaining the ritual gesture for Spirit-filled reconciliation with a text from Acts. The absence of chrism scarcely helps Bellarmine's case; he has already argued that Acts 8 and 19, where no chrism is mentioned, are about confirmation.

c. Conclusions

Augustine's *De baptismo* demonstrates how the imposition of hands was used as a ritual gesture at the beginning of the fifth century. The long history of the Church put the same gesture to additional usage, causing ambiguity for later theologians. One may presume Augustine's rites of initiation were similar to those described by Ambrose; they would not have celebrated confirmation as the distinct event known by later Catholics and Reformers. The misinterpretation of the patristic gesture is not unique to the texts of Augustine. The controversialists misapply the letters of Cyprian in the same way.[79] In general, the weakness of the argument is that both sides color the text with their own ritual experience and the need to interpret history in a light favorable to their respective theological positions.

E. William Duranti: *Pontificale Romanum*
1. Introduction

William Duranti (Guillaume Durand) was a bishop of thirteenth century France who had studied church law in Italy. Author of several works, he composed a book near the end of his life for the proper execution of ceremonies in his diocese. Sharing in the attention France received because of the papal court at Avignon, the Pontifical gained deserved attention and was ultimately adopted for general use in the Roman Church.

Among the tasks assigned by the Council of Trent was the publication of revised liturgical books for the entire Church. The composition and promulgation of the new texts took time, so even in the

---

[79] See Chapter III, fn. 197 and 199.

generation after Trent, when the controversialists of this study were writing, the rite of confirmation still in use was that of Duranti. Thus, when Calvin refers to the "formula," Chemnitz to "Durandus" and Bellarmine to the "Pontificale romanum," they all mean this same work. It contains the text of the rite of confirmation which had evolved from the Scripture, theology, and history so amply presented in the controversy.

> 2. And then, once hands have been lifted up and extended over those needing to be confirmed, <the bishop> says: "Almighty eternal God, Who have deigned to regenerate these servants and Your handmaids out of water and the Holy Spirit, and Who gave them remission of all sins, send forth onto them the sevenfold Holy Spirit, Your Paraclete from the heavens, the Spirit of wisdom and understanding, the Spirit of counsel and fortitude, the Spirit of knowledge and piety, fill them with the Spirit of fear of You, and having been appeased seal them with the sign of the cross of Christ for eternal life."
> 3. Then sitting on the faldstool prepared before the altar or elsewhere, after the name has been asked one by one of whichever person needing to be sealed presented to him by the godfather or godmother on bended knees and the tip of the thumb of the right hand having been moistened with chrism, the bishop makes a cross on the forehead of the person saying, "John," or "Mary," or with some other name, "I sign you with the sign of the cross and I confirm you with the chrism of salvation. In the name + of the Father and + of the Son and of the Holy + Spirit, that you may be filled with the same Holy Spirit and have eternal life." Response: "Amen." And in saying, "In the name of the Father and of the Son and of the Holy Spirit," he draws the sign of the cross before the face of the person.
> 4. And then he lightly gives him a slap on the cheek, saying, "Peace be with you."[80]

2. Usage
a. Calvin

Calvin cites the ritual twice to stress his point that confirmation is not found in Scripture. Having shown the silence of Scripture, he shows the verbosity of the rite–neither the words nor the action of confirmation originate from Scripture:

[80] See chart entry M-24 for the original text.

This confirmation is performed with anointing and with this
formula of the words, "I seal you with the sign of the holy
cross, and I confirm you with the chrism of salvation, in the
name of the Father, and of the Son, and of the Holy Spirit." All
beautifully and charmingly done. But where is the Word of
God, which promises the presence of the Holy Spirit here?
Not even an iota can they produce. From which place
therefore will they inform us that their chrism is a vessel of
the Holy Spirit?[81]

The words of the bishop which Calvin quotes from Duranti are a
contribution from the post-apostolic Church, and for Calvin they
confound the sacramental nature of confirmation. The use of oil does too
for the same reason. Calvin sees in the phrase "oil of salvation" a
rejection of the salvific powers of Christ:

But if they may succeed in proving that they imitate the
Apostles by this imposition of hands (in which they have
nothing in common with the Apostles except I don't know
what preposterous *kakozêlian* <perverted zeal>), nevertheless
from where comes the oil, which they call "of salvation"?
Who taught them to seek salvation in oil? Who taught them
to attribute to it the power of strengthening? Was it Paul, who
draws us far away from the elements of this world (Galatians
4, 9; Colossians 2, 20), who condemns nothing more than
clinging to little observances? But I proclaim this not from
me, but boldly from the Lord: Those who call oil the oil of
salvation abjure the salvation which is in Christ, they deny
Christ, they have no part in the kingdom of God.[82]

For Calvin, then, the ritual of Duranti betrays a departure from
Scripture and orthodox Christology. It lends no credence to the
sacramentality of confirmation and reveals those who receive the rite
as heretics who deny Christ.

[81]   "Peragitur haec confirmatio unctione, et hac verborum formula: consigno te signo
sanctae crucis, et confirmo chrismate salutis, in nomine patris, et filii, et spiritus sancti.
Pulchre omnia et venuste. Sed ubi Dei verbum quod spiritus sancti praesentiam hic
promittat? Ne iota quidem obtendere possunt. Unde ergo nos certiores facient, chrisma
suum esse vas spiritus sancti?" 5, CR 30:1069.

[82]   "Quod si manuum impositione apostolos se imitari evincant (in qua nihil cum
apostolis simile habent praeter nescio quam praeposteram *kakozêlian*), unde tamen
oleum, quod vocant salutis? Quis eos in oleo salutem quaerere docuit? quis vim roborandi
illi attribuere? An Paulus, qui nos ab elementis huius mundi longe abstrahit (Gal. 4, 9;
Col. 2, 20), qui nihil magis damnat quam talibus observatiunculis haerere? Hoc vero non
a me, sed a Domino audacter pronuntio: qui oleum vocant oleum salutis, salutem quae in
Christo est abiurant, Christum abnegant, partem in regno Dei non habent." 7, CR 30:1071.

b. Chemnitz

Chemnitz's analysis of Duranti is not limited to the rite of confirmation. He includes the rites of baptism and the blessing of oil, as well as the theological work, *Instructions et constitutions*.[83] Regarding confirmation, Chemnitz argues that the rite is a non-scriptural creation and the theology of its texts detract from the meaning of baptism.

First Chemnitz describes the rite of confirmation from the ritual. In understated sarcasm he shows the absurdity of the many elements which make up this simple rite.

> But they teach that the form of confirmation is these words, "I sign you with the sign of the cross, and I confirm you with the chrism of salvation, in the name of the Father, and of the Son, and of the Holy Spirit." And they define that confirmation itself is an anointing or smearing of consecrated chrism, which is done by the thumb of a bishop, on the forehead of the person baptized; not in the very action of baptism, but afterwards in a special sacrament, through the manner or figure of a cross, with the pronunciation of those words, "I sign you with the sign of the cross, etc." But in the action itself other prayers are also added with set words, and "Peace be with you" is said. And after that smearing, the bishop executes a slap onto the face first with the thumb of the chrisms, then with the whole hand. But the forehead having been smeared with ointment is wrapped with a white band which is removed on the seventh day after, lest the fresh ointment either flow away or be wiped off. And at length the person is entrusted to guardians. This is the action of confirmation.[84]

Next he turns to the prayer of the bishop petitioning the sevenfold gift of the Spirit. Chemnitz cautions that in asking for the Spirit, the prayer impoverishes the theology of baptism.

---

[83] See M-23 through M-26.

[84] "Formam vero confirmationis, tradunt esse haec verba: Signo te signo crucis, et confirmo te chrismate salutis, in nomine Patris, et Filii, et Spiritus sancti. Et ipsam Confirmationem definiunt esse inunctionem sive illinitionem chrismatis consecrati, quae fiat ab Episcopi pollice, in fronte hominis baptizati: non in ipsa actione Baptismi, sed postea in peculiari Sacramento, per modum seu figuram crucis, cum pronuntiatione illorum verborum: Signo te signo crucis, etc. In ipsa vero actione, adduntur conceptis verbis aliae etiam orationes, et dicitur, Pax tecum. Et post illam delibationem, Episcopus pollice primum chrismatum, tota deinde manu, alapam in faciem cedit. Frons vero unguento delibuta, panno albo qui septimo post die deponitur, circumcingitur, ne recens unctio vel defluat, vel deleatur. Et tandem commendatur susceptoribus. Haec est actio Confirmationis." 2, Preuss:285.

And the reader should remember that this is the state of the question what confirmation does confer that baptism does not have. Their Clement says that the baptized person finally receives through confirmation the sevenfold grace of the Holy Spirit, and otherwise he cannot be a perfect Christian at all, nor have a seat among the perfected, even if he will have been baptized, unless he has been signed with chrism by the bishop. Clement says these things. However they perceive a sevenfold grace of the Spirit as they are accustomed to number seven gifts of the Spirit. For in confirmation the bishop prays over the one to be confirmed among other things in this way, "Send forth onto him Your Holy Spirit, the Paraclete of your sevenfold grace. . . ."[85]

Returning to sarcasm, Chemnitz contrasts the coming of the Spirit in the New Testament with the ritual of confirmation.

Christ (they say) promised the Apostles the power of the Spirit through baptism in Luke 24 and Acts 1, and fulfilled that promise on the day of Pentecost when the Holy Spirit had been sent in the form of tongues of fire. Also, the Apostles imposed hands on the baptized who thus received the Holy Spirit (Acts 8 and 19). As a result, now in the Church the forehead of the baptized must be smeared with chrism consecrated as is described in the Pontifical, with that form of the words which has been described above, and the effects recounted above will follow.[86]

He sees no relationship between the two events of Pentecost and confirmation.

He further shows the disparity of confirmation with Pentecost by insisting the form was not instituted by Christ. In fact, the rituals record the form in different ways—evidence to Chemnitz that it has no common source, as words of Christ would have provided.

[85] "Et meminerit lector, statum disputationis hunc esse, quid Confirmatio conferat, quod Baptismus non habeat. Clemens ipsorum dicit, baptizatum per Confirmationem demum percipere septiformem gratiam Spiritus sancti, et aliter perfectum Christianum esse nequaquam posse, nec sedem habere inter perfectos, etiamsi baptizatus fuerit, nisi sit chrismate ab Episcopo consignatus. Haec Clemens. Septiformem autem gratiam spiritus intelligunt, sicut solent numerare septem dona spiritus. In Confirmatione enim, sic inter alia orat Episcopus super confirmandum: immitte in eum Spiritum sanctum tuum, septiformis gratiae tuae paracletum. . . " 3, Preuss:285.

[86] "Christus (inquiunt) Apostolis per baptismum promisit virtutem spiritus, Luc. 24. Act. 1 et illam promissionem die Pentecostes, misso in specie linguarum ignearum Spiritu sancto implevit. Apostoli etiam baptizatis manus imposuerunt, qui ita acceperunt Spiritum Sanctum. Act. 8 et 19. Ergo nunc in Ecclesia chrismate, sicut in Pontificali describitur, consecrato, linienda est frons baptizatorum, cum forma illa verborum, quae supra descripta est, et sequentur effectus supra recitati." 10, Preuss:288.

But what about the form of confirmation, "I sign you, etc."? It cannot be proved from Scripture, can it, either that Christ instituted or that the Apostles used that form of the words? Certainly this cannot even be imagined; indeed neither among the old writers nor in the canons has that form of the words been expressed. . . . And from this it happens that that form is not the same in those Pontificals. For Gabriel <Biel> recounts that certain ones say "the chrism of sanctification" in place of "the chrism of salvation." <Jean> Gerson has this form: "I fortify you with the sign of the cross and chrism, etc."[87]

For Chemnitz then, Duranti shows the creation of a ritual far from the events of Pentecost and the promises of Christ. He believes the texts detract from the theology of baptism.

c. Bellarmine

Bellarmine cites Duranti for three separate arguments. He shows that, contrary to the opinion of the adversaries, it is a continuation of the action of the Apostles; he shows the appropriateness of the rite for discerning the cause and effect of the sacrament; he uses it to describe the ceremony of confirmation. Thus for him the rite exemplifies contemporary theology and practice as it continues an ancient tradition.

The adversaries complained that the apostolic imposition of hands was deleted from the Roman rite of confirmation. Bellarmine insists that two gestures remain which continue this apostolic tradition:

> . . . <It> is false that the imposition of hands has been rejected. For twice the bishop imposes hands on those needing to be confirmed, as can be understood from the Roman Pontifical: once when he extends hands over them and prays, and again when he signs and anoints them on the forehead.[88]

---

[87] "Quid vero de forma confirmationis. Signo te, etc. Nunquid ex scriptura probari potest, vel Christum instituisse, vel Apostolos usurpasse illam formam verborum? Certe ne fingi quidem hoc potest: imo nec in vetustis scriptoribus, nec in canonibus, forma illa verborum expressa est. . . . Et inde fit quod in ipsis Pontificalibus non eadem est illa forma. Gabriel <Biel> enim recitat, quosdam pro chrismate salutis, dicere chrisma sanctificationis. <Jean> Gerson habet hanc formam: Firmo te signo crucis, et chrismate, etc." 13, Preuss:289-290.

[88] ". . . falsum est rejectam esse manus impositionem. Bis enim episcopus manus imponit confirmandis, ut ex pontificali Romano intelligi potest, semel cum super eos manus extendit, atque orat: et rursum cum signat in fronte, atque ungit." 2, Battezzati:216.

Later, in reflecting on Duranti's form of the sacrament, Bellarmine shows how the words support scholastic theology's interpretation of the causes and effect of confirmation.

> These words are the form of this sacrament, "I sign you with the sign of the cross, and I confirm you with the chrism of salvation, in the name of the Father, and of the Son, and of the Holy Spirit." Nor can it be doubted that this is an appropriate form, since it explains openly both the principal cause, which is the Holy Trinity, and the ministerial cause, which is he who pronounces the words themselves, and then the effect of the sacrament, which is to make a soldier of Christ by engraving him with the cross, and to strengthen and to arm by confirming with chrism. This form is found with eloquent words in the Council of Florence, in the Roman Pontifical, and with St. Thomas in part 3, question 72, article 4.[89]

Finally, when Bellarmine presents the ceremony of confirmation, there is no better source than the ritual.

> But now in confirmation itself besides the essential ceremony of anointing and signing the forehead with a cross, there are also employed eight other ceremonies. First, that there be present a guardian, as at baptism, who offers the one needing to be confirmed to the bishop. . . .
>
> Second, various prayers are said over those needing to be confirmed, and indeed with the imposition of the hand, which rite alone the adversaries do not rebuke.
>
> Third, that the peace is given by the bishop to the one confirmed, for a sign of the grace of the Holy Spirit having been received, whose effect is peace.
>
> Fourth, that the bishop strike the one confirmed lightly with his hand that he may understand he must be armed especially with patience against ignominy and scourges[90] needing to be born for Christ.[91]

[89] "Forma hujus sacramenti sunt haec verba: 'Signo te signo crucis, et confirmo te Chrismate salutis in nomine Patris, et Filii et Spiritus sancti.' Neque dubitari potest, quin haec sit conveniens forma, cum aperte explicet, et caussam principalem, quae est sancta Trinitas, et caussam ministerialem, quae est ille, qui verba ipsa profert, et denique effectum sacramenti, qui est facere Christi militem insigniendo illum cruce, et roborare, atque armare confirmando Chrismate. Habetur autem haec forma disertis verbis in concilio florentino in pontificali romano, et apud s. Thom. 3. par. quaest. 72. art. 4." 10, Battezzati:228.

[90] Surely Bellarmine means verbera, not verba.

[91] "Jam vero in ipsa Confirmatione praeter caeremoniam essentialem ungendi, et signandi frontem cruce; adhibentur etiam aliae octo caeremoniae. Prima ut susceptor adsit, sicut in Baptismo, qui confirmandum offerat episcopo. . . .

He concludes with other traditional ceremonies not included in the Roman Pontifical.

For Bellarmine, then, this book is a font for the theology of confirmation as well as a description of a ritual which continues the apostolic tradition for his contemporary Church.

3. Analysis
a. The Reformers

Once again the love of the Reformers for Scripture moves them to analyze confirmation in the light of the Bible. Using the framework of the scholastics, they argue that neither form nor matter in the Pontifical is scriptural. In defending the primacy of baptism, they keep confirmation from cheapening it.

These are strong arguments. On scholastic territory they question essential components of this rite. The Scriptures contain no such anointings nor do they use the words of the ritual. The celebration of confirmation poorly resembles what the Roman Church says is its original form, the imposition of hands in Acts. And the rite does not clearly distinguish the ways the Spirit is received in baptism and confirmation, thus inviting the objection that the latter's value presupposes the former's inadequacy.

There are weaknesses. Calvin's conclusion is brash, that whoever accepts confirmation denies Christ. In truth, the heart of the rites of initiation and indeed of any ecclesial rite is accepting Christ. Underlying the argument is an old impass between Catholics and Reformers: To what extent may the Church promote the events of Scripture into sacramental rituals?

b. Bellarmine

Bellarmine uses Duranti's text to answer objections of the Reformers and to explain the composition of the sacrament.

What is strong is his use of a liturgical text to explain the

---

"Secunda, ut variae preces dicantur super confirmandos, et quidem cum manus impositione; quem ritum solum adversarii non reprehendunt.

"Tertia, ut confirmato pax detur ab episcopo, in signum acceptae gratiae Spiritus sancti, cujus effectus est pax.

"Quarta, ut confirmatum episcopus manu leviter cedat, ut is intelligat se contra ignominiam, et verba <sic> pro Christo ferenda, patientia praecipue armandum." 13, Battezzati:233.

theology of his tradition. This method of theology is used sparingly here when compared with other means, e.g., quoting other theologians. For a brief moment here Bellarmine lets the liturgy explain theology. Against the Reformers who place such primary importance on Scripture this will not prove convincing on its own, but it does introduce another dimension to his argument.[92]

But there are weaknesses. It is true that the bishop's extended hands over the confirmands is a remnant of the apostolic imposition of hands, but the sign is secondary to the anointing each receives individually. And to call the application of the thumb to the forehead an imposition of hands is absurd.

c. Conclusions

Although Bellarmine and even Chemnitz give a theological reflection based on the liturgical text, the entire controversy is lacking a studied examination of this and other liturgical texts in the history of confirmation. This is more understandable from the Reformers' point of view, which simply rejects the assistance of the texts out of hand since the form is not found in Scripture. The treatment is superficial. Bellarmine does not respond to the criticisms about the prayer for the sevenfold gift of the Spirit, he keeps alive the "soldier of Christ" analogy of confirmation (which as a controversialist at the theologically militant time of the Reformation he surely found appealing), and simply details the steps of the rite to describe the ceremony at the end of his presentation. In short, this is a replay of the old Scripture versus tradition controversy, which is ineffective because the Reformers have ended the argument before they begin, and the Catholics do not explore the texts to full potential.

F. Summary

The controversy over the sacramentality of confirmation is a microcosm of the great Reformation struggle over the issue of Scripture and tradition. It wrestles with the questions of what the Scriptures say, what was in the mind of Christ, how the early Church interpreted the Scriptures, and how the tradition of the Church maintained the early practice. Reformers and Catholics alike called upon witnesses to

---

[92] See pp. 232-233 for a fuller presentation on this subject.

support their preference in sacramental practice.

The study of sources in this chapter has revealed these points:

1) The Scripture texts alone give full support to neither the Catholic practice of anointing at a mature age nor the Reformers' practice of an examination of faith.

2) The disputants are formed by the influence of scholastic argumentation and, especially on the Catholic side, by the influence of canonical legislation. Church law had a tremendous impact on sacramental theology, which the Reformation was only beginning to question.

3) Many historical sources contain ambiguous references both to the rites of confirmation and to its theology which make them open to support either side of the controversy.

4) Each side interpreted these sources by screening them through its personal experience of tradition and liturgy.

5) Many texts are treated superficially. The controversialists are not interested in historical accuracy. They take advantage of any source which supports their side.

6) Finally, there is no satisfactory treatment of the distinction between the gifts of the Holy Spirit at baptism and the gifts of the Spirit at confirmation.

If this summary leaves one with the unhappy conclusion that the controversy is little better off at the end than at the beginning, that is partially correct. After all, the two traditions continue to celebrate the rites according to their preference to this very day. But the collection of texts they offer may give some hope for building and interpreting rites of confirmation in harmony with Scripture, tradition, and even one's adversaries.

G. Conclusions

The post-Reformation confirmation controversy remained unsatisfactorily resolved in several areas: what confirmation is, what it does, how it differs from baptism, what its true origin is and whether or not it was faithfully preserved, what forms that preservation took. To evaluate the result one must know the intentions of the controversialists: What were they hoping to achieve? Then one can ask, did they achieve it?

Calvin's address to the reader of the *Institutio* does not give one the impression he is dealing with much of a controversy. The tone is one of a man surprised by the success of his work, thankful to God for its contribution.[93] Calvin's attitude is of deferential piety. He has tried to declare and maintain the pure doctrine of the faith. An important purpose of his work is to prepare and instruct those who study theology. He accepts this task to give them easy access to the Scriptures so they may profit from them. The tone is deeply spiritual. Calvin has learned the beauty of the Scriptures and longs to serve them in integrity. He wrote first for the inspiration and inner growth of the reader. Controversies with those who hold other opinions are a necessary servant to the goal of explaining the Scriptures.

In the particular controversy regarding confirmation, this goal is obscured because of the nature of this section. There are other parts of the *Institutio* where Calvin's teaching for spiritual enrichment is more evident. Here the secondary aspect of controversial theology plays the more important role. He needs to refute the theology of the Catholics to preserve the pure integrity of the Scriptures. By the end of the controversy, Calvin has helped the reader understand the scriptural passages better, and to this extent he succeeds in his goal. But the controversy became far broader than just the Scripture texts – including other sources and subtle theological expressions. Calvin's comparatively brief exposition on confirmation should help the reader achieve the primary goal of profiting his or her spiritual life through access to the Scriptures, but the goal is overwhelmed by the broader issues at stake.

The purpose of Chemnitz's work is best expressed in its title: It is an examination. The theology of Andrada and the canons of Trent were the catalysts for his book. Although he feels the oppression of the Roman Church, Chemnitz insists he is not trying to pick a fight; he wants to speak a voice of doctrine according to the norm of Scripture lest people wander from the true faith. Earlier in his life, Chemnitz was the reconciler for the Lutheran community. Here, too, he offers these examinations of the canons and openly invites the Roman Church to respond to his theology, again according to the norm of the Scriptures. He feels that the "mysteries" of the Council of Trent will then be brought to light.[94]

Of all the controversialists, the result of Chemnitz's work seems the most tragic. His hopes are not fulfilled. He has been in

---

[93] "Ioannes Calvinus lectori," CR 30:1-4; "Jean Calvin au lecteur," CR 31:5-8.
[94] "Prefatio," Preuss:3-4.

disagreement with the Jesuits before and he invites them to respond again. He opens his section on confirmation with a lengthy presentation of the Catholic position in the words of his adversaries so the reader may weigh the situation for himself. One gets the feeling from the *Examen* that Chemnitz actually hoped to achieve something by his work: a productive discussion on the issues. Perhaps this hope was inherited from his predecessor Martin Luther who yearned not for a new Church, but for a restoration of the old one according to the norms and teaching of Scripture. The examination of the canons of Trent is most provocative, and the tragedy is that it was met not with openness but with the same authoritative assuredness which accompanied the anathemas of the Council.

At the very beginning of the *Disputationes*, Bellarmine explains to the reader three reasons why he has brought the work to light: First, to accept the responsibility the Church has to fight in great numbers against the heresies of any time; second, to compile the many extant controversies into one volume for quick reference; and third, to put in writing the lectures he had given in Rome for students returning to Germany and England to impede the growth of the Reform.[95] The expressed goal, however, is not to convert heretics or convince them of their errors. It is to dispute, to fight, to train other warriors to meet the danger, to gather evidence so the weapons are ready at hand. Bellarmine's tone and vocabulary are warlike: He intends to use logic as a weapon, not for conciliation.

To this extent, he too achieves what he sets out to do: He prepares his side to answer the attacks of the opponents. And this kind of approach logically leads to the conclusion of this dispute: Each side is more convinced of its own rightness, and reconciliation is unachieved.

The role of the sources quoted is different for each writer. For Calvin they help shed light on Scripture. For Chemnitz they help examine the canons of Trent against Scripture and tradition. For Bellarmine they dispute the theology of the Reformers and uphold the true Catholic tradition. None of them approaches the sources of the controversy with an open mind: They analyze them with the purpose of applying them to a pre-ordered argument. These are not works of textual criticism, they are works of controversy.

An evaluation of the success of the results depends on the goal of the research. As works of controversy, the results intended are the

---

95 "Ad lectorem," Battezzati I:9-10.

results achieved: The strengthening of the host position against that of the adversary. But as works of ecumenism or reconciliation they are unsatisfactory. Now, just as one can criticize the sixteenth century theologians for poor textual criticism of their sources, twentieth century theologians can be criticized for poor textual criticism of their predecessors. In fact, the goal of the controversialists (with the possible exception of Chemnitz) was more to contend than to reconcile. Hence it is not so much the results of the controversy that are unsatisfactory to the modern reader but its goals.

The methodology chosen by the controversialists befits the purpose: They summoned witnesses from Scripture and tradition to tip the balance of the argument in their favor. To analyze the sources too critically would stray from the central point of gathering many witnesses to support a given interpretation of sacramental theology.

This theology, in turn, reflects an ecclesiology. The Reformers express the position that the Church needs to return to the pristine forms allowed only by Scripture. At its heart, it is a static interpretation of the Church and her role in history vis-a-vis culture. Yet at the same time they espouse a celebration of confirmation which is unique in history: a non-sacramental imposition of hands accompanying the examination of faith of an adolescent. They do so thinking this is in keeping with tradition and force an application of the Scriptures to support its practice. In fact, the rite is in keeping with the tradition of Luther and Melanchthon, and except for its non-sacramental nature, with the tradition of the medieval Roman Catholic Church. The Catholic position espouses a view of the Church as evolutionary in time, but so much so, that the Reformers had to call her back to her roots. The Church of the post-Reformation prized her tradition and justified her sacraments by it. But it was healthy for her to be called to reflect on the information originally handed down from the New Testament. Certainly a good sense of ecclesiology can blend these two strains: The Church is neither static, unmoved by the march of time, nor so evolutionary that she leaves her roots behind. Rather, like the seed planted in good soil, she bears fruit as the elements contribute to her growth.

The key to understanding the unresolved nature of the dispute is hermeneutics. It is hermeneutics which caused the forming of two sacramental theologies—one based on Scripture, the other on tradition. It is hermeneutics which governed the interpretation of sources—interpreted not for their own meaning but for how they contribute to one side. It is hermeneutics which preserves an unhappy resolution–two sides remaining opposed because they are content to look no farther for answers.

For the twentieth century theologian, a satisfactory resolution to the controversy would require new goals, new methods, new ecclesiology, and a new hermeneutic. Inspired by the Church's spirit of ecumenism and prayers for unity, the goal is not to fight the error of the foe, but to search for truth together, to see error where it exists on each side, and to work toward reconciliation. The examination of sources should be to learn from their own hermeneutic, not from one of later history; let the hermeneutic of historical integrity govern methodology. A community of faith best uses logic not as a weapon, but for nourishing its fragile trust in God. A Church who knows her origin, her history, her culture, and her future hope of glory will work with new spirit to heal the wounds of the past and live in unity and peace.

CHAPTER V:

Confirmation

The first four chapters have presented the dispute over confirmation especially through the writings of three controversialists in the early years after the Reformation. Thus far, this study has focused on this period of history to analyze the theology and criticize the method of these writers.

This final chapter will build on the historical and methodological data to examine their significance for the contemporary Church. The Christian Churches represented in this study still practice a rite of confirmation. This chapter will analyze the lingering problems from the controversy in the light of today's theology and practice of confirmation to seek avenues toward a mutually acceptable celebration of confirmation in harmony with history.

The chapter is in four parts: It reviews the problems remaining from the post-Reformation controversy, it analyzes the growing convergence in the celebration of confirmation between Catholics and Lutherans, it presents the problems still extant in contemporary practice, and it offers proposals for the Churches to help resolve them.

A. Controversy and Opposition

First a review is in order. The Reformers, motivated by the testimony of the Scriptures and a theology of sacrament derived from the words of Jesus, deny that confirmation is a sacrament. They reason that to accept it as a sacrament draws efficacy from baptism. They also believe that history is on their side. They call confirmation a rite for the examination of the faith of children baptized as infants who are old enough to make a profession of faith before the pastor and the assembly. This celebration would remind the participants of their baptism and give them strengthening grace.

The Catholics, inspired by the example of the Apostles, recognizing the practice of history, preserving the sacramental tradition, believe that confirmation is a sacrament which confers sanctifying grace and strengthens the soul against evil. It imprints a character, they say, and inscribes one into the army of Christ. Where the Reformers turned to Scripture for a decision over the sacramentality of confirmation, the Catholics looked at the tradition which interpreted the Scriptures as well. In fact, Bellarmine says the witnesses in the history of the Church "prove" that confirmation is a sacrament.

The two sides differ on the sacramental nature of confirmation and also the purpose of the rite – whether it examines faith or imparts the Holy Spirit. The effects perceived are also different, but it is deceptive in this controversy to ask what the effects of confirmation are. From the Reformers' point of view, confirmation is not only a celebration which brings about a desired effect, it is also the celebration of an effect already achieved: the mature acceptance of faith. What confirmation does is to stir up faith through an affirmation of baptism, but of equal importance to what confirmation does is what the Christian does: accepting the faith through a time of preparation and a rite of examination prior to profession before the community in confirmation. Thus to ask the Reformers what are the effects of confirmation is to ask for incomplete information concerning its purpose.

On the other hand, the Catholics express the effects of confirmation as a gift of the Holy Spirit which imprints a character to prepare one to defend the faith. Explanations about how this differs from baptism are vague. The traditional response that baptism forgives sins and confirmation arms one for spiritual combat was unacceptable to the Reformers who believed baptism itself achieved both those effects. Bellarmine himself seems content with the ambiguity of his position. For him the faith of the Church that there are two distinct sacraments is enough to justify their celebration, even if the effects are not clearly distinct.

In expressing the relationship between confirmation and baptism the Reformers say confirmation reminds one of baptism, while the Catholics stumble to separate the gifts of the Spirit. Yet both believe they are following the best witness of the Scriptures and Christian tradition. Both value Christian witness, historical fidelity and sacramental integrity, but hermeneutics kept the traditions apart.

The controversy of the sixteenth century leaves a task to the modern Church to resolve several questions which remained open. Is it possible to find a *via media* on the problem of Scripture and tradition? Can the question of confirmation's sacramentality be thus resolved? How do the effects of confirmation differ from those of baptism? Does the contemporary celebration of confirmation in Catholic and Lutheran Churches reflect its purpose?

B. Convergence in Liturgy

The positions which seemed irreconcilable at the time of the Reformation have retained their opposition through the generations since. However, a study of the liturgical practices of the two sides reveals a remarkably growing convergence. Liturgical texts, which played a minor role in the controversy, today reveal a surprising similarity in practice. This section will focus on the successors to Bellarmine and Chemnitz. The liturgical convergence is less evident with those of Calvin, although it exists in some ways because of the similarity in the positions of the Reform and Lutheran Churches in the controversy in opposition to the Catholics.

1. The Reformers

To represent the contemporary practice of the tradition of Luther and the Reformers this chapter examines the *Lutheran Book of Worship*[1] (LBW) prepared by the Churches participating in the Inter-Lutheran Commission on Worship: Lutheran Church in America, the American Lutheran Church, the Evangelical Lutheran Church of Canada, and The Lutheran Church – Missouri Synod.

Two rites need to be surveyed: baptism and confirmation. First, in the rite of Holy Baptism, after the baptism itself a hymn is sung while the group moves to the altar. This rubric and prayer follow:

> Those who have been baptized kneel. Sponsors or parents holding young children stand. The minister lays both hands on the head of each of the baptized and prays for the Holy Spirit: "God, the Father of our Lord Jesus Christ, we give you thanks for freeing your sons and daughters from the power of

---

[1] Minneapolis: Augsburg Publishing House, 1982. I have chosen a book from the Lutheran tradition because of its convergence with the Catholic celebration. Calvin's successors take a position similar to the Lutherans regarding the non-sacramental nature of confirmation, but their celebration differs. The liturgy analyzed here belongs to the successors of Luther and Chemnitz.

sin and for raising them up to a new life through this holy sacrament. Pour your Holy Spirit upon (name): the spirit of wisdom and understanding, the spirit of counsel and might, the spirit of knowledge and the fear of the Lord, the spirit of joy in your presence."[2]

The similarity to the confirmation prayer of Duranti is striking.[3] Both praise God for the new life of baptism and freedom from sins, then invoke the sevenfold gift of the Holy Spirit. The Lutheran prayer substitutes "spirit of joy in your presence" for "piety" and inverts the order of the last two gifts. It gives the prayer a more upbeat finish. This prayer originates in the fourth century for reconciliation of heretics or imposing hands on neophytes.[4] In the tenth century Roman Ordo for the Easter Vigil it accompanied confirmation which immediately followed baptism.[5] The prayer of Duranti cited by the controversialists is from the confirmation of children, a rite separate from baptism. Here in the Lutheran tradition, the prayer has been restored to the rite of baptism and does not carry the sense of Duranti's confirmation. The *Manual on the Liturgy* for the LBW explains,

> The inclusion in this service of the laying on of hands with the prayer for the gift of the Holy Spirit signals a return to the liturgical fullness of the ancient church that was lost when confirmation became a separate rite.[6]

Another commentary on the rite explains that the prayer has been restored here to a more proper place:

> In recent times, this ancient prayer for the Spirit's gifts was identified with confirmation. In the *Lutheran Book of Worship*, it is restored to Baptism to make clear that Baptism is full initiation into the people of God. No additional action is needed later.[7]

[2] "Holy Baptism," 13, LBW:124.

[3] M-24, Chapter III.

[4] Louis Ligier details the prayer's history in *La Confirmation: Sens et conjoncture oecuménique hier et aujourd'hui*, Théologie Historique 23 (Paris: Beauchesne, 1973), p. 98.

[5] M-67.

[6] Philip H. Pfatteicher, Carlos R. Messerli, *Manual on the Liturgy: Lutheran Book of Worship* (Minneapolis: Augsburg Publishing House, 1979), "Holy Baptism: The Laying on of Hands," p. 184-185.

[7] Eugene L. Brand, *By water and the Spirit: Preparing for Holy Baptism According to the Rite of the Lutheran Book of Worship*, ed. S. Anita Stauffer (Philadelphia: Parish Life Press, 1979), p. 27.

The rite continues with a suprising suggestion:

> The minister marks the sign of the cross on the forehead of each of the baptized. Oil prepared for this purpose may be used. As the sign of the cross is made, the minister says: "(name), child of God, you have been sealed by the Holy Spirit and marked with the cross of Christ forever." The sponsor or the baptized responds: "Amen."[8]

The permission for the use of oil marks another similarity to the Roman rite of confirmation.[9] The *Manual* explains,

> According to a custom of long standing in the church the cross may be traced in oil on the forehead. At an early time, perhaps to demonstrate physically the New Testament's description of Jesus as the Christ (the Greek equivalent for the Hebrew *anointed* by God) and also the conviction that the Christian is anointed with the Holy Spirit, the church began to anoint the baptized with oil. The seal of the Spirit is a sign for the future, a promise of the eschatological kingdom (Ephesians 1, 13-14; Revelation 9, 4). The material used for this anointing is olive oil or another vegetable oil into which is often mixed a fragrant oil such as that of balsam. The oil is stored in a small cruet or bowl. It is applied with the thumb, a small cloth, or a bit of cotton.[10]

The Lutherans' tolerance for the use of oil is inspired by an awareness of history and a sensitivity to scriptural imagery. Again, this is baptism, not confirmation, and what is sacramental is the pouring of water.

In addition to baptism, the Lutherans have a rite of confirmation. The LBW describes it as a profession of baptismal faith.

> Confirmation marks the completion of the congregation's program of confirmation ministry, a period of instruction in the Christian faith as confessed in the teachings of the Lutheran Church. Those who have completed this program were made members of the Church

---

[8] "Holy Baptism," 14, LBW:124.

[9] This aspect of liturgical convergence does not always hold for the successors to Calvin. The Presbyterian order of worship, for example, carries this instruction at the moment of baptism: "While saying these words, the minister shall baptize the child with water alone, without adding any other ceremony," *The Constitution of the Presbyterian Church (U.S.A.): Part II, Book of Order,* (New York: Offices of the General Assembly, 1981), p. 173.

[10] *Manual,* "Holy Baptism: Sealing," p. 186.

in Baptism. Confirmation includes a public profession of the faith into which the candidates were baptized, thus underscoring God's action in their Baptism.[11]

Confirmation is one of three variations of a single rite called "Affirmation of Baptism." The other variations are for other Christians entering the membership of the Lutheran Church and for baptized members desiring again to participate actively in the life of the Church. Affirmation consists of a calling, a renewed confession of baptismal faith, prayers of petition, and a professed intention to continue the commitment of baptism. Finally, the minister prays,

> Gracious Lord, through water and the Spirit you have made these *men and women* your own. You forgave them all their sins and brought them to newness of life. Continue to strengthen them with the Holy Spirit, and daily increase in them your gifts of grace: the spirit of wisdom and understanding, the spirit of counsel and might, the spirit of knowledge and the fear of the Lord, the spirit of joy in your presence; through Jesus Christ, your Son, our Lord.[12]

(Once again, the similarity to Duranti's confirmation prayer, invoking the sevenfold gift of the Spirit, is noteworthy.) Of the three variant forms of Affirmation, only confirmation continues as follows: The minister imposes hands on the head of each person and prays,

> Father in heaven, for Jesus' sake, stir up in (name) the gift of your Holy Spirit; confirm *his/her* faith, guide *his/her* life, empower *him/her* in *his/her* serving, give *him/her* patience in suffering, and bring *him/her* to everlasting life.[13]

Each answers "Amen" and all exchange a sign of peace.

What the Lutheran Church has preserved here is their tradition of confirmation – a public confession of faith before the minister and the assembly. And as one of the three rites of Affirmation of Baptism, confirmation is related to a form of reconciliation. As Augustine, Cyprian, and others imposed hands for reconciliation, the Lutherans use virtually the same rite for the contemporary version of the same phenomenon – restoring people to active life in the community. The Affirmation of Baptism is linked to initiation by title and profession of

---

[11] "Affirmation of Baptism," 3, LBW:198.

[12] "Affirmation of Baptism," 15, LBW:201.

[13] "Affirmation of Baptism," 16, LBW:201.

faith, but it is a later celebration, a mature confession of faith for the baptized who have undergone a special course of instruction.[14]

However, the *Manual* says that the meaning of the rite has not always been so clear.

> Confirmation has been seen as a time of instruction in the essentials of the faith as set forth in the *Small Catechism*. It has been seen as a means of church discipline by which one surrenders oneself to Christ and submits to the church's rule. It has been seen as a quasi-sacrament which added to Baptism the fuller presence of the Holy Spirit and which bestowed church membership on the recipient who now was entitled to receive Holy Communion and enter upon the undefined "spiritual privileges" of the church. It has been seen as the subjective acceptance of Christ as personal Lord, a decisive conversion experience. It has been understood as the completion of an educational course, a kind of graduation ceremony. There was no one understanding which could be shown to be distinctively "Lutheran."[15]

To define what confirmation is, the *Manual* cites the 1970 Joint Commission on the Theology and Practice of Confirmation, representing the American Lutheran Church, the Lutheran Church in America, and the Lutheran Church – Missouri Synod:

> Confirmation is a pastoral and educational ministry of the church which helps the baptized child through Word and Sacrament to identify more deeply with the Christian community and participate more fully in its mission.[16]

The commission calls confirmation a ministry, not a rite or celebration, and it is explained in terms of degree – it helps one already baptized participate "more" in the Church.

In keeping with the thought of the Reform, the *Manual* cautions lest confirmation draw attention away from baptism, but then it makes a suggestion which takes that theology a step further: Confirmation is repeatable.

---

[14] The Presbyterian manual cited above (fn. 9) also contains a rite of affirmation of baptism, but it includes neither a prayer for the gift of the Holy Spirit nor an imposition of hands, pp. 181-183.

[15] *Manual*, "Confirmation: Meanings," p. 340.

[16] Cited in Manual, p. 340.

> In the practice of Confirmation, therefore, great care
> must be taken that Confirmation neither implies joining the
> church nor overshadows Baptism. It is an affirmation of
> Baptism, a way of saying "Yes" to Baptism. It is not therefore
> an unrepeatable, once-for-all act but something that can be
> done at several points in one's life.[17]

Allowing the celebration to be repeated further sets the contra-distinction with the Catholic rite and separates this celebration completely from the notion of sacramental character. The Reformers of this study did not express an opinion about how many times one could be confirmed.[18]

The *Manual* envisions that the celebration of confirmation will be more a profession of faith than an examination of faith:

> The public examination of candidates has largely
> disappeared from Lutheran prctice, although it was once
> common. It was often perfunctory and meaningless with
> questions and answers all carefully memorized beforeheand.
> But the value of having a congregation listen to some
> questions and answers regarding the faith would be useful in
> teaching the congregation again the fundamentals of the
> faith. Some kind of public review of the fundamentals of
> Lutheran Christianity should be arranged at a time prior to
> the Affirmation. It need not be done at a service of the
> congregation and might be a presentation of the *Small
> Catechism* with comment and interpretation.[19]

This separation of the rites of examination and affirmation departs from the sixteenth century practice. In fact, where the early Reformers called confirmation an examination the *Manual* calls it an affirmation.

In summary, the Lutheran Church has preserved two rites sharing the history of confirmation in the Roman Church: a rite of sealing which forms part of baptism, and a rite of affirmation in which the mature Christian professes faith.

---

17 *Manual*, "Confirmation: Meanings," p. 340-341.

18 Repeating the ritual of imposing hands was one possible interpretation to be drawn from Augustine's *De baptismo*, but the *Manual* does not draw the connection. See chapter IV, fn. 64 and 68.

19 *Manual*, "Confirmation: Preparing for the Service," p. 342.

2. The Catholic Church

The practice of confirmation in the Catholic Church is found in two distinct moments of Christian Initiation: the Rite of Christian Initiation of Adults and the Rite of Confirmation.

a. Christian Initiation of Adults

Confirmation immediately follows baptism in the initiation of adults in the revised rites of Vatican Council II. The celebration proceeds in this manner:

> The celebrant speaks briefly to the neophytes in these or similar words:
> "My dear newly baptized:
> "Born again in Christ by baptism, you have become members of Christ and of his priestly people. Now you are to share in the outpouring of the Holy Spirit among us, the Spirit sent by the Lord upon his apostles at Pentecost and given by them and their successors to the baptized.
> "The promised strength of the Holy Spirit, which you are to receive, will make you more like Christ and help you to be witnesses to his suffering, death, and resurrection. It will strengthen you to be active members of the Church and to build up the Body of Christ in faith and love."
> Then the celebrant ... says:
> "Let us pray, dear friends, to God the all-powerful Father, that he will pour out the Holy Spirit on these newly baptized, to strengthen them with his abundant gifts and anoint them to be more like Christ his Son."
> All pray in silence for a short time.
> Then the celebrant (and the presbyters associated with him) lays hands upon all who are to be confirmed. The celebrant alone says:
> "All-powerful God, Father of our Lord Jesus Christ, by water and the Holy Spirit you freed your sons (and daughters) from sin and gave them new life. Send your Holy Spirit upon them to be their Helper and Guide. Give them the spirit of wisdom and understanding, the spirit of right judgment and courage, the spirit of knowledge and reverence. Fill them with the spirit of wonder and awe in your presence. We ask this through Christ our Lord." R. "Amen."
> ... The celebrant dips his right thumb in the chrism and makes the sign of the cross on the forehead of the one to be confirmed as he says:
> "N., be sealed with the Gift of the Holy Spirit."
> Newly confirmed: "Amen.
> " The celebrant adds: "Peace be with you."
> Newly confirmed: "And also with you."[20]

[20]   "Rite of Christian Initiation," Chapter I, "Rite of the Catechumenate Received in Stages: Third Stage – Celebration of the Sacraments of Initiation,

Imp.

K

This rite speaks of confirmation as the seal of the Holy Spirit. Also, the Spirit which was given at Pentecost is given in confirmation to make the baptized "more like Christ" and a "witness" to Him, active to build up the body of Christ. The Ritual preserves Duranti's prayer, but the words accompanying the chrism have changed to a form borrowed from the East.[21]

5 Look up

b. Confirmation

A theology for the rite of confirmation is found within several liturgical documents: the Apostolic Constitution on the Sacrament of Confirmation by Paul VI, the introduction to the rite, and the texts of the rite themselves. From these sources three theological issues arise: the Gift of the Holy Spirit, the degree of the gift, and the seal or character.

In the Apostolic Constitution for the rite of confirmation, Paul VI describes the essence of the sacrament, "through which the Christian faithful receive the Holy Spirit as a Gift."[22] He explains this gift as follows:

> Through the sacrament of confirmation, those reborn by baptism receive the inexpressible Gift, the Holy Spirit Himself, by which "they are enriched... with special strength" (Lumen gentium, 11).[23]

The introduction to the rite concurs that confirmation gives the Spirit of Pentecost:

Celebration of Confirmation," 229-231, *The Rites of the Catholic Church as Revised by Decree of the Second Vatican Ecumenical Council and Published by Authority of Pope Paul VI*, trans. The International Commission on English in the Liturgy (New York: Pueblo Publishing Co., 1976), p. 103-104. This approved translation is based on the text from *Ordo initiationis Christianae adultorum*, Rituale Romanum ex decreto sacrosancti Oecumenici Concilii II instauratum auctoritate Pauli PP. VI promulgatum, 229-231 (Vatican City: Typis polyglottis Vaticanis, 1972), pp. 95-96.

21 The post-Reformation controversy over form contended that there were many forms for the same rite. In the revision, yet another form accompanies the anointing, taken from the Eastern tradition. Ligier describes its origins, pp. 25-26, fn. 2.

22 "... per quem christifideles ut Donum accipiunt Spiritum Sanctum," Pope Paul VI, "Constitutio Apostolica de sacramento confirmationis," *Ordo confirmationis*, Pontificale Romanum ex decreto sacrosancti Oecumenici Concilii Vaticani II instauratum auctoritate Pauli PP. VI promulgatum (Vatican City: Typis Polyglottis Vaticanis, 1973), p. 8.

23 "Per Confirmationis Sacramentum Baptismo renati Donum ineffabile, ipsum Spiritum Sanctum, accipiunt, quo 'speciali... robore ditantur,' (Conc. Vat. II, Const. dogm. *Lumen Gentium*, n. 11, A.A.S. 57 <1965>, p. 15.)," Ibid., p. 10.

> <In this sacrament> they receive the Holy Spirit poured out, who was sent upon the Apostles by the Lord on the day of Pentecost.[24]

The homily suggested for confirmation speaks the same way:

> You, therefore, who have already been baptized will now receive the power of His Spirit and be signed with His cross on your forehead.[25]

The homily also marks a distinction between the visible and invisible gifts of the Spirit:

> Although today the coming of the Holy Spirit is no longer manifested with the gift of tongues, nevertheless by faith we know that He through Whom the charity of God is poured forth in our hearts and we are gathered in the unity of faith and the multiplicity of vocations, is received by us invisibly for sanctification and achieves the unity of the Church.[26]

No mention is made of the original gift of the Spirit at baptism, nor are the gifts distinguished. In fact, the texts almost set a dichotomy between baptism and the gift of the Holy Spirit, which is given (one wonders, only?) in confirmation.

The documents also speak of the Gift of the Spirit as a difference in degree. Paul VI writes about this degree, but reserves full incorporation into the Body of Christ for the Eucharist:

> . . . and having been signed by the character of the same sacrament <confirmation>, "they are bound more perfectly to the Church" (Lumen Gentium, 11) and "they are more strictly obliged at once to spread and to defend the faith by word and by deed as true witnesses of Christ" (Ibid.; see Ad gentes, 11).

---

[24] "<In hoc sacramento> effusum accipiunt Spiritum Sanctum, qui super Apostolos die Pentecostes a Domino missus est," Ibid., "Praenotanda" 1, p. 16.

[25] "Vos ergo, qui iam baptizati estis, nunc accipietis virtutem Spiritus eius et cruce eius in fronte signabimini," Ibid., "Ordo ad confirmationem intra missam conferendam," 22, p. 24.

[26] "Etsi hodie adventus Spiritus Sancti dono linguarum non amplius declaratur, fide tamen scimus illum, per quem caritas Dei in cordibus nostris diffunditur et in unitate fidei et multiplicitate vocationum congregamur, a nobis accipi invisibiliterque ad sanctificationem et unitatem Ecclesiae operari." Ibid., pp. 23-24.

Finally, confirmation is so united with the Holy Eucharist (Presbyterorum Ordinis, 5) that the faithful, already signed by holy baptism and confirmation, are fully grafted on to the body of Christ through the participation of the Eucharist.[27]

The language of degree occurs again in the introduction to the rite:

With this giving of the Holy Spirit the faithful are more perfectly conformed to Christ and strengthened with power, so that they may hold out the witness of Christ for the edification of His Body in faith and charity.[28]

Finally, these texts explain the theology of the seal, or the character imprinted in confirmation. The homily uses the language of degree to describe its effects:

The giving of the Holy Spirit which you are about to receive, most beloved, will be a spiritual seal by which you will become more perfectly like Christ and members of His Church.[29]

And the introduction says the seal is the sign that confirmation cannot be repeated. This is one clear hallmark of the Catholic position:

But the character or dominical seal is so imprinted on them that the sacrament of confirmation cannot be repeated.[30]

The fonts of the Catholic Church now include not simply liturgical texts but also administrative ones. The revised Code of Canon Law describes confirmation as one of the sacraments:

---

27   ". . . atque, eiusdem Sacramenti charactere signati, 'perfectius Ecclesiae vinculantur' <Conc. Vat. II, Const. dogm. *Lumen Gentium*, n. 11, A.A.S. 57 (1965), p.15> et 'ad fidem tamquam veri   testes Christi verbo et opere simul diffundendam et defendendam arctius obligantur' (Ibid., cfr. Decr. *Ad Gentes divinitus*, n.   11, A.A.S. 58 (1966), pp. 959-960). Demum Confirmatio cum Sacra Eucharistia ita cohaeret (Cfr. Conc. Vat. II, Decr. *Presbyterorum   Ordinis*, n. 5, A.A.S. 58 <1966>, p. 997), ut fideles, iam Sacro   Baptismate et Confirmatione signati, plene per participationem Eucharistiae Corpori Christi inserantur (Cfr. Ibid., pp. 997-998)," Ibid., "Constitutio," p. 10.

28   "Hac donatione Spiritus Sancti fideles perfectius Christo conformantur et virtute roborantur, ut testimonium Christi perhibeant ad aedificationem Corporis eius in fide et caritate," Ibid., "Praenotanda," 2, p. 16.

29   "Donatio Spiritus Sancti, quem accepturi estis, dilectissimi, signaculum erit spiritale, quo vos Christi conformes et Ecclesiae eius membra perfectius fietis," Ibid., "Ordo ad confirmationem," 22, p. 24.

30   "Ipsis autem character seu signaculum dominicum ita imprimitur, ut sacramentum Confirmationis iterari nequeat," Ibid., "Praenotanda," 2, p. 16.

The sacrament of confirmation, which imprints a character and by which the baptized, continuing the journey of Christian initiation, are enriched by the gift of the Holy Spirit and bound more perfectly to the Church, strengthens and more strictly obliges the same ones that by word and deed they be witnesses of Christ and spread and defend the faith.[31]

Except for the unique character confirmation imprints, its role is described here in terms of degree, an increase of something gone before. The Christian "continues," "is enriched," and "bound more perfectly" to the Church; confirmation "strengthens" and obliges one "more firmly" to witness for Christ. This description fits a celebration removed from the rites of initiation, at a more mature age. It thus shows some accord not only with Paul VI and *Lumen Gentium*,[32] but also with the Lutheran Church's definition of confirmation.[33] In fact, in speaking of those to be confirmed, the Code does not speak openly of newcomers to the faith who receive sacraments of initiation together, but only of those previously baptized:

Each one and only one baptized and not yet confirmed is capable of receiving confirmation.[34]

And again,

The sacrament of confirmation should be conferred on the faithful at about the age of discretion unless the conference of bishops will have determined another age or there be danger of death or in the judgment of the minister a grave cause may urge otherwise.[35]

[31] "Can. 879 – Sacramentum confirmationis, quod characterem imprimit et quo baptizati, iter initiationis christianae prosequentes, Spiritus Sancti dono ditantur atque perfectius Ecclesiae vinculantur, eosdem roborat arctiusque obligat ut verbo et opere testes sint Christi fidemque diffundant et defendant," *Codexx iuris canonici* (Vatican City: Libreria editrice Vaticana, 1983), p. 160.

[32] See fn. 23 and 27 above.

[33] See *Manual*, fn. 16 above.

[34] "Can. 889 – 1. Confirmationis recipiendae capax est omnis et solus baptizatus, nondum confirmatus," *Codex*, p. 162.

[35] "Can. 891 – Sacramentum confirmationis conferatur fidelibus circa aetatem discretionis, nisi Episcoporum conferentia aliam aetatem determinaverit, aut adsit periculum mortis vel, de iudicio ministri, gravis causa aliud suadeat," Ibid.

Although the Code requires confirmation for full Christian initiation,[36] when it speaks of confirmation alone it envisions an event separate from initiation.

In summary, these liturgical and canonical texts present three theological issues: the gift of the Spirit, the degree of the gift, and the seal. First, confirmation is the Gift of the Holy Spirit. But the language about the Holy Spirit is maddeningly imprecise: Not only does it not distinguish between the gifts of baptism and confirmation, it almost presumes there was no Spirit at baptism at all. The texts do not even call this a second gift, or a deepening of the one gift. How simply such a clarification could have dispelled the concern of other Christian Churches.

Second, the language of degree has replaced the image of enlisting in the army of Christ. The analogy of maturity is not to a soldier, but to being more like Christ and living more fully the Christian life.

Finally, the character of confirmation is an expression of the seal of baptism and by the Church's tradition is bound to its non-repeatable nature. It is an effect of the sacrament unique to Catholic theology.

c. Catechesis

The tradition of separating confirmation from infant baptism by some years has been preserved among both Catholics and Reformers. Since for Catholics the Code of Canon Law permits a conference of bishops to determine the age for confirmation,[37] many have opted for a later age, around the middle to late teens, for the celebration of the sacrament. The very selection of an age reveals a theology of confirmation.[38]

---

[36] Can. 842 – 2, Ibid., p. 154.

[37] See fn. 35 above.

[38] As an episcopal conference, the American bishops never established a national age for confirmation, and according to one news report, it was precisely because of this point. Mary Jo Murphy described the meeting: "More bishops spontaneously spoke out on this topic than any other issue that came to the floor. Archbishop Edmond Szoka of Detroit astutely pointed out that if the bishops voted for any age it would give the appearance of taking a theological position. His statement turned the tide. The amended committee motion was defeated, and the bishops approved a new motion stating the age of confirmation is to be determined by the local ordinary." "Voting on Confirmation," *Florida Catholic*, (Diocese of St. Petersburg), 15 February 1985, p. 2. The bishops refrained from appearing to take a theological position.

In the United States, an April, 1983 survey of almost 80% of the nation's dioceses revealed that over half (67 out of 131) normally celebrate confirmation at ages 14-18.[39] Some dioceses strove to relate this celebration of mature commitment to initiation. Archbishop Rembert Weakland of Milwaukee explains,

> By leaving Confirmation near to an adult age, it seems to me one is coming closer to the original intent of the whole process of rites that accompanied the initiation of adults in the early Church. . . .[40]

The archdiocese of Indianapolis, in trying to call confirmation at maturity an initiation rite, stresses the person's response more than the divine gift.

> Confirmation is considered as closely related to the total initiation process of baptism/confirmation/eucharist, yet justifies its separation in time. While the divine initiative is affirmed, it is concerned with response and spiritual readiness.[41]

Similarly, the diocesan policy in Phoenix chose a later age so the candidate might choose confirmation freely:

> <The new policy> stresses not only a reaffirmation of baptismal faith, but also an instruction which reanimates that faith, a free choice on the part of candidates, and the dynamic involvement of the local parish community.[42]

Many others emphasize the role of the parish community in preparation. The diocese of Cheyenne explains the role of parents:

[39]   This survey was taken from *The Catholic Exponent* of Youngstown, Ohio, as cited by "U.S.A.: New Policies Raise Confirmation Age," Celebration 13 (Kansas City: The National Catholic Reporter Publishing Company), October, 1984.

[40] *Confirmation Guidelines* (Milwaukee: Archdiocese of Milwaukee, 1981), p. 3.

[41]   *Confirmation Policy for the Archdiocese of Indiana and Guide for Implementation* (Indianapolis: Archdiocese of Indianapolis, 1980), p. i.

[42]   *Resources I: Confirmation and Youth Catechesis* (Phoenix: Roman Catholic Church of Phoenix, Arizona, c. 1980), p. 2.

> In terms of actually living the Christian faith, it is obvious that
> the child of 14 years is still very dependent on the spiritual life
> of his parents. Only to the extent that they have carried out
> the responsibilities accepted on the occasion of their child's
> baptism will he now be in a position to make a personal
> commitment.[43]

The diocese of Oakland explains that confirmation is initiation into a
new stage of Christian life:

> ... Confirmation closes out the sacraments of initiation but in
> no way indicates the end of growth. ... Rather, the sacrament
> is seen as the Church's sign that this person has completed
> the initiation process under the guidance of the Church and
> the Spirit and is now ready to continue his or her growth as an
> adult in the community.[44]

Newark concurs with this:

> <This process> would enable a parish to develop a wholistic
> <sic> ministry to their young people which does not view the
> Confirmation program as the culmination of its dialogue with
> its youth, but one which invites and sets an environment
> where they can continue to grow and enter ever-more fully
> into the life of the Church.[45]

In most cases, the preparation for confirmation requires time,
catechesis, ministry, and discernment. The diocese of San Bernardino,
for example, requires two years of preparation.[46]

Similar guidelines occur in other countries of the world. In
Guatemala, the Introduction to diocesan guidelines stresses the
responsibility of adulthood in receiving confirmation:

> In the last few years there was a pastoral review which re-
> evaluated confirmation. On the one hand, it is advised to
> receive it as youth or adults, since it is a "stronger union to
> Christ and a serious commitment." And to receive it is
> necessary to be an adult, responsible person; it is not
> therefore for children.

---

[43] *Diocesan Guidelines for the Celebration of Confirmation* (Cheyenne: Diocese of
Cheyenne, 1979), p. 2.

[44] *Confirmation 1980* (Oakland: Diocese of Oakland, 1980), pp. 1-2.

[45] "Essential Elements of a Catechumenate Model Confirmation Program," *Christian
Initiation: Confirmation* (Newark: Archdiocesan Office of Divine Worship, 1977), p. 24.

[46] *Confirmation: Model Preparation Program* (San Bernardino: Diocese of San
Bernardino, 1980), p. 2.

On the other hand, it has been steeped in the Theology of the Spirit and in His most important role for the life of the Church and of each Christian, as He ceases to be the "great unknown" (Acts 19, 2).[47]

In Germany, the sacrament is celebrated by young people on the threshold of adulthood:

> The youth have freely presented themselves for confirmation. . . . Now that the youth stand on the threshold of adulthood, they encounter through confirmation a conscious decision for the Church and their faith.[48]

Now, many of these developments are healthy because they exhibit reflection on the history and theology of confirmation. They emphasize the role of the community and the readiness of the person for confirmation. However, having examined the controversy of the post-Reformation, it is increasingly obvious that the Catholic interpretation of confirmation is coming more and more to resemble the rite envisioned by the Reformers: Catechesis (preceding an examination of faith) enjoys a central role. Emphasis on the candidate's own free response in faith replaces the false comfort *ex opere operato* offers. Calvin suspected that the preparation for examining children's faith would influence the faith of the family, and his insight is echoed in modern Catholic preparation.

But this leaves a question. Even though Catholics and Reformers have grown together in the centuries since the Reformation in the preparation and even celebration of this rite, have the faiths grown

---

[47] "En los últimos años ha habido una revisión pastoral y se ha revalorizado la Confirmación. Por una parte se aconseja recibirlo de jóvenes o adultos, ya que es una 'unión más firme a Cristo y un compromiso serio'. Y para aceptarlo es necesario ser persona adulta, responsable; no es por tanto para niños.
"Por otra parte se ha profundizado en la Teología del Espiritu y en su papel importantísimo para la vida de la Iglesia y de cada cristiano, dejando de ser el 'gran desconocido' (Hech. 19, 2)." "Introduccion", *Aviva el fuego de los dones que Dios te dio* (Morales-Izabal: Centro Apostólico, c. 1980).

[48] "Die Jugendlichen haben sich zur Firmung freiwillig gemeldet. . . . Jetzt, da die Jugendlichen an der Schwelle zum Erwachsensein stehen, treffen sie durch die Firmung eine bewußte Entscheidung für die Kirche und ihren Glauben." Franz Pitzal, *Die Firmung: Ein Vorbereitungsbuch* (Regensburg: Verlag Friedrich Pustet, 1984), p. 9.
France, on the other hand, has long enjoyed a tradition of a celebration of profession of faith for youth separate from confirmation. A new catechetical instrument for confirmation in high school is *Vers la confirmation: Itineraire de préparation*, ed. Odette Sarda and Louis-Michel Renier (Angers: Editions du Chalet, 1983).

together in a true expression of what confirmation is? Time and time again Catholic preparation manuals insist that confirmation is part of initiation. Time and time again they place it not at a moment of initiation, but long after initiation, or more accurately, at the beginning of adult commitment. The delayed celebration of confirmation is really not initiation at all. It is, to use the term of the LBW, a reaffirmation of baptism, but not part of the initiation rite. Delaying confirmation expresses more the individual Christian's mature acceptance of the demands of faith than a celebration of the freely given gift of the Holy Spirit as part of initiation into God's family. This leaves ecumenism with an uncomfortable accomplishment: There exists a growing convergence among the Christian faiths and practices of confirmation, but the convergence is not in keeping with its meaning.

Thus a consideration of the various texts which address the theology of confirmation reveals that the Catholic Church retains a rather broad interpretation of what the sacrament is. In fact, it encompasses two meanings for the two instances of celebration: one a rite of initiation, the other a rite of strengthening.

C. Problems Unresolved

Having traced the growing convergence in the practice of Catholics and Lutherans, one may now see more clearly the theological problems which remain. This section presents them in two groups – one methodological (how one discerns sacramentality), the other theological (the meaning of confirmation).

1. Hermeneutics and Analogy

The heart of the disagreement between the faiths is the question of institution by Christ. Everyone agrees sacraments must be instituted by Christ, but each differs on just what that means. For Luther, it meant there must be a promise and a sign in the Scriptures. Chemnitz stressed the need for a command from the lips of Christ to repeat the action. For the Roman Church, the ministry of the Apostles was evidence enough that Christ commanded confirmation, even though there is no written proof.[49]

---

[49] Incidentally, the Church argued in a similar way in our day with regard to another issue. See Sacra Congregatio pro Doctrina Fidei, "Declaratio circa quaestionem admissionis mulierum ad sacerdotium ministeriale (Inter insigniores)," 2-4, 15 October 1976, AAS 69 (1977):102-108.

Since Trent stated that all seven sacraments were instituted by Christ, many have tried to reinterpret the doctrine in light of more recent theology. The Modernists unsuccessfully promoted the belief that the sacraments were instituted by the apostolic Church according to the mind of Christ. Pius X listed among the errors of the Modernists:

Sacraments originated from that which the Apostles and their successors understood to be some idea or intention of Christ, as circumstances and events were urging and moving.[50]

Karl Rahner said Christ Himself instituted the sacraments by His institution of the Church:

If we say that by the fact that Christ instituted the Church (directly of course), the sacraments were already instituted, any intermediary who can decide concerning the institution or non-institution of the sacraments is already excluded by that very fact. The institution of the sacraments by Christ is, therefore, an immediate one.[51]

Specifically, to show the institution of confirmation, he argues that since confirmation is historically and theologically united to baptism, the institution of one presumes that of the other.

We can thus say that Christ instituted the sacrament of confirmation with this: It is sufficient that He willed an initiation of visible form into the Church, which confers on humanity that which is essential for this Church: the remission of sins and the plenitude of the Spirit.[52]

---

[50] "Sacramenta ortum habuerunt ex eo, quod Apostoli eorumque successores ideam aliquam et intentionem Christi, suadentibus et moventibus circumstantiis et eventibus, interpretati sunt." Petrus Palombelli, Sacrae Congregationis Romanae et Universalis Inquisitionis Notarius, "Decretum, Quo sub 65 propositionibus reprobantur ac proscribuntur praecipui errores reformismi seu modernismi. Feria IV, die 3 Iulii 1907 (Lamentabili)," 40, ASS 40 (1907):475.

[51] "Wenn wir sagen: Dadurch, daß Christus die Kirche (natürlich unmittelbar) stiftet, sind die Sakramente schon gestiftet, ist eine Mittelinstanz, die über die Stiftung oder Nichtstiftung der Sakramente verfügen könnte, eo ipso schon ausgeschlossen. Die Stiftung der Sakramente durch Christus ist also eine unmittelbare." Kirche und Sakramente, QD 10 (1960):56, fn. 4.

[52] "Wir können also sagen: Damit Christus des Sakrament der Firmung eingesetzt hat, genügt es, daß er eine Initiation greifbarer Art in die Kirche gewollt hat, die dem Menschen das verleiht, was für diese Kirche wesentlich ist: die Nachlassung der Sünden und die Geistfülle." Ibid., p. 52.

Salvatore Marsili echoes this opinion and adds that if institution pertains more to Christ as the fundamental sacrament of salvation, the sacraments are not bound to a written command:

> Christ is the institutor-author of the sacraments of the Church, *because* he is the great sacrament of salvation. In this way the sacraments remain bound to Christ not by means of a simple command and they do not appear as rites generically manifestive of the faith of Christ, but they depend on the same sacramental being of Christ (cf. Augustine, *In ep. Ioan.* 3, 6), as on a sacramental font from which passes to the sacraments that salvation which, being a "revealed" reality, always needs "signs" to be perceived by humanity.[53]

What makes a resolution so difficult is two sources, Scripture and the council of Trent. One said too little, the other too much. Scripture, although alluding to sacraments, does not define them or use the term in reference to them. The Reformers are caught in the predicament of arguing a non-scriptural term out of scriptural data. Despite the absence of scriptural proof, Trent defined that the sacraments were instituted by Christ, and Catholic theologians seek a credible way to explain the canon whenever they define sacraments. So to delimit the sacraments, theologians seek sense from the silent Scriptures, while reinterpreting the data from Trent.

Once again, the problem is hermeneutics. Because the two sides held opposing views about the interpretation of Scripture, they fell into irreconcilable sacramental theologies. René Marlé writes,

> The Reformers and the Roman Church were essentially opposed on two theories concerning the interpretation of Scripture, in other words on two hermeneutic doctrines. To the Reform's "scriptural" principle of *Sola Scriptura* the Council of Trent responded by the principle of *Scriptura et Traditione.* For the Reformers, Scripture accompanied by

---

[53]   "Cristo è l'istitutore-autore dei sacramenti della chiesa, *perchè* è il grande sacramento della salvezza. In questo modo i sacramenti restano legati a Cristo non per via di un semplice comando e non appaiono come riti genericamente manifestativi della fede in Cristo, ma dipendono dallo stesso essere sacramentale di Cristo (Cfr. Agostino, In ep. Ioan. 3,6 <PL 35,2000>:   'Cristo è il nome di un sacramento, come quando si dice profeta e si dice sacerdote'), come da una fonte sacramentale dalla quale passa nei sacramenti quella salvezza, che, essendo una realtà 'rivelata', ha sempre bisogno di 'segni' per essere percepita dall'uomo." "Sacramenti," *Nuovo Dizionario di Liturgia*, ed. Domenico Sartore and Achille M. Triacca (Rome: Edizioni Paoline, 1983), pp. 1276 and 1285.

"interior witness of the Holy Spirit," ought to produce by itself its sense in the spirit of the believer. Scripture is not only the object of faith, it is the unique rule of it and should for that reason remain "interpreter of itself" *(sui ipsius interpres)*. For the Council of Trent, on the contrary, the sense of Scripture can only be encountered in truth in the interior of the Church under the movement of her tradition, authenticated by the magisterium.[54]

To ask for agreement on the sacraments is to ask for a change in hermeneutics.

In the end, there is no solution to the problem as posed unless one side accepts the definition of the other. As long as the Reformers insist on written scriptural data and while the Catholics argue from history and theology, the two sides cannot agree. The two positions have been almost immovably cemented by the influence of two writers: Peter Lombard and Martin Luther. One said there were seven sacraments, the other two. The history of the conflict comes down to a defense of these men, and if a resolution is to be found, one must step beyond their influence.

There are ways of approaching a resolution. One would be for the Catholic Church to explore the two "levels" of sacraments in her tradition. It is no small point that the Church gives Eucharist and baptism a special dignity. This is evident not simply from their institution in Scripture, but also from theology. Paul VI taught that the Church keeps the Eucharist as her most precious treasure.[55] *Lumen gentium* cites Mark 16, 16 and John 3, 5 to show the necessity of baptism for salvation.[56] Even though there are seven sacraments according to

54   "Les Reformateurs et l'Eglise romaine se sont essentiellement opposeés sur deux théories de l'interprétation de l'Ecriture, autrement dit sur deux doctrines herméneutiques. Au principe 'scripturaire' du *Sola Scriptura* de la Réforme le concile de Trente a répond par le principe du *Scriptura et Traditione*. Pour les Réformateurs l'Ecriture, accompagnée du 'témoignage interieur du Saint-Esprit', devait produire par elle-même son sens dans l'esprit du croyant. L'Ecriture n'est pas seulement objet de la foi, elle en est l'unique règle, et doit pour cela rester 'interprète d'elle-même" *(sui ipsius interpres)*. Pour le concile de Trente, au contraire, le sens de l'Ecriture ne peut être rencontré en vérité qu'à l'intérieur de l'Eglise, sous la mouvance de sa tradition, authentifiée par le magistère." René Marlé, *Herméneutique et ecriture*, class notes, pp. 3-4.

55   ". . . thesaurum, quo nihil pretiosius," *Mysterium Fidei*, AAS 57:753.

56   *Lumen gentium*, 14. Sacrosanctum Oecumenicum Concilium Vaticanum II, *Constitutiones, decreta, declarationes*, Ed. Secretaria Generalis Concilii Oecumenici Vaticani II (Vatican City: Typis Polyglottis Vaticanis, 1974), p. 118.

Catholic doctrine, baptism initiates one into Christian life and Eucharist sustains one there. Among the seven, these two enjoy more dignity than the other five. Is this not a beginning from which the Church could make a distinction among sacraments in agreement with other denominations? Catholics are not blind to the supremacy of baptism and Eucharist as the Reformers feared when they examined Gratian's canon from the council of Orleans: Contrary to the canon, Catholics do not believe confirmation is necessary for being a Christian. Nor does confirmation enjoy the same dignity as baptism and Eucharist as Bellarmine implies: Just because Cyril imposed hands after baptism and before Eucharist he did not necessarily regard it as a sacrament equal to the other two. At least this much is clear: Among the seven sacraments of the Catholic Church there are two kinds – those which bear a scriptural institution from the words of Jesus, and those which do not. And if Catholics can say that among the seven there is none greater than the Eucharist and that baptism is necessary to receive it, they have already established a superior theological order over the other five. This approach affirms Luther's use of Scripture to set apart baptism and Eucharist and Calvin's philosophy of symbol for determining sacraments.

The Reformers could profitably question the source of sacramental efficacy. They bind the efficacy of sacraments to the recorded words of Jesus. Henry VIII's objection still goes unanswered: If that were true, how does one account for the celebration of sacraments by the early Church in the days before the Scriptures were written? Sacraments have been validly celebrated without a written word on the strength of the oral tradition of the community. And just as the Reformers feared confirmation robbed baptism of its power, there is a danger that limiting sacraments to Scripture robs the Church of her intermediary though indispensable role of realizing the sacraments.

Another resolution to the hermeneutical problem may be through an understanding of sacramental analogy. Reflecting on the sacraments as signs, one may confess that, of them all, the Eucharist most perfectly expresses Its reality, the Body and Blood of Christ. The other sacraments, including baptism, are sacramental signs in that they are analogous to the sign of the Eucharist. A recognition of this theology might also open the door to continued dialogue on the sacraments.[57]

---

[57] Coming to an agreement on the institution of sacraments would still leave unresolved other issues, for example the problem of sacramental causality in Calvin with the Lutheran and Catholic traditions. See Chapter II, fn. 61.

Whatever the approach, the ecumenical dialogue needs to go beyond the influence of Lombard and Luther to the insights of Scripture and the early Church (especially Augustine) for a clearer understanding of the meaning of the word "sacrament" and the full richness of its application. The true spirit of the Reformation grounds its theology in Scripture, not in Luther.

For confirmation, it is impossible for the two sides to agree on the question of its sacramentality without a mutually agreed-upon approach to the nature of sacraments and to the method of using sources.

2. Sealing and Recommitment

A further difficulty in the controversy is that the word "confirmation" has come to be applied to two different realities: sealing of initiation and recommitment to Christian life. In both the Lutheran and Catholic traditions, the history of confirmation has been handed down in two different rites – one attached to baptismal initiation, and one celebrated later. Although Catholic texts repeatedly insist that confirmation celebrated later is still an act of initiation, it is so only by analogy, and a weak one at that.

The definitions of confirmation consistently return to two words: seal and strengthening. The former better describes confirmation as initiation; the latter, as mature acceptance of faith. In the Lutheran Church, these two rites are given different names: sealing and confirmation. The seal of the Spirit is applied at baptism: one's faith is strengthened later in a rite that may be repeated. Perhaps this distinction could be of assistance to the Roman Church as she struggles to be faithful to her own tradition, to history, and to the Scriptures. The two celebrations she calls confirmation actually have different purposes: one to seal initiation, the other to strengthen faith. The liturgical text is ambiguous enough to cover both events.[58]

The theological distinction between these rites was no clearer at the time of the Reformation: Confirmations were celebrated not at baptism but administered later by a bishop. The Reformers objected to the sacramentality of confirmation of maturity. One may presume they would have denied the sacramentality of confirmation as initiation

---

[58]   For the sake of completion, one may recall that the evangelical Churches would resolve the distinctions in favor of believer's baptism. By delaying baptism to an age when the person states a belief in Christ, the Churches find no need for a later celebration of commitment.

because there is no institution narrative for it either, but the issue never arose. The confirmation which the Reformers adapted as a non-sacramental rite was confirmation of maturity – an opportunity to strengthen faith, not to seal the baptismal covenant. Thus, when they had the opportunity to revise the rite to its pristine form, the Reformers opted for a later version. This relates back to the problem of method: The practice of confirming at a later age better fit the theology of the Reform than the earlier practice of conducting the rites of initiation together. The interpretation of historical sources for the sake of polemics instead of for historico-critical hermeneutics preserved the muddled perception of what confirmation is.

Even though the origins of confirmation are with initiation, making it more seal than strength, one may object as the Reformers might have, that baptism is so powerful a sacrament it does not need to be sealed. This is true, in that it is not so much baptism itself that confirmation seals but the covenant of grace behind it. In addition, although confirmation is not necessary for becoming a Christian, it is a sign of God's abundant love for His people that He seals the grace of baptism anyway by pouring out the grace of the Holy Spirit. Because through confirmation God gives more than what is needed, it is an excellent sign of His grace.

 Confirmation is the coming of the Holy Spirit through the imposition of hands. It seals the gift of the Spirit at baptism. These elements can be traced to the scriptural foundation of the imposition of hands and the development of the practice in the early days of the Church. The coming of the Holy Spirit at Pentecost and through the apostolic imposition of hands was more a rite of initiation for newcomers to the Christian faith than a celebration of commitment delayed some years after baptism. Although strength may be given with the seal, as the homily for the rite observes, the theological emphasis is on the seal.

 What is the difference between the gift of the Spirit at baptism and the gift of the Spirit at confirmation? In one sense there is no difference since there is only one Spirit. In another sense the means and demands of the gift are different because the gift is given in a second instance. One might ask what is the difference between the gift of the person in the exchange of marriage vows and the gift of the person in sexual intercourse. In one sense the gift is the same since the person is one. But the gift comes by different means and brings new demands for accepting the fruitfulness of love. In confirmation the Holy Spirit Who came at baptism through the pouring of water comes through the imposition of hands. This renewed gift of the Spirit demands a readiness to witness the Gospel of Christ. Not that one who is baptized is not called to witness the Gospel, but one who is confirmed has received a seal of the same Holy Spirit with new demands to accept this fruitfulness of faith.

Emmanuel Lanne proposes from his study of confirmation in the West that three traits separate it from baptism: It is the gift of the sevenfold Holy Spirit who gathers different vocations into the unity of the Church. It gives a particular strength to the Christian for spiritual combat and witness. It creates a special conclusive bond with the Church through the intervention of the bishop and the doctrine of the character.[59] These are not exclusive to confirmation – elements appear in baptism and Eucharist, but their ensemble, he says, is unique. His conclusions are especially helpful when underlined with the prerequisite role of baptism, which confirmation seals.

In addition to the problems resulting directly from the controversy, a new problem arises from the contemporary situation. Throughout the post-Reformation confirmation controversy, the Reformers charged that the theology of confirmation impoverished baptism. Now both traditions should beware lest the theology of confirmation impoverish Eucharist.

In the rites of initiation, it is Eucharist which completes the process. Eucharist is the summit of Christian life and the ultimate symbol of unity with the Church. But Catholics making confirmation the third step after baptism and first Eucharist call it the culmination of initiation. Many diocesan directives express this opinion, and seemingly even the Congregation for Divine Worship in its decree on confirmation:

> Through the sacrament of confirmation the Apostles themselves and their successors the bishops have handed on to baptized persons the special gift of the Holy Spirit, promised by Christ the Lord and poured out upon the Apostles on the day of Pentecost. By this strength the initiation of the Christian life is thus completed so that the

---

[59] Emmanuel Lanne, "Les sacrements de l'initiation chrétienne et la confirmation dans l'Eglise d'Occident," *Irenikon*, 57 (1984):336.

faithful, strengthened by heavenly power, may become
genuine witnesses of Christ both in words and in examples,
and likewise be bound with the Church by a more complete
bond.[60]

But to say confirmation "completes" initiation and to receive Eucharist
before one is fully initiated is to minimize the effect of communion and
to elevate confirmation to a historically unprecedented level of
attention.[61] Among the sacraments of initiation confirmation must
decrease that Eucharist may increase.

The Lutheran tradition does not connect confirmation with first
Eucharist: Confirmation is commitment, not part of initiation.[62] This
leads the *Manual* for the LBW to state,

> First communion is theologically and liturgically
> unrelated to Confirmation. No form is provided to mark the
> occasion, for the gift of Communion is the birthright of the
> baptized.[63]

This statement reveals how the word "confirmation" is used
equivocally by the Churches. In the Catholic tradition, "confirmation"
as initiation is inseparable from first Eucharist.

The World Council of Churches' document *Baptism, Eucharist and
Ministry* upholds the Lutherans' position saying that nothing should
be interposed between baptism and Eucharist:

[60] "Peculiare Spiritus Sancti donum, a Christo Domino promissum et super
Apostolos die Pentecostes effusum, ipsi Apostoli eorumque successores Episcopi
baptizatis hominibus per Confirmationis Sacramentum tradiderunt. Cuius ope
christianae vitae initiatio ita perficitur, ut fideles, superna corroborati virtute, Christi
testes sinceri, tum verbis tum exemplis evadant, itemque arctiore cum Ecclesia vinculo
astringantur." Sacra Congregatio pro Cultu Divino, "Decretum, Prot. n. 800/71," *Ordo
Confirmationis*, p. 5.

[61] Paul VI says it is Eucharist which fully incorporates, see fn. 27 above.

[62] Theóbald Suss, however, argues that Luther, Melanchthon, and Chemnitz
implied a connection between confirmation and preparation for first Eucharist,
"Remarques sur le problème de la confirmation," *Positions Luthériennes* 3 (July 1957): pp.
181-185.

[63] *Manual*, p. 341.

If baptism, as incorporation into the body of Christ, points by its very nature to the eucharistic sharing of Christ's body and blood, the question arises as to how a further and separate rite can be interposed between baptism and admission to communion. Those churches which baptize children but refuse them a share in the eucharist before such a rite may wish to ponder whether they have fully appreciated and accepted the consequences of baptism.[64]

But history shows that confirmation is part of the one initiation rite with baptism, and the Churches may rather ask if in omitting confirmation between baptism and Eucharist they have fully appreciated the consequences of confirmation.[65] If it is celebrated after Eucharist, it loses its place as initiation, and becomes, as in the Lutheran Church, an affirmation of baptism.

An agreement on the meaning and nature of confirmation would expedite a resolution to the controversy between Catholics and Reformers.

D. Proposals

In conclusion there follow proposals for a celebration of confirmation which attempt to reconcile the controversies of the post-Reformation while being faithful to Scripture, tradition, and theology.

1. Imposition of Hands

The description in the Scriptures for what the Church came to call confirmation is so explicit in its reference to imposition of hands that it is no wonder the Reformers were puzzled by the Church's tradition of anointing.

Bellarmine explained how imposition of hands was still part of confirmation, and the rite of Vatican II underlines its importance, but the essential elements of confirmation are the words of sealing and anointing with oil. Paul VI explained that although imposition of hands was always prescribed as part of the rite, anointing held the preferred place.

---

[64] "Baptism," Commentary 14b, *Baptism, Eucharist and Ministry*, Faith and Order Paper No. 111 (Geneva: World Council of Churches, 1982), p. 5.

[65] Ligier argues this point, pp. 270-279. He concludes, ". . . il faut dire qu'on

From these things which we have recalled to mind, it is clear that in the action of confirming in the East and the West, chrismation, which in a certain way represents the apostolic imposition of hands, had occupied the first place, in a different way, soundly, with reason. But since this anointing of chrism appropriately signifies the spiritual anointing of the Holy Spirit, Who is given to the faithful, We desire that the existence and importance of the same be confirmed.[66]

However, Louis Ligier argues through his book *La Confirmation* for the primacy of imposition of hands. He says in Acts it was the essential sacramental act,[67] and that in history the imposition of hands became reserved for orders to distinguish it from confirmation.[68] He observes that the description of the essential elements in the Apostolic Constitution came from the Congregation for the Doctrine of the Faith, not from the liturgical commission which prepared the rite and altered the words accompanying the anointing which now omitted a direct reference to chrism.[69]

Although the Church has stated the primacy of the anointing for centuries, she has always retained imposition of hands as part of the rite, almost as insurance for its proper administration. And although the Lutherans have become tolerant of the use of oil in the post-baptismal rite of sealing, it is the imposition of hands which holds primacy for them. Whether one examines Scripture, the history of the practice, or the contemporary practice in all Christian Churches, one cannot minimize the importance of imposing hands for the administration of this rite.

n'accède normalement á l'Eucharistie qu'après avoir ètè confirmè. Les Pasteurs doivent le savoir. L'exemple des Eglises orientales est là pour les rassurer. Il n'est pas absolument nécessaire que l'initiation a l'Esprit soit accompagnée d'une expérience spirituelle parfaite. L'important est que cette expérience, souvent infirme à sés debuts, soit portée à son épanouissement par la vie de l'Eglise."

66 "Ex iis, quae in memoriam revocavimus, liquet in actione confirmandi in Oriente et Occidente, alia sane ratione, primum locum obtinuisse chrismationem, quae apostolicam manuum impositionem quodam modo repraesentat. Cum autem ea chrismatis unctio spiritualem Sancti Spiritus, qui fidelibus datur, unctionem, apte significet, Nos confirmatam volumus eiusdem exsistentiam et momentum." "Constitutio," *Ordo Confirmationis*, p. 13.

67 Ligier, p. 226.

68 Ibid., p. 163. There is a notable contrast between Ligier's almost exclusive dependence on liturgical sources and the spare use employed by the controversialists.

69 Ibid., pp. 25-26.

2. Confirmation as Sealing

To return to the problem of the last section, if there are two distinct rites of confirmation with separate purposes (initiation and commitment), which is more faithful to Scripture and tradition? Are both a sacrament? The Catholics' peculiar identification of the character with the sacrament is the best clue. If the nature of the character is the seal of the Spirit on the grace of baptism, then it is best expressed in the confirmation of initiation. The character, traditionally bound to the nonrepeatability of confirmation, better fits a once-only initiation than a recommitment which the faithful may make spiritually many times. As mentioned before, whereas the seal at initiation does strengthen, the confirmation of maturity strengthens more than it initiates and is a weaker expression of the impact of the seal.

Another clue to the true meaning of confirmation comes from a historico-critical analysis of sources. This method would reveal that the earliest celebration of confirmation by the post-apostolic Church was in the context of initiation. For the sake of resolving controversy and for theological insight into the meaning of confirmation, the method of using sources to defend a later theological position yields to the method of letting the sources speak to the Church from their own ecclesial experience.

It may be argued that the imposition of hands in Acts 8 was separated from the time of baptism, but it would be countered that the two happened together in Acts 19. Does this permit two occasions for the celebration of the rite?

Ritual is not history. The events of history become celebrated in ritual to make them understandable and applicable to the community. Ritual interprets history. The rites of initiation in the early Church interpreted the historical events for the people and applied them to their lives in a way that made the beginning of Christian life and the gift of the Holy Spirit understandable through signs. Even though the historical events may have happened in separate moments, the ritual celebration may be one to express their unity.

The separation of the rites was a historical development. The Church may ask if it is time to restore the rites to their original unity in the light of theological discernment, the knowledge of history, and the pastoral demands of the age.

What makes the restoration difficult is that there exist for both Catholics and Reformers two separate rites with names and two realities behind those rites. The Lutherans call them sealing and confirmation, the Catholics call both confirmation. One is initiation, the other recommitment; one is sealing, the other strengthening. The problem is that the Catholics apply the name "confirmation" in one instance to a reality the Lutherans call sealing, and in another instance to a reality that expresses the original sacrament by analogy.

This situation is being prolonged by the trend to raise the age of confirmation in the Catholic Church while trying to retain its identity as a sacrament of initiation. This corresponds to the desire of many dioceses which seek a rite of recommitment for youth. It was a need perceived by Calvin and Chemnitz, and is still a pastoral concern for the Church. What the Catholic Church is really developing, though, is a rite of affirmation of baptism and commitment to a life of witness in the Church. Both traditions are applying the word "confirmation" to a reality different from the rites of initiation, and the Catholics call it a sacrament.

This rite of affirmation has already been developed in the Lutheran Church, and not without historical precedents. St. Augustine applied the imposition of hands and even the text from Acts to the reconciliation of heretics. Surely the author of De baptismo would applaud the insight of the Lutheran practice: The affirmation of one's baptism can take several forms – confirmation, reception of new members, restoration of lost membership. The imposition of hands at the moment of baptismal affirmation is a historically supportable use of the apostolic gesture, but it is not a rite of initiation, it is a rite of affirmation. The same gesture is profitably used in initiation, where it has the full meaning of sealing the baptismal gift of the Holy Spirit.

Augustine's imposition of hands in De baptismo is actually closer to the Catholic sacrament of penance than to confirmation. It reconciles those who have fallen away. And here, dioceses which seek a rite to help their youth might look again. Do they need imposition of hands which is confirmation, or do they need reconciliation, or even affirmation? The textbooks for confirming youth prepare them to re-affirm the promises of baptism and to assert their readiness to accept the challenges of adult Christian life. Such a rite may be accompanied by imposition of hands, but it is confirmation as commitment, not as initiation. If the sacrament of sealing were reserved for initiation, other possibilities arise: Christian youth could celebrate reconciliation, or an affirmation of faith. They could be thus introduced to a rite which would be repeatable at a later moment in life when they might seek another confirmation of faith. One wonders if rather than answering the needs of youth, dioceses do not damage the possibility of growth by celebrating with them a rite which may happen once only for a phenomenon that recurs throughout life: the need to reaffirm baptismal faith.

Regarding the practice of the Churches, the post-Reformation confirmation controversy has taken a surprising twist: Both sides are developing similar rites: Lutherans allow anointing, Catholics encourage a personal affirmation of faith. But from the principles which formed the basis for the controversy – love for Scripture, respect for history – are these rites developing in the best fashion? It would rather seem that a restoration of the unity of the rites of initiation at whatever age would restore the sacrament of sealing to its pristine form and meaning, while the development of rites of affirmation for the Churches would provide an opportunity not only for youth, but for all who feel the need to return to the faith more strongly. (This division is more a need in the West than in the East, which celebrates confirmation with baptism.) For the Catholic Church this could be accomplished through a thoughtful use of the sacrament of penance for youth or the development of rites of baptismal affirmation for those who wish to recommit themselves to Christ and the Church. Either could be coupled with an extended period of preparation, in the former case perhaps a restoration in some form of the "order of penitents" which offered a parallel to the catechumenate for believers in the community; this would provide a repeatable celebration of Christian maturity. For the Reformers, restoring the full initiation rite could mean recognizing the rite of sealing as the descendent of Pentecost and underlining its importance for Church membership.

The Churches could also work toward eliminating the equivocation over the term "confirmation". It is used to cover a spectrum too broad. For the Catholics it means initiation and commitment, sealing and strengthening. The solution of the Lutheran Church is a good beginning: "sealing" for initiation, "confirmation" for commitment. These terms could be adopted, but two others, e.g. "confirmation" and "recommitment," would preserve the original usage of the term "to confirm." This study proposes the following divisions:

Confirmation is a part of the sacraments of initiation. It is the sacramental celebration of Pentecost, the gift of the Holy Spirit upon the Apostles which they shared with others through the imposition of hands. It is a freely given gift of God's abundant love, not necessary for salvation. Together with baptism, it entitles Christians to the Eucharist and enables them to bear witness to the faith through the sevenfold gift of the Holy Spirit. It is administered with baptism by the bishop, or in his absence, by the priest who baptizes. It includes anointing with oil and the imposition of hands. It imparts a character since it works with baptism as a unique moment of initiation to express the ecclesial relationship.

Recommitment is a celebration of strengthening the Christian witness. It represents a mature acceptance of the faith, preceded by catechetical review and/or conversion of heart, and makes one more like Christ. A repeatable celebration, it celebrates an increased degree of identity with Christ and the Church.

Such a distinction would eliminate the confusion inherited from the checkered history of confirmation and urge Christian Churches toward fitting celebrations of the mysteries of the Spirit.

Author's Conclusions

There are really two controversies which inspired this book. One is four hundred years old. The other is quite modern. The former was a child of a larger struggle against the Catholic Church, the latter is part of a larger discernment within the Church. One asked if confirmation is a sacrament, the other asks more fundamentally what is its meaning. I believe that these debates of an earlier age shed light on the wonderment of our own.

To examine the meaning of confirmation more clearly, this study focused on a time of great theological activity, the controversies of the post-Reformation. I began with some pre-history, to show the roots of the struggle: How Martin Luther refashioned the sacramental system and how the Catholics reacted. Then I presented the theologians whose writings would enter a contest on the pages of Bellarmine's *Controversies*: the Jesuit cardinal himself who authored the work, and his adversaries John Calvin and Martin Chemnitz. These early chapters explained the history of the theology of confirmation at the time of the Reform.

To show the complexity of the controversy, I presented the fruits of my research into the sources employed by the protagonists – a chart of 446 entries exposing the full "arsenal" of the dispute. The same chapter continued with an analysis of how the combatants used these weapons at their disposal. Then, I presented five of the sources which were treated repeatedly in the dispute and commented on the success of the outcome.

Finally, I examined the material from the later controversy, the meaning and celebration of confirmation for the Churches today who are successors to the sixteenth century dispute. This chapter investigated the growing convergence in the liturgical practice of Catholics and Lutherans, and the problems which still need to be resolved.

Ending this work I reflect on the aspects which caught my

attention at the beginning of the project. I saw the study as an opportunity to research a broad range of the history of a limited topic which touched on areas of interest to me – the theology of sacraments (and specifically the meaning of confirmation) and the field of ecumenism. It is my hope, then, that this study fulfills several objectives beyond the description of a single controversy of the sixteenth century.

First, regarding ecumenism, it is clear what poverty can result when theology is studied in isolation from the ideas of other Churches. Neither the Catholics nor the Reformers held a theology of confirmation in the sixteenth century which was so perfect it would confound the beliefs of the adversaries. One result of this work has been to underline this position: Both traditions stand to gain from a constructive rereading of their own opposing positions. The theological insights of all Christians will contribute toward the spiritual advancement of any single group.

Second, regarding the contemporary practice of confirming, historical study is essential for celebrating with understanding. The growing convergence in liturgical practice seems to have happened in spite of the controversy, not out of the pure desire of any Church to resolve its differences. Praiseworthy as the convergence is, it is time to examine its meaning for those who celebrate confirmation. Because we share a common history, the decisions we make about the practice of confirmation are statements about the interpretation of that history. The responsibility for renewed liturgical practice cannot thus be taken lightly.

In particular, regarding this point, I have a concern for the growing tendency among Catholics to celebrate confirmation at a later age out of the desire to make a pastoral application of its theology. To me, this pastoral application seems directed more toward the present need to respond to the drift of young people from the Church than toward the actual theology of confirmation. Theology must be made pastoral, but pastors must not ignore theology. The diocese or episcopal conference which selects an age for confirmation is not simply responding to the needs of its own people. It is part of a larger scene which includes the history of confirmation, its practice in non-Catholic Christian Churches, the differences in the Eastern rites, and the genuine needs of young people whose faith must be nurtured from the moment of baptism throughout all their lives.

Besides these primary points, this work may also assist students of the Reformation, of the history of confirmation, and of the protagonists of this study, their theology and method. For the rest of us who share in baptism and are confirmed for a life in the Spirit, I hope we have penetrated more deeply the mystery of our calling and feel moved to work together for the upbuilding of the Church and the healing of our divisions. This is still the post-Reformation, and the controversy lingers. May the Spirit Who seals the covenant of our baptism in Christ bring the Church to the unity and peace for which it prays, from hearts confirmed in faith.

Appendix

There follows a listing of the sources of the controversy in chronological order. Entry numbers refer to the chart in Chapter III.

DATES	NAME	ENTRY
BC	The Old Testament	S-1/S-11
70-19 BC	Virgil	X-2
AD	The New Testament	S-12/S-86
61-114	Pliny the Younger	X-1
91-101	Clement of Rome	P-3/P-7
c. 150-215	Clement of Alexandria	G-5/G-8
155-220	Tertullian	L-68/L-74
+ 165	Justin	G-41
+ 180	Theophilus Antiochenus	G-50
c. 185-253	Origen	G-42/G-43
200-258	Cyprian	L-40/L-44
251-253	Cornelius	P-9
c. 263-340	Eusebius	G-25/G-28

DATES	NAME	ENTRY
295-373	Athanasius	G-2
305	Elvira	C-9/C-10
314	Arles I	C-1
314-325	Neocaesarea	C-17
315-367	Hilary of Poitiers	L-50
c. 315-387	Cyril of Jerusalem	G-9/G-14
c. 315-403	Epiphanius	G-23/G-24
325	Nicaea	C-18/C-19
c. 330-379	Basil	G-3/G-4
c. 330-390	Gregory Nazianzen	G-29/G-30
331-419	Jerome	L-52/L-58
c. 333	Rome	C-22
334-397	Ambrose	L-1/L-8
c. 335-394	Gregory of Nyssa	G-31
c. 343-381	Laodicea	C-13/C-14
c. 344-407	John Chrysostom	G-33/G-38
345-410	Rufinus	L-67
348-405	Prudentius	L-65/L-66
354-430	Augustine	L-9/L-39

DATES	NAME	ENTRY
fl. 365	Optatus	L-61
366-384	Damasus	P-10/P-11
390	Carthage II	C-5
+ c. 392	Pacianus	L-62/L-64
c. 393-466	Theodoret	G-44/G-49
+ c. 394	Amphilochius	G-1
+ c. 397	Filastrius	L-46
c. 398	Carthage III	C-6
c. 398	Carthage IV	C-7
398	Toledo I	C-25
5th c.	Pseudo-Dionysius	G-15/G-22
401-417	Innocent I	P-24/P-25
402	Milevis	C-16
440-461	Leo	P-29/P-32
441	Orange	C-20
442	Vaison-la-Romaine	C-33
442-506	Arles II	C-2
+ c. 450	Hesychius	G-32
461	Tours	C-27

DATES	NAME	ENTRY
+ c. 492	Gennadius	L-48
492-496	Gelasius	P-15
6th c.	Gelasius (Decretum)	L-47
515-580	Martin of Braga	L-60
516	Terracina	C-24
537-555	Vigilius	P-39
538-594	Gregory of Tours	L-49
560-636	Isidore	L-51
563	Braga I	C-3
572	Braga II	C-4
590-604	Gregory	P-16/P-19
7th c.	Eusebius Gallicanus	L-45
619	Seville II	C-23
653	Toledo VIII	C-26
654-657	Eugune	P-12
673-735	Bede	M-11/M-14
c. 675-749	John Damascene	G-39/G-40
680	Constantinople III	C-8
715-731	Gregory II	P-21

DATES	NAME	ENTRY
735-804	Alcuin	M-1/M-2
757	Decretum Compendiense (Verberie)	M-21
776-856	Rabanus Maurus	M-74/M-75
c. 780-850	Amalarius	M-5/M-6
795-816	Leo III	P-33
9th c. ?	Pseudo-John III	P-28
9th c. ?	Pseudo-Council of Orleans	C-21
845	Meaux	C-15
847-852	Pseudo-Isidore	M-55/M-61
858-867	Nicholass	P-36
868	Worms	C-35/C-36
10th c.	Ordo Romanus	M-67
c. 1050-1108	Theophylactus	M-79
1075-1129	Rupert of Deutz	M-78
1090-1153	Bernard	M-15
12th c.	Gratian	M-31/M-51
c. 1100-1160	Peter Lombard	M-71/M-73
+ 1142	Hugh of St. Victor	M-53/M-54
fl. 1145-1151	Nicholas of Clairvaux	M-65

DATES	NAME	ENTRY
+ c. 1150	Herveus	M-52
+ c. 1156	Arnaldus of Bonnevaux	M-9/M-10
c. 1186-1245	Alexander of Hales	M-3/M-4
1198-1216	Innocent III	P-26/P-27
13-14th c.	Ripelin, Hugues	M-77
c. 1217-1274	Bonaventure	M-16/M-17
c. 1225-1274	Thomas Aquinas	M-80/M-82
1227-1241	Gregory IX	P-22/P-23
c. 1230-1296	Duranti, William	M-23/M-26
c. 1275-1334	Durandus Saint-Pourçain	M-22
1277-1342	Palud, Pierre La	M-69
1300-1360	Richard Armachanus	M-76
c. 1330-1384	Wyclif, John	M-85
1330-1396	Marsilius of Inghen	M-63
1363-1429	Gerson, Jean	M-29/M-30
c. 1377-1430	Netter, Thomas	M-63/M-64
1401-1464	Nicholas of Cusa	M-66
c. 1420-1495	Gabriel Biel	M-27/M-28
1439	Florence	C-11/C-12

DATES	NAME	ENTRY
1458-1464	Pius II	P-37
1469-1534	Cajetan	R-22
1478-1541	Faber, Johannes	R-61
1483-1546	Luther, Martin	R-66/R-67
1484-1531	Zwingli, Ulrich	R-74
1485-1528	Hubmaier, Balthasar	R-64
1485-1546	Franciscus Victoria	R-73
1486-1543	Eck, John	R-60
1490-1552	Nausea, Friedrich	R-69
1495-1560	Dominic Soto	R-70
1497-1560	Melanchthon, Philipp	R-68
1499-1570	Brenz, Johannes	R-20/R-21
1503-1559	Gropper, Johannes	R-62
1509-1564	Calvin, John	R-23/R-37
1522-1523	Adrian VI	P-1
1522-1578	Surius	R-71/R-72
1522-1586	Chemnitz, Martin	R-38/R-58
1527-1588	Hesshusen, Tilemann	R-63
1528-1578	Andrada, Diego	R-1

DATES	NAME	ENTRY
1540	Colloquy of Ratisbon	R-59
1542-1621	Bellarmine, Robert	R-3/R-19
1544	Antididagma	R-2
1547	Trent	C-28/C-32
1548	Leipzig Interim	R-65

Bibliography

A. THE CONTROVERSY

Bellarmine, Robert. "Liber Secundus, de sacramento confirmationis," *Disputationum de Controversiis Christianae fidei adversus hujus temporis haereticos*. 6 vols. Naples: Josephum Giuliano and Milan: Natale Battezzati, 1857-1862. Vol. 3, (1858):209-234.

Calvin, John. "De confirmatione," *Opera quae supersunt omnia: Institutio Christianae religionis*. Ed. William Baum, Edward Cunitz, and Edward Reuss. CR 30 (1864):1068-1075.

Chemnitz, Martin. "De confirmatione," *Examen Concilii Tridentini*. Ed. Ed. Preuss. Berlin: Gust. Schlawitz, 1861. Pp. 284-298.

B. PRIMARY SOURCES NOT LISTED IN CHAPTER III

Augustine. *De catechizandis rudibus*. CChr.SL 46 (1969).

Baptism, Eucharist and Ministry. Faith and Order Paper No. 111. Geneva: World Council of Churches, 1982.

Biblia Sacra iuxta Vulgatam Clementinam. Ed. Albertus Colunga and Laurentius Turrado. Nova editio. BAC:1946.

Bucer, Martin. *Censura Martini Buceri Super Libro Sacrorum Seu Ordinationis Ecclesiae atque Ministerii Ecclesiastici in Regno Angliae ad petitionem R. Archiepiscopi Cantuarensis Thomae Cranmeri Conscripta*. Alcuin Club Collections, No. 55. Great Wakering: Mayhew-McCrimmon, 1974.

_____. *De Regno Christi*. Opera Latina, Vol. 15. Ed. Francois Wendel. Paris: Presses Universitaires de France, 1955. ,

Calvin, John. *Petit Traicté de la Saincte Cene de Nostre Seigneur Iesus Christ*. Geneva, 1541. CR 33:429-460.

_____. *Les Actes de la iournée imperiale tenue en la cité de Regespourg, aultrement dicte Ratispone*. 1541. CR 33:509684.

_____. *Le Catechisme de l'Eglise de Geneve, 1545*. CR 34:1-160.

_____. *Articuli a facultate sacrae theologiae parisiensi determinati super materiis fidei nostrae hodie controversis. Cum Antidoto.* 1544. CR 35:1-44.

_____. *Interim adultero-germanum: cui adiecta est vera christianae pacificationis et ecclesiae reformandae ratio.1549-1550.* CR 35:545-686.

_____. *Instruction et confession de foy dont on use en leglise de Geneve.* CR 50:25-74.

_____. *Commentarius in Acta Apostolorum.* CR 76: 1-574.

_____. *Commentarius in epistolam ad Hebraeos.* CR 83:1-198.

_____. *Institutes of the Christian Religion.* The Library of Christian Classics, 21. Ed. John T. McNeill. Trans. Ford Lewis Battles. 2 vols. Philadelphia: The Westminster Press, 1967.

_____. *Tracts and Treatises in Defense of the Reformed Faith.* Trans. Henry Beveridge. 3 vols. Edinburgh: Calvin Translation Society: 1851; reprint ed. Grand Rapids, Michigan: Wm. B. Eerdmans Publishing Company, 1958.

Catechismus Romanus ex decreto sacrosancti concilii Tridentini. Ed. Pius V. Rome: Typis Sacrae Congregationis de Propaganda Fide, 1796.

Chemnitz, Martin. *De dvabvs natvris in Christo: De hypostatica earvm vnione: De commvnicatione idiomatvm, et aliis qvaestionibus inde dependentibus libellvs.* Leipzig: 1600.

_____. *Examination of the Council of Trent.* Trans. Fred Kramer. 2 vols. St. Louis, Missouri: Concordia Publishing House, 1971.

_____. *The Two Natures in Christ.* Trans. J. A. O. Preuss. St. Louis: Concordia Publishing House, 1971.

Code of Canon Law: Latin-English Edition. Trans. Canon Law Society of America. Washington, D.C.: Canon Law Society of America, 1983.

Codex iuris canonici. Second edition. Vatican City: Libreria Editrice Vaticana, 1983.

Confutatio Confessionis Augustanae, "Ad artic. XIII.," CR 27:114.

Documenta Mag. Joannis Hus, vitam, doctrinam, causam in Constantiensi Concilio actam et controversias de religione in Bohemia annis 1403-1418 motas. Ed. Franciscus Palacky. Osnabrück: Biblio-Verlag, 1869; reprint ed., 1966.

Eck, John. *Enchiridion locorum communium adversus Lutherum et alios hostes ecclesiae (1525-1543),* CCath 34 (1979).

_____. *Enchiridion of Commonplaces Against Luther and Other Enemies of the Church.* Trans. Ford Lewis Battles. Grand Rapids: Baker Book House, 1979.

Erasmus. "Paraphrases in N. Testamentvm," *Desiderii Erasmi Roterodami Opera Omnia.* Lyons: Petrus Vander Aa, 1706. Vol. 7.

Henry VIII. *Assertio septem sacramentorum adversus Marti. Lutherum.* London: Pyrson, 1521. Reprint ed., Ridgewood, NJ: The Gregg Press Incorporated, 1966. "De confirmatione," pages not numbered.

Hermann, Ertzbisschof von Köln. *Einfaltigs bedencken warauff ein Christliche inn dem wort Gottes gegrünte Reformation an Lehr brauch der Heiligen Sacramenten vnd Ceremonien Seelsorge vnd anderem Kirchen dienst biß avff eines freyen Christlichenn Gemeinen oder Nationals Concilij oder des Reichs Teutscher Nation Stende im Heiligen Geist versamlet verbesserung bei denen so unserer Seelsorge befohlenn anzurichten seye.* Marpurg: Antonium Tirolt, 1544.

Hubert, Friedrich. *Die Strassburger Liturgischen Ordnungen im Zeitalter der Reformation.* Göttingen: Vandenhoeck & Ruprecht, 1900.

Hus, Johannes. *Mag. Joannis Hus opera omnia: Super IV. Sententiarum.* Ed. Wenzel Flajshans & Marie Kominkova. Osnabráck: Biblio-Verlag, 1966. Vol. 2.

Kühn, Johann. (Henricus Artopoeus.) *Ad theologogastrorum Coloniensium censuram responsio.* Grenoble: Petrus Cephalius Duromontanus, 1561.

Leo X, "LI.: Ex supernae dispositionis." *Bullarum Diplomatum et privilegiorum sanctorum romanorum Pontificum.* Ed. Collegium Adlectum Romae Virorum S. Theologiae et SS. Canonum Peritorum, Taurinensis editio. 22 vols. Turin: Seb. Franco et Henrico Dalmazzo, 1860. Vol. 5, pp. 773-775.

Luther, Martin. "Ein Sermon von der heiligen hochwürdigen Sakrament der Taufe, 1519." WA 2 (1884):727-737.

_____. *An dem christlichen Adel deutscher Nation von des christlichen Standes Besserung. 1520.* WA 6 (1888):404-469.

_____. *De captivitate Babylonica ecclesiae praeludium. 1520.* WA 6:497-573.

_____. *Ein Sendbrief an den Papst Leo X. Von der Freiheit eines Christenmenschen. 1520.* WA 7 (1897):3-38.

_____. *Zu der frue Christmeß Epistell Pauli.* WA 10,1,1 (1910):95-128.

_____. *Welche Personen verboten sind zu ehelichen, 1522.* WA 10,2 (1907):263-266.

_____. *Vom ehelichen Leben, 1522.* WA 10,2:267-304.

_____. *Predigt am Sonntag Lätare Nachmittags (15. März 1523).* WA 11 (1900):65-67.

_____. *Von Der Widdertauffe an zween Pfarherrn. Ein brieff Mart. Luther.* WA 26 (1909):144-174.

_____. *Deudsch Catechismus (Der Große Katechismus). 1529.* WA 30,1 (1910):123-238.

_____. *Commentariolus in epistolam divi Pauli Apostoli ad Hebreos – 1517.* WA 57,3 (1939):95-236.

_____. "Luther an Spalatin. Wittenberg, 18. Dezember 1519. Nr. 231." WABr 1 (1930):594-596.

_____. "Luther an Gregor Solinus in Tangermünde, Wittenberg, 13 September 1540, Nr. 3534." WABr 9 (1941):230-233.

Luther's Correspondence and Other Contemporary Letters. Trans. and ed. Preserved Smith. Philadelphia: The Lutheran Publication Society, 1913. Vol. I, 1502-1521.

Luther's Large Catechism. Trans. J. N. Lenker. Minneapolis: Augsburg Publishing House, 1967.

Luthers' Works, American Edition. General editors Jaroslav Pelikan and Helmut T. Lehmann. St. Louis: Concordia Publishing House and Philadelphia: Fortress Press, 1958ff.

Melanchthon, Philipp. *Loci Theologici,* CR 21 (1854); reprint ed., 1963.

_____. "Confessio Augustana Ipsa." CR 26:263-336.

_____. "Apologia Confessionis Augustanae," CR 27 (1859):419646. Reprint, 1963.

Reformatio Wittebergensis (Wittenbergische Reformation). CR 5:584.

Simler, Iosias. *Bibliotheca institvta et collecta primvm a Conrado Gesnero, Deinde in Epitomen redacta et nouorum Librorum accessione locupletata, iam vero postremo recognita, et in duplum post priores editiones aucta, per Iosiam Simlerum Tigurinum.* Zürich: Christophor Forschover, 1574.

C. LITERATURE

Alberigo, Giuseppe. "Du Concile de Trente au tridentinisme." *Irenikon* 54 (1981):192-210.

_____. "Dinamiche religiose del Cinquecento italiano tra Riforma, Riforma cattolica, Controriforma." *Cristianesimo nella storia* 6 (October, 1985):543-560.

Aviva el fuego de los dones que Dios te dio. Morales-Izabal: Centro Apostólico, c. 1980.

Baudrillart, A. "Calvin, Jean." *Dictionnaire de théologie Catholique.*

Bibliographia Brentiana: Bibliographisches Verzeichnis der gedruckten und ungedruckten Schriften und Briefe des Reformators Johannes Brenz. Nebst einem Verzeichnis der Literatur über Brenz, kurzen Erläuterungen und ungedruckten Akten. Ed. Walther Köhler. Berlin: 1904; reprint ed., Nieuwkoop: B. de Graaf, 1963.

Bibliothèque de la Compagnie de Jésus. Ed. Augustin DeBacker, Auguste Carayon, Carlos Sommervogel, et al. Bruxelles: Oscar Schepens, 1890. S. v. "Bellarmino, Robert," Vol. II, col. 1151-1254.

The Book of Concord: The Confessions of the Evangelical Lutheran Church. Trans. and ed. Theodore G. Tappert et al. Philadelphia: Muhlenberg Press, 1959.

Brand, Eugene L. *By Water and the Spirit: Preparing for Holy Baptism According to the Rite of the Lutheran Book of Worship.* Ed. S. Anita Stauffer. Philadelphia: Parish Life Press, 1979.

Brodrick, James. *The Life and Work of Blessed Robert Francis Cardinal Bellarmine, S.J., 1542-1621.* 2 vols. London: Burns Oates and Washbourne, Ltd, 1928.

_____. *Robert Bellarmine: Saint and Scholar.* Westminster: The Newman Press, 1961.

Cayré, F. *Manual of Patrology and History of Theology*. Trans. H. Howitt. Paris: Society of St. John the Evangelist, Desclée & Co., 1935. Vol. 1.

Cicognani, Amleto Giovanni. *Canon Law*. Second, Revised Edition. Philadelphia: The Dolphin Press, 1935.

Clavis Patrum Latinorum. Sacris Erudiri, Jaarboek voor Godsdienstwetenschappen 3. Editio altera. Brugge: Firma Karel Beyaert, 1961.

Confirmation Guidelines. Milwaukee: Archdiocese of Milwaukee, 1981.

Confirmation: Model Preparation Program. San Bernardino: Diocese of San Bernardino, 1980.

Confirmation 1980. Oakland: Diocese of Oakland, 1980.

Confirmation Policy for the Archdiocese of Indiana and Guide for Implementation. Indianapolis: Archdiocese of Indianapolis, 1980.

The Constitution of the Presbyterian Church (U.S.A.). New York: Offices of the General Assembly, 1981. Part II: Book of Order.

Deluz, Gaston. "Le Baptême d'eau et d'Esprit ou le problème de la confirmation." ETR 22,3-4 (1947):201-235.

Diocesan Guidelines for the Celebration of Confirmation for the Diocese of Cheyenne. Cheyenne: Diocese of Cheyenne, 1979 .

Dizionario dei Concili. Ed. Pietro Palazzini. Rome: Città Nuova Editrice, 1966.

Dudon, Paul. "Bellarmine (Saint François-Robert-Romulus)." *Dictionnaire d'histoire et de géographie ecclésiastiques*.

"Essential Elements of a Catechumenate Model Confirmation Program." *Christian Initiation: Confirmation*. Newark: Archdiocesan Office of Divine Worship, 1977.

Fisher, J. D. C. *Christian Initiation: The Reformation Period. Some Early Reformed Rites of Baptism and Confirmation and Other Contemporary Documents*. Alcuin Club Collections, No. 51. London: S.P.C.K., 1970.

Franzen, August. "Monheim, Johannes." *Lexikon für Theologie und Kirche*. 1962 ed. Franzen.

Galeota, Gustavo. "Bellarmini, Roberto (1542-1621)." *Theologische Realenzyklopädie*.

Ganoczy, Alexandre. *Calvin: théologien de l'eglise et du ministére.* Unam Sanctam 48. Paris: Les editions du Cerf, 1964).

Garnier, François and Viard, Gabriel. *Vers la confirmation: Itinéraire de préparation.* Ed. Odette Sarda and Louis-Michel Renier. Angers: Editions du Chalet, 1983.

Grönvik, Lorenz. *Die Taufe in der Theologie Martin Luthers.* Göttingen-Zürich: Vandenhoeck und Ruprecht, 1968.

Gulik, Wilhelm van. *Johannes Gropper (1503 bis 1559): Ein Beitrag zur Kirchengeschichte Deutschlands, besonders der Rheinlande im 16. Jahrhundert.* Freiburg im Breisgau: Herdersche Berlagshandlung, 1906.

Hareide, Bjarne. *Die Konfirmation in der Reformationszeit: Eine Untersuchung der lutherischen Konfirmation in Deutschland 1520-1585.* APTh 8 (1971).

Huby, Joseph. "Une Exégèse faussement attribuée à Saint Cyprien." *Biblica* 14 (1933):96.

Iserloh, Erwin; Jedin, Hubert; Glazik, Joseph. *History of the Church.* Vol. 5: *Reformation and Counter Reformation.* Ed. Hubert Jedin and John Dolan. Trans. Anselm Biggs and Peter W. Becker. A Crossroad Book. New York: The Seabury Press, 1980.

Jaffé, Philippus. *Registra Pontificum Romanorum ab condita ecclesia ad annum post Christum natum MCXCVIII.* Second edition, ed. Gulielmus Wattenback. 2 vols. Leipzig: Viet et Comp., 1885.

Jorissen, Hans. *Die Entfaltung der Transsubstantiationslehre bis zum Beginn der Hochscholastik.* Ed. Berhard Kötting and Joseph Ratzinger. Münsterische Beiträge zur Theologie 28, 1. Münster Westfalen: Aschendorffsche Verlagsbuchhandlung, 1965.

Klaiber, Wilbirgis. *Katholische Kontroverstheologen und Reformer des 16. Jahrhunderts.* Reformationsgeschichtliche Studien und Texte. Münster Westfalen: Aschendorff, 1978.

Klassiker der Theologie. Ed. H. Fries & G. Kretschmar. Munich: C. H. Beck, 1981. "Robert Bellarmin (1542-1621)," by Gustavo Galeota. Vol. 1, pp. 346-362.

Kretschmar, Georg. "Firmung." *Theologische Realenzyklopädie.*

Kuckhoff, Joseph. "Monheim, Johannes." *Lexikon für Theologie und Kirche.* 1935 ed.

THE MEANING AND PRACTICE OF CONFIRMATION

Lanne, Emmanuel. "Les sacrements de l'initiation chrétienne et la confirmation dans l'Eglise d'Occident." *Irenikon: Revue des Moines de Chevetogne trimestrielle* 57 (2nd trimester, 1984):196–215; (3rd trimester, 1984):324-346.

Le Bachelet, X. "Bellarmin, Francois-Robert-Romulus." *Dictionnaire de théologie Catholique.*

Leclercq, J. "Les collections de sermons de Nicolas de Clairvaux." RBen 66 (1956):269-302.

L'Estrange, Hamon. *The Alliance of Divine Offices.* Library of Anglo-Catholic Theology. Fourth edition. Oxford: John Henry Parker, 1846.

Lightfoot, J. B. *The Apostolic Fathers.* London: Macmillan and Co., 1890. Vol. 1, part 1.

Ligier, Louis. *La Confirmation: Sens et conjoncture oecuménique hier et aujourd'hui.* Théologie Historique 23. Paris: Beauchesne, 1973.

Loevenbruck, L. "Chemnitz (Chemnitzius, Kemnitz) Martin." *Dictionnaire de théologie Catholique.*

Lutheran Book of Worship. Ed. Inter-Lutheran Commission on Worship: Lutheran Church in America, The American Lutheran Church, The Evangelical Lutheran Church of Canada, and The Lutheran Church – Missouri Synod. Minneapolis: Augsburg Publishing House, 1982.

Lutheran Cyclopedia. S.v. "Lutheran Confessions." Ed. Erwin L. Lueker. St. Louis: Concordia Publishing House, 1954.

Mahlmann, Theodor. "Chemnitz, Martin (1522-1586)." *Theologische Realenzyklopädie.*

Marcel, Pierre. "Théologie Réformée de la confirmation," RRef 63 (1965/3).

Marsh, Thomas A. *Gift of Community: Baptism and Confirmation.* Ed. Monika K. Hellwig. Message of the Sacraments. Wilmington: Michael Glazier, Inc., 1984.

Marsili, Salvatore. "Sacramenti." *Nuovo Dizionario di Liturgia.*

McDonnell, Kilian. *John Calvin, the Church, and the Eucharist.* Princeton: Princeton University Press, 1967.

McShane, E. D. "Interims." *New Catholic Encyclopedia.*

Milner, Austin P. *The Theology of Confirmation.* Theology Today 26. Cork: The Mercier Press, 1972.

Mitchell, Leonel L. *Baptismal Anointing*. Alcuin Club Collections, No. 48. London: S.P.C.K, 1966.

Morin, Germain. "La collection gallicane dite d'Eusèbe d'Emèse et les problémes qui s'y rattachent." *Zeitschrift für die Neutestamentliche Wissenschaft und die Kunde der Älteren Kirche* 34 (1935):92-115.

Nijenhuis, Willem. "Calvin, Johannes (1509-1564)." *Theologische Realenzyklopädie*.

Nomenclator literarius recentioris theologiae catholicae theologos exhibens qui inde a Concilio Tridentino floruerunt aetate, natione, disciplinis distinctos. Ed. Hugo Hurter. Innsbruck: Wagner, 1871-1886.

Ordo Confirmationis. Pontificale Romanum ex decreto sacrosancti Oecumenici Concilii Vaticani II instauratum auctoritate Pauli PP. VI promulgatum. Editio typica. Vatican City: Typis Polyglottis Vaticanis, 1973.

Ordo initiationis Christianae adultorum. Rituale Romanum ex decreto sacrosancti Oecumenici Concilii Vaticani II instauratum auctoritate Pauli PP. VI promulgatum. Editio typica. Vatican City: Typis Polyglottis Vaticanis, 1972.

Ortolan, T. "Confirmation." *Dictionnaire de théologie Catholique*.

The Oxford Dictionary of the Christian Church. Second edition. S.v. "Melanchthon."

Paquier, J. "Melanchthon, Philippe." *Dictionnaire de théologie Catholique*.

Pfatteicher, Philip H., and Messerli, Carlos R. *Manual on the Liturgy: Lutheran Book of Worship*. Minneapolis: Augsburg Publishing House, 1979.

Pitzal, Franz. *Die Firmung: Ein Vorbereitungsbuch*. Regensburg: Verlag Friedrich Pustet, 1984.

Poll, G. J. Van de. *Martin Bucer's Liturgical Ideas: The Strasburg Reformer and His Connection with the Liturgies of the Sixteenth Century*. Assen: Van Gorcum & Comp. N.V., 1954.

Rahner, Karl. *The Church and the Sacraments*. Quaestiones Disputatae. Trans. W. J. O'Hara. New York: Herder and Herder, 1963.

_____. *Kirche und Sakramente*. QD 10 (1960).

Repp, Arthur C. *Confirmation in the Lutheran Church.* St. Louis: Concordia Publishing House, 1964.

Resources I: Confirmation and Youth Catechesis. Phoenix: Roman Catholic Church of Phoenix, c. 1980.

Reuter, Karl. *Das Grundverständnis der Theologie Calvins: Unter Einbeziehung ihrer geschichtlichen Abhängigkeiten.* Beiträge zur Geschichte und Lehre der Reformierten Kirche. Ed. Paul Jacobs et al. Vol. 15, 1. Neukirchen: Verlag des Erziehungsvereins GmbH, 1963.

Richgels, Robert William. *Robert Bellarmine's Use of Calvin in the "Controversies": A Quantitative Analysis.* Ann Arbor, Michigan: University Microfilms, 1973.

The Rites of the Catholic Church as Revised by Decree of the Second Vatican Ecumenical Council and Published by Authority of Pope Paul VI. Trans. The International Commission on English in the Liturgy. New York: Pueblo Publishing Co., 1976.

Schaff, Philip. *The Creeds of Christendom, with a History and Critical Notes.* Fourth edition, revised and enlarged. 3 vols. New York: Harper & Brothers, 1919.

Smith, Preserved. *Luther's Correspondence.* Philadelphia: 1913.

Soden, Hans Freiherr von. "Die Cyprianische Briefsammlung Geschichte ihrer Entstehung und überlieferung." TU 10,3 (1904).

Suss, Théobald. "Remarques sur le problème de la confirmation." PosLuth 3 (July, 1957):179-197.

Swaans, W. J. "A propos des 'Catéchèses Mystagogiques' attribuées à S. Cyrille de Jerusalem." *Le Muséon: Revue d'Etudes Orientales* 55,1 (1942):1-43.

Tavard, Georges. *Protestantism.* Ed. Henri Daniel-Rops. Trans. Rachel Attwater. Twentieth Century Encyclopedia of Catholicism 137. New York: Hawthorn Books, 1959.

Thurian, Max. *La Confirmation: Consécration des laïcs.* Neuchâtel: Delachaux & Niestle, 1957.

_____. *Consecration of the Layman: New Approaches to the Sacrament of Confirmation.* Trans. W. J. Kerrigan. Baltimore: Helicon, 1963.

Umberg, Johannes Bapt. *Die Schriftlehre vom Sakrament der Firmung: Eine Biblisch-Dogmatische Studie.* Freiburg im Breisgau: Herder & Co., 1920.

Vischer, Lukas. *La Confirmation au cours des siècles: Contribution au débat sur le problème de la confirmation.* Trans. Jean Carrère. CTh 44 (1959).

Walker, Williston. *John Calvin: The Organiser of Reformed Protestantism (1509-1564).* Bibliographical essay, John T. McNeill. New York: Schocken Books, 1969.

Wendel, Francois. *Calvin: Sources et évolution de sa pensée religieuse.* Etudes d'histoire et de philosophie religieuses publiées par la faculté de theologie protestante de l'Université de Strasbourg 41. Paris: Presses Universitaires de France, 1950.

_____. *Calvin: The Origins and Development of His Religious Thought.* Trans. Philip Mairet. New York: Harper & Row, 1963.

Whitaker, E. C. *Martin Bucer and The Book of Common Prayer. Censura Martini Buceri Super Libro Sacrorum Seu Ordinationis Ecclesiae atque Ministerii Ecclesiastici in Regno Angliae ad petitionem R. Archiepiscopi Cantuarensis Thomae Cranmeri Conscripta.* Alcuin Club Collections, No. 55. Great Wakering: Mayhew-McCrimmon, 1974.

_____. *Sacramental Initiation Complete in Baptism.* Grove Liturgical Study 1. Bramcote Notts: Grove Books, 1975.

Wicks, Jared. "Recensiones: Johannes Eck, *Enchiridion locorum communium adversus Lutherum et alios hostes Ecclesiae (1525-1543),* CCath 34...," AHP 19 (1981):386-390.

Williams, George Huntston. *The Radical Reformation.* Philadelphia: The Westminster Press, 1962.

Wisløff, Carl F. *The Gift of Communion: Luther's Controversy with Rome on Eucharistic Sacrifice.* Trans. Joseph M. Shaw. Minneapolis: Augsburg Publishing House, 1964.

Herbert W. Basser

MIDRASHIC INTERPRETATIONS OF THE SONG OF MOSES

American University Studies: Series VII, Theology and Religion. Vol. 2
ISBN 0-8204-0065-3   326 p.   paperback US $ 28.85*

*Recommended price - alterations reserved

This work provides a translation of, and a commentary to the text of *Sifre Ha'azinu*. Finkelstein's edition (1939, reprinted JTS 1969) and selected readings of the London manuscript of this midrash appear in translation with full notes covering textual observations, philological inquiries and exgetical problems. The following ideas are discussed within the course of the work: midrashic forms, the use of Scripture in midrash, the dating of the traditions and of the recording of this midrash, the use of apologetic and polemic in midrash. An *Introduction* and *Conclusion* have been provided which discuss the items in this midrash which are relevant to the academic study of Judaism. The literary aspects of this midrash on Deut. 32 are used to exemplify *midrashim* on poetic Scriptures.

Contents: Introduction discussing literary, theological, historical aspects of midrash – Translation and analysis of the midrash to Deut. 32. Sifre Deuteronomy – Conclusion summing up the findings in the work.

PETER LANG PUBLISHING, INC.
62 West 45th Street
USA – New York, NY 10036

Blasi, Anthony J.

A PHENOMENOLOGICAL TRANSFORMATION OF THE SOCIAL SCIENTIFIC STUDY OF RELIGION

American University Studies: Series VII, Theology and Religion. Vol. 10
ISBN 0-8204-0235-4   205 pp.   hardback US $ 27.85

Recommended prices - alterations reserved

This book develops a theoretical methodology for the scientific study of religion, from the principle of meaning adequacy. Religion is to be understood adequately when the character of its presence in the mind of the religious person is described. This methodology is used to address some major issues in the study of religion in new ways – defining religion, understanding ritual, the connection between religion and morality, religious social morality in the third world, pietism, the value problem in scientific accounts of religion, and types of religious mentalities. These discussions comprise a substantive phenomenology of religion, and a distinctive sociology of religion.

Contents: After developing a phenomenological methodology for the study of religion, the book addresses major issues in the social scientific study of religion. Among these are ritual, morality, and conversion.

PETER LANG PUBLISHING, INC.
62 West 45th Street
USA - New York, NY 10036

John D. Laurance

"PRIEST" AS TYPE OF CHRIST

The Leader of the Eucharist in Salvation History according
to Cyprian of Carthage

American University Studies: Series VII, Theology and Religion. Vol. 5
ISBN 0-8204-0117-X   256 pp.   hardback US $ 30.80

Recommended price - alterations reserved

Behind much of the turmoil in the Church since Vatican II is the question.
«What is a priest?» *«Priest» as Type of Christ* turns to the time-honored witness
of Cyprian of Carthage on this question, asking. «What is the connection between the bishop or presbyter's imitation of Christ and Christ's consequent
presence at the Eucharist?» In the course of this investigation biblical typology.
Tertullian and Cyprian's use of *«sacramentum,»* and the roles of the baptized
and of the martyr in the Church are all seen in light of Christ's saving presence throughout human history. *«Priest» as Type of Christ* is thus not only
a study in liturgical and sacramental theology, but also in the early Church's
overall theology of salvation history.

Contents: *«Priest as Type of Christ»* studies Cyprian's grasp of biblical typology,
«sacramentum», eucharistic leadership vis-à-vis the baptized and the martyr,
all in light of Christ's saving presence throughout history.

PETER LANG PUBLISHING, INC.
62 West 45th Street
USA - New York, NY 10036